The Terms of our Surrender

The Terms of our Surrender
Colonialism, Dispossession and the
Resistance of the Innu

Elizabeth Cassell

Published by University of London Press

Human Rights Consortium
Institute of Commonwealth Studies
School of Advanced Study, University of London
2021

ISBNs:
978-1-912250-45-5 (paperback edition)
978-1-912250-46-2 (.epub edition)
978-1-912250-47-9 (.mobi edition)
978-1-912250-48-6 (.pdf edition)

University of London Press
School of Advanced Study
University of London
Senate House
Malet Street
London WC1E 7HU

Cover image: Shutterstock_1620652243

Contents

Part Five: 'Citizens Plus' or parallel paths?

Acknowledgements

I owe an immeasurable debt of gratitude to the Innu people of Matimekush Lac John, Maliotenam and Uashat who trusted me with their history and shared with me their wisdom, their beliefs and their warm hospitality. In particular my thanks are due to Chief Réal McKenzie who invited me to Matimekush Lac John and to Chief Negotiator Lucien McKenzie whose proposal it was that I should undertake an oral history of his community and their struggle to retain their land rights. Innu lawyer and activist Armand Mackenzie proved an excellent guide and shared his knowledge and experience of Innu culture and politics as well as providing insightful interpretations of the interviews. Thanks are also due to Mike Cluney, who also acted as interpreter, for his growing interest in his people's history and culture so that elders were keen to pass on their knowledge to him and thus to me.

Danielle Descent has been a mentor, guide, an excellent host with her husband Sylvain Vollant, and a true friend. Yvette Mackenzie and Bruno Ouellet lent me their house in Matimekush where I could work in peace and comfort. On my third visit they were at home and welcomed me, providing great hospitality and valuable insights. Mani Aster and Jean-Marie Mackenzie took me into their family and I gained much from Mani's wisdom and Jean-Marie's non-judgmental approach to life on reserve. Rita McKenzie and Adrian Cluney also gave me great encouragement, helpful suggestions and introductions and many cups of coffee.

My introduction to the Innu way of life came in 2008 at the 4ème Seminaire Nordique at Mushua Nipi, Northern Quebec. Elizabeth Ashini, Serge Ashini-Goupil, Philippe Messier and Anne-Marie Andre organised a multicultural, multidisciplinary conference which enabled wide-ranging discussion of the issues which affect the life of the Innu today. They took time to answer my many questions and to explain complex aspects of resource extraction from Innu lands. I am truly grateful for their encouragement and friendship. But above all, I am indebted to those who agreed to speak to me, who were, like all Indigenous people, meticulous in their need to give a full and truthful account of their people's history so that this could be recorded in order that future generations should know how they fought to prevent the extinguishment of their rights.

In Sheshatshiu, my thanks are due for the guidance of Anthony Jenkinson and Marcel Ashini and for my continued contact with Napes Ashini who, with Marcel and Tony, maintains his fight for the rights of Innu hunters despite the ratification of the New Dawn Agreement in Principle.

Professor Colin Samson has provided immense help and support throughout my years of study. This work has benefitted greatly from his suggestions and constructive criticism and his generosity in sharing sources and contacts and, most of all, his own experience. Through him, I joined a group of doctoral students who have formed close bonds and offer mutual support and encouragement: Pierrot Ross-Tremblay, Suzanne Robinson, Katya Brooks, Carlos Gigoux and Rebecca Fan.

I am grateful to the staff in the libraries I used, especially to Caroline Checkley, law librarian at the University of Essex, and Annalise D'Orsi at the Tshakapesh Institute in Uashat. Thanks are also due to the library staff at the Institute of Advanced Legal Studies, University of London, the Bibliothèque Nationale in Montreal, and Université Laval, Quebec City, in particular to their film archivist.

Damien Short, Robert Davies and the team at the University of London Press have provided strong and very helpful guidance, especially Juliet Chalk, whose careful editing illuminated my prose.

My family, David Cassell, Miranda and Mark Andras and Beth and Holly Andras, have supported my work with encouragement and forbearance, putting up with long absences, reading my drafts, correcting my spelling and grammar and providing love and laughter.

Any inaccuracies are all my own.

Terminology

The indigenous peoples

The Innu who live in Quebec refer to themselves simply as Innu (the 'people'), a name which includes their relatives who live across the border in Labrador. Sometimes they call themselves Montagnais, the name given to them by Jesuit missionaries, indicating those who live in the south of the Ungava Peninsula. Those who lived in the North, and who had not converted to Christianity, were referred to by the missionaries as Naskapi. Frank Speck made no distinction between Innu and Naskapi and, in his seminal work, named them all Naskapi. In its policy of divide and rule, the Canadian federal government named the Mushuau Innu who settled in Lac John Naskapi and, under this name, they became signatories of the North Eastern Quebec Agreement. Where the context permits, I have referred to the indigenous peoples under their chosen name.

Nation is a Canadian concept, used to identify 633 individual groups of indigenous people. Similarly, Band Council is a Canadian term for the governing body of each reserve equivalent to a town council. Reserve is the Canadian name for the villages in which indigenous peoples were sedentarised. Although these terms are used to identify individual groups of people and their settlements, and sometimes for convenience, these are not indigenous terms or constructs. Where possible I have used the term village to describe a people's settled habitation.

The Innu with whom I worked referred to indigenous peoples by the term *Indiens* or *autochtones,* which translates into English as 'natives'. They rarely used the term 'First Nations', another Canadian term which the Innu consider meaningless as long as Canadians deny them their rights to ancestral lands. I have used the terms native, indigenous and aboriginal interchangeably, according to context, but have avoided where possible the term First Nations.

Matimekush Lac John and Schefferville

Matimekush and Lac John are now two separate reserves served by the same Band Council. The Innu who live in these two villages settled together when the new town of Schefferville was created in 1950 to house the Iron Ore Company's offices and employees. This is the municipality to which, in

Canadian terms, Matimekush and Lac John belong. The Innu inhabitants who settled originally spent their summers in Uashat and Maliotenam (Innu name Mani-utenam) on the North Shore of the Gulf of St Lawrence near Sept-Iles. Around 1956, they were joined by Mushuau Innu from Fort Chimo (now Kuujjuaq) who were moved there by the Canadian government. Two separate Innu villages were created when the Indian Agent tried to move those Innu and Naskapi living in Lac John onto a new reserve outside Schefferville. Some Innu campaigned successfully to remain in Lac John, where they had provided housing for themselves. On the closure of the Iron Ore Company mine in 1982, the Naskapi received land on which to build a new village, Kawawachikamach and, after a successful negotiation, the Innu moved into vacated housing in Schefferville, although some chose to stay on the old reserve and in Lac John. Since the move into the town, Schefferville has been used by the Innu who live there interchangeably with Matimekush. The Innu from Matimekush Lac John are part of the negotiating table with Uashat and Maliotenam, together first as members of the Conseil Attikamekw-Montagnais, then as the Ashuanipi Corporation (named after a lake shared by all Innu and other indigenous peoples but now ceded to the Crown under the New Dawn Agreement) and now as the Strategic Alliance.

Note: Where I have quoted from French-language texts, for ease of reading I have translated the quotation into English.

Glossary

fee simple	Absolute title to land
Innu-Aimun	The Innu language
Innu-Aitun	Innu culture – their way of life; their world view; their ideas, beliefs and values, handed down from generation to generation; their skills; their artefacts – everything which gives them their identity
Innu Nation	Until 2011, this name was used to indicate all Innu resident in the two government villages, Sheshatshiu and Natuashish, Labrador. The 'Nation' will come into being as a government-sponsored body when the New Dawn Final Agreement is ratified. After the ratification of the Agreement in Principle, however, the Innu resident in Central Quebec also adopted this name, to which they were equally entitled but as a separate negotiation organisation
Nitassinan	The Innu homeland
nutshimit	The open country including all aspects of Innu life lived out on the land
Strategic Alliance	Negotiating body formed in 2009 to represent the villages of Uashat, Maliotenam, Matimekush and Lac John following the breakdown of negotiations for the recovery of their James Bay lands
sui generis	Unique, in a class of its own
terra nullius	Vacant land with no true owner, free for the taking
time immemorial	The common law date from which absolute title to land is measured – in the case of indigenous land from before the time of contact
Tshash Petapen	The New Dawn Agreement
Turtle Island	The indigenous name for North America
usufruct	The right to gather the fruits of land; a right which does not amount to ownership of the land

Abbreviations

AFN	Assembly of First Nations
AIP	Agreement in Principle
CAM	Conseil Attikamekw-Montagnais
CF(L)Co	Churchill Falls (Labrador) Company
CLCP	Comprehensive Land Claims Policy
CCP/CLCP	Comprehensive Land Claims Process
DIAND	Department of Indian Affairs and Northern Development, subsequently **AANDC**, Aboriginal Affairs and Northern Development Canada, then **INAC**, Indigenous and Northern Affairs Canada. The Department is now divided into two bodies: **CIRNAC**, Crown–Indigenous Relations and Northern Affairs Canada, and **ISC**, Indigenous Services Canada
FPIC	Free, prior and informed consent
HBC	Hudson's Bay Company
IBA	Impacts and Benefits Agreement
ICEM	Institut Culturel et Educatif Montagnais
IRS	Indian Residential Schools
JBA, JBNQA	James Bay Agreement, James Bay and Northern Quebec Agreement (full title)
LIL	Labrador Innu Lands
LISA	Labrador Innu Settlement Area
Nalcor	The Newfoundland Labrador Corporation
NEQA	North Eastern Quebec Agreement (the agreement signed by the Naskapi)
RCAP	Royal Commission on Aboriginal Peoples
TK, TEK	Traditional knowledge, traditional environmental knowledge
UCRA	Upper Churchill Redress Agreement
UNDRIP	United Nations Declaration on the Rights of Indigenous Peoples

Maps

Preface

Based on the experience of the Innu resident in Quebec and Labrador, this book is intended to be a work of advocacy for the full extent of the rights of indigenous peoples whose landholdings have been devastated in the Canadian land claims process. As things stand at present, the Innu who are resident in government villages in Quebec have lost their rights to all their land and this makes them almost unique among indigenous groups in Canada. Those peoples who, unlike the Innu, have signed land deals purporting to grant them rights over their own land have, in effect, lost 90 per cent of their ancestral land. Using the experience of the Innu as a template, I shall question Canadian sovereignty over indigenous lands which have been taken without the free, prior and informed consent of the indigenous peoples concerned. More important, my aim is to demonstrate the disconnect between the negotiation process and the reality of human suffering which loss of land entails for the Innu of the Ungava Peninsula and other indigenous peoples.

In 2008, I was invited to observe the land claims negotiations of the Innu of what was then known as the Ashuanipi Corporation, which represented the Innu of Central Quebec who live in government-built villages at Uashat, Maliotenam and Matimekush Lac John. They had two negotiations in progress with the Canadian federal government and the provinces of Quebec and Labrador. The first was to recover land rights which had been extinguished over their heads under the James Bay and Northern Quebec Agreement of 1975. The second was to establish their rights to land which they have owned for millennia across the provincial border in Labrador. The name of the corporation was significant in that it is the name of a lake and has been a meeting place for all Innu and other indigenous peoples of the Ungava Peninsula for at least 4,000 years. Now it is to be ceded to the Crown under the terms of the Tshash Petapen (New Dawn) Agreement signed only by the Innu who are settled in two villages in Labrador. Thus, having chosen to negotiate with only two of the 11 Innu communities who formerly shared the land, the Crown will receive land for which it has no current use in relation to any of the 'public interest' purposes such as resource extraction and hydro-electricity which are permitted under the line of judicial decisions starting with *R v Sparrow*[1] and expanded in *Delgamuukw v British Columbia*[2] and subsequent cases (see Chapter 9).

In 1972, all 11 Innu communities on both sides of the Quebec–Labrador border walked away from the negotiation table for rights to the land taken for the James Bay hydro-electricity project. They held to their firm belief that land is not a commodity to be bought or sold, but something which is held in trust for six generations of ancestors and the six generations to come. Land is given to be shared by all and humanity has a duty to take care of it and to conserve it. Although these beliefs are also held by the Cree, in 1972 the Grand Council of the Cree joined with the Inuit, first to assert their land rights through the courts and then to negotiate a settlement which recognised their right to the land but at the same time extinguished the land rights of non-participating indigenous peoples, including the Innu.

In the negotiation process in both these instances, so far as the governments are concerned, the rights to the land of the Innu settled in Quebec have been conclusively extinguished by the parties to the James Bay agreements. The Ashuanipi Corporation and its predecessors spent more than 30 years negotiating for the recovery of the lost James Bay lands. The federal government insisted that any renegotiation must take place between the indigenous parties concerned, but when in 2009 there seemed to be a breakthrough in these negotiations the government closed them down on a pretext. By the time I returned to observe the negotiations, they had ended and the Innu, now reconstituted as the Strategic Alliance, had begun to pursue a court case.

When I returned in March 2009, my purpose was to work on an oral history, in an effort to try to understand the human consequences of such a loss, which would recount the effects of denial of land rights on a people whose identity is defined by land. This aim coincided with the Matimekush Lac John Band Council's proposal that I record the efforts they had made to recover the James Bay lands so that their descendants would know that they had not willingly given up the territory which in the future should rightfully belong to them. I had also hoped to uncover new arguments in favour of Innu ownership of the land, but the research and documentation prepared by the Innu for the negotiation process presented a very comprehensive case for Innu ownership of the land both in Quebec and in Labrador. This evidence is set out in Chapter 16.

With the aid of interpreters and a recording engineer provided by the Band Council, I conducted interviews with 48 people from a population of approximately 800, who collectively were able to give voice to highly relevant factors which are never raised at the negotiation table – where much indigenous testimony is lost in Euro-centric processes involving lawyers and consultants

1   *R v Sparrow*, [1991] 1 SCR 1075.
2   *Delgamuukw v British Columbia*, [1997] 3 SCR 1010.

who speak on behalf of the Innu. My work with the Innu shows that, to those I worked with in Matimekush Lac John, land is not a commodity that *can* be bought and sold. Their past and future are tied up with the love they have for the land and their duty to protect it. The land belongs to every culture but to no individual or group and should be available for all to use. They can define the difference between the Innu and non-Innu attitude. As one Innu explained, 'Canadians cherish a country, not the land'.[3] Non-natives treat land as a commodity, an investment. To the Innu, one said, the land is everything while to the settler it is only money. The land is the Innu life, their culture and their home. It is their nourishment in every sense of the word.

Theirs is a two-way relationship: not only do they own the land on the basis of being the first to occupy it and to continue that occupation, but they also belong to the land and have a duty to protect it from the environmental disasters that come in the wake of Canadian resource development. Without the need for ownership by individuals, the land is their wealth. It provides food, medication, clothing and shelter – but only if it is respected. Further, it has given them the transferable skills of close observation, patience, endurance and flexibility, which are stifled by an existence on welfare payments.

When the Quebec–Labrador border was drawn, in 1927, it had no significance to the Innu, who had walked the entire peninsula together for generations and whose families live in both provinces. At the time they were not even told about the division of the peninsula. It only came to light nearly 50 years later during discussions with the governments and Hydro-Québec over the James Bay Agreement. As was pointed out by one Innu elder, the provincial border had no significance for the anthropologist Frank Speck either when, in 1935, he published his work on the Naskapi and the Montagnais.[4] He allocated the whole peninsula to bands of indigenous people. French priests named the Innu 'Naskapi' and 'Montagnais', depending on whether they were from the North – the Mushuau Innu, whom they called Naskapi; or from the South – the people of the mountains whom they called Montagnais. To themselves they are simply Innu – 'the people'.

The Innu of Uashat, Maliotenam, Matimekush and Lac John are isolated, the other Innu reserves having signed agreements for the exploitation of resources on their land. While there have always been tensions between the Matimekush Lac John Innu and the Labrador game wardens, in 2008, when the signing of the New Dawn Agreement in Principle was imminent, Innu hunters were threatened that, if they did not get off their lands in Labrador, their hunting cabins would be burned down. This threat was quickly withdrawn but the Innu have been denied the peaceful enjoyment of their land.

3   Interview MD2, Sept. 2009.
4   Speck, F., *Naskapi: The Savage Hunters of the Labrador Peninsula* (Norman: University of Oklahoma Press, 1935).

The Matimekush Lac John Innu live in the heart of the Quebec-Labrador Peninsula, right on the provincial border. This has enabled them to keep close to the earth and to all it means to them. They are constantly reminded of the stark difference between life in the interior and life on reserve. To sign a treaty extinguishing their rights is also to sign away their obligations to the land but, unless and until they do, they see the prospering all around them of communities who have signed extinguishment agreements and taken the benefits.

At the same time, in Matimekush Lac John the Innu are starved of resources and their children are failed by the standard of education provided in federal rather than provincial schools. They remain wards of the Crown, like children unable to control their own destiny, and deprived of the power to protect their environment. The chiefs and elders at the time of the James Bay Agreement were strong in their culture and, for them, agreement to extinguishment of their rights was impossible in the face of deeply held spiritual convictions. The community was kept informed and consulted about the negotiations, and support for refusal to sign any such agreement was virtually unanimous.

Settler Canadians identify indigenous peoples by where they live on reserve but, historically, the Innu and many others lived out on the land in the interior, only coming to summer meeting places to trade and to escape the mosquitoes and blackfly which make life unendurable to hunters and caribou alike in the two summer months. This was the mindset I encountered on reserve in Matimekush Lac John. Most of the people I interviewed, including the school students, indicated that they were settled in the government villages against their will and that their identity depended on their connections with the land which, even in the face of all government attempts at assimilation, remain strong.

There is a firm basis for indigenous land claims in the Royal Proclamation of 1763 (reproduced in Appendix A), in which George III of the United Kingdom undertook to protect the land of the indigenous peoples of North America from the incursions of other empire-building nations and from waves of settlers from Europe. The Proclamation decreed that it was made for the protection of the indigenous people and that no indigenous land could be purchased or taken in any way other than through the British Crown.

This undertaking was never revoked and it was recorded both in the Treaty of Niagara of 1764 and in the wampum belts which were widely distributed and which embody the indigenous understanding of the terms of this Treaty – that settlers and indigenous peoples should live side by side, following parallel paths which preserve their respective cultures, joined in mutual respect, peace and friendship. Where the indigenous peoples believed the arrangement to be a treaty of peace and friendship, however, those who signed on behalf of the Crown described it as a treaty of offensive and defensive alliance. At the time, the Crown was dependent on its indigenous allies in its wars with the French, and subsequently with the independent states of America.

By the beginning of the 19th century, however, the British were firmly established in what was then British North America, north of the 49th parallel. They no longer had need of allies for war. They needed land for settlement and later for resource extraction. This book is an account of the ways in which the Crown in Right of Canada set out to circumvent the promises given in the Royal Proclamation.

The decisions taken by the Crown on behalf of the native peoples to whom it had offered protection took no account of the fiduciary duty it had assumed under the Royal Proclamation. Negotiators sent by the British North American authorities to bargain for land which belonged to the natives failed to observe the duties of utmost good faith assumed by the Crown under the Royal Proclamation. Negotiations took place according to settler custom under the common law. There were no words in indigenous languages for the terms which were eventually written down, under which the land was taken by the Crown in absolute ownership in exchange for a small annuity, supplies, education and medicine which in no way represented the value of the land which had been ceded. This is exactly the sort of situation which the law on fiduciary duties is intended to prevent. Here the Crown, as the dominant party, took advantage of its superior bargaining power and the special relationship which the Royal Proclamation created with the indigenous people.

Unable to see any worth in the cultures of the indigenous peoples with whom they treated, the Crown assumed that they would soon be assimilated into settler society. In order to accelerate this process, native children were taken from their families and sent to residential boarding schools where they were deprived of their language and culture in the most brutal way, and most were so damaged by the experience that they were left with no future either in settler society or in their own families. Following Confederation in 1867, steps were taken to settle native peoples into villages owned by the government – which later became the model for concentration camps in the South African Boer War and subsequently in Germany.

Under this process, the Crown claimed that it was observing its fiduciary duty by making the 'Indians' wards of the Crown, i.e. treating them as minors, unable to make decisions for themselves. Indigenous destinies lay in the hands of an Indian Agent who had virtually unlimited power to decide who could leave the village, and who was to receive seeds and farming implements to allow them to lead a sedentary life. Far from being allowed to pursue their parallel existence in an atmosphere of respect, peace and friendship, the indigenous peoples of Canada were deprived of their land, language and culture and thus their identity. They had no control over their own destiny. This in no way represents the nature of the fiduciary duty imposed by the Royal Proclamation

– which is founded on an undertaking given nation-to-nation regarding land, and between parties of equal standing.

Through the lens of the common law and, in particular, the law of trusts and fiduciary duties this book examines the devices used by the Crown to deprive the indigenous peoples of their lands. It will demonstrate that there is no need to look to indigenous law to make a case that indigenous land to this day is owned outright by indigenous people. Under the terms of the Royal Proclamation, the British Crown had assumed responsibility for all dealings in indigenous land. This was the basis of the fiduciary duty. The party who assumes a fiduciary duty may never take advantage of that position and must act always in the best interests of the party to whom the duty is owed. This precludes all dealings in land and other assets and information obtained as a result of the relationship. Thus the Crown is prohibited from dealing in indigenous land for its own benefit without the free, prior and informed consent of its indigenous owners. Any interpretation of the Crown's duty to the indigenous peoples which falls short of this is a stain on the honour of the Crown, a concept discussed at length in Chapter 8. Having observed such duties in my professional life and subsequently having impressed their fundamental importance on generations of law students, it became a personal imperative that I make an attempt to clarify this issue.

The indigenous rights decisions heard by the Supreme Court of Canada, while acknowledging the existence of such rights, would balance them against the general public interest of those who had settled in Canada. Similarly, the Canadian and provincial governments negotiate with individual indigenous peoples whom the governments have called 'nations' on a 'take it or leave it' basis, purporting to grant rights to rather than to receive rights from the indigenous people concerned. The Canadian legal system seems not to be able to conceive of solutions to these intractable problems of indigenous land rights from an alternative world viewpoint to its own. It appears to see no value in the indigenous system of landholding whereby land is shared by all.

Intent on acquiring the land for development, the governments and their commercial partners will pay sums of money which hold the promise of a better future for Innu youth. On closer examination, however, the payments are divisive and destructive of communities. The Innu I interviewed were fearful of the large sums of money which would be available in the village following the reopening of the mines. They knew that drugs and alcohol would threaten the relative stability which the community had enjoyed in recent years.

In the court cases from *Delgamuukw* onwards the land claims settlement process is said to be one of reconciliation – the reconciliation of indigenous rights with Canadian sovereignty. Yet a system under which the governments provide a set agenda on a 'take it or leave it' basis and take 90 per cent of aboriginal land on the pretext of granting rights to 10 per cent cannot work towards a long-term solution of the 'Indian problem'.

Across Canada, land settlement agreements are couched in remarkably similar terms. Any attempt to allow indigenous peoples to continue a life based on subsistence are firmly resisted. For governments, it is preferable to assume the huge cost of keeping indigenous people in idleness on reserve rather than to allow them to continue their hunting life, which is the antidote to the epidemics of drug misuse, alcoholism, diabetes and domestic violence that plague native communities. What the Canadian governments are seeking is not reconciliation but an updated version of assimilation.

In 2007, all but four UN member states endorsed the United Nations Declaration on the Rights of Indigenous Peoples. Canada was one of the four. Yet the Declaration simply spelled out the duties already assumed by the Crown in Right of Canada through the Royal Proclamation. Finally, in 2010, Canada endorsed the Declaration. So far as can be ascertained, the Innu resident in Labrador were never advised of the significance of the Declaration vis-à-vis the Tshash Petapen Agreement in Principle, ratified in 2011. Despite the parliamentary apology to the Indian Residential School survivors, which would have provided an ideal opportunity, the Declaration has never passed into Canadian law, although Prime Minister Justin Trudeau has issued his own apology for the catastrophic effects of the Indian Residential Schools system and Bill C-15, An Act respecting the United Nations Declaration on the Rights of Indigenous Peoples was only introduced on 3 December 2020. British Columbia had introduced similar legislation in November 2019.

New hope has also been given to indigenous peoples across Canada who are 'negotiating' land claims with the delivery of the Supreme Court decision in *Tsilhqot'in Nation v British Columbia*.[5] The position of the Innu who live in Quebec has been fully vindicated. The Supreme Court of Canada in a unanimous decision of the eight senior judges who heard the case has confirmed that aboriginal title includes title to land used by nomadic and semi-nomadic peoples and that, once title is acknowledged, the consent of the claimants must be obtained for any incursions onto that land. This decision could finally bring the overlong period of fruitless negotiations to an end and lead to a land claims settlement which does not require the Innu to agree to the extinguishment of their rights.

Although *Tsilhqot'in* comes close to confirming that the Canadian governments must hold fast to their fiduciary duty, Chief Justice McLachlin nevertheless maintains the principle laid down in *Sparrow* which permits governments and corporations to proceed without consent with schemes on native land for the general public good, which include hydro-electric projects and resource extraction. In Chapter 9, I dispute the validity of such an exception.

5   *Tsilhqot'in Nation v British Columbia*, [2014] SCC 44.

The approach taken in *Sparrow* demonstrates the inability of governments and courts to conceive of a true reconciliation between settler and native peoples where the undertakings given in the Royal Proclamation are fully honoured. Academic writers who have long supported the indigenous peoples in their struggle for recognition of their rights also draw back from full restoration.

The concluding section brings together the legal and sociological analyses of the foregoing material. In order to do this, I examine texts which propose solutions to the situation in which settlers and indigenous peoples find themselves today. None of these authors fully support the proposals of the Royal Commission on Aboriginal Peoples, namely of two separate peoples living side by side.

The indigenous peoples of Canada set out, in the Report of the Royal Commission on Aboriginal Peoples (RCAP), their requirements for a true reconciliation of the differences between Canada and the original peoples. To date this vital document has been largely ignored. In the wake of the Report of the Indian Residential Schools Truth and Reconciliation Commission, there have been renewed calls for the implementation of the recommendations of both the RCAP Report and the United Nations Declaration on the Rights of Indigenous Peoples. In spite of its declared intention to do so, we must wait to hear how far the present Liberal government is prepared to go along this road.

Outline of the book

Part One: The Innu

This section of the book is intended to bring to the fore the severe consequences for indigenous peoples of the way in which the Canadian federal and provincial governments seek to deprive them of their land. Drawing on the oral history I conducted in 2009, I recount the treatment of the Innu and the many broken promises which were made to them. In Chapter 1, their voices tell the story of the move north to the new town of Schefferville. Chapter 2 tells what happened when the iron mines closed in 1982 and Chapter 3 what life is like in the villages today. Nevertheless, I demonstrate that the Innu culture and way of life are strong despite the ravages of the fur trade, residential schooling, mining and the activities of game wardens – which are discussed in Chapter 4 – and racism, recounted in Chapter 5. All chapters in the book are interleaved with Innu perceptions of their fate at the hands of the governments and corporations, as well as at the hands of other indigenous groups, which deprived them of their rights.

Part Two: The Royal Proclamation and questions of trust over Canadian indigenous land

This part explores the nature and extent of the fiduciary duty owed by the

Crown, traces it to its logical conclusion and sets out the implications for the ownership of indigenous land in Canada. It examines the duty to obtain the Innu's free, prior and informed consent to any transaction or resource extraction concerning their land as enshrined in the United Nations Declaration on the Rights of Indigenous Peoples, which fully reflects the duties of a fiduciary.

Chapter 6 sets out the historical background of European land acquisition on the American continent and sets the Royal Proclamation in context. Chapter 7 explains the nature of the fiduciary duty owed by the Crown, while Chapter 8 demonstrates how the Crown in Right of Canada circumvented its fiduciary duty and traces the treaties and court decisions through which this was done. This chapter also discusses the validity of the *Sparrow* decision and I suggest that, under section 35(1) of the Constitution Act 1982, there can be no justification for exploiting indigenous land for the public good without the free, prior and informed consent of the original owners of the land. Chapter 9 examines the nature of the 'honour of the Crown', a fundamental principle which has been revisited recently by the Supreme Court of Canada in a line of cases culminating in *Tsilhqot'in*.[6]

Part Three: The modern treaties and Canada's Comprehensive Land Claims Policy

This part of the text examines the relationship between the Quebec government and the indigenous peoples whose lands they sought to use for a massive hydro-electric project centred on James Bay, the southern arm of Hudson Bay. The provincial government proceeded with no acknowledgement whatsoever that indigenous rights to the land might exist. The Cree and the Inuit sought an injunction to stop work on the project and the ensuing Malouf judgment formed the basis of the James Bay Agreement.

Chapter 10 gives the background to the project, describes the life of the Cree and Inuit who shared the land with the Innu before construction started, and describes the James Bay project and the political reasons for its implementation. Chapter 11 describes the application for an injunction brought by the Cree and Inuit and provides an analysis of the judgment handed down by Judge Albert Malouf in these proceedings. The reasons for the decision in this case are very rarely discussed in depth, as they are in this chapter. Chapter 12 follows the ensuing negotiations for what was to be the first modern land claims settlement. Chapter 13 provides a review of the implementation of the James Bay Agreement and its consequences for the Innu, who shared the land with the Cree and the Inuit. Chapter 14 covers the developing Comprehensive Land Claims process of successive Canadian governments.

6 [2014] SCC 44.

Part Four: The Innu experience of the Comprehensive Land Claims process

Chapter 15 describes and analyses the 40 years of fruitless negotiations in which the Innu of Central Quebec have tried to recover their lost James Bay lands. In Chapter 16, I look at the Comprehensive Land Claims process across the border in Labrador, where Quebec Innu land rights have been ignored or written out. I analyse the terms of the New Dawn Agreement in Principle (AIP) and the subsidiary Impacts and Benefits Agreements, examining the extent of the land which has been sold to Canada for the Lower Churchill Falls hydro-electric project. I trace the process of ratification of the AIP and raise questions as to its validity through two lenses: the duty to consult the aboriginal group and the fiduciary duty to uphold the honour of the Crown. I also look at the duties of indigenous representatives, lawyers and consultants involved in the negotiation process and the impact of the AIP on the Innu resident in Quebec. In Chapter 17, I examine the position of the Innu resident on the other side of the border in Quebec who are seeking to establish their rights over the New Dawn lands. Finally, in Chapter 18, I look at the consequences of constructing the dam at Muskrat Falls, with its ensuing dangers to life, without a Tshash Petapen Final Agreement in place.

Part Five: 'Citizens Plus' or Parallel Paths?

Chapter 19 reviews the work of settler writers who have been influential in directing current perceptions on the question of indigenous rights in relation to the *de facto* sovereignty claimed by the Crown in Right of Canada. I review the work of J.R. Miller and Alan Cairns, political scientists who propose that indigenous peoples be treated as 'Citizens Plus' – Canadian citizens with additional rights. I contest the assertions of Tom Flanagan, a former adviser to the Conservative Harper government, that indigenous peoples have few rights in the land they occupied long before first contact with Europeans; and also the assertions of his former student, Christopher Alcantara. I dispute the opinion of Widdowson and Howard that there is an 'aboriginal industry' which inappropriately fuels the conflict over such rights, an argument used in support of Christopher Alcantara's thesis that reconciliation of indigenous rights is fully served by the terms of the New Dawn Agreement. None of these writers acknowledge the full impact of the promise given in the 1763 Royal Proclamation. In Chapter 20, I compare their views with those of indigenous scholars such as John Borrows, Taiaiake Alfred, Vine Deloria and Calvin Helin. Finally, in Chapter 21, I give my own conclusions.

Throughout the text, I try to give priority to indigenous voices in order to reflect their arguments should they ever be properly represented at the negotiating table. This text should be read as a proof of evidence, and thus I have interleaved the chapters with direct quotations from the people of Matimekush Lac John, Municipality of Schefferville, Northern Quebec. Consistent with this approach, **at no time have I contacted the lawyers and consultants advising the Innu Nation of Labrador.**

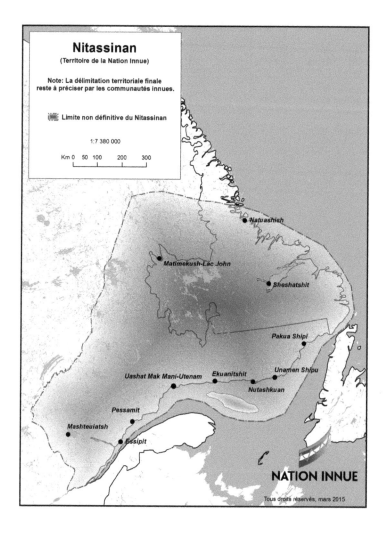

Map 1: Territory of the Innu Nation. Note: The final territorial delimitation remains to be defined by the Innu Communities. The shaded area represents the non-definitive limit of Nitassinan.

If we go back to the values and the actions of our traditional leaders, they were always looking for ways to bring food to the table. It was always survival mode. Trying to bring something good for the family, whether it was only to bring flour from the trading post. They would try to bring something back for the family so they could live throughout the year. I believe that the leaders, the elected leaders nowadays, have to do the same in trying to bring food to the tables of the families who are living in this community. Nowadays we are stuck in between two different lifestyles, the traditional life and this modern life, and we are always stuck in between these two roads and we are not totally fit for the non-Innu way of life and many of our young people are not fit for the traditional way of life. So we are stuck in between and we have to find a junction or a balance between the two lives to bring wealth or food in our community and, for that, a leader has to be wise and they have to have the wisdom to find the balance between the Innu way of life and the non-Innu way of life; and, to have wisdom, the elected leaders would work closely with the communities, the grassroots people: they should work very closely with the community. It is as if they are disconnected from their community, their people.

Part One
The Innu

Chapter 1

Innu/Canadian relations in their social context

Although one travels on a train named for the wind, *Tshiuetin* in Innu-Aimun, the journey north on the Quebec North Shore and Labrador Railway is a slow one. Passengers arrive very early in the morning at the railway station in Sept-Iles with luggage unimaginable for a more southerly North American train journey – canoes, fridges, cartons of provisions, insulated containers, blankets and sleeping bags for the long journey – much like the old expeditions the Innu used to make to their northern lands with heavy loads and long portages. Now the train whisks them to their destination 350 miles away in a mere 12 hours. For most Innu, the train is the only connection between the northern and southern communities. There are no roads and air travel is prohibitively expensive.

When I travelled on the train between 2008 and 2011, it was very much a family train, linking the Innu who had moved north to their villages around Schefferville with their cousins who continued to live along the North Shore of the St Lawrence. It is a friendly train. Children moved along the carriages with confidence, greeting friends, relatives and strangers alike. My friend Danielle Descent prepared me a picnic for my journey – bannock and partridge. When I opened my lunch, which had been packed in the Innu way into a clean white cloth bag, the contents drew appreciative murmurs and I made new friends over morsels of partridge and bannock, a friendship sealed when they saw I was reading An Antane Kapesh's account of their grandparents' generation and how they settled in Matimekush and Lac John.[1] These encounters served me well when I began my series of interviews to try to convey to future generations of Innu how present-day Innu had fought to retain their land and to protect it from the incursions of the governments and corporations who were destroying it for the sake of a few years' resource extraction.

This train is a symbol of the lived experience of the Innu of Matimekush Lac John. It was built to enable iron ore from the Iron Ore Company mines to be transported from Schefferville to the port at Sept-Iles. It was an instrument of the devastation of their lands and of their lives as nomadic subsistence hunters.

---

1   Kapesh, A.A., *Je suis une maudite sauvagesse*, trans. (into French) by J. Mailhot, assisted by A.-M. André and A. Mailhot (Ottawa: Editions Lemeac, 1976)

The purpose of my work in Matimekush Lac John was to try to reach a clearer understanding of the consequences of denying the rights of indigenous peoples who have walked the land for millennia. I have tried to be as true as possible to the accounts I was given in the Band Council offices and around the kitchen tables of homes in the two villages. I intend that the information given in these chapters should be given the same weight as a proof of evidence.

'Suffering' is a term which has entered the academic debate on land claims and indigenous rights.[2] However, the term is rarely used at the negotiating table, certainly not by government and company negotiators. These chapters are an attempt to bring home to those sitting round the land settlement negotiation tables the true cost of what they demand of the Innu and other indigenous peoples – in exchange for the sale of their land at a gross undervalue together with a very few employment opportunities for their children.

The Innu

The Innu are an indigenous people related to the Cree and speaking an Algonquin language, Innu-Aimun. For the Innu, Quebec and Labrador are alien concepts. The land of the Ungava Peninsula is Nitassinan – 'the peoples' land' – the homeland shared by all indigenous peoples of the area, but with sovereignty over certain areas of territory acknowledged to be held by individual groups such as the Innu. This land is described in Innu-Aimun as *nutshimit* – land which encompasses a whole way of life – religion, nourishment, moral values – in which people live in harmony with their surroundings, and are not regarded as a superior species but have a responsibility to maintain the balance of nature.

The Innu identify themselves as hunter gatherers who, until the middle of the 20th century, lived in the interior and only journeyed to the coast in the two summer months when the flies drove both humans and caribou away. The Innu who have contributed their stories for this text made the annual 750-mile round trip on foot, by canoe and with difficult portages, returning to Uashat and Maliotenam on the North Shore in the two summer months. They found everything they needed for survival through hunting, fishing and gathering, although conditions could be very hard in times when the animals did not come.

Until 1975, Nitassinan had never been ceded or conquered and the Innu and other peoples who shared the peninsula were able to retain much of their traditional way of life, albeit adapted in order to provide high-quality skins for the fur trade. In any event, apart from land along the North Shore of the Gulf

---

2   See, for example, G.M. Sider, *Skin for Skin: Death and Life for Inuit and Innu* (Durham, North Carolina: Duke University Press, 2014); and S. Irlbacher-Fox, *Finding Dahshaa: Self-government, Social Suffering, and Aboriginal Policy in Canada* (Vancouver: UBC Press, 2009).

of St Lawrence, initially their territory was inhospitable to the non-indigenous peoples coming from Europe.

The Innu claim to the land is that they walked the land, etching deep trails into the rocks with their footsteps, travelling the whole of the Quebec-Labrador Peninsula, meeting up by the coast in the two summer months. Families travelled 750 miles a year on a round trip from Uashat to the Caniapiscau region over the ten months of hunting. One man talked of being taken by his father from Matimekush to Sheshatshiu on the Labrador coast without the aid of a map. His father knew the Innu name of every lake on a Canadian map of the Quebec-Labrador Peninsula.[3] Out with his father in the bush many years ago, another elder discovered a birch bark canoe from generations ago.[4] Some of the hunting camps used by today's Innu are situated in the clearings made by their ancestors. The stone hearths are preserved as archaeological sites and as memorials to hunters long gone.

The Innu way of life was threatened, however, with the discovery of iron ore in Nitassinan which was exploited after World War II. When the Iron Ore Company opened its mine in Schefferville, Innu from Uashat and Maliotenam were persuaded to come north to settle on the new reserves at Matimekush Lac John. They were attracted by this move not only because of the offer of jobs and housing but also because the new reserve was on their traditional hunting grounds and this would save them much of their annual travel. A railway was built along their ancient trail to the north. However, when they got to Schefferville, there was little or no housing for the Innu, there were not enough jobs and the open-cast mine workings destroyed the landscape and drove the caribou away.

All the hunters speak of a feeling of peace and safety out on the land. Now the hills nearest to Matimekush have become a place of danger. The land will never recover from the top-slicing of the earth for the open-cast mines. Recently, the reserve has been the subject of a film, *Une Tente Sur Mars*,[5] which shows the effect of the mining operation on the community and what it means to have the land for which the Innu are responsible ravaged in the Canadian rush to exploit its resources. Thirty years after it opened, the mine closed in 1982 and the Matimekush Lac John Innu were abandoned on their spoiled land. The Iron Ore Company was not even required to make the land safe when it left. Now new mines have opened, but the Matimekush Lac John Innu will be the last in the queue to benefit. The 11 Innu communities on either side of the Quebec–Labrador border, who have stood together to fight encroachment on Innu land wherever it occurs, are divided. The Innu who live in Labrador are on the brink of signing the New Dawn Final Agreement,

3   Interview MA8, March 2009.
4   Interview MD6, Sept. 2009.
5   M. Bureau and L. Renaud (Productions Thalie, 2009).

but the governments and their commercial partners have already constructed the dam they need to exploit the waters of the Lower Churchill Falls without the Final Agreement in place. Further, new iron ore mines have opened on the Labrador side of the border at Schefferville.

The move to Schefferville

After World War II, with the preparations for the opening of the Schefferville mine, the Quebec government and the Iron Ore Company encouraged the Innu to move from their summer home on the coastal reserves of Maliotenam and Uashat and to settle permanently on a new reserve on the outskirts of Schefferville. First, labour was needed for the building of the railway and a hydro-electric dam on the Menehek Lake, together with a camp for the prospectors. An elder explained: 'With all the construction going on in Schefferville, hunters started to stay here and to become more and more sedentary, abandoning the nomadic way of life in the sense that nobody was buying fur from the trading posts so people somehow had to rely on some form of revenue from working at the mine. They abandoned the traditional way of life.'[6]

An Antane Kapesh, one of the Innu who came to Matimekush on the promise of better access to land and a more secure future, in her book *Je Suis Une Maudite Sauvagesse* speaks of the hardships which the Innu faced when they first settled in Schefferville, for example having to live in tents despite the promise of new modern housing. She recounts how, when no permanent housing was provided after several months, the Innu bought up the temporary buildings, now abandoned by the Iron Ore Company, for greatly inflated prices.[7] When her family could afford to buy a building, all they could get was the toilet block, which was nevertheless sold to them at an exorbitant price.

Once the Innu settled into the housing, which they had had to provide for themselves, the mine officials decided that they should be moved away from the town to Lac John because, they claimed, the Innu were polluting the water supplies. In fact, the Innu were moved on to Lac John because the land they occupied was designated for the new airport.[8]

In 1956, the federal government removed a northerly Mushuau Innu group (known by Europeans as Naskapi[9]), from Fort Chimo in the far north of the Quebec-Labrador Peninsula, to settle in Lac John with the Innu. There was no consultation with either the Naskapi or the existing community.[10] Like the

6   Interview MFD7, Sept. 2009.
7   Kapesh, *Maudite sauvagesse*, pp. 187–9. See also J. Silberstein, *Innu: A la rencontre des Montagnais du Québec-Labrador* (Paris: Editions Albin Michel, 1998), p. 246.
8   Silberstein, *Innu: A la rencontre*, p. 191.
9   I shall use this term because this group, following the signing of the North Eastern Quebec Agreement, became known as the Naskapi Nation.
10 Interview MFC6, March 2009.

Innu, the Naskapi came with nothing and, at this time, they were altogether poorer than the Innu. Jules d'Astous, regional supervisor of Indian Agencies in Quebec, wrote at the time that the group transferred to Schefferville were 'sick, totally destitute and now living almost solely on relief'.[11] There was considerable resentment between the two indigenous groups, particularly as the government provided housing for the newcomers, whereas it had failed to do so for those already there despite its initial promise.[12] A former non-Innu schoolmaster who taught at Schefferville School in the 1980s suggested that the Naskapi were moved south following an exchange at the United Nations when Canada challenged human rights practices in the Soviet Union and the Russians replied that the Canadians housed their northern peoples in dustbins (probably unused containers from the local air base near Fort Chimo).[13]

There came a time when it was no longer cost-effective to provide services to the community at Lac John and pressure was put on the people who lived there to move nearer to Schefferville. The authorities met with considerable resistance from the Innu families, who were now settled in Lac John, and the community was divided. While some families moved into new accommodation on the new Matimekush reserve on the other side of Lake Pearce from Schefferville, others chose to stay. At this time, the affairs of the reserve were overseen by an Indian Agent whose power over the community was seen as malevolent.[14] According to one interviewee, the Indian Agent was deeply insulting to her because of her leadership of the group who wished to stay in Lac John. She spoke of the pressure that was put on the families who wished to stay:

> They even proposed to me that the government would build me a big fancy house and furnish it just to bribe us because we were at the head of the committee against relocation. They thought we would convince other families that it was acceptable now to move. They thought probably that by bribing the head of the movement that somehow the group would follow. But they didn't understand that it was the group that gave us the strength.[15]

Speaking to Jil Silberstein, the same interviewee described what was left of the Lac John community as a ghost town, with only six families remaining.[16]

11   Quoted in M. Wadden, *Nitassinan: The Innu Struggle to Reclaim Their Homeland* (Vancouver/Toronto: Douglas & McIntyre, 1991), p. 31.

12   Silberstein, *Innu: A la rencontre*, p. 246; but see also Sider, *Skin for Skin*, pp. 194–5, where he says that no housing was provided for the Naskapi.

13   Conversation with delegate to the Arctic Frontiers Conference, Tromsø, Norway, 10 Jan. 2010.

14   For an account of the Indian Agent system, see R. Brownlie, *A Fatherly Eye: Indian Agents, Government Power, and Aboriginal Resistance in Ontario, 1918–1939* (Toronto: Oxford University Press, 2003).

15   Interview MC6, 25 March 2009.

16   Silberstein, *Innu: A la rencontre*, p. 291.

Before World War II, the Innu were able to maintain their seasonal round
and their traditional ways of living off the land with relatively little interference.
José Mailhot describes how the land of the Ungava Peninsula was shared by
all Innu. Hunting parties were usually made up of related families travelling
together. She describes how they had access to lands occupied by the wider
family, which included in-laws.[17]

In 2009, a 45-year-old hunter told me about that life, a life which he still
pursues today:

> When you live off the land you live according to the rhythm of the
> seasons and the rhythm of the animals. There are certain seasons of
> the year when it is good to live off the land. I try as much as possible
> to share whenever I have a good kill. I try to share as well with other
> people the knowledge that I have.
>
> When you live off the land you see your day, you see your life. Your life
> is filled with very positive things. You work a lot. When you burn the
> fat [to sear the skin of the geese before cooking], all the bad things that
> you had when you were on the reserve are burnt in that process and you
> do a lot of physical activities. You start your day when the sun rises and
> you see your day filled with activities, hard work; you are a free man.
> You want to go on the lake and see a good place where you can lay a
> net or gather some fish – you can do it. You are filled with happiness
> because your whole body exudes happiness when you live on the land.
>
> I was among elders when I learned those skills and there was not a
> single time when I was bored. There is a lot of peace and pleasure and
> happiness when I think of that life.[18]

This man is one of the few today who spend most of their time hunting. The
traditional way of life and culture of the Innu – *Innu-Aitun* – is significantly
diminished, the knowledge of living the seasonal round out on the land resting
in the hands of a few elders, now well advanced in years. However, fortunately
there are plenty of young people eager for a chance to learn these skills.

The Innu agreed to be settled in Schefferville because they were promised
that they would have greater access to their hunting land as well as modern
living conditions and a proper education for their children. When they got
there, there was no housing, and no sooner were they settled in one place
than they were moved on. Having been promised easier access, they were
systematically driven off their land. Further, as discussed below, even today the
education on a reserve where its inhabitants are wards of the Crown is inferior
and a hindrance to the development of young Innu.

Life settled near a town exposed the Innu to alcohol and drugs for the first
time. Alcohol formed no part of their life in the country. An Antane Kapesh

17   J. Mailhot, *The People of Sheshatshit: In the Land of the Innu*, trans. A. Harvey (St.
     John's: Institute of Social and Economic Research Press, 1998).
18   Interview MD6, 14 Sept. 2009. See also Silberstein, *Innu: A la rencontre*, p. 311.

speaks of the devastation caused by drink, bringing about the ruin of many young Innu.[19] She also tells of the discrimination and brutality of the police in dealing with the resulting problems.

In his 1983 film *Mémoire Battante*,[20] Arthur Lamothe follows the family of Matthieu André out onto the land and records the caribou hunt. When no caribou appear, the old man puts the scapular bone of a caribou onto the fire and reads the whereabouts of the caribou from the marks which appear on the bone, a practice recorded by Frank Speck as scapulamancy. Lamothe records all the hunting skills passed down from generation to generation of Innu. Other footage records the transition which was taking place in Matimekush family events, which owe more to western culture.[21] Lamothe remarks on the consistent racism towards the Innu which he encountered among settler Canadians living in Schefferville.

Writing of the Innu who live in the two Labrador villages of Utshimassits (Davis Inlet) and Sheshatshiu, whose treatment at the time was similar to that of their relatives across the Quebec–Labrador border, Colin Samson observes that:

> ... it was important that the first generation to live in the villages on a permanent basis be educated to accept the various assumptions on which Euro-Canadian society was beginning to develop on the Labrador–Quebec peninsula, particularly the need to economically exploit the resources of the area. If they were to function in the society of those who were about to bring such drastic changes to them, the socialization of children could not be left up to Innu parents, the hunters who were deemed to have only a fragile grip on the skills, attitudes and knowledge which the Euro-Canadian world demanded.[22]

As will be seen, this forced transition to a settled life within a cash economy resulted in a loss of identity which could not be fixed by an underfinanced education system.

Work at the Iron Ore Company mine

In 1982, after less than 30 years of exploitation, the mine closed – the market price for iron ore having fallen, making it uneconomic to continue the operation at that time. The mine and the services which supported it had provided jobs for the Innu and made most of them as dependent on wage labour as they were on hunting. François Aster, 99 years of age, a respected hunter and staunch defender of Innu land rights, was one of several interviewees who spoke of

19   Kapesh, *Maudite sauvagesse*, Chapter 6.
20   K Films, 1983, Quebec, Canada.
21   Audio archive of the University of Laval, Quebec City.
22   C. Samson, *A Way of Life That Does Not Exist: Canada and the Extinguishment of the Innu* (London: Verso Books, 2003), p. 173.

working at the mine: 'I got a certificate for working with dynamite. It was only Indian people who were allowed to carry dynamite. It was harder working [in the mine] because you had to work with time rather than with the daylight. Even in weather like this you had to be there.' (The outside temperature was −39 degrees at the time of the interview).

Another hunter said that when the Innu mineworkers had worked five years they got a vacation for three months, which was the only time when they could go hunting. Very few Innu workers had sufficient education to get the skilled jobs in the mine.

Nevertheless, as we shall see in the following chapter, when the mine closed the resilience of the Innu enabled them to fight successfully to remain in their town despite the efforts of the governments to move them south again.

The land is being sold everywhere. We are stuck in a corridor that is getting narrower. We are stuck on a land where everyone is making deals. We should occupy the land and strive to pass it on to our young people.

Dad went to the trading posts scattered all over. We lived off the land and hunted all the year round.

If food was scarce, we would share.

When I was young I was taught to learn all kind of skills like cooking Indian food, preparing food, knowing how to cut food, where to cut it, how to prepare the skin and how to prepare the animal and how to cut up the animal. We had to learn the preparation for different animals, cooking and preparation. Those are the things that a young girl would know. Then of course, I had the teachings about domestic skills, like trying to help out, making handicrafts, moccasins, gloves, clothes, even snowshoes. Learning how to do what a woman does. To accompany her man in the forest so you have to have all those skills as well. I also learned how to pray – how to read the bible and the prayer book and then learning it by heart which was important back then. All these skills, including prayer, helped me to go through my life up to today.

I guess there will be some remnants – something will remain of our culture – but as years go by no one will care much about it. But there will always be someone who knows about the traditional way of life.

You didn't hunt immediately around your home or *teepee* because you wouldn't use up all the resources around your *teepee* – you would go as far as possible in case you were sick so you wouldn't have to travel far, and for the women as well, so that they could use the resources next to the *teepee*: so there was a strategy, for instance you won't cut wood for your fire or use the trees next to your *teepee* to cut wood for your fire. You would have to go a bit of a distance so that you don't use up all the resources next to your *teepee* in case you get sick, or to facilitate the work of the women as they were staying behind.

Chapter 2

The Innu left to their fate in Schefferville

When the Schefferville mine closed, the federal government, according to one informant,[1] first considered and then rejected the idea of moving the Innu sedentarised in Sheshatshiu into Schefferville town.[2] Subsequently, the Iron Ore Company and the Quebec government sought to close down the town. Jil Silberstein suggests that this was to be an incentive for the Innu to move back to Maliotenam and Uashat on the North Shore. He describes the town as 'a sinister town, almost a ghost town surrounded by a mutilated landscape, immense craters reddened by the abundance of iron, abandoned hangars, rusty machinery. Hideous. And then there are the Innu, shocked and stricken after having been humiliated.'[3]

The vast majority of the non-Innu moved south again, but the Innu wanted to stay. The hunters went back to living off the land, but they had a fight on their hands to keep the facilities which had been provided for the white workers. At the Tshakapesh Institute (formerly ICEM) in Uashat, there is a file of letters and reports pleading the case for keeping the town open – but the bulldozers moved in and the hospital and sports facilities were demolished, after which they began to bulldoze housing which was urgently needed for Innu families.

Negotiations for the survival of Schefferville

The closure of the town itself was announced in June 1986, and Bill-67 was passed by the Quebec government to facilitate this. The Innu saw the closure of the town as an opportunity both to move from their cramped reserve into the white workers' houses, and for their own economic development. At first the Ministry of Indian Affairs was encouraging but, with the departure of a key figure who stepped down from the ministry, the governments pressed for compulsory purchase of the Schefferville houses and Ottawa delegated to Quebec the task of visiting Schefferville to inform the Innu that they would not

1   Interview MAS5.6.E5.64, 23 Sept. 2009.
2   Ibid.
3   Silberstein, *Innu: A la rencontre*, p. 248.

after all be allowed to buy the houses of the miners. Instead the Matimekush reserve would be enlarged. The Band Council organised a petition signed by the Innu population which expressed clearly that they wanted to move into Schefferville.

On 9 February 1988, there was a meeting between the Innu and the Naskapi with the Ministers of Mines and Indian Affairs at which it was decided that everything was negotiable, whereupon the Band Council expressed its willingness to negotiate and handed the file to the Conseil Attikamekw-Montagnais (CAM), the body which was negotiating on behalf of the Innu to recover their lost James Bay lands. While the Quebec government accepted, the federal government refused to negotiate on the grounds that:

- it did not want a negotiated solution which would open the door to other Indian groups who wanted to negotiate the enlargement of their reserves;

- Quebec was using the Innu request as a pretext to preserve the urban environment and thus keep the town open, but hiding this behind the Innu demands;

- the request was a political move for the enlargement of the reserve and not a desire for relocation; and

- there was no money for such a project.

Instead, the federal government proposed a working party to find solutions for the enlargement of the reserve. A public meeting was held in Schefferville on 5 April 1988, at which the Innu approved the strategy of the Band Council to force the two governments to sit down at the negotiating table. The government of Quebec agreed to the negotiation. A meeting was arranged in Ottawa but neither government attended. At a meeting with representatives of the Prime Minister's office, the Department of Indian Affairs and Northern Development (DIAND) agreed to work with the Innu and a further meeting was arranged to take place in Schefferville, followed by a tripartite negotiation which was held on 26 and 27 April 1988 and at which a working plan was presented.

This plan set out the process for the closure of Schefferville and the transfer of the town by the governments to the Matimekush Lac John Band Council. It encompassed issues including the boundaries of the new territory acquired; the maintenance of essential services; the rehousing of the Innu in the town and the provision of education, health and leisure facilities; and the development of employment creation schemes.

It was made clear that the Quebec government had no intention to keep the town open. There were further discussions between the Quebec and federal (Ottawa) governments, following which the Quebec representative let it be known that Quebec had no further objection to Innu settlement in the town and would engage in serious negotiations with the Band Council. The federal government made no such commitment. Thus the Innu became well versed in the government's tactics of prevarication and procrastination intended to wear down their resolve.

With no further employment in the mine and having abandoned the practice of walking the land for ten months of the year, hunting became prohibitively expensive because of the need for fuel for vehicles and seaplanes. Life on reserve degenerated into a cycle of dependency on benefits, empty days and a loss of the ethic of sharing and mutual support. This is in sharp contrast to the life of purpose and action out on the land. Only short and brief expeditions were possible. Jil Silberstein[4] remarks that very few Innu had jobs and thus they 'vegetate thanks to public assistance which arrives in the form of a monthly cheque'. He describes the system as 'humiliating, depressing … especially as 60% of the Innu are under 25. Corollaries to this forced idleness are family violence, delinquency, suicide and addiction. Quarrels between clans make the atmosphere tense, sometimes fed by the *métissage*[5] of the population.'[6]

Living off the land

One interviewee described how, following the closure of the mine, she and her husband went on to set up an outfitter's business which would maintain their connection to the land:

> When we wanted to build our project to have an outfitter's licence for our family hunting grounds, we thought we would not have much difficulty in obtaining this licence – we invested ten thousand dollars travelling back and forth to Ottawa, Quebec City, Schefferville, to try to convince the government that we should have a licence to operate as outfitters. Nevertheless, we learned the sad news that we couldn't do it because of the Naskapi Agreement. We couldn't operate on our family hunting ground offering these facilities without the consent of the Naskapi.

> We wanted to do something to realise a project that all of us would be proud of, you know, a modern facility to keep our connection to the land, and that government person tells us we have to ask permission from the Naskapi and we reply, 'I would be a fool to ask the Naskapi permission to be on our own hunting grounds'.

> We hear all kinds of sayings or labelling, we hear about people labelling the Indians as being drunks, always having a case of beer, that's all we hear – that they are drunk, they are lazy, they don't do anything. But we tried to be the opposite. We had all our evidence, all our papers, everything, travelling to Ottawa, Quebec and back to Schefferville with our own money and we tried to see the Minister … and he said he wouldn't have time for us. I said, 'Well, I can come back here tomorrow

4 Silberstein, *Innu: A la rencontre*, p. 248.
5 'Attempted assimilation'.
6 Silberstein, *Innu: A la rencontre*, p. 15.

with reporters, the movie film-makers and I will tell them about the treatment you are giving to the Indian people here if we don't see the Minister, if we don't see anything, any concrete result about our request for a licence.

The next day, someone knocked at the door saying that a fax would be sent shortly and there it was – a letter confirming that we would have a licence and permit. We could operate our outfitting facilities on our family hunting ground.

By getting our permit or licence, we thought that this is another closed file and then we started another round of battles against the government. They would send their game wardens flying over, landing next to our cabin, asking us to pay a licence and some other fees attached to the licence. We asked, 'Why would we have to pay that? We are the rightful owners.' And then he said, 'Well, if you don't pay, guys, your clients might be sent to jail because you don't pay those fees.' So, in order not to cause harm to our clients, well, we finally agreed to pay the licence fee but then, again they would come and harass us, come after us, chasing our clients, being very annoying to us. I finally got upset with this and said to the game wardens, 'Next time you come, bring the Minister.' I wanted to talk to this guy because he didn't know about the history of this land: we are the rightful owners, the rightful occupants of these hunting grounds.

Well, at the very end we saw the game wardens coming again. I said 'You guys, just arrest us and imprison us because there is nothing more that we could ask than to be in prison because we want to defend our land and maintain our relationship to the land. We are doing nothing wrong. We are doing no harm. We just want to get a decent livelihood from our family hunting grounds. So, have us arrested and then I'll be very proud of the grounds upon which you would arrest us. I'd be very proud to say to the world that we want to lead a decent life and live in peace on our land.'[7]

The business is now well established and is still running successfully 35 years on.[8]

When the mine closed in 1982, some of the hunters once again put food on the table by going back to hunting full-time. However, the landscape was changing. The mine itself has scarred the mountains above Matimekush, slicing through the hillsides and leaving deep and dangerous holes. The area around Schefferville is still littered with old machinery and the site is dangerous. The Iron Ore Company failed to decommission the site satisfactorily. Bears which once fed on the berries which grow on the site of the old mine now feast across

7 Interview MFC6, 26 March 2009.
8 Another interview with the same interviewee, recorded in the 1990s, can be found in the 'Autochtone' section of the Museum of Civilisation in Quebec City.

the road at the garbage dump. Though they were once revered by Innu hunters, I was shown the bears as a kind of tourist attraction.[9]

There have been many summonses issued when Matimekush Innu have been found hunting on their traditional lands which have now been allocated to other peoples under the James Bay, North Eastern Quebec and New Dawn Agreements. The firearms are confiscated. There are many stories of confrontations with game wardens, some resulting in imprisonment for the hunters. One elder described the effect of such harassment on his own life:

> I try to be a good father to my children. I try to give the best to my children. I try to give them good traditional food, but I see by the actions of the government the total lack of respect for our people. The government doesn't think that by taking our food off the table, that the hunter, the father, will have to go back on the land to replace that food. The government doesn't think about the hardship it creates for the Innu. So, I am trying to be a good father but at the same time I see the Crown ruining the future of our children. Basically, they have ruined our children.[10]

The Innu are being driven off their lands to make way for sports hunters from the United States, Canada and Europe, mainly Germany. Gérard Simeon, an elder from Mashteuiatsh, Lac St Jean, told Jil Silberstein[11] that, from the moment that white sporting clubs were opened in that region, the restrictions imposed by the game wardens had become extremely severe 'in order to protect the game'. No such restrictions applied to the sports hunters, however. In Matimekush they observe that, while it is permissible to hunt for sport, it is forbidden to the owners of the land to hunt to provide themselves with food. At the same time, the vast majority of the community lives on benefits in run-down housing and with nothing to do all day. It is hardly surprising that bingo is the highlight of their week.

The food provided by the hunters and the gatherers who are seen picking the blueberries and cranberries on the hillside is exactly the sort of food which workers at the health centre would like to see in the diet of Matimekush families. When I was gathering interviews in March 2009, there was nearly always a rich aroma of partridge or other small game being cooked on the stove – but I was listening to a small group of Innu who had managed to keep their culture strong.

Caribou has become a much rarer source of food. The schoolmaster to whom I spoke at the conference in Tromsø could not find words to describe the vastness of the George River herd of caribou which came to Matimekush each

---

9   See also C. Samson, *A World You Do Not Know: Settler Societies, Indigenous Peoples and the Attack on Cultural Diversity* (London: Institute of Commonwealth Studies, 2013), pp. 121–3.

10   Interview MFC6.

11   Silberstein, *Innu: A la rencontre*, p. 33.

autumn in the years before the Iron Ore Company mine closed. According to government statistics, the George River herd numbered 800,000 in 1990. By 2012, there were only 27,000.[12] When Jil Silberstein stayed in Matimekush in 1998, the caribou could be found a 15-minute truck ride away.[13] In 2009, the Matimekush Innu had to travel 80 miles to find them, and in that year and the subsequent years to 2012, there were few caribou to be found anywhere. Even the small game has been driven away by the opening of new mines, over-killing by sports hunters and by climate change.

There are now plans to build dams on every major river of the Quebec-Labrador Peninsula, which will have a devastating effect on the hunting territories and on the ecology of the region generally. Because of these disturbances, the great George River herd of caribou has ceased to come to Schefferville on its annual migration.

In the face of the governments' opposition to the Innu refusal to be moved on once more from their northern village, the Innu remain faithful to their core beliefs. In the next chapter we shall examine their day-to-day lives as wards of the Crown.

12   Quoted in M. Blaser, 'Is Another Cosmopolitics Possible?', *Cultural Anthropology*, 31(4) (2016): 545–70.
13   Silberstein, *Innu: A la rencontre*, p. 302.

Another teaching that I received was never to be afraid in the forest because nothing can hurt you in the forest, unlike here in the city or in the village up here in the community. You won't hear any noise – you just hear the sound of nature. And then there was no animal who would try to hurt you, because if you pay respect or respect animals they won't chase you or do you harm.

> The animals won't come up to you or come close to you, because they are afraid, and if you respect the animals, they won't touch you – they won't come chasing after you.

The attitudes are changing now that we live in houses. Like when a child doesn't want to eat, you send him away from the table and say, 'Well, if you don't want to eat, just get down from the table and go in the other room.' Well, you punish the kid for not eating. That wouldn't happen when we were living in a tent, according to our way of life.

> So that's how an Innu child was raised and he or she would learn by looking, through example. He wouldn't use a pen or take notes. The child would only use his memory to learn: by touching, by smelling, by hearing, that child will learn from his or her parents the Innu way of life.

That's how the Innu would live. They would spend all year, all winter, here in this area, in the hunting grounds, and they wouldn't think they were living a miserable life or in poverty or in difficulty, living a bad kind of a life – even though it was tough. Once they were in Sept-Iles or Uashat, on the coast, they would look forward to coming back to their hunting grounds, to come back again to live according to the Innu way of life.

> Before coming back to our times, before telling how we live today, I would say the Innu pretty much enjoyed living their way of life because there was a lot of sharing involved. People would share their food and there was a lot of solidarity back then. And for that reason people would enjoy that way of life.

The Innu would help one another as well and they could tell where they were supposed to be at a certain time of the month, what area you were supposed to be in – and if they didn't hear back from you, from your comrades or your friends, then you would start worrying and you would look for help or look out for … try to reach that person to find out if they were sick or needed food or if there was an accident. If something happened to these people, you would find out. You would try to find out. And that's how people would live back then. Helping one another.

Chapter 3

Matimekush Lac John today

Health issues

The senior health worker in the Matimekush Lac John health centre told me of the cycle of alcoholism in the area. Alcoholics appear in the clinic with the shakes or hallucinations. The staff take care of them and dry them out. They go home and are lonely. Then they go out to see their friends and the drinking begins again. Yet, many elders here and elsewhere have spoken of the disappearance of alcohol dependency without any intervention when the Innu go back to the land.

The health worker also spoke of the poor diet of the people in Matimekush, mainly because the prices at the store are double what they are in Sept-Iles on account of the town's poor transport links. As in many aboriginal communities, one of the main health problems is diabetes. When the Innu are not working:

> Money is used for all sorts of marginal things – smoking, alcohol, gaming, drugs. If both the man and the woman smoke a packet of cigarettes a day each, that's $500 a month. Two or three beers a day – $30–50 per month. All you hear on the radio is bingo – if they play two or three times a week that's $500 a month. So, in this way $1,000 a month goes on marginal activities.

> If you take the money for things like that, there is very little money left for eating fruit and vegetables or proteins, to make a choice for your children. They don't make a life choice. They eat to survive. So, the food that is prepared at home is not so good and they don't have time to prepare it so they think it is better to get it outside the home because they don't have time to make a good meal at home. And so they have malnutrition – not undernourishment but malnutrition. There is obesity here.

> The amount they smoke is another cause of diabetes – I would say that 80% of people smoke in this town. The secondary students at the school, they all smoke – 100% of the children. Some of the primary children also smoke. So, there is cancer and pulmonary

disease, coronary disease – we are moving towards a generation who hypothetically will destroy their health. Because of their way of life. Because of the food, the smoking and there is also alcoholism. It's a vicious circle.[1]

Nevertheless, he did say that nowadays levels of domestic violence were low and that there had only been two suicides in the community in the past five years.

As Colin Samson notes:

Illness to the Innu is not simply a biological malfunction. It follows from community life. For them, the severing of a permanent link with the land, which is the flip side to their confinement to villages, has had a huge bearing on their well-being. The collective loss of autonomy occasioned by these processes acts as a sort of benchmark against which they situate illness and healing.[2]

Writing in 2013, he observes the descent of the Innu into the world of fast food and plasma televisions, which the non-Innu residents in the two Labrador villages claim is a 'necessary evil of advancement and a temporary dip in the upward movement of progress'.[3] That 'temporary dip' has, so far, lasted more than 60 years and, despite the attempts at land deals and resource extraction, there are no signs of improvement in the everyday life of those Innu not tied up in the business deals. Samson further points out that: 'Cable TV and satellite dishes arrived for the people of Davis Inlet about a decade before toilets and running water.'[4]

Education

Donat Jean-Pierre, Principal of Schefferville School, and the first Innu to hold that post, spoke of his dilemmas in funding.[5] Unlike the Naskapi school in Kawawachikamach, where the North Eastern Quebec Agreement handed responsibility for the reserve's education budget to the provincial government, the federal funding for his school is much lower. Moreover, with only 144 students, the *per capita* grant is inadequate for the improvements he would like to make to the curriculum. He cannot join forces with the Kawawachikamach school because that school is anglophone and the Schefferville school is francophone.

Two Canadian teachers, who clearly had respect for the students they taught, spoke of the lack of parental interest in education. I asked whether that

1   Interview ME3.
2   Colin Samson, *A Way of Life*, p. 255.
3   Colin Samson, *A World*, p. 22.
4   Ibid., p. 23.
5   Interview MAS4, Sept. 2009.

might be because of the parents' own education and they agreed that this was a factor.

Jil Silberstein speaks of the 'vampirisation'[6] of Innu youth by the introduction of western culture. On my earlier visit to Matimekush, one young mother had said:

> It is hard to break that cycle [of resistance to education], because what I see is that the problems here are with cocaine and gambling. For example, the parents are playing bingo. They spend money on X-boxes and video games, bingo. Small kids have motor bikes. Just material things and I don't think that's what the children need. They give the things to the kid just to get rid of the kid and in the meantime the parents play card games and bingo.[7]

Colin Samson observes that, 'Many people believe that television influences young people to believe that the values of North American society, including violent retribution, greed for money and material possessions, and the ideals of romantic love, are normal and preferable to the values that Innu people have for sharing, generosity, and an outdoor hunting lifestyle.'[8]

I was surprised and impressed by the level of response from a group of 14–16-year-olds who, in a history lesson at school, responded to my questions about hunting and living on the land with a lively interest. They enthusiastically noted down the URL of Memorial University, St. John's, Newfoundland, where they could find the history of their own people. I am not used to such a response in English schools from students of the same age. When I saw them in the corridor after the session, they were equally responsive and polite when their teachers were not there.

Yet, even if the students stay the course and finish school, their certificates do not have the same recognition as those from a provincial school because they must retake a year if they fail it. An interviewee who runs the café where many of the children go for their lunch told me that she never asks the children their age or grade for fear of embarrassing them in front of their peers.[9] Earlier that week I had seen a girl of 12 or 13 years of age in the café alongside her classmates who could not have been more than nine years old. Sometimes they retake the year three or four times. They are labelled as failures even before they step out into the adult world. Yet they are trying their best. I spoke to a young Metis man who was determined to finish his schooling and go on to an accountancy training. He was 23 and his hopes were high: 'Unfortunately, my education has been very prolonged – I am twenty-three and I am still trying to pass my exams so that I can work in accountancy. I am very determined and I

6   Silberstein, *Innu: A la rencontre*, p. 68.
7   Interview FAS.5, 2009.
8   Samson, *A Way of Life*, p. 211.
9   Interview FAS.15, Sept. 2009.

keep trying. I have had some periods when I have given up but I've gone back again and hope to finish in the next year or so.'[10]

The parents I spoke to were also concerned about the standard of education provided by federal schools. Two young women were thinking of moving away when their children reached secondary level:

> I am afraid. If I stay here I am afraid for myself or my baby because the fact that there is always bingo affects the mindset of the people. It's like being brainwashed and all they have in mind throughout the day is bingo. At some point it gets into the kids as well. That's all they hear – life is bingo. If I stay here, I hope that my kids will have a good education but I don't think that will happen. You are given a diploma or certificate. But once you leave this community it is not good enough. You always miss a couple of credits so you can't get success – you always have to do more to catch up.[11]

This mother had made the effort to finish her own education in Sept-Iles and had travelled through Canada in order to learn English. She had also travelled in Peru. She returned to live in Matimekush because she wanted to learn the traditional skills.

A 31-year-old mother told me how, when she was at school, there were programmes on how to sew in the Innu way and how to clean caribou. She would welcome a return of these programmes.[12]

The social worker, health worker, school principal, teachers and parents all remarked on the way they felt the young people of Matimekush Lac John were let down by the governments' aboriginal policies. There is very little teaching at the school on Innu culture and tradition – perhaps two short courses each lasting a week. However, there were classes in Innu-Aimun to keep the language alive. The children speak Innu-Aimun at home and are taught in French at school, unlike their cousins on the North Shore of the St Lawrence who have almost lost their language. This gives the North Shore Innu an advantage in the job market because their French is much stronger and this impacts on education and interviews for work.[13]

An Innu teacher to whom I spoke on a previous visit, who has since left the school, told me she felt the young people had no heroes, no role models. She was trained in theatre studies and had a teaching qualification. She wanted to introduce the students to the characters from their Innu history and legends through drama education. She had come to Matimekush because she had spent happy summers with her grandparents there and she wanted to give

---

10   Interview MAS10, Sept. 2009.
11   Interview FAS5, Sept. 2009.
12   Interview FB3, March 2009.
13   Interview SAS.7, Sept. 2009.

something back but, before I returned, she had gone back to Quebec City for family reasons.[14]

The Royal Commission on Aboriginal Peoples described education as follows: 'Education is the transmission of cultural DNA from one generation to the next. It shapes the language and pathways of thinking, the contours of the character and values, the social skills and creative potential of the individual. It determines the productive skills and creative potential of a people.'[15]

This is an area in which the elders and the Band Council in Matimekush could and should intervene, to create an environment in which success in the classroom in both Canadian and indigenous skills is valued and recognised. The Canadian provincial and federal governments cannot afford to continue to starve indigenous communities of good education when the Canadian demographic of a rapidly ageing population urgently needs the human resources which a well-educated indigenous youth could provide. Perhaps the standard of education in Matimekush will improve with the influx of non-indigenous families to take jobs in the mines. Then education will no longer be segregated.

Employment

For the years between 1982 and 2010, the main sources of employment within Matimekush Lac John were controlled by the Band Council. As well as an office administration, they have a team of workers who maintain the housing stock and carry out decoration and repairs. There are jobs at the school and the health centre, and at the airport and the Northern Stores, but there are not nearly enough jobs to go round. The Innu Band Council manager who was responsible in 2009 for employment and job creation schemes explained the situation:

> I said I wanted to help the community and I started to work for the Band Council. I work to implement projects. I meet people from the community who are in difficulties. They come to my office and talk about their life and maybe I help some people. They want a job and I have to say, 'I have no jobs'. I have no money to help create jobs and after the person has explained their problem, I change my role and become a psychologist to help the person go home stronger. Another person with the same problem says to me, 'I have no food.' I say, 'I am sorry, I have no money or job [for you]. Maybe in two months when the Band Council gets money.' I have seen 400 people like this. I think I started to take drugs to freeze my emotions when people couldn't get jobs. I get very tired. I don't think I shall be working here long because I have a

14 Interview FX5.28, March 2009.
15 *Report of the Royal Commission on Aboriginal Peoples* (Ottawa: Government of Canada, 1996), Chapter 5.

dream to set up a company, to work for myself. They all have problems. They tell me their problems. They bring their problems here.[16]

The projects are job creation schemes providing temporary work in construction and maintenance for a few weeks each year. If administered successfully so that the work is shared out, the projects enable participants to claim benefits for the rest of the year. Someone who previously held this administrative position noted that, even though the participants in the projects had more money in their pockets while working, they had less need to drink while they had an occupation.[17]

Two Innu women to whom I spoke had tried to qualify as professionals in order to return to work with the Innu, one as a librarian and the other as a nurse.[18] Both had passed their respective examinations comfortably but, when it came to the work experience part of their course, were marked down and have so far not received the qualifications to which they are patently entitled. The nurse told me that she failed her practical assessment because she spoke to her Innu patients in Innu-Aimun and the other medical staff could not understand what she was saying. The nurse is about to make her third attempt to qualify, this time in Quebec City where she hopes that, in a more cosmopolitan environment, she will not meet with the racial prejudice she has encountered so far.

The opening of the new mines in 2010 has provided 100 new jobs. When I asked the school students what they wanted to do when leaving school, they said they hoped for jobs at the mine. Now that the mines are open, some are quitting school to take menial jobs. Others who complete their secondary education are offered training for the skilled jobs. No one on drugs can be offered employment at the mine because of the dangers of operating machinery. This has a significant effect on the numbers who are eligible to take the few jobs available.

The couple with whom I stayed in 2011 both took up jobs with the newly opened mines in Schefferville, one as an office worker and the other as a machine operator. Both expressed their ambivalence at taking wages from an organisation which would destroy the land they revered and loved.

In August 2016, Tata Steel announced a new scheme for its Schefferville mine under which it would employ more Innu and give them better training for more senior jobs. This project was endorsed by the federal minister responsible for aboriginal affairs.

The future lies with young Innu

There were three things upon which everyone I spoke to agreed: that they had a prior and superior title to their traditional land, that things could not go on

16 Interview MC2, March 2009.
17 Interview MAS5, Sept. 2009.
18 Interview F0D1, Oct. 2011.

like this within the community for much longer, and that the key to the future lay with the community's young people.

If the young people, say those under 40 years of age, are to take this community forward, they must not be denied their Innu identity. This was the opinion of everyone I spoke to, young or old. They point out that the Innu values and principles have been swept away with the attempts at assimilation and nothing has been put in their place – so the children and young people are left to their own devices, watching TV all day or playing on X-box, and the only values they have now are the values of consumerism. Yet, having been told that the young were losing their culture, when I asked the students at the school whether they all had seen a caribou, they looked at me as though I was mad – of course they had, and eaten caribou too, they said enthusiastically. 'Would you like to learn the skills of the old hunters?' I asked. Yes, they said. The idea of teaching the school children and their parents the traditional ways, and by doing so introducing the values of caring for the land, caring for each other and sharing, and of being proud of their Innu heritage, seemed to both elders and young people to be the way forward.

One young woman told me of her longing to learn the traditional skills. She had been a voluntary youth worker in the community and she could see the need for the young people to be taught the values handed down to her by her mother and grandparents:

> I saw my mother as a hard-working woman, never giving up, and I saw that and from that experience I learned and it gave me some values. I was very closely connected to my grandparents; they knew a lot about the traditional way of life. I had a lot of connections [to the land] through meeting them, talking to them, visiting them. I recall that I was frustrated by the fact that my younger brother was the one who was privileged in terms of the teaching of the traditional way of life. Of course, I knew the legends, stories, the language and our history but not all the skills needed for an Innu woman to sustain and support her traditional way of life. My younger brother was always the one sent to live off the land with the grandparents. I was sent to school. I was very upset about this situation because I lacked the skills. I know now the reasons why my younger brother was chosen to learn those skills – because now he can support us, he can give us food and share all the game that he hunts – provide us with food.[19]

A young man whose family was strong in its hunting tradition told me:

> The land is, it is like life. In the land, you have your food, person, harmony and it is the Innu identity. You can't imagine destroying the land. The land is all. For a long time, we have respected the land. I remember going on my land. I am Innu. If you go onto the land you become another person. When I come back to my land, I am not the

19   Interview FD5, Sept. 2009.

same person, I am alone and I feel a different person. I feel free and I
think there is no danger. On the land, you have good energy, nobody
stresses you, there is harmony. Our brothers in Labrador, they will make
treaties in Labrador over my father's land for another dam. For water to
flood the land. If I don't hunt, I will lose my land. It's my grandfather's
land and it's flooded and we can do nothing about it. Some morning I
will wake up and I will lose my identity because there will be no land
for my children. It's not good. It is very like I have a duty.[20]

The Band Council

In nearly all the interviews, comparisons were made between conditions in
Kawawachikamach, the Naskapi village, and in Matimekush. Whereas, on the
closure of the Schefferville mine in 1982, the Iron Ore Company bulldozed the
swimming pool and sports facilities in Matimekush, by contrast the Naskapi,
with the lump sum received on the signing of the North Eastern Quebec
Agreement in 1979, were put in charge of their own budget. The town has
excellent modern facilities including an Olympic-sized swimming pool. It also
has a development corporation which uses the lump sum for new enterprises
and which bids for government contracts denied to the Innu in Matimekush
unless and until they sign away their rights.

By contrast, the Band Council in Matimekush has no control over its
budget, which until recently ran at a considerable deficit. The Band Council
has few powers as the Matimekush Innu remain wards of the Crown and their
affairs are controlled by the Department of Indigenous Affairs. As the health
worker explained to me:

> The Band Council is there just for implementing white policy. They
> have no power and I have the impression that no one can change
> anything. Families think the Band Council should provide food and
> clothing for them, that they [the Band Council] should pay. They
> don't control their budget. All the money comes from outside and the
> Band Council can't implement an aboriginal programme. The power
> lies with the Director General [of Aboriginal Affairs] who oversees all
> the Band Councils. We need another system of management before
> anything will improve.[21]

As things stand, unless and until there is an agreement in place extinguishing
Innu ancient rights to the land, the Innu will never have autonomy; and the
impression of those who manage the community's essential services is that the
federal government, which has a fiduciary duty to all its aboriginal peoples,
never gives enough funding to get to the root of the problems they face.

Both the health centre and the school have excellent new buildings but
they have no funding for programmes to strike at the heart of the reserve's

20   Interview MC2, March 2009.
21   Interview ME3 Sept. 2009.

problems of drug and alcohol abuse, smoking, poor diet and childcare due to poverty and to the legacy from family members who were taken away to Indian Residential Schools. One interviewee also mentioned lack of care for elders, something which would have been unthinkable even 20 years ago.[22] Much of the housing is in a depressing state of dilapidation and very little has been done to the roads since the mine closed in 1982. The dusty open spaces are littered with broken glass.

So far as housing is concerned, the Band Council has done its best on its very limited (and often negative) budget, and it took on an expensive task when it improved the houses in Schefferville to rehouse those who had been living on the old Matimekush reserve in homes of an unacceptable standard. But as a former chief explained:

> When I was chief, I said to Indian Affairs 'Just give us the $2 million extra necessary for the next 15 years and we will do a pretty good job.' Through the last 50 years, we were told what to do, what was good for us, as if we were incapable of managing our own affairs. With that extra $2 million we could repair and give some form of redress to our society and we could probably do something good. But of course, we didn't get that. And even the chiefs ... when I met the chiefs they were always talking about the future and all the future was aimed at educating the young people. But how can you educate them with their loss of culture? They can't get a decent education when they don't know who they are.[23]

He was asking for capital funding to attempt a long-term solution to the town's social problems, but capital funding seems only to be available to the communities which sign away their rights. He also complained of the stifling bureaucracy and the constant visits of auditors. Calvin Helin points out that[24] 'the search for a real solution must begin outside the current dependency mindset', in the hands of the indigenous peoples acting for themselves, independently of the federal government. This is precisely what the former chief was seeking to achieve. The settlements with the mining companies, which at present do not compromise the land rights of the Innu, have provided a small fund. To date, the Innu have been required to eliminate the deficit in the Band Council's budget and, such was the trauma of the bulldozing of the town's facilities with the closure of the mine, they initially gave priority to the building of a sports facility and swimming pool for the reserve to match that in Kawawachikamach, rather than on new enterprises to boost the economic independence of the reserve. However, many of the people I spoke to recognised the need for better sports facilities: they saw that the principal

22   Interview FAS15, Sept. 2009.
23   Interview MAS5.6.E5, Sept. 2009.
24   C. Helin, *Dances with Dependency: Out of Poverty Through Self-Reliance* (California: Ravencrest Publishing Inc., 2006, 2008), p. 29.

reason for drinking and gambling was that there was nothing else to do. The provision of sports facilities, especially indoor ones when winter is nine months long, lies at the heart of any preventative programme, whether for health, addiction, diet or dysfunctional families. Eventually, the mining companies contributed to this provision.

There is mistrust of the way in which the Band Council handles its finances within the community too. Several people gave examples of nepotism when it came to allocating jobs and houses, for example. People spoke of the system of job allocation, which supports family members and keeps bright young minds from the key jobs in the community, stifling the innovation on which the reserve depends for its renewal.[25] There was also talk of the expensive trips taken by Band Council members to negotiations. These were accusations which dismayed the two former chiefs I spoke to and they were at pains to explain that they felt caught between the demands of their constituents and the pressures from the governments.[26]

The reasons for this mistrust of the Band Council are well founded. The system of local government through chiefs and Band Councils is a federal government construct, introduced to replace the Indian Agents. Innu self-governance depended traditionally on a leader being selected only for the task in hand – typically the annual journey north or a major hunting expedition. Decision-making was consensual within the group of families travelling together and no one put themselves forward to lead the others. The idea of elections of chiefs and councillors is no part of Innu culture, particularly as these officials take precedence over the elders.[27] At the same time, the Band Council has no proper power of its own to make the decisions which the community requires of it – everything is controlled by the Department of Indigenous Affairs until the Innu buy their freedom by selling their land. The Band Councils are an arm of the state. As Colin Samson observes: 'the band councils ... are now integral to the political nexus of the state and find themselves reacting to Canadian policies that assume sovereignty over their lands and dictate the terms upon which they are able to respond.'[28]

Renée Dupuis[29] claims that the replacement of traditional governance had

25   Interviews FD5, FAS15, MFC6; Calvin Helin notes the nepotism which facilitates queue-jumping in the administration of the Band Councils' housing lists (*Dances with Dependency*, p. 123).
26   Jil Silberstein was also told of nepotism on the reserve at Mashteuiatsh (Silberstein, *Innu: A la rencontre*, p. 123)
27   For a full comparison of the Innu and non-Innu systems see Samson, *A Way of Life*; see also Silberstein, *Innu: A la rencontre*, p. 42ff.
28   Samson, *A World*, p. 25.
29   R. Dupuis, *Justice for Canada's Aboriginal Peoples*, trans. R. Chodos and S. Joanis (Toronto: James Lorimer & Company Ltd, 2002), p. 16.

a destabilising effect on indigenous communities, and Pamela Palmater goes further:

> One of the most devastating impacts to our nations has been the impact on our traditional governance structures. Successive ministers of Indian Affairs, under the authority of the Indian Act, imposed multiple election-based systems in many communities within our larger nations – not only dividing us geographically but politically as well. Our large powerful nations were divided into smaller communities, often relocated at great distances from one another and on less valuable land. Our people were exchanged for government-controlled bureaucracies that were forced to account only to the Minister of Indian Affairs.[30]

Clans

Père Gérard, then priest in charge at Schefferville, told Jil Silberstein of his surprise on arriving in Matimekush at the strength and aggression of each clan to towards the others, suggesting that this started with the dispute over the move from Lac John.[31] One sociological study[32] concludes that:

> the main problem is that lack of productive employment has undermined traditional role and status relationships, especially for male members, most of whom have lost their important role as food providers for their family or kin group. They are denied an opportunity to validate their self-worth by contributing to the survival and well-being of their family and community through work. The idleness of unemployment has devastated morale and undermined Indian cultures. This in turn has bred extraordinary levels of social pathologies.

José Mailhot traces the origins of the powerful McKenzie family in her genealogical work on Sheshatshiu, Labrador.[33] She identifies four separate groups of Innu who settled in Sheshatshiu, the first three of which are the Uashaunnuat (people from Sept-Iles), Mashkuanunnuat (people from Musquaro to the south of Sheshatshiu) and Mushuaunnuat (the people of the tundra, also later known as the Naskapi). There was a further sub-group of the Uashaunnuat, the McKenzie. A hierarchy developed among these groups with the McKenzie at the top and the Mushuaunnuat at the bottom.[34] She was told of bullying of Mushuaunnuat by the children of the McKenzie clan because

---

30 P. Palmater, *Indigenous Nationhood: Empowering Grassroots Citizens* (Halifax and Winnipeg: Fernwood Publishing, 2015), p. 3.

31 Silberstein, *Innu: A la rencontre.* p. 287.

32 M. Boldt, *Surviving as Indians: The Challenge of Self-Government*, (Toronto: Toronto University Press, 1993), p. 223; quoted in Helin, *Dances with Dependency*, p. 110.

33 Mailhot, *The People of Sheshatshit.*

34 Ibid., p. 54ff.

their speech was difficult to understand.[35] Maillot attributes the premier ranking of the McKenzie firstly to the fact that they were the descendants of the Metis Alexandre McKenzie and secondly to the benefits they enjoyed from the patronage from Père Arnaud, one of the influential Jesuit priests who worked with the Innu in Sept-Iles.[36] Alexandre and Gaston McKenzie of Matimekush Lac John are the descendants of the explorer Alexander Mackenzie.

By contrast the Mushuau Innu (Naskapi), living away from contact with settlers, hunting caribou instead of trapping for the fur trade, were on the lowest rung of the social structure in Sheshatshiu. They were dark-skinned woodsmen. Relations between the two divisions at the top and bottom of this structure were already troubled even before the Naskapi were forcibly settled into the Lac John Innu community in the 1950s.

José Mailhot comments that the McKenzies and the other Sept-Iles Innu settled in Sheshatshiu enjoyed a higher status, thanks to their more frequent contact with Europeans, and that there was a 'flagrant' inequality between the two groups in the 1970s.[37] This relationship seems to have been similar in Lac John – but the situation was soon to be reversed on the signing of the North Eastern Quebec Agreement by the Naskapi.

In 2009, the family-based factions in Matimekush Lac John were still apparent, surfacing again over tensions arising as Chief Réal McKenzie closed negotiations over the lost James Bay Agreement lands and opened negotiations for a share of the profits and jobs with Labrador Iron Mines. From the interviews given to me in 2009, it is apparent that there are five identifiable factions in Matimekush, three of them among the descendants of the five McKenzie brothers who effectively ruled the reserve in the early days. Calvin Helin calls this 'lateral violence': unable to strike at those who control their lives, people trapped in the depths of society internalise their frustration and lash out at their peers.[38] The reserve had turned on itself in what Calvin Helin describes as 'grieving mode',[39] locked in its dysfunction, unable to identify the pragmatic steps which would give its residents the ability to reconstruct their lives. There is some evidence that the Innu who live in Matimekush Lac John are now emerging from this dysfunction, in the lower domestic violence and suicide rates. The choice of a sports hall and swimming pool as the first purchases with funding which came to the reserve is an example of this, since the choice reflects the rivalry between the Matimekush Lac John Innu and the Naskapi which has existed since the signing of the North Eastern Quebec Agreement in 1979.[40]

35 Ibid., p. 72.
36 Ibid., p. 62.
37 Mailhot, *The People of Sheshatshit*, p. 78.
38 Helin, *Dances with Dependency*, p. 125.
39 Ibid., p. 166.
40 The sports facilities also represented a replacement of what was lost when the town was bulldozed by the Iron Ore Company following closure of the mine.

The then chief negotiator for the Strategic Alliance (himself a controversial member of one of the Matimekush clans) observed that there was much in the way of infrastructure which could have been demanded instead of or as well as a cash settlement. For example, with the construction vehicles on site, the chief could have asked the mining companies to build them tracks through the country to give them better access to their hunting cabins. The reserve which this negotiator represented had, in a recent negotiation with Hydro-Québec, been offered C$300,000 in infrastructure, including much-needed housing.[41] Significantly, that community voted against the settlement; many of them saying that, in view of past dealings, they would never enter into a deal with the predatory hydro company.[42]

Gerald M. Sider sees the emergence of an elite within Innu society which tends to become the ally of the dominant group when its members are offered the rewards which resource development brings in its wake.[43] There also seems to be an emerging career path for those who negotiate on behalf of their individual Band Councils and are then invited to oversee negotiations for another, larger group.

Resilience

Speaking to the Royal Commission on Aboriginal Peoples in Montreal in 1993, Innu Chief Jean-Charles Pietacho of Uashat summed up the predicament of the Innu:

> Collective despair, or collective lack of hope, will lead us to collective suicide. This type of suicide can take many forms, foreshadowed by many possible signs: identity crisis, loss of pride, every kind of dependence, denial of our customs and traditions, degradation of our environment, weakening of our language, abandonment of our struggle for our aboriginal rights, our autonomy and our culture, uncaring acceptance of violence, passive acknowledgement of lack of work and unemployment, corruption of our morals, tolerance of drugs and idleness, parental surrendering of responsibilities, lack of respect for elders, envy of those who try to keep their heads up and who might succeed, and so on.[44]

The Royal Commission on Aboriginal Peoples points to the negative effects of maintaining the indigenous status quo: the human cost of the inability of indigenous people to obtain jobs with reasonable incomes, and the burden on the taxpayer to provide the remedial services such as they are[45] to help indigenous people cope with their history of domination and discrimination.

41 Interview M02, Oct. 2011.
42 Interview FX4, Oct. 2011.
43 Sider, *Skin for Skin*, pp. 39–40.
44 Quoted in Dupuis, *Justice for Canada's Aboriginal Peoples*, p. 22.
45 Helin, *Dances With Dependency*, p. 58.

Calvin Helin points out that, with its ageing population, Canada cannot afford to exclude its indigenous young people from the workforce at a time when it is having to bring in workers from China, and when the indigenous population of working age is increasing three to five times as fast as the mainstream population in the same age group.[46]

One elder thought that Innu tradition could help the children with their schooling too:

> We should have more *Innu-Aitun* presented in the school. For example, I went to a school in Saskatchewan and when the young people want to get out of school they have a choice either to drop out or to go to 12 elders of their community at the school, so that's an option that they have – they can get out of school or go to see the elders; and they would spend time with the elders or discuss with the elders and finally end up going back into the school system. That's a way of doing things. I believe that Indian culture should be more present in school.[47]

This approach has the dual advantage of giving aboriginal value to the teachings of the school, and of letting the students know that there is a disciplinary procedure for truancy which operates independently of the school. At least in this way children begin to get the message that school is important. This is also a measure that need not cost anything, although there are stories of elders asking to be paid for their knowledge – something which makes sense in the world they live in today, but something that would never happen in their traditional way of doing things, which imposes a duty to impart knowledge.[48]

One Innu initiative is seeking to put new generations in touch with traditional Innu values. Tshakapesh, the giant child of Innu legend, and of the legends of many other indigenous nations stretching as far as Montana and Siberia, is walking the land again. Anne-Marie André's brother, Jean St Onge, has constructed a giant puppet with which she introduces the legends to new generations.[49] The stories of Tshakapesh are the creation stories of the Innu and other peoples. Anne-Marie André believes they tell of Cro-Magnon times and date back to the Ice Age.[50] They are stories to instruct listeners in their

---

46 Ibid., pp. 43–57.
47 Interview MA11, March 2009.
48 Colin Samson (*A World*, p. 154) notes that Innu elders in Labrador asked to be paid by visiting researchers and were paid C$200 for their contributions to the Voisey's Bay Environmental Impact Assessment. I was asked to pay for interviews in Matimekush, but reached a compromise by making a donation for each interview to a fund to help pass on traditional skills to the young.
49 For the stories of Tshakapesh as told by Pien Peters, an elder from Saint-Augustin, see R. Savard, *La Voix des autres* (Montreal: Editions de l'Hexagone, 1985).
50 Interview FD11, Sept. 2009.

origins and culture.[51] Denis Clément has noted the accuracy of the anatomical information contained in the stories.[52]

The giant puppet has been taken to schools in aboriginal communities and also to Montreal. In Montreal, Tshakapesh was used in a suicide prevention programme for children. The children are first told of a little boy who went to Mushuau Nipi (a traditional meeting place of aboriginal peoples on the George River). He had suicidal thoughts and a spirit came to him. The spirit was his grandfather. He told the grandfather about his troubles and he felt calmer. Then the children are invited to tell of their own suicidal thoughts and in return they are given the stories of Tshakapesh.

One health worker spoke of the effects of the Truth & Reconciliation Process on Residential Schools, in which former students of the residential schools are called on to give testimony on their treatment at the hands of the staff. For the first time, as adults, Innu men in their forties discovered that their friends and neighbours had suffered the same abuse. They had lived together in a small community (not Matimekush Lac John) for years and had never known that the others had also been victims.[53] The health worker arranged a series of meetings with them and then a camp by the Moisie River to begin to reconnect them with each other and with their lost culture. She has taken groups of recovering alcoholics and drug addicts up the trails of the Moisie taken by their ancestors for hundreds of years (and once by Henry Youle Hind).[54] She makes them undertake the portages and carry the heavy bundles just as their ancestors did. In this way, they begin to understand their heritage and to recover their identity.[55]

Identity seems to be the key to so many of the problems which beset Matimekush Lac John, and Innu identity is rooted in the land. There is a need for everyone to maintain contact with the land if they are to recover their sense of self. None of the people I spoke to were urging a return to the life of even 70 years ago – they have welcomed the technology which has made life easier and safer for them. Nor do they wish to turn non-Innu off their land; but they do ask for peaceful enjoyment of their lands for themselves, their families and their guests without harassment from game wardens and police.

Innu beliefs

When I talked to those who had lived on the land in earlier times, not only elders but their children and grandchildren, many of them broke down in

---

51 Interview MD12, March 2009.
52 Denis Clement, Environmental Adviser to Matimekush Lac John Band Council, Interview Sept. 2009.
53 The priest in charge of the residential school stayed on to be the parish priest.
54 H.Y. Hind, *Explorations in the Interior of the Labrador Peninsula* (Labrador: Boulder Publications, 2007) (first published London, 1863).
55 Interview FX5, March 2009.

tears over the loss of the freedom to move on their own land. I could hear the deep sadness in the voices of others. Often Innu religious belief was dismissed by missionaries as animistic.[56] Yet Innu beliefs are not based on the spirits of the animals, rocks, rivers and lakes – they are based on the land itself, which is held in trust for future generations. Respect for the animals and other aspects of the land is only one part of a much wider concept. The deep sense of loss experienced by these recent generations stems from the fact that they have been forced to break the trust vested in them by letting go of the land.

Rémi Savard[57] believes that the European antipathy to aboriginal hunting is derived from the fact that at the time of first contact, in Europe, particlularly in England, hunting was an occupation reserved for the aristocracy, and anyone else who took animals from the land was severely punished. Savard's work is principally concerned with analysis of the Innu myths and legends, which the missionaries cited as examples of heathen practices, or dismissed as wicked, blasphemous nonsense. Savard calls on non-indigenous people to examine the place of their own myths in their own culture before denigrating the Innu for theirs, and refers in particular to the resurgence of German identity when the brothers Grimm started to collect and examine their fairy tales. However, this comparison only leads to further confusion between oral history based in truth, and myths and fairy tales which are symbolic.

Through the work of Père Babel and Père Arnaud, the elders have adopted the Catholic faith as part of their identity and have mingled it with their traditional beliefs[58] but, although the parishioners conduct their own services, there is no longer either a priest or nuns working in the Matimekush Lac John community. I asked one 78-year-old what happened when the community needed the priest: 'The only way is when he comes for a few days, but there should be one here permanently. It's hard when someone dies. What happens to a child who is not baptised? Two people died and there was no priest to help.'[59]

For a community beset by so much sadness and so many problems, many of them caused by the missionaries and the nuns who ran the residential schools, it is extraordinary that the church can only send a priest for a few days every few months. One person I spoke to saw the lack of a priest to guide the young as another factor in their lack of discipline, saying that the priest's was another adult voice which could encourage children and their parents to improve school attendance and behaviour outside school. An active church is also a rich source of activity in a community.[60]

56 Savard, *La Voix*, Chapter 1.
57 Ibid., p. 30.
58 Interviewee F10 cited her Catholic faith as part of her traditional culture.
59 Interview MC5, March 2009.
60 Amateur footage of Schefferville posted on Facebook showed three church buildings in the town before the mine closed in 1982.

One of the strong influences in the community is adherence to Indian Spirituality. This is a movement which has come to Canada from the United States. Indian Spirituality has encouraged aboriginal people of many nations to return to ancestral practices – although not necessarily the practices of their own ancestors – and to return to the values of their culture. This has enabled many to turn away from addiction and rediscover a form of their Innu identity. They have returned to the sweat lodge and use prayerful ceremonies. At the beginning of one interview, sage and tobacco were burned and a prayer was offered for the success of the work we were doing together. At the end of another I was given an eagle feather which generated the tingling feeling of the passing of *chi*. It sits on my desk as I write.

One interviewee told me that those who came from the US to propagate the new spirituality were particularly interested in the Innu because their hunting tradition remained so strong and there was much to be learned from it.[61] One adherent of Indian Spirituality summed up religious practice in Matimekush Lac John, Christian and traditional:

> I am afraid that somehow the government or the Crown has managed to make us like white people. But we will go back to our traditions and our spirituality and in this way try to regain some sense of who we are and some force. They almost succeeded in making sure that we would not go back to our traditional spirituality but somehow we managed to hang on to our connection to the land, our sacred pipe ceremony, sweat lodge and so on because [speaking of Catholicism] the way people pray here today, they pray in [Innu-Aimun] but it is just a translation of another person's spirituality. It is not our traditional teachings so we managed just about to lose the spirituality but we have been able to salvage it and other elements of our culture.[62]

Due to the resilience of the community, there is ample evidence that the Innu culture, language and tradition are alive; but at present they are not flourishing.

There is a great deal which the community must do for themselves to repair the damage of the last 70 years, and there are influential figures in the community – young and old – who are ready to take on that challenge. If the Innu in Matimekush were free of the reins of the Department of Indigenous Affairs and were given the capital funding necessary to enable them to give their young people a future, and if aboriginal education were put on the same footing as non-aboriginal education, the will to change is there, ready to move the community to a brighter future. However, without a change of outlook on the part of the federal and provincial governments, these remain faint hopes and all Canada suffers because the courage, tenacity and intelligence of indigenous communities like Matimekush Lac John are going to waste. Moreover, in a matter of decades, land which has been protected by their good stewardship

61 Interview FX5, March 2009.
62 Interview MFD7, March 2009.

for countless generations is being destroyed. The other big lesson to be learned from the contact between our peoples is that progress is not the only principle on which a balanced life should be based. In the next chapter, we will attempt to unlock the depth of the suffering inflicted on this resilient people and their comrades across Canada.

Everyone closed their eyes to the transition.

My grandmother died of depression because she could not take the transition.

We were moved from place to place like cattle.

When they built the town, they wanted us all to leave.

There was something going on on Naskapi land so the government sent them here like refugees.

When you go hunting you feel good, but when you are on the reserve you are locked in with a lot of problems.

My father came to work here first and sent money for us to come. He never took lunch to work – he left it for us because we were too poor – there were 15 children.

My father worked in the mine pushing a broom.

We are all locked in – whenever you start something, the government tries to interfere.

I can see a lot of changes in the values and lifestyles of people – changes in attitude, lack of respect towards themselves. I see a bleak future because people don't have values.

I had a hard, hard childhood – my dad died and my mum had to cope alone – she turned to alcohol but she did teach us values. I had to be responsible for my young sister and brothers.

I worked in the mine but we were unskilled labour and did not have certificates. The good jobs were reserved for white people.

The mine disturbs the environment – it is not safe. Someone will fall into the holes left – some are as big as 600 feet. Our environment is destroyed.

The last hunters became very disciplined working people in the mine.

All you hear on the radio is bingo.

Chapter 4

Legacies of the past: barriers to effective negotiation

While the treatment of the Matimekush Lac John Innu on reserve has been a catalogue of broken promises and bad faith on the part of governments, there are three further factors in the history of Innu/non-Innu relations which have created an overwhelming barrier of mistrust for the Innu: the introduction of game wardens to deny them their long-held rights to hunt on their own land, the fur trade, and Indian Residential Schools. These factors are disastrous enough individually, but their effects also cumulate with a history of cultural genocide which included the introduction of disease, the extinction of the animals upon which indigenous peoples relied for their subsistence, and profound racism. Yet despite this constant adversity nothing in this dark history has succeeded in severing the deep connection of the Innu to their land.

Harassment by game wardens

One elder gave me a more personal description of what the activities of game wardens meant for his family:

> I recall myself, when I was young there were 14 of us, and I remember my mother – she would cook a meal, prepare a meal and then when we were starting to smell the cooking we would all gather around anxious to eat because we knew that it would be good, we would be healthy and it would be something nice – that's what I recall when I was young. But an incident happened here 20 years ago whereby there was an Innu family and I am very upset when I talk about it. The game wardens or the representative of the Crown, the representative of the government of Newfoundland and Labrador, the authorities, came to a family and they looked at what the family were eating, they looked at the pot, the meal and they took away the meal while the kids were eating and, while the kids were crying, afraid, a helicopter landing next to their tent and they took the meal, they took the cooking pot and then they took away the food of the family just as if we were in a war or something – and I'm telling you, I'm very upset about that incident when I think about it, when I talk about it, I'm very, very upset.

> If this had happened to me, to my family, seeing authorities, game wardens, come to me, to my tent, come to my family and take away the

food that I hunted for my children, I would have been very upset, up to the point where I would probably have taken my firearm and fired on the helicopter. That's how disrespectful the government is towards the Innu and the lack of respect that they show and lack of compassion – towards the Innu family. I am very upset, and very saddened when I think about that too.

They took the father's firearm – they took the gun away and by doing so, in Innu culture, they were trying to kill that family and I am not saying there is genocide here – there are rules, laws against it, but in a way they try to come up with something with a similar result, acting in a way that will compromise our life as a people, they will compromise our culture – so that's how evil the government of Newfoundland and Labrador is.

It is as if they are trying to kill the people by doing all these actions and then we would live ten months out of 12 in the year in Labrador – they would live in Labrador, they would get a decent livelihood by hunting, surviving off the land and they find all these tricks and actions to undermine the Innu – for example the eviction orders that they sent to families, threatening to burn down the cabins of the Quebec Innu who had cabins in Labrador – they threatened to burn down our cabins, our camps, which is very unfortunate, I'm very upset by it. It is as if they are trying by all means to kill the Innu.[1]

Historically, the Newfoundland Labrador government has a record of resistance to Matimekush Innu's access to their land. The claim of Innu resident in Quebec to the lands they own in Labrador is set out in a document prepared for a court case by Pierre Grégoire.[2] Annexed to the brief report were a series of documents including a map of the traplines allocated to the Sept-Iles and Schefferville Innu in 1949, as augmented in 1951 and 1952, together with a list of the families to whom they were allocated. Grégoire claims that the map shows that no account was taken of the Quebec–Labrador border when the traplines were allocated. Grégoire deduces that hunting activity only became of interest to the Newfoundland government after the opening of the iron mines at Labrador City and Wabush, when the activity of game wardens was significantly increased in the area frequented by the Sept-Iles Band (at that time the Innu of Uashat, Maliotenam and Matimekush Lac John). At this time, members of the Sept-Iles Band were stopped and the maps which they carried with them showing the locations of beaver lodges were confiscated. In 1960–61 there were negotiations on the difficulties the Innu living in Sept-Iles

1   Interview MFC6, March 2009.
2   P. Grégoire, *Relations entre le gouvernement de Terre-Neuve, le Ministère des Affaires Indiennes et les Montagnais, enregistrés à Sept-Iles au sujet de la trappe et de la chasse au Labrador 1960–1970 (document préparé pour les comparutions en cour, novembre 1979)* (Conseil Attikamekw-Montagnais, Nov. 1979).

were encountering in hunting and trapping in Labrador and an agreement was reached on the subject of caribou. Hunting permits were sent from Ottawa to allow the Innu to hunt on their traditional lands. Thereafter, the Sept-Iles Band members were treated by the Newfoundland government as residents of Labrador for these purposes. The only difference was that hunting and trapping was by permit and the skins were identified as coming from Labrador. A letter from the Ministry of Indian Affairs to Matthieu André of Schefferville dated 23 March 1961[3] tells the Innu that, while they are permitted to transport provisions and furs by the train which passes Lake Ashuanipi in Labrador, one of the principal hunting areas of the Matimekush Innu, they are prohibited from carrying caribou meat on the train. This was clearly another ploy to detach the Innu from their subsistence way of life. The train would have provided a very cheap means of transport to assist hunting in a community where time out on the land had become restricted by work in the mines. The alternative was air transport, which was prohibitively expensive. In 1961, the correspondence shows that the permits required to trap in Labrador arrived in Schefferville only after the trappers had left for the winter, and in 1962 that officers of the mining companies were acting to stop trapping by Matimekush Innu in Labrador.

Correspondence from 1969 shows that at that time the Sept-Iles Band were still considered residents of Labrador so far as trapping was concerned, but at the same time the right to hunt caribou was abolished by the Newfoundland government. On 22 July 1969, the Ministry of Indian Affairs wrote to the Director of Wildlife for the Department of Mines in St. John's, reminding him that aboriginal rights to hunt in the area were subject to the Royal Proclamation, and pointing out that in other regions in Canada game wardens treated native hunters with leniency. The Innu living in Matimekush continued to purchase permits to trap and to hunt small game up until around 1976–77. The following year they requested the permits but were refused.

In 1979, Chief Alexandre McKenzie of Matimekush sent a telegram to the Minister of Indian Affairs requesting him to intervene to protect the Innu from Matimekush from acts of discrimination by the Newfoundland government authorities,[4] saying that the Newfoundland government did not respect the rights of the Innu to hunt on their territories in Labrador.[5] The Minister replied that these interests had to be taken into consideration alongside those of other indigenous groups. Alexandre McKenzie also sought help from the Regional Director of Indian Affairs for Quebec and eventually a tripartite

3   This correspondence is attached to Grégoire, *Relations entre le gouvernement de Terre-Neuve* (Fonds d'Archives CAM, Boîte 5800-6-2).

4   This correspondence is summarised in a document titled *Démarches éffectuées dans le cadre des litiges entre les Indiens Montagnais concernant la chasse au Labrador* (Fonds d'Archives CAM, Boîte 5800-6-4).

5   *Historique du dossier des activités traditionelles de chasse et de trappe des Montagnais au Labrador* (CAM archives, on file at Tshakapesh Institute, Uashat).

meeting was arranged to address the issues. In 1980 another telegram was sent by the President of the Conseil Attikamekw-Montagnais (CAM) to the Regional Director of Indian Affairs in Quebec asking him to intervene to stop the court cases brought by the Newfoundland government against the Innu from Schefferville who were hunting in Labrador. Another meeting was called to organise a regime under which all native people could trap on their lands in Labrador. Again, the Newfoundland government was resistant, claiming that the numbers of caribou in Labrador had fallen to a low level.

Representatives of CAM wrote to the Newfoundland and Labrador government in the comprehensive land claims negotiations, telling the government that their comprehensive claim had been validated in 1979 and that this included territory in Labrador, some of which overlapped with claims from the Naskapi-Montagnais Innu Association based in Utshimassits and Sheshatshiu. It was proposed to set up a working group to resolve the overlapping interests. Despite support from the Ministry of Indian Affairs in Quebec, its proposals were rejected by the Newfoundland government in August 1980 in a letter which defined the Sept-Iles Band (which included Innu from Matimekush Lac John) as non-residents of Labrador. At a meeting between representatives of CAM and the Deputy Minister for Tourism for Newfoundland, it was announced that the Newfoundland government was prepared to look at the requests for the reinstatement of the pre-1969 situation, under which hunters who lived in Quebec were considered to be residents of Labrador for both hunting and trapping purposes. In November 1980, in a demonstration of solidarity, Greg Penashue, then President of the Naskapi-Montagnais Innu Association in Labrador, wrote to the Prime Minister of Newfoundland protesting at the 'continued harassment and callous actions' against Innu families from Quebec 'performed in your attempts to enforce a border on our people which is not recognised by nor of relevance to the Innu'.[6] In the same month, CAM asked Prime Minister Pierre Trudeau to intervene on their behalf and the Minister of Indian Affairs in Ottawa wrote to the Newfoundland government asking that they should revise their trapping regulations and permit the Sept-Iles Band to trap as if they were resident. In reply, the Newfoundland Director of Hunting wrote to CAM saying that the Sept-Iles Band would have resident status but must obtain non-resident permits. However, on 9 October 1981, the Minister of Indian Affairs for Quebec had to write again to the Newfoundland minister to complain that trappers from the North Shore of the Gulf of St Lawrence were being prevented from hunting in Labrador. Meetings were held and nothing was achieved, but the Newfoundland minister had hopes that a further meeting would be successful.

6   Undated letter from Greg Penashue to the premier of Newfoundland Labrador, received 18 Nov. 1980 (CAM Archive, Tshakapesh Institute, Uashat).

This seemed to be the pattern set by the Newfoundland government: one of prevarication and inaction which kept the Innu from their lands.

When in 1986 the federal Minister of Indian Affairs called for a negotiation table to settle the matter, again the Newfoundland government prevaricated, saying it preferred first to negotiate with the Innu who lived in Labrador and then to consider the position of those who lived in Quebec. Between 1987 and 1989 hunters living in Quebec were routinely being arrested and harassed, fined C$1,000 for each offence, and their hunting equipment and snowmobiles confiscated.

In 1989, Clyde Wells, Prime Minister of Newfoundland Labrador, having met with representatives of CAM, was invited to join the comprehensive land claims negotiations so that the conflicts between Labrador and Quebec could finally be resolved within the context of the wider negotiation.[7] The President of CAM pointed out that a framework agreement for negotiation had been in place since September 1988, to which the Newfoundland Labrador government had given no response; and there is no response on file to this repeated request.

In March 1990, there was a further demonstration, initiated by the Innu of Saint-Augustin on the North Shore and supported by CAM, for which there is a plan of action on file.[8] The stated purposes of the demonstration were listed as:

- to alert the public to the discrimination suffered by the Montagnais when visiting their territories in Labrador;

- to encourage the opening of discussions between the two governments and the Montagnais who live in Quebec with a view to reaching an interim agreement relating to the practice of traditional activities on the territory concerned; and

- to motivate the Newfoundland and Quebec governments to negotiate an agreement relating to the 1927 frontier between Quebec and Labrador.

They proposed three hunting parties of occupation in the territory to last for seven to ten days, with the Sept-Iles Band – including those from Schefferville – tasked to work with the Innu from Sheshatshiu, Labrador to demonstrate together at a location of their choice. CAM envisaged that the Newfoundland government might refuse to budge; that it might make its presence felt with helicopters, planes and visits to camps in order to show that it was on the alert, but without engaging in a confrontation; that it might arrest everybody

---

7   Letter to Clyde Wells, newly elected Premier of Newfoundland Labrador, from George Bacon, President of CAM, dated 16 Oct. 1989 (CAM Archives, Tshakapesh Institute, Uashat).

8   Conseil Attikamekw-Montagnais, *Plan d'action: Occupation territoriale du Labrador par les Montagnais* (undated) (CAM Archive, boîte 5800-6-7, Tshakapesh Institute, Uashat).

engaging in an 'illegal act'; or, depending on the public reaction, that it might agree to talks.

In a letter dated 21 October 1991, when CAM was considering a court case to settle its differences with the Newfoundland government, Peter Penashue, then President of the Innu Nation in Labrador, advised by lawyer John Olthuis, suggested that CAM join forces to discuss an approach to the Newfoundland government in the light of the recent decision in the *R v Sparrow*[9] case. This approach stemmed from a fear that any court case might prejudice the future of a working group set up in Labrador to address similar issues with regard to the Labrador Innu Nation.

In 1991, the National Chief of the Assembly of First Nations, Ovide Mercredi, following the decision in the *Sioui*[10] case, called on the government of Quebec to recognise aboriginal land rights, and on the government of Newfoundland to settle the rights to hunt and trap of Innu who live in Quebec.[11] He declared that the government of Canada was in breach of its fiduciary obligations in allowing the 'constitutional rights of the Montagnais to be trampled upon', concluding: 'These people, who had lived with the caribou since time immemorial, know what is best required to maintain the survival of the caribou, the ecology of the region and their way of life, while governments attempt to impose offensive criteria upon them. Real negotiations, based upon principles of justice and equity, must take place if this matter is to be resolved.'

Nevertheless, on 2 December 1991, the Newfoundland Intergovernmental Affairs Secretariat wrote to Chief Alexandre McKenzie of Matimekush rejecting his proposal of a buffer zone around Schefferville in which the Innu could hunt and trap without interference. He said that hunting and trapping rights for the Innu of Schefferville should be treated as a separate issue, and at the same time rejected any notion of Newfoundland involvement in the comprehensive land claims negotiation.[12]

Immediately following yet another meeting with Premier Clyde Wells of Labrador in which he sought information but promised no action,[13] on 24 February 1992 Peter Penashue of the Innu Nation wrote once more suggesting the setting up of a joint committee representing the Innu Nation, CAM and the Schefferville Montagnais to arrange for joint management of the George River Caribou Herd, which was under threat from 'more and more industrial

---

9   [1990] 1 SCR 1075.
10 [1990] 70 DLR (4th) 427.
11 Statement by National Chief Ovide Mercredi, 9 Sept. 1991 (CAM Archive, box 5800-6-8, Tshakapesh Institute, Uashat).
12 CAM Archive, box 5800-6-8, Tshakapesh Institute, Uashat.
13 Office of the Prime Minister, St. John's, *Agenda for meeting with the Honourable Clyde Wells, Prime Minister of Newfoundland Labrador*, Wednesday 19 February 1992 (CAM Archive, Tshakapesh Institute, Uashat).

projects imported from the south'.[14] These included hydro-electric dams, roads, military flight training and new mining operations.

There was further trouble between the Innu of Uashat, Maliotenam and Matimekush Lac John (the 'Strategic Alliance') and the Newfoundland Labrador government in the run-up to the ratification of the New Dawn Agreement in Principle, under which the Innu resident in Labrador agreed to sign away the rights of all Innu from either side of the Quebec–Labrador border to vast tracts of Innu land. There was a group of Innu hunters called Tshikapisk who opposed the Lower Churchill Falls project and the hunting ban which the Newfoundland Labrador government was proposing in order to protect declining caribou numbers. At the same time, the Innu of the Strategic Alliance wished to assert their right to hunt on their lands in Labrador. In order to do this, the Strategic Alliance organised a hunt of 100 Innu hunters who between them killed 250 caribou. This provoked outrage in the Newfoundland and Labrador press, but the Strategic Alliance pointed out that these numbers were justifiable as representing the average size of catch for this number of hunters. Mario Blaser[15] suggests that the issues of the Agreement in Principle and the ban on indigenous hunting are intertwined. The protest hunt came only after the Newfoundland Labrador government threatened to burn down Innu cabins in Labrador. The main thrust of Blaser's article is the failure of the Newfoundland Labrador authorities to appreciate the spiritual aspects of Innu hunting and also the spiritual taboos which, for the Innu, surround the dam construction at Muskrat Falls.

The fur trade

From early contact onwards, the Hudson's Bay Company (HBC) and its predecessors required that time and effort be diverted from the major task of subsistence hunting towards the trapping of fur-bearing animals such as marten and, most important, beaver. This new hunting activity provided an alternative source of livelihood in the years when the caribou did not come, but this advantage was outweighed by the negative impact of the cash economy. Eleanor Leacock describes the change in the way of life of the Innu which the fur trade demanded:

> The Seven Islands Indians ... have completely adopted the white trapper's system in all its essentials. The white trapper has several hundred traps which are left where they are set from year to year. He has usufruct rights to his line as long as he continues to use it ... He has several 'tilts' along his line, each a day's journey from the next, and he travels continually back and forth. He leaves his family at the

14   CAM Archive, box 5800-6-8.
15   Blaser, 'Another Cosmopolitics?', pp. 545–70.

coast and, in the interest of efficiency, generally works alone, although
maintaining regular contact with the trappers whose lines border his.[16]

This represented a very significant break with the nomadic life related to the
caribou hunt which required the Innu to travel north with their families and
in small groups. It also entailed a dietary change in that the Innu became more
dependent on store-bought food like flour and lard, and less reliant on country
food. One hunter in the Mistassini region told Eleanor Leacock that traded
supplies were 'essential': 'Wherever possible, meat and fish are served together
with banock [sic], the Indian bread, but quite frequently, the bannock is the
only food available.'[17]

Gerald Sider points out that the most valuable pelts were found in the
autumn and early winter, at the time when the caribou hunt takes place. But
the fur-bearing animals could only be found in locations which were a long
way from the migration paths of the caribou, which meant that indigenous
people became bound into an unjust system and so a climate of distrust began
in dealings with white people.

An Innu elder commented:

> The reality that affected our land use and our way of life was the coming
> of the trading posts. We noticed a change in the traditional lifestyle in
> the sense that we depended more and more on the products that were
> offered by the trading posts in exchange for furs – flour, sugar, things
> like that, and our ancestors felt obliged to get as much as possible in
> furs, to bring them back to the trading posts and to get something back
> – new products that we were not used to having before. This greatly
> affected our traditional lifestyle in the sense that we were trapped in a
> way in some form of dependency towards the trading posts.
>
> I don't think they gave a fair price for all the amount of fur that was
> given or traded at those posts, according to what I have heard through
> the oral tradition. I heard that the fur was piled very high for a small
> amount of goods given back to the Innu, just the essential basics, tea,
> flour, just the basics. When they were leaving the trading posts they left
> owing something back to the trading posts. They were already getting
> things on credit and they had to spend the whole year trapping to pay it
> back and then they ended up again owing money. I don't think that the
> Innu made a profit out of this process of economic exchange. I think
> the profit was on the side of the fur trade company, the HBC. Those
> are the ones who got all the wealth and got a lot of money. The money
> didn't stay here in this community.[18]

Others spoke of instances when, in lean years, having failed to produce enough

16   E. Leacock, 'The Montagnais "Hunting Territory" and the Fur Trade', *American
     Anthropologist*, 56 (1954): part 2, memoir no. 78.
17   Leacock, 'Montagnais "Hunting Territory"', p. 39.
18   Interview MSA5, Sept. 2009.

furs, members of their family had been turned away empty-handed by the HBC manager and left to starve.

Colin Samson defines this relationship:

> Although the fur trade enabled the continuation of hunting via trapping fur-bearing mammals, the purpose of hunting was changed by making it commercial. In order to acquire furs, traps and guns were needed and the only way of obtaining these tools was by entering into a quasi-market exchange or debt peonage relationship with traders. Hunters quickly saw that this equipment, and later snowmobiles, outboard motors and even planes were useful to them. The desire to use such technologies combined with the advent of individual traplines that accompanied fur trading in many places, facilitated the decollectivisation of trapping and encouraged more individual or small group-based hunting activities that potentially made hunters as reliant on the trader as upon each other.[19]

Yet the trader could never be relied upon. Gerald Sider claims that starvation of the hunters was a deliberate policy of the HBC to force the Innu to do more trapping. At the same time, traplines were exhausted by over-exploitation. Further, the HBC posts introduced diseases into defenceless populations, but no medical assistance was available at the posts. HBC factors also provided alcohol to the indigenous hunters, a further means of binding them to the trading post.[20] To use Sider's term, the trappers were disposable. Georg Henriksen records the deaths of 200 Innu over the course of two seasons.[21]

A.P. Low, who was stationed at the Fort Chimo HBC post in the 1890s, observed the Innu women, when reunited with other families at the post in the spring: 'Instead of joyous greetings, the women clasp one another and indulge in a period of silent weeping ...'[22]

Indian Residential Schools

The Innu are aware that it was only when iron ore was found on their territory, and their lands became of importance to the non-Innu, that the authorities took an interest in their schooling. It was not until iron ore was discovered around Sept-Iles on the St Lawrence North Shore, and inland at what became Schefferville, that parents were pressured to leave their children behind so that they could attend the Maliotenam Residential School. Some children were sent further afield to Jonquière. This meant that residential schools came comparatively late in the history of the Innu.

19 Samson, *A World*, p. 29.
20 Sider, *Skin for Skin*, p. 67ff.
21 G. Henriksen, *Hunters in the Barrens: Naskapi on the Edge of the White Man's World* (New York and Oxford: Berghahn Books, 1973), p. 4.
22 Quoted by Sider at p. 117.

Those people I interviewed between the ages of 40 and 70 had either experienced residential school themselves or had siblings or parents who had undergone the indignities and privations which such schooling entailed. Since the Innu still lived the nomadic life in whole or in part as late as the 1970s, not all children in a family were necessarily sent away, or left behind when it was time to return to the interior after the summer break on the coast. In some families, only the children who had *not* proved themselves to be excellent hunters were sent to school.

Thus, the experience of the Innu is different from that of indigenous peoples elsewhere in Canada, where residential schooling often started as early as the 1870s and where most children in any community were taken away. There are many accounts of the experiences of children who suffered in this way[23] and, in 2005, an Indian Residential Schools Settlement Agreement was reached, under which C$1.9 billion in compensation was set aside for Indian Residential School survivors, and a Truth and Reconciliation Commission was set up in order to educate settler Canadians about this dark episode in their shared history.

Innu now see the schooling not only as an attempt at assimilation but also as an attempt to break their connection to the land. Père Babel and Père Arnaud had built a relationship of trust between the church and the Innu which led the Innu to accept the church's offer of education. In addition, it was difficult to feed a large family in Nutshimit so the promise of board and lodging as well as education in residential schools had its attractions. It is also suggested that, with money constantly owing to the HBC, the hunters could get more fur if their children were cared for elsewhere. Parents also feared that they would be sent to jail if they did not allow their children to be taken away to school.

A hunter told me of his family:

> I was very fortunate not to go to residential school. But when I think about my older brothers and sisters, it basically killed our identity, our connection to the land. Imagine all these people who went through the residential schools, today they would probably be skilled hunters. They would be able to transmit our way of life to the younger generations, so basically it cut off our connection to the land.
>
> We lost all these people, all these minds and workforce, in the sense that probably many of them would know about our handicrafts. The

23   For an overview of Indian Residential Schools in Canada see: A. Grant, *No End of Grief: Indian Residential Schools in Canada* (Winnipeg: Pemmican Publications, 1996); Chrisjohn, R., Nicholas, A., Craven, J., Wasacase T., Loiselle, P. and Smith, A., 'A Historic Non-Apology, Completely and Utterly Not Accepted', *Upping the Anti: A Journal of Theory and Action*, 2008, https://kersplebeded.com.an-historic-non-apology; and J.R. Miller, *Shingwauk's Vision: A History of Native Residential Schools* (Toronto: University of Toronto Press, 1996).

> women would be able to use all the traditional skills, to do all the crafts that we had – they would be able to sew, many of them able to do all the traditional skills like making snowshoes. The men would have been good carvers, making canoes, snowshoes, and [would have been able] to use the Innu tools to carve the wood. Therefore, I think we lost a lot: we lost generations, and people just got brainwashed and they lost all confidence, all pride in themselves and who they are. They began to deny who they are.

> In terms of who we are as Innu it is as if we would have to start all over again – we would be in the kindergarten of our way of life, of the Innu school, and we must struggle to gain back this identity, the skills and it's a tremendous task [he laughed] – in terms of the language, like a vision or Utopia. It's a huge, huge task.[24]

Although the inducement was an education which would allow their children to become doctors, lawyers, priests and teachers, the education did nothing to prepare the Innu to take their place in mainstream Québécois society and, at the same time, robbed them of their own culture and the skills required to lead the nomadic life which would have been their choice.

While there is an acknowledgement among those who had turned to Indian Spirituality that not all priests were bad, the psychological, physical and sexual abuse at the hands of the priests and nuns was reinforced by an institutionalised racism which scarred the recipients for life. The only way they could cope on returning to the reserve was to resort to alcohol and drugs. In many cases, the ability to lead a normal family life was taken away and a deep mistrust of education was passed on to succeeding generations. One woman told me: 'Because of residential school, I don't know how to sew, how to clean the caribou. But also I don't know how to live with white people. I am nobody.'[25]

Everything that the Innu held dear, they were told, was bad, heathen, conjuring, sorcery, primitive; to the extent that they began to believe it themselves and they were cut off, not only from their families, but from the roots of their culture. Having stayed in schools for ten years of their lives, they lost the ability to walk the long trails, the knowledge of where the animals, fish and birds could be found, the sense of freedom and the self-reliance enjoyed in the country. In return, they got dependency on benefits, ridicule and rejection by mainstream society. As many said, they were totally lost.

A woman elder told me: 'I drank because of residential school. I got married and had a child but I was still drinking. My mother couldn't understand why. I

---

24 Interview MD6, Sept. 2009.
25 Interview FD11, Sept. 2009.

was mad at my parents because I had lost my culture. I stopped drinking when I realised I was passing it on to my grandchildren.'[26]

Stephen Harper's apology[27] to the victims of the residential school system did not begin to address the wrongs the former students and their families have suffered and continue to suffer to this day. Matimekush Lac John had to wait a long time before the Indian Residential Schools Truth and Reconciliation Commission (TRC) sent people to take their testimony, very late in the day, by which time those giving evidence were very anxious. The compensation received under the Indian Residential Schools Settlement Agreement was never enough to change lives – just enough to buy a plasma TV, a truck or a skidoo – and there was friction in the families over how the money was to be spent. No compensation was paid to the community as a whole. The apology did not come from the perpetrators – no priest or nun offered a personal apology. Western psychology did not provide answers to the continuing trauma.

At the end of a long interview with a former chief, I asked him what he thought of Stephen Harper's recent apology to Indian Residential Schools survivors. I reproduce his answer in full because it is such a comprehensive picture of the damage caused by this experiment in assimilation. It took him an hour to reply:

> I guess it all started with the residential schools in the sense that most of my family, my older brothers, my sisters, my younger sisters, we all went to the residential school and somehow there was this threat that if the child didn't go to the residential school our parents would be jailed or sent to prison. So, there were all these veiled threats.
>
> Basically, what happened is that one would expect that you would glean something from the residential school, that you would get some form of education to have a better life, and then that's what the parents were hoping, that somehow we would get better lives because of course living off the land, the parents knew that there were hardships. Nevertheless, we entertained for a while this illusion that we would get something back from the residential schools or there would be some positive outcome. We entertained this for a while up to the moment that we realised that we didn't learn much.
>
> In fact, instead of gaining something we were losing a lot, our culture, we were losing everything, every aspect of our culture was being lost and the residential schools even changed the life of our parents in the sense that they couldn't go on the land any more. They were prevented somehow [by the game wardens and the construction workers from the new railroad] from going on the land.

26 Interview FBS1, Sept. 2009.
27 S. Harper, *Statement of Apology to Former Students of Indian Residential Schools*, 11 June 2008, https//:www.rcaanc-cirnac.gc.ca.

But they were very torn – the decision to send the kids to the residential school was very difficult for them. They thought we would get better lives. We didn't get any form of education. My dad probably would have liked me to learn about all these Innu traditional skills, but I couldn't and I lost a lot and my parents lost a lot in this whole thing. They lost pretty much their lifestyle, because we were told, 'Go and live in Sept-Iles. We will build a house for you. Your kids will be taken care of and you guys won't need to worry about food any more because you will get coupons [probably worth about C$20] to buy food. You won't need to worry about living off the land any more.'

That's what residential school did. That's how it changed the fabric of Innu society. We entered into some form of identity crisis. It screws you up a lot. You don't know. You are totally lost. At some point you don't identify yourself with your culture. You don't believe in your culture and you believe somehow you are making this illusion that you will get something much better than your culture. You go through some form of identity crisis. You are totally screwed up for years. You don't know what to do and it takes you a very long time to get your life back together. That's the extent of how residential school changed our lives.

The apology doesn't cover all the things lost through the residential school experience. We lost so much, so much in terms of culture, our identity, our traditional knowledge, our traditional skills. It disturbed a lot of our society, the families, the relatives, the kinship. I remember at times when I was young I was hoping that I would see my parents just like the students who lived in Sept-Iles; their parents were living in Sept-Iles and they could see their parents. But it wasn't possible for us to see our parents. So we were deprived of their affection, of their love. A kid needs to be taken care of, to be hugged, to be cuddled, and we were cut off from all those experiences that a child needs, we were deprived of this as well.

And then all the effects of the residential schools went on throughout all our life – all the students who went experienced the effects of the residential schools through many, many aspects of our lives. Because you were told you were bad, Indians were bad. Your lifestyle was bad. And you ended up believing that you were bad as well, that your parents were bad and your culture and your people, they were just bad. In terms of society, the choice that society was making, that your people were making, the choices were bad as well. So, therefore, you denigrate or dismiss or despise your own culture. You don't like your parents, you don't like your culture. You end up believing that you are in the wrong place and the wrong time.

So it goes on throughout your life and it took me a long time, personally I probably lost, like, 20–25 years of my life because of the experiences I had to do with the residential schools. I didn't succeed in my professional life, even though I was good at school. I always thought that I had the skills, the certificates and everything to get a decent job but I couldn't because I was an Indian and I was told that I was bad and that I wasn't good enough to fulfil the position. I was just an Indian even though I had a certificate. I wasn't good enough. And it went on and on through my life and even coming back here I lost the ties and the kinship and everything of my sense of being Innu. I lost my language, so I couldn't speak to my cousins or uncles or people. I was not able to talk to them.

So you lose a lot – your culture, your language, your traditions, your traditional knowledge and with the money, the compensation – it's not enough to compensate for all the things that you lose in a person's life.

And the effects go on to the other generations in the sense that because you screwed up through all these years, you were not a good parent to your own children because you didn't know how to take care of them. We don't know what to transmit – what kind of knowledge you will transmit. You lose trust. You don't have that. My parents had to learn values, their own principles. I didn't have any because I was totally screwed up. I didn't know where to go. I was not an Indian. Who was I? You can't teach your kids to be an Indian because being an Indian is bad, you know. So how do those kids relate to one another and how do they define themselves? They define themselves by what they are witnessing today. It's like pot smoking, gambling, alcohol, drugs. That's what they are looking at. The only models that they have. They don't have any other models because the parents are totally screwed up.

In my professional life, I tried to do something good. I tried to help out my community – as a chief, as a Band Council manager back then, or band administrator because all of our business was taken care of by white people, by Indian Affairs, and probably I was the first one or one of the few who were educated enough or who had the non-Innu skills to go and look at the book-keeping for instance, to look at the papers, write things, fill out the forms and so on. Even there I had my own doubts because the non-Indian colleagues would say 'You're not good enough to take care of your own matters. You will never know how to manage. You will never be able to take care of your own affairs up there.' And then it ends up in a subtle way that you start believing that and you question yourself professionally. Then we start to think, yes, we are not up to that. And we will always be these screwed-up people who are bad people, with no skills, with nothing good to offer.

It goes on like that, on and on, and because of that I was looking at those things when I was band manager, and I even tried to ask for help from my wife. I asked her to help me out into the wee hours, trying to perform professionally, do a good job and then I failed miserably because I didn't have all the resources, human resources or financial resources to manage properly. I didn't have the help because Indian Affairs didn't give you all the resources to do a good job, to perform well. They always give you just enough to be in the same loop of misery day after day, month after month, season after season, year after year. Just enough to be in the same misery of your own. So I didn't get any help.

What was the end of that? Well I was even more screwed up and I ended up drinking – when I was younger I had started drinking because I felt so bad and then professionally because I was screwed up because I was a bad Indian or a bad Indian manager (I couldn't do what the white people were doing). I ended up drinking because I questioned myself. I wasn't good enough for anyone. I was of no help to anyone. I wasn't good enough for the white people and I wasn't good enough for my own people. So I lost probably 25 years of my life because of the experience of the residential school and I am so upset about this because nothing will compensate this, the years lost, traditional knowledge, all the skills, all the strength that my parents and ancestors had. They could rely on themselves and had the skills to survive for thousands of years. They were brilliant people, survivors with all the intelligence to survive in difficult situations and nowadays, even if I have an axe, I can't do a proper job. My parents could do those things and they didn't have axes, they had their own tools to survive off the land with their own skills, their own intelligence, their own ways – they were capable of surviving off the land all year long.

So this is a long answer to your question. I got carried away but those apologies will never compensate all the loss we face and all the loss we went through because of the experience of the residential schools.[28]

Since Newfoundland Labrador did not join the Confederation until 1949, the survivors of the residential schools system within the provincial boundary were excluded from the Indian Residential Schools Settlement Agreement of which the Innu resident in Quebec were beneficiaries. They were also excluded from the proceedings of the TRC. However, on 7 November 2016, the Supreme Court of Newfoundland and Labrador approved a Settlement Agreement following an action brought by five former residential school students who attended either International Grenfell Association or Moravian schools.[29] Under the negotiated settlement, the survivors were awarded C$50 million to be shared between 1,200 survivors. However, the survivors will only receive C$32 million once lawyers' fees have been paid.[30] There is provision for commemoration events similar to those which have taken place in the other provinces of Canada. The settlement was endorsed by the federal government, despite the fact that it had formerly argued that it bore no responsibility since the schools were not run on its behalf. Having been excluded from Stephen Harper's apology, finally the residential school survivors of Newfoundland

28   Interview MAS5, Sept. 2009.
29   *Anderson v Canada (Attorney General)*, [2016] NLTD(G) 179.
30   B. Herbert, Canadian Aboriginal Law blog, 13 May 2016.

and Labrador received one from Prime Minister Justin Trudeau on 24 November 2017.[31]

On its very first page, the Report of the Indian Residential Schools Truth and Reconciliation Commission names the residential schools project cultural 'genocide', which it defines as follows:

> Cultural genocide is the destruction of those structures and practices that allow the group to continue as a group. States that engage in cultural genocide set out to destroy the political and social institutions of the targeted group. Land is seized and populations are forcibly transferred and their movement is restricted. Languages are banned. Spiritual leaders are persecuted, spiritual practices are forbidden, and objects of spiritual value are confiscated and destroyed. And, most significantly to the issue at hand, families are disrupted to prevent the transmission of cultural values and identity from one generation to the next. In dealing with Aboriginal People, Canada did all these things.[32]

The residential schools system was the enabler for all Canada's assimilation policies, which would rid them of 'the Indian problem'. Taking the broadest interpretation of its remit, the Commission's Report also concludes that the general Canadian public's ignorance of the consequences of the Comprehensive Land Claims Policy reinforces racism, and 'makes for poor public policy decisions'.[33] One poor public policy decision was to refuse to release key documents to the TRC which were relevant to its inquiries.[34] The Report sets out 94 'calls to action' which would begin to redress the balance in favour of indigenous nations.[35] It declares the doctrine of discovery, under which Europeans claimed indigenous land, to be null and void.[36] It also calls for the immediate implementation of the United Nations Declaration on the Rights of Indigenous Peoples.[37]

Historic trauma

In its work with Indian Residential School survivors, the Aboriginal Healing Foundation identified a phenomenon which greatly amplifies the losses suffered, the harms done and the grief experienced by those who were caught

---

31 APTN National News, 'PM to apologise to residential school survivors in Newfoundland and Labrador', 11 Aug. 2017; G. Bartlett, 'Tearful Justin Trudeau apologises to NL Residential School survivors', 24 Nov. 2017, https//:www.cbc.ca.

32 Truth and Reconciliation Commission of Canada, *Final Report of the Truth and Reconciliation Commission of Canada, Volume One: Summary* (Winnipeg, MB: Government of Canada, 2015), p. 1.

33 Truth and Reconciliation Commission of Canada, *Final Report*, p. 8.

34 Ibid., p. 27.

35 Ibid., p. 2 and p. 39ff.

36 Ibid., p. 191.

37 Ibid., p. 186.

up in the Indian Residential Schools process. They use the term 'historic trauma' to describe the cumulative effect of all the catastrophic interactions between settlers and indigenous peoples which led to loss and death.[38] Historic trauma leads to 'the creation of a nucleus of unresolved grief that has continued to affect successive generations of indigenous people'.[39] This study demonstrates the incidence of disease, loss of land, loss of flora and fauna and attempts at assimilation which led to the wiping out of indigenous populations from 1493 onwards, and links these events to the waves of colonisation of the North American continent. The writers identify historic trauma as a disease in itself.[40] They piece together this history of devastation in an attempt to 'remind people that indigenous social and cultural devastation in the present is the result of unremitting personal and collective trauma due to demographic collapse, resulting from early influenza and smallpox epidemics and other infectious diseases, conquest, warfare, slavery, colonization, proselytization, famine and starvation, the 1802 to the late 1960s residential school period and forced assimilation'.[41]

What happened to indigenous peoples in the waves of colonisation was unspeakable – it is so horrific that it cannot be spoken of. The memories are so traumatic that those affected could not speak of what they had endured. In the opinion of the authors, 'This nucleus [of unresolved grief] is so condensed with sadness, so pregnant with loss, so heavy with grief that its very weight constitutes a good reason why people often do not talk about it or, as one aboriginal woman said, "It is probably too horrible to turn our gaze in that direction".'[42]

The writers classify this shared experience of intergenerational grief as a form of post-traumatic stress disorder, leaving indigenous peoples in a state of chronic sadness. Gerald Sider compares the dislocation of indigenous society in the wake of these catastrophic events with the impact of the Black Death in Europe.[43] As noted above, the elders in Matimekush referred to the loss of key skills when children were 'educated' in residential schools. Further, the impact of pandemics meant that elders were not there to pass on the oral history of their people, which could have transmitted much invaluable (traditional) knowledge. The epidemics were so catastrophic that there was no one left even to bury the dead.

Sider notes that continuous waves of famine and epidemic meant that indigenous peoples lived with uncertainty as to their future.[44] He describes the

38   See Wesley-Esquimaux and Smolewski, *Historic Trauma*.
39   Ibid., p. iii.
40   Wesley-Esquimaux and Smolewski, *Historic Trauma*, p. iv.
41   Ibid., p. 1.
42   Ibid., p. 10.
43   Ibid., pp. 77, 96–7.
44   Sider, *Skin for Skin*, p. 70.

Spanish flu epidemic of 1918 which ravaged impoverished native communities in Labrador – what he calls the 'White Plague'.[45] He compares the effects of the flu in St. John's, Newfoundland, where there were sufficient medical facilities and the death rate was one per cent, with Labrador where there was little or no medical access and the population was devastated. He attributes this in part to the long history of famine, epidemics, forced relocation and provincial bans on hunting and fishing.

As the interviews carried out in Matimekush Lac John show, the shattering of culture and identity manifests itself in alcoholism, drug addiction, suicide, all forms of abuse, physical and mental illness, apathy and fatalism, all markers which the writers of the historic trauma study identify as the consequence of post-traumatic stress.[46] As Gerald Sider points out:

> We might usefully appreciate the fact that 'doing' drugs and alcohol is, among other things, an expression of one's autonomy, and it produces the social connections with others rooted in this autonomy. The starting point here is that people who engage in what the dominant society calls 'substance abuse' usually know full well that it is 'wrong', know that it is not approved, know that it is illegal, know that it is destructive, whatever. So to do it is to express one's freedom and autonomy from such strictures, such control, such dominant statements about yes and no – even though it is also the case that the users themselves know it is destructive to themselves and others. They are, at least for the moment and beyond the compulsions and satisfactions of addictions, making their own lives as they choose, even though … even though …[47]

Sider maintains that the historic trauma suffered by indigenous peoples can never be considered to be in the past. It is in the present and in the future too. He tells us that many of the catastrophes are socially produced, not natural phenomena,[48] especially in the experience of the Inuit and Innu of the Quebec-Labrador Peninsula. In particular, he cites the activities of the HBC and the Moravian missionaries, and later the Newfoundland Labrador government, and the resulting acts of self-destruction among the Inuit and Innu themselves, seeking oblivion in alcohol, drugs and suicide.[49] He also notes the colonisers' tendency to 'blame the victims'.[50] While still recognising the long history of suffering at the hands of the colonisers, he attributes the waves of self-destruction to the forced settlement of the Inuit and Innu into government villages. Despite the building of new villages with relatively better conditions, the epidemic of suicide and other pathologies of deprivation

45   Ibid., p. 98ff.
46   Wesley-Esquimaux and Smolewski, *Historic Trauma*, p. 24.
47   Sider, *Skin for Skin*, p. 71.
48   Sider, *Skin for Skin*, p. 2.
49   Ibid., p. 6.
50   Ibid., p. 9.

have persisted.[51] Yet the Canadian answer to the dysfunction of indigenous communities remains 're-education'.[52]

Speaking of the tuberculosis epidemic and the current suicide epidemic among the Inuit of Nunavut, Lisa Stevenson tells of the different meaning of death for the settler Canadians who came north to treat the Inuit. The priority of the incoming health workers was to keep people alive. Once they were dead, they ceased to matter. She says their work is directed at populations, not individuals.[53] Through a series of interviews with Inuit living in Iqualuit, Nunavut, she describes the impact of this point of view on the Inuit left behind when their kin were taken south for treatment and, later, when a village had suffered a suicide. Because the Inuit see no separation between life and death, they need to know the circumstances of the death, what the loved one said in their final moments and to know where they have been laid to rest.[54] Inuit would do everything they could to avoid being taken south on the *C D Howe*, the boat which took them to the sanatoria. If they died in the south, they would be buried in unmarked graves and news of their deaths might never reach their loved ones. The patients were given military dog tags with numbers and their names lost significance. To this day, the Innu of Natuashish and Sheshatshiu, Labrador make an annual pilgrimage to the graveyard of the former sanatorium at St. Anthony, Newfoundland where their relatives were taken and from which they never returned. Lisa Stevenson remarks on the contradiction that Canadian health workers impose a duty to live and at the same time have an expectation that native peoples will inevitably die. Further: 'Although the norms of cleanliness, tidiness and deference were taught and modelled assiduously by social workers, nurses, doctors, missionaries and others, the Inuit (from the perspective of the colonial agents) could never quite manage to live up to the standards set by their white counterparts.'[55]

Whether in homes, in health centres or at the negotiation table, the attitude of Canadian settlers towards indigenous peoples is one that is reflected in the concept that they are wards of the Crown – they are viewed as incapable of knowing what is best for themselves. This is a presumption that amounts to institutionalised racism.

Sider says that the solutions offered to native communities are only ever partial and are subject to the domination of governments and corporations. While some undoubtedly thrive in their new circumstances, inevitably others in the indigenous group suffer: 'what was done ... has led to the increasing

51 Ibid., p. 11; see also Samson, Wilson and Mazower, *Canada's Tibet*.
52 L. Stevenson, *Life Beside Itself: Imagining Care in the Canadian Arctic* (Oakland: University of California Press, 2014), p. 82.
53 Ibid., p. 3.
54 Stevenson, *Life Beside Itself*, Chapter 1.
55 Ibid., p. 66.

differentiation of Native societies'.[56] This is evident in the Labrador villages of Sheshatshiu and Natuashish, which have entered into the land claims process, and as a result are more prosperous than the Central Quebec villages which have refused to sell their land. Sider sees displacement of indigenous peoples, whether physically or by being deprived of their means of survival, as another form of imposed dependence. Displacement, he says, makes native peoples vulnerable to domination.[57] He suggests that, in this context, the term 'post-traumatic stress disorder' be abandoned and the term 'continued trauma stress' be used instead. He points out that this is not a disorder, since the chaos caused by their history is not the fault of the native peoples. Further, he says, the silencing of these 'continually re-created memories of domination' is one of the core untruths of power, central to the political violence which is the fate of indigenous communities.[58]

On 25 August 2017, the United Nations Committee on the Elimination of Racial Discrimination (CERD) denounced Canada for its ongoing violation of indigenous land rights. Its report called for indigenous peoples to be recognised as decision-makers and that free, prior and informed consent be obtained for all matters concerning their land rights.

In response, in his address to the United Nations on 21 September 2017, Prime Minister Justin Trudeau finally acknowledged the truth of what the United Nations had been reporting for years. He acknowledged the devastating legacy of the forced removals, broken treaties and residential schools, and continued:

> For indigenous peoples in Canada, the experience was mostly one of humiliation, neglect and abuse … There are, today, children living on reserve in Canada who cannot safely drink, or bathe in, or even play in the water that comes out of their taps. There are indigenous parents who say goodnight to their children and have to cross their fingers in the hopes that their kids won't run away or take their own lives in the night … And for far too many indigenous women, life in Canada includes threats of violence so frequent and severe that Amnesty International has called it a 'human rights crisis'.

> That is the legacy of colonialism in Canada.[59]

Another legacy of colonialism, however, is procrastination so far as indigenous projects are concerned. Despite the fine words, any assistance to indigenous communities seems to be directed to exploitation of natural resources on their land.

56 Sider, *Skin for Skin*, pp. 12–13.
57 Ibid., p. 27.
58 Ibid., p. 110.
59 www.bbc.com-world-us-canadas-41342434.

The people of Matimekush Lac John have refused to agree to the extinguishment of their land rights in exchange for the freedom to manage their own affairs. They have kept faith with their forebears and have, insofar as they are able, managed the land and its flora and fauna for future generations, just as their ancestors did for them. In 70 years, much of their land has been ruined by developments without consultation and without their consent. Yet their way of life has survived all the incursions from non-aboriginal society and the disastrous attempts to assimilate them into mainstream culture.

As Commissioner of the Mackenzie Valley Pipeline Inquiry, Thomas Berger wrote: 'It is native peoples' profound desire to be themselves that has led to the present confrontation. Far from deploring their failure to become what strangers want them to be, we should regard their determination to be themselves as a triumph of the human spirit.'[60]

Calvin Helin observes that indigenous peoples living on reserve in dependency find this situation normal.[61] The people of Matimekush Lac John are caught in as tight a trap as the animals they depend upon: in order to escape the cycle of deprivation and dependency, they must sign an agreement with people and organisations they do not trust, which extinguishes the rights to lands they have held for thousands of years. This is a stipulation which is prohibited by the United Nations Declaration on the Rights of Indigenous Peoples.[62] These lands form the basis of Innu language, culture and identity, and the Innu of the Strategic Alliance are the stronger psychologically for standing by their beliefs.

There is a marked absence of the sacred around land claims negotiations tables. Proceedings may begin with a sage-burning or smudging ceremony but the spirit of these ceremonies in no way impacts on the conduct of the meetings. Indigenous representatives are encouraged to enter into the corporate mindset and to step away from the fundamental belief that land is the basis of their identity.

The troubles of the Innu resident in Quebec are by no means behind them. When asked to participate in the land claims negotiations, they refused as soon as they realised that any settlement would entail extinguishment of their rights to the land.

However, their relatives in Labrador decided that their future and that of their children lay in a settlement which recognised their absolute right to a proportion of their land and promised future employment and a degree of self-governance. While the Innu of Matimekush Lac John respect their cousins' right to do this, they are saddened that this entails the loss of their own land rights.

60   Quoted in Wadden, *Nitassinan: The Innu Struggle*, pp. 43–4.
61   Helin, *Dances with Dependency*.
62   Articles 8(1)(c) and 26.

Our rights to hunt and fish are taken away by game wardens.

Now non-Innu cabins are built on Innu land.

The government is taking food from our mouths by preventing us from caribou hunting.

It is as if they are trying to kill the people by doing all these actions. Then we would live ten months out of 12 in the year in Labrador – they would live in Labrador, they would get a decent livelihood by hunting, surviving off the land – and [now] they find all these tricks and actions to undermine the Innu: for example the eviction orders that they sent to families, threatening to burn down the cabins of the Quebec Innu who had cabins in Labrador – they threatened to burn down our cabins, our camps, which is very unfortunate, I'm very upset by it. It is as if they are trying by all means to kill the Innu.

They put a book on the table and told me that that was our [trap]line. I told them why would I follow their line? They said in the US I would be afraid to talk to them like that. I said why would I be afraid? We've got to talk to them if they want to understand – and all the things they took, fishing things they took off us, we never saw them again. They sent them away. I told them they would have to pay me for what I had to buy.

They sent [my hunting equipment] home to me with the meat on them. When I opened it, it was all rotten. Even the line was rotten. It was only the hook that was still good.

I have a nephew who lives near Kujjuuaq – he sent me a message that he was going to kill a caribou and some fish to send to my father. There is a boundary – James Bay Agreement boundary – and a few minutes from the boundary we have Matimekush and Kawawachikamach. He works for the mining company from Toronto. He went ten months ago and he sent me an email saying he was going to send the caribou and fish. It was yesterday that I heard by the CB [radio] that we use in the country that the game wardens had taken the food because my nephew is Montagnais.

Harper may have apologised but the priests who abused us never have.

Chapter 5

Racism

Added to the sense of entitlement on the part of Canadian settlers is their schizophrenic image of native people, as explained by Daniel Francis in *The Imaginary Indian: The Image of the Indian in Canadian Culture*.[1] Francis describes the reaction of Duncan Campbell Scott as he led a party of European intellectuals across Canada in the year following the negotiations for Treaty 9. Scott explained to them that, 'In the early days the Indians were a real menace to the colonization of Canada.' When they visited the Cree and Ojibwa, this party was surprised to find that they were peaceable. Scott attributed this to western education and 'contact with a few of the better elements of our society' – never, Francis remarks, to the nature of the people themselves.[2]

In his conclusion Francis observes:

> Our responses to Native peoples reveal more than racism, fear and misunderstanding. It is more complicated than that. Our thinking about Indians relates to our thinking about ourselves as North Americans. Despite the stories we tell ourselves about 'discovering' an empty continent, stories told mainly to console ourselves for getting here second, we have to admit that we were latecomers. Native people claim the land by virtue of it being their home. For Whites, the issue has been more problematic.

Francis counterposes the cinematic image of the noble savage against the primitive, work-shy, alcoholic figure perpetuated by the press. This last image took no account of months spent out on the land coping with harsh conditions and long heavy portages. Most settlers live close to the 49th parallel and few venture onto the Canadian shield to experience these conditions for themselves. Henry Youle Hind, one of the few Europeans who did so, describes a portage:

> At 4am we dispatched the men with a load, instructing them to carry it as far as a beaver meadow on a high valley between conical hills about half a mile from our camp, and then return for breakfast … After breakfast, the canoes were sent forward to the beaver meadow, and we broke up camp. It was heavy work carrying them up the steep

1   D. Francis, *The Imaginary Indian* (7th edn) (Vancouver: Arsenal Pulp Press, 2004).
2   Ibid., pp. 198–9.

[hill], 320 feet up an incline of 45 degrees, the remains of former landslides, thinly covered with slippery black mould. This morning's work
bruised the shoulders of the men and damped their spirits. We were
compelled to use the line with the big canoe and haul it inch by inch
up the steepest parts.[3]

It is hardly surprising that, on emerging from the interior, the Innu had little
time or energy for the wage economy. Moreover, until very recently, almost
all settlers were unaware of the ravages of the residential schools on native
communities – they attributed the alcoholism, violence and abuse to weakness
rather than to a social experiment gone very badly wrong.

Giving an aboriginal perspective on Canadian human rights, Krista
McFadyen refers to the findings of the Aboriginal Commission on Human
Rights & Justice in 2009. Aboriginal people interviewed by the Commission
reported, among others, the following experiences:

- I experience discrimination in public at least once every single day
  of the week.

- Discrimination has become normalised in society; it begins with
  the media.

- Education is the worst! I experienced bullying, teasing and name-
  calling when I was in school. Teachers ignored it.

- As soon as hospital [staff] noticed my last name, I felt categorised.
  Their tone changed and I didn't get assistance.

- From my childhood I experienced discrimination in foster homes
  I was placed in. Now I experience it in general community almost
  daily.

- Discrimination can be very subtle, difficult to name or prove.

- There is another form of discrimination – perceptions from non-
  natives that you're not the right 'type' of aboriginal, they think that
  you are not Native enough.[4]

Of the 303 aboriginal people interviewed, 100 per cent had experienced
discrimination in the past ten years, 63 per cent had experienced it in the last
year and 33 per cent had experienced it in the last month.

Krista McFadyen concluded from the Commission's Report that:

While systemic discrimination through education, employment, or by
police was considered to be the most commonly cited reason for human
rights violations, most respondents also experienced discrimination
from mainstream people such as racist jokes, offhand comments or
differential treatment in informal settings such as shopping centres

3   Hind, *Explorations in the Interior*, pp. 117–18.
4   K. McFadyen, 'An Aboriginal Perspective on Canada's Human Rights "Culture"',
    Cultural and Pedagogical Inquiry, 4(1) (2012): 27–42, at p. 31.

or social settings. In addition, discrimination within and among Aboriginal community members and leaders was also cited.

We might postulate that these examples are relatively consistent across Canada. Therefore, it may be appropriate to suggest that oppression against Aboriginal people is ongoing, that Canadian institutions discriminate, that mainstream Canadians are socialized to perpetrate human rights violations on a daily basis, and that Aboriginal people experience human rights violations in all aspects of their lives and on an ongoing basis.[5]

Professor Patricia Monture-Angus delivered a paper recounting her own experience of racial discrimination as a Mohawk law student and subsequently in the academy.[6] She tells us:

When I finished law school, I quite often described the feeling at graduating as the same feeling of relief combined with fear I had after leaving an abusive man. It felt like I had been just so battered for so long. Finishing law school is an accomplishment, yet I did not feel proud of myself – I just felt empty. This feeling forced me to begin considering why I felt the way I did. It was through this process that the ways in which law is fully oppressive of Aboriginal people began to be revealed.

...

Everything that we survived as individuals or as 'Indian' peoples, how was it delivered? The answer is simple, through law. Every single one of the oppressions I named [collective oppressions through the justice system, the taking of our land, the taking of our children, residential schools, the outlawing of ceremonies], I can take you to the law library and I can show you where they wrote it down in the statutes and in the regulations. Sometimes the colonial manifestation is expressed on

---

5   Ibid., p. 32. See also M. O'Neal, 'Aboriginal Woman Wins Favourable BC Human Rights Decision', 28 March 2007, *First Nations Drum*, firstnationsdrum.com (accessed 10 May 2021); A. Hildebrands, 'Aboriginal peoples, Muslims face discrimination most: poll', *CBC News*, 5 March 2010, www.cbc.ca/news; J. Barrera, 'Iranian President Ahmadinejad's top aide rebukes Canada in letter to AFN candidate Nelson', 24 April 2012, *APTN National News*; 'Aboriginal People File Hundreds of Human Rights Complaints', 18 June 2012, *CBC News, https;//www.cbc.ca-canada-news-aboriginal-people* (accessed 10 May 2021); 'Discrimination against aboriginal women rampant in federal prisons', 25 July 2003, PrisonJustice.ca, www.vcn.bc.ca/august10/politics/1018discaborig.html; 'Prison Ombudsman accuses prison system of "institutionalised discrimination"', 16 Oct. 2006, *CanWest News Service*.

6   P. Monture-Angus, 'Considering Colonialism and Oppression: Aboriginal Women, Justice and the "Theory" of Decolonization', *Native Studies Review*, 63 (1999) 12(1).

the face of the statute books, other times it is hidden in the power of bureaucrats who take their authority from those same books.[7]

Patricia Monture-Angus cites the Indian Act 1876, under which the federal relationship with indigenous people in Canada was changed from partnership to status as wards of the Crown with no more powers than minors, as a target for resistance to racism. Speaking long before there were calls in Parliament for the replacement of the Indian Act by the United Nations Declaration on the Rights of Indigenous Peoples (UNDRIP), she calls for its repeal, saying that as long as it remains on the statute book, colonialism will remain a vibrant force.[8] She links the Act to the presence of poverty, suicide, child welfare interventions, lack of education and an unfair justice system.[9] Later, she points to chronic underfunding and under-resourcing of indigenous communities, which in turns leads to infighting and favouritism as instruments of oppression: 'These conditions perpetuate our oppression because they step on our hopes that things will change'.[10]

She points out that colonialism leads to a relationship of dependency in which one side is dependent on the other. In the case of aboriginal people, this leads to a stereotype in which they are seen as weaker, backward, uncivilised and non-human, etc.[11] The stereotype 'carries with it the personal pain of many individuals'. This, she says, is wrong. Later she points to the discriminatory way in which history is told:

> History carries with it a credibility, a cloak of truth-telling, that hides the privilege of the discourse and who has done the telling. Aboriginal peoples do not have history, we have 'oral history'. It is a variant, or some slice of what is real, that is history. Oral history is not seen as a complete thing (that is, that inferiority stereotype again). There has been very little rigorous examination of the conditions and consequences (the emotional impact and all other effects) on the colonizer. I see this denial as one significant source of the problem and why Canada has never been able to successfully eradicate 'the Indian problem'. There needs to be a commitment to truth and truth-teaching.

In November 2013, the Department of Indian Affairs in Quebec ran a consultation process through which a governmental Action Plan to Combat Racism and Discrimination Towards Aboriginal People was to be established.[12]

---

7   Patricia Monture-Angus, 'Considering Colonialism and Oppression: Aboriginal Women, Justice and the 'Theory' of Decolonization', *Native Studies Review*, 1999, iportal.usask.ca/docs/Nativestudies_review/v12/issue1.
8   Monture-Angus, 'Considering Colonialism', p. 70.
9   Ibid., p. 73.
10 Ibid., p. 74.
11 Ibid., p. 77.
12 Secretariat de Quebec, *Action Plan to Combat Racism and Discrimination Towards Aboriginal People*, Consultation Paper, Oct. 2013, https://cdn-contenu.quebec.ca.

In her introduction, Elizabeth Larouche, Minister for Aboriginal Affairs, said:

> This event will provide an opportunity for sharing concerns and experiences and for coming up with potential solutions to the problems that deny thousands of Aboriginal citizens in our society the opportunity to develop their potential. In their daily lives and in almost all areas of public life, many Aboriginal people have to contend with prejudice and stereotyping. In the workplace, at school, and in the media, Aboriginal people are sometimes faced with a mindset and behaviour that, regrettably, are tainted with racism, discrimination, and harassment.

The stated aims of the consultation were to develop an understanding of the issues surrounding discrimination and racism and to identify potential solutions. Whether these recommendations will be heeded any more than previous attempts remains to be seen. Much has been written on possible ways of solving the 'Indian' problem.

When, in October 2013, Special Rapporteur James Anaya visited Canada, he reported[13] on the present human rights abuses and significant inequality which beset indigenous peoples, finding no improvement since the visit of his predecessor in 2004. He noted the disparity in incomes, provision of services and infrastructure, health, education and other amenities. The report also pointed to the social consequences of the resulting poverty and deprivation: very much higher incarceration rates, murder rates and negative social indicators such as alcohol and drug abuse and domestic violence. He drew attention to the unexplained disappearance of aboriginal women.

The report also highlighted Canada's failure to honour aboriginal treaties and to involve indigenous leaders in consultation and decision-making processes over new legislation which concerned them, all of which reinforced indigenous mistrust of government.

As Chief Perry Bellegarde, then a member of the Assembly of First Nations and now National Chief, pointed out in 2012: 'Canada is number six [in the world quality of life index] but if you apply the same statistics to Indigenous Peoples, we end up being number 63, so there's a great socioeconomic gap between Indigenous Peoples and the rest of society.'[14]

Personal and institutionalised racism is the lived experience of many, if not all, indigenous people in Canada. The province of Quebec has a clear intention to address these issues but will this, like the Royal Commission on Aboriginal Peoples (RCAP) and UNDRIP, be another dead letter as settler Canadians continue to stand by?

13   J. Anaya, *The Situation of Indigenous Peoples in Canada* (New York: United Nations, 2014).
14   Quoted in G. Courey Toensing, 'UN: Canada continues discrimination against indigenous peoples', 14 March 2012, *Indian Country*.

In the next section, we shall examine the history of colonialism in North America and trace the roots of a system under which governments and corporations believe they can take indigenous land with impunity.

If an Indian does something bad, you will hear it in the news, that an individual would commit something bad in society. The media will put the Indians all in the same basket – all the Indians will be responsible even if it's the act of only one individual. They say, 'It's all the Indians.' You do your own thing, lead your own life, but you are put in the same basket and the Indian will be told, 'It's all you Indians who are responsible.' For the actions of the individual it's a collective betrayal because a negative image has been given of Indians.

> The Indian people will always be labelled or portrayed in a very negative way. They will always be looked at as if there are only the negative aspects of being an Indian that you will see on TV. You won't see or hear about the good side, the good actions and achievements of the Indian people. The media portrays negative images only and the government should do something about it.

Unfortunately even if I have a nice house, this house doesn't belong to me. It belongs to the Crown. It belongs to the Band Council. I will never be able to mortgage it and use it as leverage for economic purposes because the banks will say, 'The house doesn't belong to you. It belongs to the Band Council.' Even though I have paid rent all my life, it will never belong to me. I will never own it. If I leave this community to go somewhere else, I leave all the money that I gave here for this house, all the rent that I paid over the years. I won't get it back.

> If we don't do something now, we will be really poor – they don't know we are here.

Young people are leaving because we don't have adequate housing and because of financial problems.

> The church is a tool of assimilation.

Part Two
The Royal Proclamation and questions of trust over Canadian indigenous land

Chapter 6

Historical background

At the end of the 15th century, in 1492, having driven the Moors from Spain, the Castilian king and queen commissioned Christopher Columbus to undertake a voyage of exploration to the west for the purpose of discovering a trade route to China and the Indies. Columbus landed on the island in the Caribbean which he named Hispaniola, and thus began the European annexation of America. Soon after, England sent John Cabot, commissioned by Henry VII, who landed in Newfoundland in 1497, and the French despatched Jacques Cartier, who made landfall at Gaspé at the mouth of the Gulf of St Lawrence in 1534. The Dutch and Portuguese also made expeditions to the new continent. These were not the first Europeans to reach these shores. They were preceded by sailors and fishermen whose journeys were not recorded and by Norse parties sailing out of Greenland in the 11th century.[1]

When Columbus arrived, the continent was already inhabited by a population estimated by Charles C. Mann[2] at 90–112 million and by James Tully at 80–100 million – as compared to a population of the whole of Europe of 60–70 million. In both North and South America there were sizeable cities. However, these societies were decimated by the diseases which spread through indigenous populations after European contact. As a result, James Tully estimates the indigenous population of the United States and Canada to have dropped to 8–10 million in 1600 and just 500,000 in 1900.[3]

Tully observes that the indigenous nations were well used to making treaties between themselves for the sharing and partition of land and, when Europeans sought to move onto their lands, they treated them no differently.[4] European incursions into the American continent were ostensibly as much to do with the Christian religion as with the European nation-states involved. Spanish exploration in Central and South America was sanctioned by five papal bulls

1 C.C. Mann, *1491: New Revelations of the Americas Before Columbus* (New York: First Vintage Books, 2006), p. 103.
2 Ibid., p. 104.
3 J. Tully, *Strange Multiplicity: Constitutionalism in an Age of Diversity* (Cambridge: Cambridge University Press, 1995), p. 19.
4 Tully, *A Discourse on Property*, pp. 121–2.

in 1493, and another in 1539 when Pope Paul III decreed: 'We trust that ... you will compel and with all zeal cause the barbarian nations to come to the knowledge of God ... by force and arms, if needful, in order that their souls may partake of the heavenly kingdom.'[5]

François I of France issued a commission to Jean de la Rocque in 1541 requiring that he should 'inhabit the aforesaid lands and countries and build there towns and fortresses, temples and churches, in order to impart our Holy Catholic Faith and Catholic Doctrine, to constitute and establish law and peace, so that they [the Native Americans] may live by reason and civility.'[6]

The chosen vehicle for this conversion of the native peoples was trade, so that priests travelled aboard merchant ships bound for the New World. Even the English, Anthony Pagden tells us, based their claim to legitimacy in America on their kings' and queens' assumed title of Defender of the Faith. The Charter of the Virginia Company of 1609 stipulated its purpose to be to propagate the Christian religion 'to such peoples who, as yet, live in darkness and miserable ignorance of the true knowledge and worship of God ...'[7] Alongside conversion, however, the English had two further aims: trade and settlement. Many of these settlers along the eastern seaboard of North America were Puritans who followed a Calvinist creed. They had no real desire to welcome the native people into their religious circles.

The European nations who now sought to colonise the New World had legal systems which all derived from Roman law. Anthony Pagden suggests that they had inherited from the Romans the concept of *imperium*: a duty to spread citizenship and to 'crown peace with law, to spare the humbled, to tame the proud in war'.[8]

By the time of Charles II's restoration to the throne of England, theories of the bond between the church and the monarchy had been severely tested and those Christian settlers on the American eastern seaboard were more interested in establishing settlements than in converting the 'savages'. Having realised that there was no gold to be found in eastern North America, the colonisers turned their attention to settlement and agriculture. They justified their seizure of native land for these purposes through the application of principles developed by John Locke, who had been commissioned by Charles II to write the new constitution of the Carolinas.

It had previously been established by the Royal Commission of 1665 that the only legitimate way in which Europeans could settle on aboriginal land in

5   Quoted in P. Seed, *American Pentimento* (Minneapolis: University of Minnesota Press, 2001), p. 100.
6   Quoted in A. Pagden, *Lords of All the World: Ideologies in Spain, Britain and France, c1500–c1800* (New Haven: Yale University Press, 1995), p. 33.
7   Ibid., p. 35.
8   Pagden, *Lords of All*, p. 19.

America was with the consent of the aboriginal people.[9] Since the aboriginal people were unwilling to give such consent, John Locke's *Two Treatises,* written 15 years later, provided a solution to enable settlers to take the land without consent. Written in reply to a treatise by Sir Robert Filmer, who favoured renewed recognition in England of the divine right of kings and their sovereign power, Locke proposed that, in order to own land, the claimant had to work the land. This would create what Tully calls 'a form of popular sovereignty'[10] to accommodate the restoration of the English monarchy without its divine right.

Locke's argument has three stages. First, he classifies indigenous peoples as the most primitive, in a state of nature. As hunters and gatherers, native people merely acquire rights in the animals they kill and the nuts and berries they gather,[11] a usufruct.[12] They do not work the land and therefore do not have rights in it. Europeans are in the most advanced, civilised, stage. Only they can exercise sovereignty.[13] Since the indigenous people are in a state of nature, the civilised Europeans can take their land without their consent so long as it appears to Europeans to be uncultivated and unimproved – waste land: '*As much Land* as a Man Tills, Plants, Improves, Cultivates, and can use the Product of, so much is his *Property.* He by his labour does, as it were, inclose it from the Common.'[14]

The Report of the Royal Commission on Aboriginal Peoples (the 'RCAP Report') comments that: 'These kinds of arguments, which distorted the reality of the situation and converted *differences* into *inferiorities,* have had surprising longevity in policy documents and in court proceedings up to the present day. As modified by the courts, they are at the heart of the modern doctrine of Aboriginal title which holds that Aboriginal peoples in North America do not "hold" their lands ...'[15]

Since this land is vacant (*terra nullius*), common land, each may only take according to their need. To be owned, land must be cultivated according to European agricultural practices under which it is essential to make full productive use of the land. If it is left unproductive, it is waste and therefore eligible to be taken and cultivated. Locke draws an analogy from God as

9   Tully, *A Discourse on Property,* p. 71.
10   Ibid., p. 72.
11   J. Locke, *Second Treatise on Government,* Chapter V, para 26, in P. Laslet (ed.), *Cambridge Texts in Political Thought* (Cambridge: Cambridge University Press, 1988), p. 286.
12   As we shall see, this position was adopted in one of the first aboriginal rights cases, *St Catherine's Milling v R* [1888] 14 App Cas.46 (P.C.).
13   J. Locke, *First Treatise on Government,* Chapter IV, para 26, in Laslett, *Cambridge Texts,* p. 159.
14   Locke, *Second Treatise on Government,* Chapter V, para 42, in Laslett, *Cambridge Texts,* p. 297.
15   Dussault and Erasmus, *Report of the Royal Commission,* vol. 1, p. 45.

Maker[16] – humans must work the land they are given. John Locke's theories provided a form of justification for taking indigenous lands.[17] He places the creation of property rights firmly in political societies who were held together by a social contract:[18] 'It was common [that] *without any fixed property in the ground* they made use of, till they incorporated, settled themselves together, and built Cities, and then, by consent, they came in time to set out *the bounds of their distinct Territories,* and agree on limits between them and their Neighbours, and by Laws within themselves, settled the *Properties* of those of the same Society.'[19]

By contrast, in 1690 Locke dismissed American Indians as 'the wild Indian who knows no enclosure and is still a tenant in common'[20] – by which he meant that the indigenous peoples shared their land and did not recognise formal individual ownership.

Locke's thesis did not envisage the sale of the products of labour, which he saw as taking more than a family needed – the only entitlement was to take as much as was needed for personal consumption, leaving more land for the rest of mankind.[21]

Having been forged initially against a backdrop of the Puritan work of leaders such as John Winthrop and John Cotton in the time of Oliver Cromwell's Commonwealth, these doctrines were enthusiastically received by a Puritan population of the new colonies who were already certain in their belief that they were a chosen people who were answering a personal calling, and that financial success, so long as it was a result of sober industry, was a sign of being one of the elect.[22] Weber observes: 'Even more striking … is the connection of a religious way of life with the most intensive business acumen among these sects whose otherworldliness is as proverbial as their wealth, especially the Quakers and the Mennonites. The part which the former played in England and North America fell to the latter in Germany.'[23] Maybe this was what led them eventually, in the interest of profit, to ignore the admonition to take only what was necessary.

---

16   Locke, *First Treatise on Government*, Chapter VI, para 53, in Laslett, *Cambridge Texts*, p. 179.
17   For a full discussion of this, see Tully, *A Discourse on Property*, pp. 70–8.
18   Tully, *A Discourse on Property*, p. 98.
19   Locke, *Second Treatise on Government*, Chapter V, para 39, in Laslett, *Cambridge Texts*, p. 295.
20   Seed, *American Pentimento*, p. 35.
21   Tully, *A Discourse on Property*, pp. 148–9.
22   See the Introduction by Anthony Giddens to M. Weber, *The Protestant Ethic and the Spirit of Capitalism*, trans. T. Parsons (London and New York: Routledge, 1992), p. xiii.
23   Weber, *The Protestant Ethic*, p. 10.

Weber notes Benjamin's Franklin's exhortations that the purpose of money is to beget money; and to frugality, punctuality and justice in all dealings.[24] Franklin sees it as man's duty to increase his capital. Weber sets this philosophy in the context of utilitarianism and concludes that: 'Man is dominated by the making of money, by acquisition as the ultimate purpose of his life. Economic acquisition is no longer subordinated to man as the means for the satisfaction of his material needs. This reversal of what we should call the natural relationship, so irrational from a naive point of view, is evidently as definitely a leading principle of capitalism as it is foreign to all peoples not under capitalistic influence.'[25]

Locke's thesis of land gained by labour resonated with Puritan ethics of 'hard, continuous and bodily labour'.[26] As Patricia Seed points out: 'Once the Puritans arrived, Native Americans lost the right of refusal ... natives did not have a right to insist upon holding on to their land or to reject Puritan rights to settle.'[27]

This practice she labels 'forcible expropriation'.[28] The English were the only nation to seek to justify their expropriation of indigenous land and they alone believed that farming gave them superiority over the native population.[29] In contrast to the Puritans, however, Patricia Seed notes that the French were not seeking to purchase land – they asked for permission to reside, which was recognised by an exchange of gifts, not of money.[30]

Accompanying the Puritan sense of being a chosen people was the contrast with those who were not chosen, those who bore the signs of eternal damnation.[31] As had been seen during the Commonwealth in England, the Puritans rejected everything that they condemned as being founded on ostentation, superstition or the pleasures of the flesh: 'And even more important, the religious valuation of restless, continuous, systematic work in a worldly calling, as the highest means to asceticism, and at the same time the surest and most evident proof of rebirth and genuine faith, must have been the most powerful conceivable lever for the expansion of that attitude toward life which we call the spirit of capitalism.'[32]

Or, as Bill Reid, sculptor of *The Spirit of Haida Gwai*, put it:

> Sometimes they [the European invaders] found great cities, homes of
> people with cultures as advanced as their own, and so beautiful they

24 Ibid., p. 15.
25 Ibid., p. 18.
26 Ibid., p. 105.
27 Seed, *American Pentimento*, p. 20.
28 Ibid., p. 21.
29 Ibid., p. 43.
30 Ibid., p. 23.
31 Ibid, p. 75.
32 Ibid, pp. 115–16.

thought they had stumbled into fairyland, so they promptly destroyed them. Sometimes they found beautiful, gentle, generous people, so they made slaves of them and killed them.

Sometimes they found people who weren't so nice, so beautiful, or gentle and generous, but were almost as avaricious as themselves. These they dealt with as allies or trading partners until they relieved them of the goods they coveted; then they destroyed them and their cultures.[33]

The Royal Commission on Aboriginal Peoples reminds us that virtually all of Canada was occupied and used by indigenous peoples at the time of contact with Europeans.[34] The nature of the land they occupied dictated the manner of settlement, so that the Pacific coast peoples who depended on fishing lived in villages, the hunters of the north pursued a nomadic life ranging over vast areas and, where the land was fertile, the peoples pursued agriculture and horticulture. Alternatively, they may have lived by a mixture of these occupations. The nature of the individual society and its governance varied but there were social and political principles common to all. As Chief George Desjarlais told RCAP:

You must recognize that although we exercised dominion over these lands prior to the coming of the foreigners, our values and beliefs emphasized stewardship, sharing and conservation of resources, as opposed to the foreign values of ownership, exclusion and domination over nature. Proprietorship over use of resources within a traditional land base was a well-established concept that influenced our relations among ourselves as a people, and with other people who entered our lands from time to time.[35]

Trade was important between indigenous nations before contact with European settlers. Control of trade between indigenous groups was a sign of superior power over them and the holders of that power traded with the European incomers in the same way.[36] The native people dictated the terms of trade according to their own rules, generally preceded by speeches and exchange of gifts, rather than following the practices of the European marketplace. The native traders, in particular the Iroquois and the Montagnais (Innu) then traded the goods on to other indigenous groups, despite their belief in sharing.[37] French merchants seeking to trade with the Huron had to learn the Huron language because of Huron superiority of numbers and of bargaining power in the 17th century.

33   Quoted in J. Tully, *Strange Multiplicity: Constitutionalism in an Age of Diversity* (Cambridge: Cambridge University Press, 1995), pp. 19–20.
34   Dussault and Erasmus, *Report of the Royal Commission*, vol. 2, part 2, p. 452ff.
35   Ibid., p. 457.
36   J.R. Miller, *Skyscrapers Hide the Heavens: History of Indian–White Relations in Canada* (Toronto: University of Toronto Press, 1991), p. 10.
37   Ibid., p. 37.

Nevertheless, relations between European settlers and their indigenous partners engendered little desire on the part of the incomers to accept or even understand the ways of the natives. This relationship has resonances in the work of Michel Foucault, particularly in the ideas discussed in *Madness and Civilisation*. Through the trope of mental illness, Foucault observes how 'civilised' societies deal with the 'Other'. He describes how the leper colonies of the Middle Ages became the lunatic asylums of the 18th and 19th centuries. He notes that, in the Renaissance, madness was perceived to be a release of the wild animal in man's nature – 'impossible animals issuing from a demented imagination become the secret nature of man'.[38] Foucault links madness to man's weakness, dreams and illusions, and to all irregularities of conduct.[39]

From the 16th century onwards, these 'madmen' had to be confined, excluded from a civilised society.[40] Foucault points out that from the middle of the 17th century, the so-called 'Age of Reason', the purpose of confining those who could not take their place in society was 'the imperative of labour'.[41] By 1657, the Hôpital-Général in Paris had adopted the practice of hunting down beggars and confining them within its precincts.[42] In England, it was proposed that the poor, a term which included all outcasts from society who refused to work, should be banished to Newfoundland.[43]

Foucault asserts that: 'The walls of confinement actually enclose the negative of that moral city of which the bourgeois conscience began to dream in the seventeenth century; a moral city for those who sought, from the start, to avoid it, a city where right reigns only by virtue of a force without appeal – a sort of sovereignty of good ...'[44]

Those who established their 'moral cities' in the New World carried these perceptions of the contrast between madness and civilisation with them. They were a chosen elite and they found confirmation of this status when they encountered peoples who lived by hunting and gathering, appeared never to till the soil or do any real work, and whose practices seemed to the newcomers to release their animality – Giorgio Agamben's '*homo hominis lupus*'.[45] The settlers lived within the walls of their settlement and they kept the Other firmly

---

38 M. Foucault, *Madness and Civilization: A History of Insanity in the Age of Reason*, trans. R. Howard (New York: Random House, 1965), p. 21.
39 Ibid., pp. 27–8.
40 Ibid., p. 37ff.
41 Ibid., p. 47.
42 Ibid., p. 49.
43 Foucault, *Madness and Civilisation*, p. 51.
44 Ibid., p. 61.
45 'A man is a wolf to another man'; G. Agamben, *Homo Sacer: Sovereignty, Power and Bare Life*, trans. D. Heller-Roazen (Redwood City: Stanford University Press, 1998), p. 106.

without. There were plenty of pretexts for taking their land and driving the native population away.

The effect of these perceptions was compounded by the European diseases which swept through defenceless populations. Hugh Brody explains that these diseases were spread through human societies via animal husbandry, which is why they had not reached hunter-gatherer populations. Brody turns received wisdom about settlers and hunter gatherers on its head, pointing out that hunter gatherers had a settled routine to get the best use out of their lands, whereas Europeans were constantly seeking to annex new land.[46] Initially, not knowing that they and their animals were the carriers of the smallpox, measles and other animal-borne diseases which ravaged indigenous peoples, Puritan settlers such as John Winthrop believed that this was the way in which God was clearing the land for their use.[47] J.R. Miller suggests that the Huron lost half their population to measles between 1634 and 1640 because they were in contact with Jesuit missionaries and French traders.

Iroquois converts told the Jesuits of their perceptions of the English and French newcomers:

> Go see the forts our Father [the French] has erected, and you will see that the land beneath his walls is still hunting ground, having fixed himself in those places we frequent, only to supply our wants, whilst the English, on the contrary, no sooner get possession of the country than the game is forced to leave it; the trees fall down before them, the earth becomes bare, and we find among them hardly wherewithal to shelter us when the night falls.[48]

Whereas the French were prepared to leave the native people to lead their lives according to their traditions, the English wanted to clear their land. Patricia Seed attributes this to the English perception that hunting was a right exercised by the nobility as part of their ownership of the land. English people of low status hunted on pain of death, whereas there was, she says, no such class distinction in France.[49]

Miller defines the 18th century, the height of the Age of Reason, as the era in which European claims to territory in the Americas were fought out. This, he says, engendered a new relationship with the native peoples who, as well as becoming trading partners, were needed as allies in war.[50] If Europeans were dependent on the indigenous nations as allies, they had to treat them as

---

46   H. Brody, *The Other Side of Eden: Hunter-Gatherers, Farmers, and the Shaping of the World* (London: Faber & Faber, 2001), p. 157ff.

47   Seed, *American Pentimento*, p. 43.

48   Quoted in Miller, *Skyscrapers*, p. 68, from an unknown source in W.J. Eccles, *The Canadian Frontier 1534–1760* (New York: Holt, Reinhart and Winston, 1969) at p. 158 and p. 68.

49   Seed, *American Pentimento*, p. 50ff.

50   Miller, *Skyscrapers*, pp. 62–3.

equals, and a different relationship was necessary in regard to their land. Thus, following the European peace settlement marked by the Treaty of Paris, George III of England made his Royal Proclamation of 1763 which acknowledged indigenous ownership of indigenous land.

It fell to William Blackstone in 1765 to enshrine the rules of colonial land ownership in law. Following the doctrines of Locke, he proposed that 'colonies of settlement' included all settlements and plantations where 'an uninhabited country be discovered and planted by English subjects'. This included land where there were very few inhabitants, land which had not been cultivated and land inhabited by 'uncivilised inhabitants in a primitive state of society'.[51] Although Blackstone never uses the term *terra nullius*, he bases his analysis on Roman law relating to unoccupied land.[52] Writing of the law applicable in the new colonies, he said: 'In conquered or ceded countries, that have already laws of their own, the king may indeed alter and change those laws, but till he does actually change them the ancient laws of the country remain, unless such are against the law of God, as in the case of infidel country.'[53]

His analysis echoes the wording of the Royal Proclamation.

As will be seen in the ensuing chapters, and as noted by Patricia Seed,[54] when 'using long-standing expressions about Native Americans, present-day judges, lawyers and citizens, intentionally or not, often carry forward meanings created by colonizers'. It was not until the Australian case of *Mabo v Queensland [No2]*[55] in 1992 that the doctrine of *terra nullius* was successfully challenged. It has now been excluded from Canadian law by McLachlin CJ's decision in *Tsilhqot'in Nation v British Columbia*.[56] Moreover, the Final Report of the Indian Residential Schools Truth and Reconciliation Commission also declares the doctrine null and void.[57]

The Royal Proclamation in context

In 1763, the indigenous people in North America were still numerically superior to the European settlers. As we have seen, they lived in structured

51 Quoted in G. Partington, 'Thoughts on *terra nullius*', *Proceedings of the Samuel Griffith Society*, (2007): 96.
52 Seed, *American Pentimento*, p. 155. For a discussion of the influences of Roman law on this doctrine, see Pagden, *Lords of All*, p. 76ff.
53 Sir W. Blackstone, *Commentaries on the Laws of England*, Book I (Oxford: Clarendon Press, 1765), p. 105.
54 Seed, *American Pentimento*, p. 165.
55 *Mabo v Queensland [No2]* [1992]107 ALR 1 (HC Aust).
56 *Tsilhqot'in Nation v British Columbia* [2014] SCC 44.
57 Truth and Reconciliation Commission of Canada, *Final Report of the Truth and Reconciliation Commission of Canada, Volume Six* (Winnipeg, MB: Government of Canada, 2015), p. 90.

societies, although not on recognisably European lines. Although their leaders recognised the sovereignty of the English king over his own people, they had no intention of ceding their own sovereignty to the British Crown. Indigenous leaders like Pontiac continued to wage war against the British and the British government began to develop an enforceable Indian policy based on principles of conciliation. This was set out in a memorandum by Lord Egremont:

> Tho' … it may become necessary to erect some Forts in the Indian Country, with their Consent, yet His Majesty's Justice & Moderation inclines Him to adopt the more eligible Method of conciliating the Minds of the Indians by the Mildness of His Government, by protecting their Persons & Property & securing to them all the Possessions, Rights and Privileges they have hitherto enjoyed, & are entitled to, most cautiously guarding against any Invasion or Occupation of their Hunting Lands, the Possession of which is to be acquired by fair purchase only …[58]

This memorandum reflects the indigenous understanding of the Treaty of Niagara of 1764.

George III was offering his protection to equals, not to subject nations. The reason for the Proclamation was to establish the Crown's supremacy over its North American territories following the Treaty of Paris of 1763. This treaty concluded the territorial settlement at the end of the Seven Years' War, the last great European war before the French Revolution. The war was fought between Great Britain, Hanover and Prussia on one side and France, Austria, Saxony and Sweden on the other. One of the principal reasons for the conflict was to settle the division of French and British rights to territory in North America.

John Borrows[59] reminds us that the Royal Proclamation and the ensuing Treaty of Niagara of 1764 were the results of a two-way negotiation process – a process during which the indigenous chiefs thought about their future. He also points out that theirs was an oral culture, so that the documents which emanated from these negotiations showed only one side of the picture. He claims that the idea of distributing the wampum belts on the conclusion of the Treaty of Niagara came from Sir William Johnson, who was the Crown's representative at the negotiations for the Treaty.[60] Yet this was a Proclamation and a Treaty with what were regarded at the time as sovereign nations, which

---

58 Egremont [Secretary of State responsible for the North American Colonies] to the Lords of Trade, 5 May 1763 in Dussault and Erasmus, *Report of the Royal Commission*, vol. 1, p. 115.

59 J. Borrows, 'Wampum at Niagara: The Royal Proclamation, Canadian Legal History and Self-Government', in M. Asch (ed.), *Aboriginal and Treaty Rights in Canada* (Vancouver: UBC Press, 1997), p. 155.

60 Ibid., p. 162.

were recognised as able to form alliances with the Crown. Borrows[61] tells us that negotiations with indigenous peoples were conducted on a 'government to government' basis and that the indigenous peoples expected and received gifts in recognition that the land was theirs to share. If the gifts did not appear, conflicts arose.

This indicates that the indigenous peoples as sovereign nations were also making an offer of protection to the settlers, and one which was of greater significance at the time as the incomers needed guides and knowledge of how to cope with the difficult terrain as well as allies for military power. Borrows[62] sees the Proclamation as an attempt to delineate indigenous territory and to define jurisdictions after a period of increasing conflict. He refers to it as 'a codification of pre-existing First Nation/Colonial practice'.[63] Yet this analysis of the relationship was more honoured in the breach than in any other way once the Crown had established military superiority. Taken at face value, such an interpretation would preclude the Crown from unilaterally requisitioning indigenous land or from entering into treaties with indigenous peoples in the absence of full information and disclosure of terms which adversely affect indigenous rights – a concept which has come down to us as 'free, prior and informed consent' in the United Nations Declaration on the Rights of Indigenous Peoples, endorsed by Canada in 2010. It would preclude the Crown from taking adversarial action through the courts to oppose indigenous land claims. And, most importantly, it would preclude the Crown from insisting that indigenous rights be extinguished on the signing of any treaty. The Crown could not deal in indigenous land without the free, prior and informed consent of all members of the group whose land is to be taken.[64]

Yet the Proclamation refers to indigenous lands as being 'such Parts of Our Dominions and Territories' – i.e. they were already to be treated as Crown lands, in breach of the fiduciary duties undertaken by the British Crown. The RCAP Report suggests that this signifies the adoption of the doctrine of discovery[65] with regard to these lands.[66] The Report goes on to note that:

> It appears that European and Aboriginal interpretations of their agreements, whether written or not, differed on some key issues. The two principal ones were possessory rights in the land and the authority of European monarchs or their representatives over Aboriginal peoples. In general, the European understanding – or at least the one that was committed to paper – was that the monarch had, or acquired through

---

61 Ibid., p. 158.
62 Borrows, 'Wampum at Niagara', p. 159.
63 Ibid., p. 160.
64 See *Boardman v Phipps* [1967] AC 46.
65 That the first 'civilised', i.e. European, people to occupy the land can claim absolute title to it.
66 Dussault and Erasmus, *Report of the Royal Commission*, vol. 1, p. 116.

> treaty or alliance, sovereignty over the land and the people on it. The
> Aboriginal understanding, however, recognized neither European title
> to the land nor Aboriginal submission to a European monarch.[67]
>
> …
>
> These incongruities could co-exist without creating conflict because,
> for the most part, the parties were unaware of the significant differences
> in interpretation. Indeed, the deep differences in world view may have
> gone unexpressed simply because they were so fundamental and so
> different.[68]

Aboriginal treaties were much more than a contractual relationship: they
created a living relationship and they required ceremonies in which they were
renewed and the parties reconciled. They evolved over time and developed and
changed as people grew to know each other better.[69] J.R. Miller tells us that
indigenous/European treaty-making was based on kinship tradition and that
the ceremonial created 'fictive kinship' so that trading arrangements were seen
as part of treaties of peace and friendship. These ceremonies were repeated each
time the parties met so that the peace and friendship was renewed and the
arrangements could be updated if necessary.[70]

Whereas in land claims indigenous people are called upon to prove
occupation of their lands since time immemorial,[71] the Canadian judiciary
has never challenged the Crown's sovereignty over indigenous land. This is
despite the fact that the Crown's negotiators of the numbered treaties (see
below) and other agreements were careless about whom they chose to represent
the indigenous group concerned, to the extent that there are questions over
the validity of these arrangements.[72] According to Colin Calloway,[73] the
indigenous peoples of Quebec never considered themselves to be governed by
the French. An Ojibwa chief told the British after the fall of Quebec: 'Although
you have conquered the French, you have not yet conquered us! We are not
your slaves. These lakes, these woods and mountains were left to us by our
ancestors. They are our inheritance and we will part with them to none.'[74]

---

67   Dussault and Erasmus, *Report of the Royal Commission*, vol. 1, p. 1255.
68   Ibid., p. 126.
69   Ibid., p. 129.
70   J.R. Miller, *Compact, Contract, Covenant: Aboriginal Treaty-Making in Canada*
     (Toronto: University of Toronto Press, 2009), p. 9, p. 33ff.
71   In the context of indigenous land rights in Canada, 'time immemorial' means
     occupation prior to first contact with Europeans.
72   See *Paulette v Registrar of Titles*, discussed below.
73   C.G. Calloway, *The Scratch of a Pen: 1763 and the Transformation of North America*
     (New York: Oxford University Press, 2006), p. 66.
74   Full quotation in Borrows, 'Wampum at Niagara', p. 157.

Borrows notes[75] that in Article 40 of the Articles of Capitulation at the end of the Seven Years' War, both the British and the French speak of the indigenous peoples as autonomous and independent. Sir William Johnson wrote to the Lords of Trade that 'having never been conquered, either by the English or the French, nor subject to the Laws, [the Iroquois and eastern Indians] consider themselves as a free people'.[76] Macklem tells us that imperial dispatches and correspondence sent out before the Proclamation gave its purpose as to demonstrate 'a Readiness upon all occasion to do them justice'[77] and to give 'Royal protection from any Incroachment on the Lands they have reserved to themselves, for their hunting Grounds, & for their own Support and Habitation'.[78]

The Royal Proclamation was confirmed by the Treaty of Niagara of 1764, a treaty of 'offensive and defensive alliance', according to Sir William Johnson who represented the Crown. The terms of the Treaty were also represented by the wampum belts presented on the signing of the Treaty. The two rows of purple beads set in a bed of white beads (signifying purity) represented the intention of the indigenous and the non-indigenous people to lead separate lives according to their own world view but joined together in mutual respect, peace and friendship. This relationship was worked out in a series of proclamations and treaties. The wampum belts, understood by all parties to the Treaty, signify the true meaning of the Proclamation because they are the record of the party which acted to its detriment in giving the Crown a degree of control over its land. Thus, the Crown owes a duty to protect the land and the whole way of life of the indigenous people. This interpretation is confirmed in the letters written by Sir William Johnson to the Lords of Trade in 1764.[79] J.R. Miller tells us that, unless wampum was exchanged, the agreement was not to be taken seriously.[80] Further, Kathryn Muller tells us, wampum 'carried an inherent spiritual power in addition to serving as mnemonic devices that record transactions.'[81]

75 Ibid., p. 159.
76 P. Macklem, *Indigenous Difference and the Constitution of Canada* (Toronto: University of Toronto Press, 2001), p. 104.
77 Circular letter from Lord Egremont to the Superintendent for the Southern Indians and several colonial governors.
78 Egremont [Secretary of State for the Southern Department] to Amherst [Commander in Chief of the British Forces in America], 27 Jan. 1763.
79 Reproduced in Borrows and Rotman: *Aboriginal Legal Issues: Cases, Materials and Commentary* (2nd edn) (London: LexisNexis Butterworths, 2003).
80 Miller, *Compact, Contract, Covenant*, p. 42.
81 K.V. Muller, *The Two-Row Wampum: Historic Fiction, Modern Reality* (MA thesis, University of Laval 2004), quoted in J.R. Miller, *Compact, Contract, Covenant*, p. 39.

Writing to General Sir Thomas Gage, acting commander-in-chief of the British Army in North America, Sir William Johnson told him: 'We should tye them down … according to their own forms of which they take the most notice, for Example by Exchanging a very large belt with some remarkable & intelligible figures thereon.'[82]

The Proclamation claims sovereignty over Quebec, East Florida and West Florida deriving from the Treaty of Paris of 1763, and purports to be the settlement of British claims to French-held American territory. This settlement was reached over the heads of the indigenous people. First, George III prohibited the Governors of his 13 American colonies from granting rights of survey over indigenous lands which were not as yet ceded to or purchased by the British. The Proclamation continues:

> And we do further declare to be Our Royal Will and Pleasure, for the present as aforesaid, to reserve under our Sovereignty, Protection and Dominion, for the use of the said Indians, also the Lands and Territories not included within the limits of our said three new Governments, or within the Limits of the Territory granted to the Hudson's Bay Company, as also all the Lands and Territories lying to the Westward of the Sources of the Rivers which fall into the Sea from the West and North West as aforesaid.[83]

The wording 'for the use of' mirrors the form of words of trust in use at the time: 'to the use of'. 'For the use of' is also the form of wording used in the numbered treaties to establish the Crown's fee-simple title over indigenous lands. John Borrows notes the ambiguity of the wording,[84] which ostensibly affords the indigenous people the protection of their way of life as indicated by the wampum belts and at the same time affords a mechanism through which indigenous lands could be acquired. Leonard Rotman[85] observes that the surrender provision enabled the Crown to monitor the activities of the French, American and indigenous peoples while keeping them apart. Furthermore, since some Indian bands were the allies of the French, it was essential that the Crown won them over to the British side.[86] But, as Borrows points out,[87] words such as 'sovereignty' and 'dominion' were inserted into the Royal Proclamation without the consent of the indigenous peoples. So far as the indigenous peoples are concerned, they can thus have no force or effect.

---

82 Quoted in Miller, *Compact, Contract, Covenant*, p. 72.
83 The full text of the Royal Proclamation is set out in Appendix A.
84 Borrows, 'Wampum at Niagara', p. 160.
85 L. Rotman, *Parallel Paths: Fiduciary Doctrine and the Crow–Native Relationship in Canada* (Toronto: University of Toronto Press, 1996), p. 28.
86 Ibid., p. 38.
87 Borrows, 'Wampum at Niagara', p. 160.

Borrows[88] describes the Royal Proclamation as confirmed by the Treaty of Niagara of 1764 and the wampum belts as 'the most fundamental agreement' and one that was 'more than a unilateral declaration of the Crown's will'.[89] He argues that the *sui generis* description (see below) leads judges to interpret treaties under the law of contract and that this interpretation should allow the court to consider the implied terms in any treaty, including those provided by the Royal Proclamation. He believes that a contractual interpretation would provide more consistency in indigenous law and would avoid the trap of perceiving the indigenous people as in any way 'subservient'. His ultimate conclusion is that colonial interpretations of the Royal Proclamation are a way of dispossessing indigenous peoples of their rights.

Yet, for valid reasons, fiduciary relationships can be arranged between parties with equal power and still leave one party more vulnerable than the other. A fiduciary relationship creates more benefits than a contractual one and is no reflection on the status of the original parties.

There are some who remain true to the fiduciary duty established by the Royal Proclamation, however. When chairing the Mackenzie Valley Pipeline Inquiry, which was established in 1974 to report on the impacts of a pipeline which was proposed for the Mackenzie Valley in the Northwest Territories, Thomas Berger chose to concentrate on the social, environmental and economic impact within the region. In doing so, he fulfilled the true role of a fiduciary, refusing to put the Crown's interests in oil and gas before those of the aboriginal people in their land. Concluding that the non-indigenous population was transitory and that the majority of non-indigenous workers would return south, he attached the greatest importance to the effect of the proposals on the indigenous way of life, concluding:

> The culture, values and traditions of the native people amount to a great deal more than crafts and carvings. Their respect for the wisdom of the elders, their concept of family responsibilities, their willingness to share, their special relationship with the land – all of these values persist today, although native people have been under almost unremitting pressure to abandon them.
>
> Native society is not static. The things the native people have said to this Inquiry should not be regarded as a lament for a lost way of life but as a plea for an opportunity to shape their own future, out of their own past. They are not seeking to entrench the past but to build on it.[90]

To the dismay of the Canadian government and the oil companies, Berger ordered

88 Borrows, 'Wampum at Niagara', p. 169.
89 Ibid., p. 169.
90 T. Berger, *Northern Frontier, Northern Homeland: The Report of the Mackenzie Valley Pipeline Inquiry* (Ottawa, Ont.: Ministry of Supply and Service, 1977), part 1, xviii.

a ten-year moratorium so that the aboriginal people could have their land claims settled and thus benefit from the revenues from oil found on their territory.

In 1981, Berger published extra-judicially his book *Fragile Freedoms: Human Rights and Dissent in Canada* and told an audience at the University of Guelph: 'In the end, no matter what ideology they profess, our leaders share one firm conviction: that native rights should not be inviolable, the power of the state must encompass them.'[91]

Patrick Macklem points to three flaws in current indigenous jurisprudence:

> First, it unreasonably restricts constitutional protection to pre-contact cultural practices integral to Aboriginal cultural identities. Second, it fails adequately to explain why interests associated with Aboriginal cultural difference merit constitutional protection. Third, and perhaps most important, it treats Aboriginal cultural difference as though it were the only aspect of indigenous difference worthy of constitutional protection, ignoring the fact that indigenous difference also includes Aboriginal prior occupancy, Aboriginal prior sovereignty and Aboriginal participation in a treaty process.[92]

The Royal Commission on Aboriginal Peoples recognised that:

> When Europeans first came to the shores of North America, the continent was occupied by large numbers of sovereign and independent Aboriginal peoples with their own territories, laws and forms of government. These nations entered into relations with incoming European nations on a basis of equality and mutual respect, an attitude that persisted long into the period of colonisation.

The Crown is in breach of its fiduciary duty to allow the indigenous peoples to live independently, unmolested on their lands. It seems the view was taken that, once peace was restored on the American continent, there was no need to respect the promises given in the Royal Proclamation. In order to accommodate the mass migration from Europe, it became expedient to deprive the indigenous people of their land and their right to maintain and develop their traditional life. It soon became expedient to override indigenous civilisations and label their adherents as savages or as simple children not ready to join sophisticated non-indigenous society.

According to Rotman:

> The process of colonialism meant that the Crown's sovereign relations with the aboriginal peoples that had been honed over centuries were left to decay in mere decades. The Crown renounced responsibility for the

91 T. Berger, *One Man's Justice: A Life in the Law* (Vancouver: Douglas & MacIntyre, 2002), p. 148. Tom Berger paid the price for this remark – the Canadian Judicial Council launched an inquiry in which Berger was sanctioned for engaging in political controversy, a challenge to his integrity which caused him to resign his judicial appointment.

92 Macklem, *Indigenous Difference*, p. 48.

sovereign alliances that it had voluntarily entered into and the resultant responsibilities that it had undertaken through the terms of various Indian treaties and compacts, in favour of achieving its long-standing colonialist goal in North America. Yet throughout the process of the decay of this unique relationship, the Crown continued to enter into treaties with the aboriginal peoples and to affirm to them the sovereign nature of their rights and status in Canada. The Crown's justification of its activities under the rule of law, however, was as faulty as the very foundations of the colonialist doctrines on which its claim to absolute sovereignty over Canada was based.[93]

Speaking of fiduciary duties in general, not just those owed to indigenous peoples, Finn[94] maintains that the recognition of a fiduciary duty is nothing more than a matter of public policy. Once the utility of the Crown's guarantee to the indigenous people of Canada ceased to be recognised, the Crown failed to honour its promises.

There is confusion between the duties which the Crown assumed by virtue of the Royal Proclamation – which are fiduciary and proprietary – and those which it created under the Indian Act, in which the Crown perceives itself as the guardian over its indigenous wards, a relationship which leaves indigenous peoples with no more powers than minors.

Yet the Royal Proclamation was addressed to, and the Treaty of Niagara was concluded with, what were regarded at the time as sovereign nations who were recognised as able to form alliances with the Crown. Thus, the personal fiduciary duty is a more appropriate interpretation of the duty owed by the Crown to its indigenous peoples. By assuming responsibility for indigenous lands, the Crown also assumed a proprietary fiduciary duty. As we shall see in Chapter 16, this is a principle as pertinent today in the interpretation of the negotiation and terms of the Tshash Petapen Agreement in Labrador as it was to the negotiation of a treaty of offensive and defensive alliance in the proceedings at Niagara in 1764. As Rotman[95] points out, 'a nation did not need to treat with its own subjects'. The provisions of the Indian Act 1876 and its subsequent amendments are a dilution of these fundamental duties, instigated after Canada's indigenous peoples had been suppressed by the treaty process and decimated by European disease, with the indigenous population reduced to one tenth of its former size. The Indian Acts were a process by which indigenous peoples were given a separate status pending full assimilation into Canadian society. Purporting to place the Crown in a position of wardship over indigenous peoples, they took away rights to self-determination and territory guaranteed by the Royal Proclamation.

93 Rotman, *Parallel Paths*, p. 64
94 P.D. Finn, 'The Fiduciary Principle', in T.G. Youdan (ed.), *Equity, Fiduciaries and Trusts* (Toronto: Carswell, 1989), p. 26.
95 Finn, 'Fiduciary Principle', p. 13.

Yet James (Sake) Youngblood Henderson points out that: 'Only positive law empires created around centralized rulers or aristocratic society can transfer total control to another ruler. This attribute was missing in First Nations. None of the First Nations had any such idea or structure. The First Nations leaders were not superiors that directed the will of the inferiors; instead, they were limited representatives of the people.'[96]

J.R. Miller elaborates on this, pointing out that indigenous peoples lived in non-state societies whose functions were misunderstood by the Crown's representatives, as was also the way in which they were governed.[97]

This is apparent in the introduction of the Indian Act in 1876, which codified existing legislation dealing with indigenous peoples and brought in a regime in which they were to be treated as wards of the Crown, with no more legal standing than children. The Crown was to make all decisions regarding their way of life – a more convenient interpretation of the fiduciary duty for the land-hungry settlers. As Miller points out:

> The trustee–ward, adult–child relationship embodied in the Indian Act was the antithesis of the kindred relationship – brother to brother, sister to sister under their mutual parent, the Great White Queen Mother – that both sides had talked about during treaty negotiations. The federal government pushed this evolution to its perversely logical end in 1880 with the creation of the Department of Indian Affairs. Ottawa had transformed First Nations into administered peoples with the Indian Act; it equipped itself with the machinery to administer them in the Department of Indian Affairs.[98]

Between 1927 and 1951, section 141 of the Indian Act even made it a criminal offence to raise money to fund challenges to treaties:

> Every person who, without the consent of the Superintendent General expressed in writing, receives, obtains, solicits or requests from any Indian any payment or contribution or promise of any payment or contribution for the purpose of raising a fund or providing money for the prosecution of a claim which the tribe or band of the Indians to which such Indian belongs, or of which he is a member; has or is represented to have for the recovery of any claim or money for the benefit of the said tribe or band, shall be guilty of an offence.

For the time being, the Crown had reneged on its fiduciary duty. There was no longer any need for a treaty process. Until the decision in *Calder v Attorney General for British Columbia* in 1973, the federal government could move settlers and corporations onto indigenous land with impunity.

---

96   J.(S.) Youngblood Henderson, 'Empowering Treaty Federalism', (1994) 58 Sask L Rev 241, at p. 251.

97   Miller, *Compact, Contract, Covenant*, p. 4.

98   Ibid., p. 190.

You can trace the change back, not to the coming of the mines, but to the first initial contact with Europeans through the fur trading – that's when we started to change our traditional way of life, when we started to abandon our traditional way of life in order to get some other form of revenue. It's not black and white – it's a gradual change. Our way of life was transformed gradually with contact with Europeans and other factors – a curve. You don't go right or left. It's a slow curve of change. It's a mindset, you know. I feel more and more voiceless, powerless compared perhaps to 30 or 40 years ago, in the sense that nobody cares much about us. People and companies and governments go on with their projects – business as usual – and it just rolls over us without considering us much or our aspirations as Innu.

> After that a lot of Innu people died because they starved. They could have made a lot of money selling furs to the Europeans and the Northern Store. My cousin starved to death.

Some people are not yet ready to talk about abuse.

> I was there for three years and then I went on for two years to the convent. Because of this I lost all my culture. They broke up our family. If I had been able to grow up there I would have known all the animals, what is there, what their names are. I would have known all about the country if they hadn't done that. If I hadn't gone there my life would have been very different. That's what I can't forgive. Now I am trying to help younger people not to feel bad like I did. I tell children where they came from, their history, about their land, their culture. That makes me feel better in myself, helping other people.

Chapter 7

The personal fiduciary duty

In 1984, after over 200 years, in the case of *Guerin v R*,[1] the Supreme Court of Canada recognised that the Proclamation created a personal fiduciary duty. The analysis in *Guerin* of the relationship between the Crown and the aboriginal peoples of Canada speaks of a personal rather than a political fiduciary obligation. Just as Canadian judges classify indigenous rights as *sui generis* (i.e. in a class of their own), the case law produces a *sui generis,* unique model of fiduciary relationship as applied to indigenous rights which has developed independently of the principles laid down in the Canadian case law dealing with non-aboriginal claims of breach of fiduciary duty, which derives from the line of English cases starting with *Keech v Sandford* in 1726.[2] According to Donovan Waters,[3] 'English equity precedents had an almost conclusive force in Canadian courts up until the 1960s. In the succeeding 30 years, however, Waters notes a trend towards 'unjust enrichment'[4] doctrines which go beyond traditional fiduciary considerations of undue influence and towards a situation where 'undesirable conduct rather than the exact character of a fiduciary relationship gives rise to a remedy'.[5]

P.D. Finn[6] defines the American and Canadian approach to fiduciary law as a 'surrogate of trusts law' as these are nations 'with a dominant commitment to individuality', whereas in England, Australia and New Zealand, which he characterises as societies committed to fostering social co-operation, the position of fiduciary 'exposes that person to the full rigour of equity both in method and in remedy'.

---

1   [1984] DLR (4th) 321, [1984] 2 SCR 355, [1984] 6 WWR 481, 59 BCLR 301, [1985] 1 CNLR 120, 20 ETR 6, 36.
2   *Keech v Sandford* [1726] Sel Cas Ch 61.
3   D.W.M. Waters, 'New Directions in The Employment of Equitable Doctrines: The Canadian Experience', in T.G. Youdan (ed.), *Equity, Fiduciaries and Trusts* (Toronto: Carswell, 1989), p. 411.
4   Where one party receives a benefit to the detriment of another without giving anything of equal in return.
5   Ibid., p. 412.
6   Finn, 'Fiduciary Principle', p. 2.

Canadian judges in indigenous rights cases have declared a political fiduciary duty which allows justification arguments and public policy concerns to override the strict application of equity and trusts law. Furthermore, a political trust is only morally, not legally, binding.[7]

By contrast, the law of trusts imposes on fiduciaries a duty of the utmost good faith and an obligation never to allow their own interests, or the interests of those to whom they owe other duties, to conflict with those of the beneficiary. The personal fiduciary's duty is one of complete loyalty. The duty, developed first in English case law and received into Canadian law, precludes any dealings in the beneficiary's property which are not entirely for the benefit of the beneficiary (in this case the indigenous people). Thus, the fiduciary can neither purchase the beneficiary's property nor make use of information or opportunities received through dealings with the property. The duty was made clear as early as 1726 in the *Keech* case, which concerned a trustee who, having failed to obtain the renewal of a lease to be held for the benefit of his beneficiary, was offered the lease for himself. The relationship of trustee and beneficiary is the prime example of a fiduciary relationship and, at English law, the case law on the duties of trustees and fiduciaries is interchangeable. In *Keech* Lord King LC observed: 'This may seem hard, that the trustee is the only person of all mankind who might not have the lease, but it is very proper that the rule should be strictly pursued, and not in the least relaxed ...

In England in 1896 Lord Herschell[8] gave three criteria by which a beneficiary can establish the existence of a fiduciary relationship:

- the defendant is actually in a fiduciary relationship with the claimant – a relationship in which it is possible to exert undue influence;

- the defendant obtains a benefit; and

- there is a causal connection between the relationship and the benefit.

As can be seen from the cases and treaties discussed below, these criteria apply to the Crown's dealings in indigenous land.

Lord Herschell went on to explain: 'It does not appear to me that this rule is, as has been said, founded upon principles of morality. I regard it rather as based on the consideration that, human nature being what it is, there is danger, in such circumstances, of the person holding a fiduciary position being swayed by interest rather than duty, and thus prejudicing those whom he was bound to protect.'

---

7   See L. Rotman, 'Taking Aim at the Canons of Treaty Interpretation in Canadian Aboriginal Rights Jurisprudence', 46 (1997) UNBLJ 1.

8   *Bray v Ford* [1896] AC 44.

This strict approach was confirmed in English law by the House of Lords in *Boardman v Phipps*,[9] and at that time the decision was further explained by Professor Gareth Jones as follows: the very fact that the fiduciary had a personal interest in the assets of the beneficiary might detract from the impartiality of his decision-making.[10]

In both the United Kingdom and in Canada, once a fiduciary duty is established, the court will declare the fiduciary to be a constructive trustee of any assets, information or opportunities obtained by virtue of the fiduciary relationship. This entails a duty to account fully to the beneficiary for any profits or losses made. This was the approach in *Guerin* to the question of compensation. The court awarded C$10 million in full compensation for the breach of fiduciary duty. The fiduciary is burdened with all the duties of a trustee and, if dealing with trust property, must exercise the standard of care of the ordinary prudent man of business acting for one to whom he is morally obliged.[11]

Rotman claims that 'whereas a trust relationship results in the existence of fiduciary duties, it is not the same thing as a fiduciary relationship. A trustee is a type of fiduciary, but a fiduciary is not necessarily a trustee'.[12] Yet in all cases other than those concerning the Crown in its dealings with indigenous peoples, if the court declares that a fiduciary relationship exists, it will declare a constructive trust over the assets of the beneficiary and treat the fiduciary exactly as if he or she were declared a trustee.

In order for a full trust over land to be declared in Canada, the three certainties whose existence validates a trust must be present:

- certainty of intention: namely, the text of the Royal Proclamation, as confirmed by the wampum belts, which sets out that indigenous lands are to be held for indigenous peoples;

- that the lands so described form the subject matter; and

- that the intended beneficiaries are clearly the indigenous peoples.

There is only one factor which prevents this situation from resulting in a full declaration of trust – the Crown has no title to indigenous land. Thus, this must be a fiduciary relationship, under which one party takes responsibility for the other's land and is subject to the duty to obtain prior fully informed consent for any proposed dealings in the property.

Following the English jurisprudence, in the Canadian case of *Frame v Smith*, Wilson J defined a fiduciary relationship as one in which:

9   [1967] 2 AC 46.
10   G. Jones, 'Unjust Enrichment and the Fiduciary's Duty of Loyalty', (1968) 84 LQR 472, at 474.
11   *Learoyd v Whitely* [1887] 12 App Cas 727.
12   Rotman, *Parallel Paths*, p. 5.

- the fiduciary has scope for the exercise of some discretion or power;

- the fiduciary can unilaterally exercise that power or discretion so as to affect the beneficiary's legal or practical interests; and

- the beneficiary is peculiarly vulnerable to or at the mercy of the fiduciary holding the discretion or power.[13]

This form of fiduciary duty is described by Finn[14] as a proscriptive rather than a prescriptive duty: its boundaries are set by what a fiduciary may not do. Until the decision in *Guerin*, in the aboriginal cases concerning the fiduciary duty of the Crown, the Crown's duties are held to be political rather than personal, leading to an analysis that the duty is a 'prescribed' one – i.e. set out in terms of justification and public policy arguments. Rotman[15] notes the courts' inability to understand the historical context of the indigenous cases and the courts' unwillingness to address the significance of this relationship. It should also be noted that elsewhere in Canadian law, if the presumed fiduciary wishes to show that the relationship does *not* fall into the category of a fiduciary relationship, the burden of proof falls on the fiduciary – but this is another principle ignored by the Canadian courts in indigenous rights cases. In *R v Sparrow*[16] (1990), it was laid down that a purposive approach (looking to the purpose of the legislation rather than to the plain words of the statute) should be taken to the interpretation of indigenous rights and treaties.

Finn[17] also raises the question of the purpose for which the fiduciary has acquired rights, powers and duties. He concludes that, to the extent that the fiduciary acquires such rights for his or her own purposes, he or she is bound by strict fiduciary duties. In the case of the Royal Proclamation, the purpose of taking control of indigenous land was to keep it from incursions from competing nations and from settlers who must hold land through the Crown, a purpose which only served the British Crown.

Macklem[18] explains that: 'vague treaty guarantees were infused with substantive meaning by unquestioned reference to a reliance on Anglo-Canadian categories of human understanding. Notions of private property and freedom of contract guided the judiciary.'

However, he recognises a more recent trend, namely a willingness 'to embrace native difference, with the acknowledgement that native expectations

---

13   *Frame v Smith* [1987] 2 SCR 99.
14   P.D. Finn, *Fiduciary Obligations* (Sydney: The Law Book Company, 1977).
15   Rotman, *Parallel Paths*, p. 140.
16   [1990] 70 DLR (4th) 385, [1990] 1 SCR 1075, [1990] 4 WWR 410, 46 BCLR (2nd) 1m 56 CCC (3d) 263m 111 NR 241m [1990] 3 CNLR 160.
17   Finn, *Fiduciary Obligations*, p. 35.
18   Macklem, 'First Nations Self-Government and the Borders of the Canadian Legal Imagination', *McGill Law Journal* (1991): 442.

concerning the meaning of treaty entitlements may well have been markedly different than those entertained by the agents of the Crown'.

Yet he concludes that the judgments still maintain a hierarchical approach to indigenous peoples and still rest on Anglo-Canadian conceptions.

On reviewing relevant case law, a question does arise as to whether a trust can be imposed on the Crown,[19] unless the Crown voluntarily and explicitly assumes that role.[20] However, in the Royal Proclamation of 1763, the Crown did exactly that and thus is precluded from denying the fiduciary relationship on this basis. In any event, the Crown should be estopped from doing so on the basis that the Crown received a benefit or benefits from the relationship created by the Proclamation and the indigenous peoples acted to their detriment in giving up freedom of alienation of their land. We know they did this willingly, because the agreement is recorded in the wampum belts, but this still allows for a fiduciary relationship because the arrangement was to the Crown's advantage and the Crown took responsibility for the alienation of indigenous land. As explained immediately below, this would place the relationship within reliance theory, although it could also be argued that the Crown's fiduciary duties also arise under property theory and inequality theory. Certainly, in later dealings, unjust enrichment theory would apply.[21] Unjust enrichment theory applies when the fiduciary has benefitted personally from the relationship, as in the case of *Keech* above. Reliance theory applies when the beneficiary has acted to their detriment in reliance on an undertaking given by the fiduciary; so the duty undertaken by the Crown in the Royal Proclamation would give rise to a strong legal case under reliance theory.

By 1812, with the end of the wars with America, the British had no need of further alliances with indigenous warriors – but they did have a great and increasing need of land for settlement: 'The association was no longer one that emphasized military alliance but rather one in which the dominant partner sought the removal of the Indian from the path of agricultural settlement … From the point of view of the European, the Indian had become irrelevant.'[22]

Squatters moved in and the authorities did little to protect the rights guaranteed by the Royal Proclamation. Miller notes that the settler population of Upper Canada rose from 95,000 in 1812 to 952,000 at the time of the census in 1851.[23]

19   See *Henry v R* [1905] 9 Ex. CR. 417.
20   See Rotman, *Parallel Paths*, p. 75ff.
21   See Rotman, *Parallel Paths*, Chapter 9.
22   Miller, *Skyscrapers*, p. 84.
23   Miller, *Skyscrapers*, p. 92.

The white people came and changed our religion.

Canadians are consumers so they rely on our resources – I would try as much as possible to protect my land rights and not extinguish them.

[Canadians] cherish a country and they cherish their piece of property because it has a value. It is an investment for them. Nitassinan is our homeland, it's our land, our way of life, our culture. It's more than a piece of property that you can sell and hope to get a better deal or more money. It's who we are.

It started in August that people would go back to their villages and they would work until the first freeze and that's where the stories started to be told in the community. Young people don't know these stories – in these stories there is education. It teaches where we came from, how animals and plants came here. It also helps young children to believe that they can do whatever they need to – like using a bow and arrow to go hunting. It's to help young people know how they came to earth.

Drugs and alcohol are the community's cry for help.

When I look at the eagle feather, that is how much I have to do in the culture [something for every strand of the feather].

We have no land to pass on – the children turn to alcohol out of hopelessness.

The government fails to tell the real story about the Indian people. They don't tell the fact that this [status] card is only useful on an Innu reserve. If I work outside the reserve I pay taxes just like the other citizens of Canada.

I have to respect the decisions that other nations made – they didn't sell their land, they just lost it. I didn't like what the Cree and Inuit did because they sold land that was not theirs – but they were under a lot of pressure from the government.

8

Bending the law to the needs of settlement

The treaties

As the Crown increased its military presence in British North America, and as the fur trade became less dependent on indigenous trappers, the incomers were less inclined to respect the covenants given in the Royal Proclamation. The RCAP Report tells us that Loyalists moving across the 49th parallel after the American War of Independence brought with them the idea of entering into land treaties with the indigenous peoples.[24] Before a treaty was concluded the Crown described the lands as 'public lands' but, once the treaty was concluded, the lands were allocated into private ownership by individuals. This was contrary to the indigenous understanding that the treaties were agreements to share the land.

Rotman notes that, as the Crown became less dependent on its former indigenous allies, the subject matter of the treaties changed from peace to land. The solution adopted by the Crown to its increasing need for indigenous land was to send out negotiators to treat with small bands of indigenous people. At the same time, the terms of Indian treaties ceased to be agreements between sovereign nations and instead became one-sided documents under which the Crown dictated terms of surrender of lands.[25]

The Robinson treaties

The treaty process began in earnest when the Ojibwa and Metis people of Lake Huron and Lake Superior began to protest at the use of natural resources on their land without their consent. In 1849, a war party took possession of a mine near Sault Ste. Marie. The governor general called in William Robinson to negotiate the two treaties which bear his name. A former fur trader, he insisted that the Ojibwa people be permitted to maintain their connection to the land because they supplied high-quality furs. These were resource-development treaties and the land taken was not suitable for settlement. Reserves were set apart for the

24   Dussault and Erasmus, *Report of the Royal Commission*, vol. 2, part 2, p. 468.
25   Rotman, *Parallel Paths*, p. 42.

Ojibwa at a rate of 640 acres per family. Nevertheless, the treaty stated that this land was to be shared with the settlers, which Robinson explained was an advantage since the Ojibwa would be able to sell them their produce![26]

The Ojibwa negotiated to receive a share of the revenues from the mines, with annuities and cash payments increasing with the increase in the revenues. However, the increase in payments did not match the increase in the revenues and when the Ojibwa demanded further increases to make up the shortfall, the Crown relied on the wording of the treaty, never shown to the Ojibwa at the time of signing, to the effect that any increases would be limited to what 'Her Majesty may be graciously pleased to order'. Although Ojibwa hunting and fishing rights were to be totally undisturbed, the written treaty provides that what has taken place is a total surrender – whereas the Ojibwa had understood that the treaty covered only the right to subsurface exploitation.[27]

Recently, the true intention behind the Robinson Treaties has come under scrutiny in the Ontario Supreme Court of Justice I *Restoule v Canada*.[28] Judge Patricia Hennessey, in interpreting the two Robinson treaties, accepted evidence of Anishinaabe methods of treaty making together with the intentions of each side in order to give a purposive interpretation, which would give the Anishinaabe a considerable sum of unpaid annuities accruing since 1874. The Anishinaabe published their Opening Statement[29] online and the respondent governments accepted the evidence of the way in which the treaty was originally negotiated.

The numbered treaties

After Canada's Confederation in 1867, each of the treaties was given a number. All of the numbered treaties contained a clause by which indigenous people 'cede, release, surrender and yield up to the Government of the Dominion of Canada ... all their rights, titles and privileges whatsoever, to the lands'. Treaty 4 was the first treaty to contain an extinguishment clause whereby all indigenous rights were wiped out unless specified in the treaty.[30]

The wording of the treaties implies that the Crown received absolute title to the land and was then obliged to grant reserve land to the peoples concerned. Yet the RCAP Report reminds us that negotiations were conducted according to

26 Dussault and Erasmus, *Report of the Royal Commission*, vol. 2, p. 481.
27 Ibid., p. 158.
28 *Restoule v Canada (Attorney General)* [2018] ONSC.
29 Court File No: C-3512-14 & C-3512-14A, Ontario Supreme Court, 2017_09_25-Opening-Statement-of-the-Plaintiffs.pdf.
30 Miller, *Compact, Contract, Covenant*, p. 172. See also M. Asch, *On Being Here to Stay: Treaties and Aboriginal Rights in Canada* (Toronto: University of Toronto Press, 2014), pp. 76–7.

the indigenous oral tradition, which had no words to express these concepts.[31] Some indigenous peoples were shrewd negotiators. They were familiar with the results of negotiations south of the 49th parallel, and used this knowledge so that they became expert negotiators themselves. They knew the value of their lands to the Crown. They also recognised the dangers: 'We see how the Indians are treated far away. The white man comes, looks at their flowers, their trees and their rivers; others soon follow; the lands of the Indians pass from their hands, and they have nowhere a home.'[32]

The peoples concerned were moved onto reserves so that their title was extinguished, releasing large tracts of land to the Crown for settlement or exploitation. Sprague[33] notes that each of the treaties corresponded to an economic interest of the government of the day. The indigenous people were led to believe that treaty provisions were created in perpetuity. On this basis, according to the indigenous point of view, the Royal Proclamation of 1763 should be read in conjunction with every subsequent treaty. By contrast, Canadian law required[34] that treaties be ratified by parliament. Further, treaty provisions were superseded by subsequent treaties. Macklem[35] maintains that, prior to the introduction of section 35(1) of the Constitution Act 1982, treaties were regarded by the Crown as contracts which permitted the Crown to extinguish existing treaty rights unilaterally but, with the introduction of section 35(1), courts changed their approach to interpretation towards one that was more understanding and accommodating of indigenous treaty expectations. Previously, treaty interpretation had been subject only to the norms of the dominant society. Nevertheless, the Crown was still under the fiduciary duty *not* to deal in indigenous land without the free, prior and informed consent of the people concerned. This is a duty which arises from the Royal Proclamation. Macklem notes James (Sake) Youngblood Henderson's words that 'aboriginal people entered the treaties as keepers of a certain place',[36] so that for them the purpose of a treaty was to regulate the sharing of the land in such a way as to protect the land and their own use of the territory concerned. However, the decisions do not reflect the indigenous primary concern that, above all, the land should be protected. Macklem[37] sees the treaty process as an alternative to the doctrine of discovery; as a foundation of Canadian sovereignty over,

31 Dussault and Erasmus, *Report of the Royal Commission*, vol. 2, p. 159.
32 Quoted in H.Y. Hind, *Narrative of the Canadian Red River Exploring Expeditions of 1857 and of the Assiniboine and Saskatchewan*, and reproduced in Dussault and Erasmus, vol. 1, p. 165.
33 D.N. Sprague, 'Canada's Treaties with Aboriginal Peoples', (1996) Man LJ 341.
34 See *R v Sylliboy* [1929] 1 DLR 307, 50 CCC 389.
35 Macklem, *Indigenous Difference*, p. 138.
36 J.(S.) Youngblood Henderson, 'Interpreting *sui generis* Treaties', (1997) 36 Alta Law Rev 46, at p. 64.
37 Macklem, *Indigenous Difference*, p. 256

and title to, the land. This might have been an effective transition had the treaty negotiations been carried out under the fiduciary obligations of the Crown. However, no attempt was made to obtain the fully informed consent of indigenous representatives authorised by the group concerned to enter into negotiations. No mention appears to have been made in the face-to-face negotiations of the extinguishment of their land rights.

In *Simon v R*[38] Dickson CJ gave four principles of treaty interpretation:

- 'Indian treaties should be given a fair, large and liberal construction in favour of the Indians';

- treaties should not be construed 'according to the technical meaning of their words but in the sense that they would naturally be understood by the Indians';

- rights to hunt should be 'interpreted in a flexible way that is sensitive to the evolution of changes to normal hunting practices'; and

- the right to hunt also comprises 'those activities reasonably incidental to the act of hunting itself'.

Sharon Venne[39] points out that the chiefs who negotiated with the Crown's representatives had no authority to enter into treaties extinguishing their rights in the land. She writes as follows of the role of the chief in Plains Cree governance: chiefs and headmen must win and maintain the respect of their followers, but there were no elections and tenure of the position is under constant review. The people made their wishes known by their actions. Indigenous representatives had been observed down the years before they are chosen and their mandate is to implement decisions made by their people. The chief had no authority to make binding, unilateral decisions. Political and legal authority rests with the people.

Venne[40] goes on to describe the treaty-making process for Treaty 6 in 1876 according to Cree oral history. The Crown treaty commissioner said that the Crown wanted a 'treaty of peace and friendship' to last 'as long as the sun shines, the grass grows and the rivers flow', which would allow the Queen's Canadian subjects to move out of their present overcrowded conditions onto Indian land. The negotiations were at arm's length and subject to no external pressure, and concluded with the smoking of a pipe. This represented a solemn undertaking before the Creator. The provision in the treaty for the payment of annuities represented the necessity of the giving of a gift in order to share indigenous land. Yet when it came to the written version of the treaty, the Cree

---

38   [1985] 24 DLR (4th) 309 (SCC).

39   S. Venne, 'Understanding Treaty 6: An Indigenous Perspective', in M. Asch (ed.) 1997, *Aboriginal and Treaty Rights*, p. 178ff.

40   Ibid., p. 187ff.

denied that they ever agreed to 'cede, surrender and forever give up title' to their lands. Such words did not exist in their language. Under Cree law, the Cree can only ever agree to share their land. The Cree have their own written version of the treaty, in two copies which are written on buffalo hide, never to be erased. These can be produced to show the original agreed version of Treaty 6. Venne also gives reasons why the Cree would never enter into a treaty for 'so long as the sun shines, the grass grows and the rivers flow' – in their collective memory, they know that such things are uncertain.

In *Paulette v Registrar of Titles (No 2)*,[41] Morrow J noted the 'ultimatum effect' of the Crown's negotiation style, which took an extreme form when the chief appointed to sign Treaty 11 at Fort Simpson refused to sign and the Crown's representatives appointed another chief without the knowledge of the indigenous people. Under the treaty, each indigenous family was to be given a piece of reserve land which was too small to sustain it. The RCAP Report tells us that the reserves promised under the terms of Treaties 8 and 11 were not built until the 1950s or even the 1970s, and this was one of the factors leading to Morrow J's decision that the indigenous rights had not been extinguished.[42] Pointing to the inferior bargaining position of the indigenous people, Morrow J held that there was doubt as to whether the full indigenous title had been extinguished.

The Crown has argued that any outbreak of hostilities extinguished treaty rights agreed between the warring parties. Yet in *Simon*, Dickson CJC confirmed the Micmac's continuing right to hunt despite the fact that hostilities had broken out between the Crown and the Micmac after the treaty was concluded. The hostilities had been initiated by the Crown. He held that the Micmac hunting rights were not 'frozen rights' but rights to hunt according to contemporary practices. He upheld Simon's right to carry a gun outside the provincially prescribed hunting season on the grounds that, by section 88 of the Indian Act, treaty rights took precedence over provincial legislation.

The Royal Commission on Aboriginal Peoples recommended treaty legislation which, *inter alia*, would affirm the jurisprudence on treaty interpretation and commit the Canadian government to treaty processes which would implement the spirit and intent of the treaty negotiations rather than the plain meaning of the words of the written treaties. If these principles of interpretation are applied, there is an arguable case for returning the lands and the rights to the indigenous people where extinguishment and expropriation were achieved by deception – since the claims would not be statute-barred (out of time).

41   [1973] DLR (3rd) 8, [1973] 6 WWR 97, [1976] WWR 193.
42   Dussault and Erasmus, *Report of the Royal Commission*, vol. 2, p. 482.

The Royal Commission on Aboriginal Peoples[43] found that the non-aboriginal people took advantage of the indigenous lack of understanding of the legal and political implications of the terms of the treaties. Further, the written terms often failed to reflect the oral agreement reached in negotiation. In particular, the written versions of the numbered post-Confederation treaties differed from the oral agreements. The indigenous peoples found themselves subject to colonial laws of which they knew nothing, despite the assurances given in the negotiations that they would continue to be independent and free to pursue their traditional life. They had little comprehension of the clauses in the written treaties under which their rights were extinguished. In the treaty documents indigenous nations were referred to as subjects of the Crown, something which they never conceded. James (Sake) Youngblood Henderson says that, since no purchase price or other consideration was given for the surrender of the rights, the Crown received a protective rather than a proprietary tenure, under which the indigenous people maintained their sovereignty and a degree of self-determination.[44]

The RCAP Report sums up the general outcome of the numbered treaty negotiations as follows:

> The Crown asked First Nations to share their lands with settlers, and First Nations did so on the condition that they would retain adequate land and resources to ensure the well-being of their nations. The Indian parties understood they would continue to maintain their traditional governments, their laws and their customs and to co-operate as necessary with the Crown. There was substantive agreement that the treaties established an economic partnership from which both parties would benefit. Compensation was offered in exchange for the agreement of First Nations to share. The principle of fair exchange and mutual benefit was an integral part of treaty-making. First Nations were promised compensation in the form of annual payments and annuities, social and economic benefits, and the continued use of their land and resources.[45]

These are the terms agreed in oral negotiations but, the Report tells us, little time was spent on discussing them in detail and the later, written, versions were silent on these provisions. The Canadians did not have any commitment to the fulfilment of the terms which the indigenous groups considered vital. The RCAP Report also points out that treaties were executive actions of the Crown and were never sanctioned by parliament through legislation. The treaties were never disseminated in government departments.[46]

---

43 Dussault and Erasmus, *Report of the Royal Commission*, Chapter 1.
44 Youngblood Henderson, *Interpreting Sui Generis Treaties*, p. 265.
45 Dussault and Erasmus, *Report of the Royal Commission* vol. 1, p. 174.
46 Ibid., p. 177.

The case law

The two cases which first defined the significance of the Royal Proclamation, and thereby the nature of indigenous land rights, concerned disputes over indigenous land between non-indigenous litigants.

Johnson v M'Intosh,[47] an American case, concerned the purchase of indigenous lands without the Government's permission. It was heard by a judge who was a land speculator; both counsels were land speculators, the parties were land speculators, and the defendant, M'Intosh, only agreed to be a party to the case to settle a score with another land speculator.[48] It is hardly surprising, therefore, that Marshall CJ upheld the doctrine of discovery as the basis of British title to indigenous land.

Chief Justice Marshall gave his interpretation of the doctrine of discovery as meaning that the nation which first discovered the aboriginal lands could claim title to them as against other European nations. It was contended that the indigenous people were repaid for their lands by being given the advantages of civilisation and Christianity. Nevertheless, the indigenous right to occupy the land by virtue of their possession was recognised under the common law. The Marshall judgment was the basis for the UK Privy Council's decision in *St Catherine's Milling v R*[49] although Chief Justice Marshall, in a subsequent case,[50] held that land could only be acquired by cession or by purchase.

St Catherine's Milling, a Canadian case, was heard in London by the Privy Council. Lord Watson dismissed the indigenous peoples' right to their own land as 'a personal and usufructuary right dependent on the will of the sovereign' – a right *in personam* rather than *in rem* and thus defeasible because the right is not attached to the land. The Privy Council held that the indigenous people had a mere licence to use the land until the Crown decided unilaterally to revoke that licence. It was held that the beneficial interest in the disputed indigenous land lay with the province of Ontario. If the indigenous people had no proprietary interest in the land, they lost the protection afforded them by the Royal Proclamation as there was no need for the surrender of the lands to the Crown if the indigenous people had a personal, non-transferable interest. This decision had far-reaching consequences: it effectively gave permission for 150 years of unilateral expropriation of indigenous lands and repression of indigenous language and culture in a failed attempt at assimilation.

As Gerry St Germain, a Metis Canadian senator, observed to the Truth and Reconciliation Commission on Indian Residential Schools: 'There can be no

---

47   [1823] 8 Wheaton 543, 21 US 240.
48   For a fascinating account of the proceedings in *Johnson v M'Intosh*, see L.G. Robertson: *Conquest by Law* (Oxford: Oxford University Press, 2005).
49   [1888] 14 App Cas. 46 (P.C.).
50   *Worcester v Georgia* 6 Pet (USSC) 515 [1832].

doubt that the founders of Canada somehow lost their moral compass in their relations with the people who occupied and possessed the land …'[51]

It was not until 1973 in *Calder v Attorney General for British Columbia*[52] that the Court reconsidered the finding in *St Catherine's Milling* that aboriginal title was no more than personal and usufructuary. The court heard evidence gathered from the historical documents of the time, including the proclamations and ordinances of the Governor of the Colony of British Columbia. In the words of Judson J: 'Although I think it is clear that Indian title in British Columbia cannot owe its origin to the Proclamation of 1763, the fact is that when the settlers came, the Indians were there, organised in societies and occupying the land as their forefathers had done for centuries.'

The Supreme Court of Canada granted the declaration sought by the Nisga'a Nation that 'the aboriginal title of the Plaintiffs … has never been lawfully extinguished'. However, there was no clear majority in their favour over the deciding issues in the case.

The court acknowledged that the Nisga'a were never conquered, nor did they enter into any treaty or surrender of their lands. They rejected the assumption which formed the basis of the Marshall judgment, namely that the aboriginal people were savages – a premise which had been accepted by the judge at first instance in *Calder*.

The judges accepted that indigenous title throughout Canada was subject to the fiduciary duty created by the Royal Proclamation of 1763, described by John Borrows as 'an Indian Bill of Rights' – it was deemed to be a law which 'followed the flag' as England assumed jurisdiction over newly discovered or acquired lands or territories. They approved dicta in *Amodu Tijani v Secretary, Southern Nigeria*[53] that, once indigenous title is established, it is presumed to continue until the contrary is proven. The court reiterated that the onus of proving that the sovereign intended to extinguish title lay with the Crown and that such an intention must be 'clear and plain'.

When deciding indigenous rights cases, the main purpose of the judiciary is to reconcile indigenous title with the common law. Asch and Macklem[54] distinguish two theories of indigenous rights: a contingent theory under which indigenous sovereignty depends on legislation or executive action for its validity, and an inherent rights theory under which indigenous rights pre-exist and are continuing rights regardless of the attempts of governments to extinguish them. The courts initially took a contingent rights approach,

51   Truth and Reconciliation Commission of Canada, *Final Report*, vol. 6, p. 23.
52   [1973] 34 DLR (3rd) 145, [1973] SCR 313, [1973] 4 WWR 1.
53   [1921] 2 A.C. 399, at pp. 409–10.
54   Asch and Macklem, 'Aboriginal Rights and Canadian Sovereignty', (1991) 29 Alta Law Rev 498, at p. 501ff.

regarding the Proclamation as having granted rights to the indigenous peoples rather than protecting existing rights.[55] Asch and Macklem note the change to a definitive inherent rights approach in *Guerin v R.*

The Canadian courts have never entertained arguments that the Crown does not have sovereignty over aboriginal lands. *R v Sparrow*[56] was the first decision in which a court was called upon to interpret section 35 of the Constitution Act 1982. Section 35(1) provides: 'The existing aboriginal and treaty rights of the aboriginal peoples of Canada are hereby recognized and affirmed.'

The judge, determined to preserve Canada's ability to encroach on indigenous land,[57] declared: 'It is worth recalling that while British policy towards the native population was based on respect for the right to occupy their traditional lands, a proposition to which the Royal Proclamation bears witness, *there was from the outset never any doubt that sovereignty and legislative power, and indeed the underlying title, to such lands vested in the Crown*' (emphasis added).

The court in this case accepted an argument that the true interpretation of section 35 (1) of the Constitution Act 1982 should have written into it a justification clause which enabled governments to requisition land for purposes which were of overriding public benefit. This argument was founded solely on a journal article by Canadian academic lawyer Professor Brian Slattery.[58]

A reading of the *Sparrow* reasons for decision shows that the Supreme Court in that case did not apply what were at that time well-recognised rules of interpretation. Instead of applying the plain words of the statute, which simply give constitutional recognition to aboriginal rights which were still in existence at the time the Constitution Act became law, the court said it intended to take a purposive approach. This approach allows the court to look at the passage of the bill through parliament in order to discover the intentions of parliament in passing the bill. The court can examine Hansard, committee papers and *travaux préparatoires*, and from these interpret the provision in such a way as to give effect to the intention of parliament. However, despite the court's stated commitment to a purposive approach, it would appear from the reasons for decision that it signally failed to adopt one.[59]

---

55   Rotman, *Parallel Paths*, p. 8.

56   [1990] 70 DLR (4th) 385, [1990] 1 SCR 1075, [1990] 4 WWR 410, 46 BCLR (2nd) 1m 56 CCC (3rd) 263m 111 NR 241m [1990] 3 CNLR 160.

57   See discussion of *Tsilhqot'in* below, Chapter 9.

58   B. Slattery, 'Understanding Aboriginal Rights', *Canadian Bar Review* (1987) 727.

59   For an explanation of the courts' duty in interpreting constitutional statutes, see David Feldman, *Factors Affecting the Choice of Techniques of Constitutional Interpretation* (Address to the round table of the International Association of Constitutional Law on Interpretation of Constitutions, in memory of Louis Favoreu, 15 and 16 Oct. 2004).

Instead, the court looked to the article by Brian Slattery entitled *Understanding Aboriginal Rights*,[60] in which he traces the development of the doctrine of aboriginal rights from the Royal Proclamation of 1763 to the Constitution Act 1982. The main thrust of his discussion of section 35 of the Act is to ascertain whether the rights 'recognized and affirmed' are those which existed at first contact, or those extant in 1982 as they have developed over the years. He suggests that the correct interpretation is 'extant', which implies that it is contemporary rights which are preserved, and he advocates an approach which allows for these rights to continue to develop.

He recognises that there must be a limited power to legislate over indigenous land, but the only such regulation which he considers valid would be of a type which applies to all Canadian land held under the Crown, namely:

- regulations that operate to preserve or advance section 35 rights (as by conserving a natural resource essential to the exercise of such rights);

- regulations that prevent the exercise of section 35 rights from causing serious harm to the general populace or native peoples themselves (such as standard safety restrictions governing the use of fire-arms or hunting); and

- regulations that implement state policies of overriding importance to the general welfare (as in times of war or emergency).

This last category was widened by the Supreme Court in *Sparrow* in such a way as to give it a meaning that was never Brian Slattery's intention, in order to fill what the court perceived to be a major and highly inconvenient lacuna in the plain words of the statute.

According to recognised applications of the 'purposive approach' in Canadian law, the parliamentary record on the progress of the Constitution Bill would have to be explicit in order for the court legitimately to interpret the provision in the way it chose to.

Furthermore, it would appear that no counter-argument was put forward, nor was there reference in the judgment to the doctrine of statutory interpretation, which would be the usual first approach considered and under which the plain words of the statute, implying no justification provision, would have to be accepted by the court. The court appears to have disregarded the fact that the power of the Crown to requisition land which Professor Slattery refers to is a power subject to national emergency.

In the same article, Slattery points out that:

> Canadian law treats the question of when and how the Crown gained sovereignty over Canadian territories in a somewhat artificial and self-serving manner. To state a complex matter simply, the courts apparently feel bound to defer to official territorial claims advanced by the Crown, or

60 *Canadian Bar Review*, vol. 66 No. 4 (1987), pp. 727–83.

the facts supporting them or their validity in international law. This judicial posture of deference is designed to leave the executive with a relatively free hand in matters of foreign policy. So a Canadian court will ordinarily recognize historical claims officially advanced by the Crown to American territories as effective to confer sovereignty for domestic purposes.

Brian Slattery's conclusion is that section 35 (1) of the Constitution Act represents:

> ... a conscious political act whereby the people of an independent Canada reaffirm the values implicit in the doctrine [of aboriginal rights]. In 1969, when the government of Canada issued its famous White Paper on Indian policy, it was possible to view aboriginal rights as the embarrassing relics of a half-forgotten colonial past, to be interred as quickly and decently as possible and certainly not to be taken as the basis for modern governmental policies. The remarkable reaction of native communities across the country [to the 1969 White Paper] was a matter of life or death for others. So, when s 35 of the Constitution Act, 1982 recognizes and affirms the existing aboriginal rights of the aboriginal peoples of Canada it constitutes a significant step toward the acceptance of the native point of view.

It was clearly not his intention to propose a justification interpretation of section 35(1).

It is sometimes claimed that Crown sovereignty over aboriginal lands is non-justiciable. This appears to rest on convention, not solid law, and it is therefore open to advocates and negotiators who represent aboriginal clients in land claims processes to re-open this issue in the light of the developing doctrine of the honour of the Crown (discussed below).

R v Badger[61] was the first case to consider the effect of section 35(1) of the Constitution Act 1982 on the interpretation of treaties. If the principles of interpretation set out in *R v Badger* are applied, however, there are considerable doubts as to British sovereignty over indigenous land. Summarising principles of interpretation from earlier cases, Cory J recognised that:

> 1. Treaty 8 represented the exchange of solemn promises between the Crown and the Aboriginal people.

> 2. Treaties and statutes must be liberally construed and provisions in the treaty must be interpreted so as to maintain the honour of the Crown.

> 3. Ambiguous provisions must always be interpreted in favour of the indigenous people and limitations on their rights must be narrowly construed.

---

61   [1996] 133 DLR (4th) 324, [1996] 4 WWR 457.

4. The onus of proving extinguishment of indigenous rights rests with the Crown and there must be strict proof of the fact of extinguishment and evidence of a clear and plain intention to extinguish treaty rights.

5. The court must take into consideration the context in which the treaty was signed.

6. Treaties must be construed in the sense that they would naturally have been understood by the Indians at the time of their signing. Because of the indigenous oral tradition, verbal promises made on behalf of the government would be binding.

Once the test was applied to the facts, however, the appeal of two of the three defendants was dismissed because the land over which they had hunted had a 'visible incompatible use' and it was held that indigenous hunting was therefore prohibited under both the oral and written terms of the treaty negotiations. This decision is incompatible with the treaty commissioners' assurance that 'they would be as free to hunt and fish after the treaty as they would if they had never entered into it'. As so often in indigenous land rights cases, although the potential right to the land is recognised, the court found other grounds on which to defeat it.

The *sui generis* fiduciary duty owed by the Crown in Right of Canada to the indigenous people as defined by the Canadian courts

Indigenous rights cases come to court piecemeal to settle issues for individual nations. The court is never asked to adjudicate on the bigger picture. It was held in *Quebec (Attorney General) v Canada National Energy Board*[62] that the court itself was not under the same fiduciary duty as other emanations of the Crown, because this would prejudice the independence of the court system; a decision which is inconsistent with current human rights principles, for example Article 6 of the (British) Human Rights Act 1998. The line of cases discussed below demonstrates the erosion of the fiduciary duty owed by the Crown.

Following the dissenting judgments in *Calder*, Dickson J in *Guerin v R* accepted that the Royal Proclamation of 1763 applied to indigenous lands in British Columbia and acknowledged that aboriginal title amounted to a *sui generis* beneficial interest, more than a personal right but less than a proprietary right; i.e. a right in the nature of a fiduciary duty owed by the Crown.

Guerin provided the circumstances which enabled the Supreme Court of Canada to define more precisely the nature of the Crown's fiduciary duty. The Musqueam Band had been committed by the District Superintendent of the Indian Affairs Branch to lease its land to the members of a golf club on disadvantageous terms which were not disclosed to Band members,

62 [1994] 1 SCR 159.

terms which they had agreed to had been varied without their consent. The misrepresentation became known to them only when the golf club applied for a renewal. At the time that the original lease was granted, developers were interested in purchasing the land. This was concealed from the Band. An official in Ottawa questioned the low rental and advised the District Superintendent to seek expert advice. When seeking this advice, he failed to disclose all the terms of the lease.

Analysing the duty owed by the Crown, Dickson J said:

> In my view, the nature of Indian title and the framework of the statutory scheme for disposing of Indian land [for the surrender of Musqueam lands to the Crown before the lease could be granted] places upon the Crown an equitable obligation, enforceable by the courts, to deal with the land for the benefit of the Indians. This obligation does not amount to a trust in the private law sense. It is rather a fiduciary duty. If, however, the Crown breaches this fiduciary duty it will be liable to the Indians in the same way and to the same extent as if such a trust were in effect.

Judge Dickson traced the fiduciary duty back not to the Royal Proclamation of 1763 *per se*, nor to the indigenous possession of the land, but only to the requirement in the Proclamation that indigenous lands be surrendered to the Crown before they could be sold or leased. This narrow definition was all that was necessary to resolve this particular case. Furthermore, it was easier to declare the existence of a fiduciary duty in a commercial rather than a constitutional case. In *Osoyoos Indian Band v Oliver (town of),*[63] Judge Iacobucci held that the fiduciary duty also applied in cases of expropriation by the Crown. Iacobucci J also rejected the contention that the Crown owed no fiduciary duty in circumstances where that duty conflicted with the Crown's public law duties, and ruled that the Crown had a duty to reconcile the conflicting interests rather than assume that the public interest automatically prevailed.[64]

Judge Dickson observed that, by the current Indian Act, the government had given the Crown discretion to decide what *were* the best interests of the indigenous people. It was the conferring of this discretion which turned the Crown's duty into a fiduciary duty. The combination of the obligation undertaken in the Proclamation and the discretionary power given by government led to the existence of a fiduciary relationship. Thus the words of the Royal Proclamation alone are sufficient to create the fiduciary duty. Because the indigenous peoples' interest in the land was an 'independent, legal interest', and the Crown's obligation did not arise by statute, the duty was a personal duty rather than a public law one.

---

63 *Osoyoos Indian Band v Oliver (town of)* [2001] SCR 746.
64 See L. Rotman, 'Wewaykum: A New Spin on the Crown's Fiduciary Obligations to Aboriginal Peoples?', 31.1 (2004) *UBC Law Review* 219, at p. 224.

Noting the *sui generis* nature of the fiduciary relationship, because of the unique features attaching to indigenous title and the historic relationship between the Crown and the indigenous people, Judge Dickson maintained that the duty is narrowed by sections 18(1) and 38(2) of the Indian Act. However, Judge Wilson said that it would be inequitable to allow the Crown to hide behind its own document (section 18(1)). Applying a proprietary estoppel argument,[65] Dickson J said that it would be 'unconscionable' for the Court to ignore the terms which were stipulated orally by the Musqueam – 'equity will not countenance unconscionable behaviour in a fiduciary'. Since there had been a fraudulent concealment of the terms of the lease, the Band's claim could not be statute-barred.

Waters[66] contends that the court could have resolved the case by looking to the correct construction of the Indian Act, arguing that it is 'functionally impossible' to hold the Crown to the fiduciary duty to avoid conflict of duties. The court can only decide a case at common law on the arguments which are presented by the parties, but the very purpose of imposing such a duty is to control the acquisitive tendencies of those in a dominant position. In order to avoid conflict of duties, the Crown must recognise that the land it controls on behalf of the indigenous people cannot be treated as if it is owned outright by the Crown. The Crown must satisfy the tests which enable a fiduciary to deal in the land of the beneficiary regardless of the potential benefits to the nation as a whole. Waters[67] argues that the court in *Guerin* was wrong to discard the trust concept, which has provided a more satisfactory solution to US dealings with indigenous nations. The court's reason for doing so was that the Musqueam's proprietary interest in the land disappeared on surrender of the land to the Crown. Yet at this point the trust attached to the proceeds of that transaction.

If Canada had accepted from the outset the clear assumption of a fiduciary duty in the Royal Proclamation, this might have tempered the conduct of the 'negotiations' for the numbered treaties discussed above. However, a trustee owes no duty of consultation to the beneficiaries and has the discretion to decide what is in the best interests of the beneficiaries. A fiduciary owes such a duty. 'Best interests' means best financial interests to the exclusion of social and moral interests, and financial interests are rarely the priority of indigenous peoples. Waters[68] accepts without question that the Crown's superior title to land rests on discovery, describing it as 'an internationally recognised claim'. At the time he was writing, *Mabo v Queensland [No2]*, the Australian aboriginal land rights case, had yet to be decided.

---

65   See Waters, 'New Directions', p. 417.
66   Ibid., p. 420.
67   Ibid., p. 423.
68   Waters, 'New Directions', p. 423.

Waters' paper illustrates the enormity of the leap of faith required of Canadian citizens to equate Crown–indigenous relations with those of any other fiduciary and beneficiary – because the Indian Act confined the Crown's duty to wardship, which is a personal, not a proprietary, duty. The consequences of acknowledging the import of the Royal Proclamation shake the Canadian founding myth to its core. Yet this is the exercise which the Crown in Right of Canada must undertake, not only to redress past injustices but to build a secure future by honouring its obligations.

'*Sui generis*' in relation to rights simply means that the rights are in their own class – they are unlike any other rights. Rotman[69] attempts to analyse the nature of the *sui generis* title of indigenous peoples in Canada. He maintains that it is rooted in the 'historical, political, social and legal interaction … since the time of contact' between the indigenous peoples and the Crown. The *sui generis* formula has been used to attempt to reconcile indigenous land rights and rights to pursue a traditional lifestyle, as guaranteed in the Royal Proclamation, with the common law doctrines of Canadian land law. It allows the court to recognise the different forms of landholding according to indigenous and non-indigenous tradition, and to depart from Judge Dickson's clear analysis of the fiduciary duty when there is a conflict of interest between indigenous and non-indigenous interests. In *Wewaykum Indian Band v Canada*,[70] Binnie J held that the foundations of the Crown's fiduciary duty rested on 'the degree of economic, social and proprietary control and discretion asserted by the Crown [which] left Aboriginal populations vulnerable to the risks of government misconduct or ineptitude'. Noting that, over the years, governments had assumed increasingly higher degrees of control over the lives of aboriginal peoples, he held that the Crown's fiduciary duty was needed to facilitate supervision of the exercise of those powers – rather than it being, as many Canadians and indigenous peoples assert, a question of paternalism. He went on to observe that the Crown's fiduciary duty was not open-ended and that courts should '… focus on the particular obligation or interest that is the subject matter of the particular dispute and whether or not the Crown had assumed discretionary control in relation thereto sufficient to found a fiduciary obligation and in a way which gave rise to a private law [personal] duty'.[71]

Binnie J confirmed the statutory limitation of 12 years in which to bring an action for breach of fiduciary duty, but this finding must be interpreted in light of the prohibition on legal action by indigenous peoples which was imposed by the Indian Acts 1927–1951. It should also be noted that time begins to run from the date of the discovery of the breach of trust or fiduciary duty. Rotman points out that beneficiaries are under no duty to enquire as to the conduct of

69   Rotman, *Parallel Paths*, p. 12.
70   *Wewaykum Indian Band v Canada* [2002] DLR (4th) 1.
71   Rotman, 'Wewaykum: A New Spin', p. 241.

the fiduciaries and that, while a finding that the action was statute-barred in *Wewaykum* was appropriate to the circumstances of the case, this might not be so in other indigenous cases.

In *Kruger v R*,[72] the majority of the Court of Appeal condoned a breach of fiduciary duty when the Department of Transport's need for a wartime airfield prevailed over the Department of Indian Affairs and Northern Development's duty to act in the best interests of the indigenous people. Urie J held that the same fiduciary duties arose on expropriation as on surrender. It was held that the Crown had competing duties and the compromise reached in the negotiation for the airfield enabled it to satisfy these duties. The Department of Indian and Northern Affairs had advocated a lease of the land to the Department of Transport, which would have fully satisfied both duties. However, the Department of Transport insisted on expropriation on what the judge described as 'niggardly terms'. Since there was no element of fraud in this case, the majority applied the statutory limitation so that in any event the claim was time-barred. Such a limitation does not apply to breaches of fiduciary duty. There followed, in *R v Sparrow*, a timely reminder that 'the relationship between the government and aboriginals is trust-like rather than adversarial'.

This is confirmed by the Report of the Truth and Reconciliation Commission, which found as follows:

> In Canada, it must be recognized that the federal Department of Justice has two important, and potentially conflicting, roles when it comes to Aboriginal peoples:
>
> 1. The Department of Justice Canada provides legal opinions to the Department of Aboriginal Affairs and Northern Development Canada (AANDC) in order to guide the department in its policy development, legislative initiatives, and actions. Those opinions, and the actions based on them, invariably affect Aboriginal governments and the lives of Aboriginal people significantly. Often those opinions are about the scope and effect of Aboriginal and Treaty rights, and often they form the basis upon which federal Aboriginal policy is developed and enacted.
>
> 2. Justice Canada also acts as the legal advocate for the AANDC and the government in legal disputes between the government and Aboriginal people. In this capacity, it takes instruction from senior officials within the Department of Aboriginal Affairs when the department is implicated in legal actions concerning its responsibilities. It gives advice about the conduct of litigation, the legal position to be advanced, the implementation of legal strategy, and the decision about whether to appeal a particular court ruling.

---

72 [1985] 17 DLR (4th) 591, [1986] 1 FC 3, 32 LCR 65. 58 NR 241, [1985] 3 CNLR 15.

The necessity both to uphold the honour of the Crown and to dispute a legal challenge to an official's or department's action or decision can sometimes give rise to conflicting legal opinions ...

Canadian governments and their law departments have a responsibility to discontinue acting as though they were in an adversarial relationship with Aboriginal peoples and to start acting as true fiduciaries.[73]

The Commission's Call to Action 51 does not go as far as this, however. It calls for transparency in disclosure of documents and opinions on which the government relies in cases concerning indigenous land. While this is a step in the right direction, it still presupposes an adversarial framework.

The very essence of a fiduciary duty is to ensure that such conflicts do not arise – the duty undertaken by the Crown in the Royal Proclamation and the subsequent treaty was to uphold indigenous title and to secure it against all incursions unless these were made with the free, prior and informed consent of the peoples concerned.

By contrast, Michael J Bryant[74] is under the mistaken belief that the court uses fiduciary principles as a tool to redress past injustices, and warns that importing such principles into indigenous law risks bringing both fiduciary law and Indigenous rights law into disrepute. He maintains that 'fiduciary law is notoriously ambiguous incorporating general notions of loyalty, trust and good faith'. Despite the courts having centuries of experience of interpreting such notions satisfactorily, it would seem that the Canadian courts are not able to do so in indigenous contexts. If the guarantee contained in the Royal Proclamation were given in any other context, a duty of the utmost good faith would be declared by the court and the fiduciary would be called upon to account fully for any profits made as a result of the breach of fiduciary duty. From the earliest days of *Keech v Sandford*, decided just 40 years before the Royal Proclamation, the duty could not have been made clearer.

It is only when courts attempt to maintain the Crown's absolute title to indigenous land that the waters are muddied. It was the court in *Guerin* which defined the relationship as *sui generis* in order to overcome the seemingly impossible task of declaring the Crown title invalid. Donovan Waters asserts that 'the difficulty is that the Crown cannot avoid the conflict; it can only lessen the ambiguity of its position.'[75] One possible solution is to apply the maxim that 'When equities are equal, the first in time prevails'. But this is also a step too far for Bryant, who categorises the surrender requirements in the Proclamation as a feature of indigenous title rather than a source of fiduciary obligation. In line with the myth of European settlement, Bryant fails to

73 Truth and Reconciliation Commission of Canada, *Final Report*, vol. 6, p. 89.
74 M.J. Bryant, 'Crown–Aboriginal Relationships in Canada: The Phantom of Fiduciary Law' (1993) 27.1 *UBC Law Review* 19–49.
75 Waters, 'New Directions', p. 419.

establish the way in which sovereignty was vested in the Crown and maintains that, at contact, numbers of colonialists and indigenous peoples were equal rather than acknowledging that at that time, the indigenous peoples were numerically superior. Bryant does not understand the concept of vulnerability as laid down in *Frame v Smith*, failing to recognise that the Crown's ability to intervene in any land transaction weakens the indigenous peoples' position over disposal of their land. Bryant recognises that the outcome of a finding of breach of fiduciary duty can be restitution of indigenous lands, but finds it unacceptable that such an outcome would bankrupt the Crown. In the interviews I carried out in Matimekush Lac John, it was made clear that the indigenous peoples are not seeking such an outcome – they want recognition of their rights and a fair resolution of their claims which does not entail the extinguishment of those rights. Indeed, the extinguishment requirement in itself is a breach of fiduciary duty.

In 1850, the first Canadian legislation was passed for the control and management of indigenous lands: 'An Act for the Protection of the Lands and Property of the Indians in Lower Canada.'[76] This vested indigenous lands in a Commissioner on trust for the indigenous peoples who occupied them. The obligation under this trust was transferred to the federal government (the Crown in Right of Canada) on Confederation.[77]

76 13–14 Vict, 1850.
77 'An Act Respecting Management of the Indian Lands and Property', 23 Vict, 1860, c151.

They were, these people, considering the amount of work, the difficulty of the geography, they were very brave hardworking people, not lazy at all. There was always a leader in the group, a captain or a chief, and they would show a direction and people would go in that direction and listen to the chief, to the captain or the leader. They would cover long distances in their journey sometimes just to sell fur and get something back. They would go to a trading post and it's amazing how our parents were fit and not lazy at all, hardworking.

> Among all those groups that are around here, I think that the government is creating a lot of prejudice against us. They undermine a lot of our rights. We are the poorest of the poorest in the sense that we are the last in line. If you look all around here – all the ore that has been exploited and the wealth generated and created, and even today, all the work that has been done on the exploration, we still haven't seen any benefit for our community and all of this is done without our knowledge or consent – without our prior consent. And this is our homeland.

The white people tell us of all the benefits and perks that we have because we are Indians. We have fiscal privileges because we are Indian. I often hear complaints from white people saying we have free housing, freebies everywhere, but the thing that they don't know is that if the white person wants to leave the community and to go to another place in another municipality, they will be able to sell the house, sell their property and they will get some money back out of it – but it is not the same with us. If I want to leave this community, I am stuck with this house. If I leave it I won't get my money back but it's different for the white people. They get their money back and are able to use it to buy another house somewhere else.

> Nowadays I feel like we are being stamped, we are numbered just like cows are numbered when the farmer brands them, and I feel like that because we are numbered. We are given a number from the government and I feel like a cow.
>
> And then with this card [Indian Status Card] came a regime whereby they place a fence around the territory of the people, the Indian people who wouldn't be allowed to get out of the reserve and the white people wouldn't be allowed to get into the reserve.

Chapter 9

The honour of the Crown, the duty to consult and the United Nations Declaration on the Rights of Indigenous Peoples

The duty to consult aboriginal communities whose land rights are infringed by governments was first fully considered by the Canadian Supreme Court in *Delgamuukw v British Columbia*,[1] although the Report of the Royal Commission on Aboriginal Peoples (RCAP) notes that Treaty 6 negotiations in 1876 began with ceremonies and declarations which represented the honour of the Crown and set the moral and spiritual context within which the negotiations were to be conducted.[2]

Delgamuukw confirmed the requirement that the fiduciary is to act always in the utmost good faith and solely in the interests of the beneficiary. This duty includes dealing in the beneficiary's property only with the free, prior and informed consent of the beneficiary. However, following the dictum of Lamer CJC in the case, where government policy can be justified, the fiduciary duty has been reduced to a duty to take the aboriginal beneficiary's interests into consideration and to place them second to government policy if the government can justify such a course of action. Thus, the duty to act only with fully informed consent has been replaced by a duty to consult, and not necessarily to act according to the wishes of the indigenous people.

In a discussion of the grounds on which governments could justify the release of aboriginal lands for resource extraction and development, Lamer CJC proposed that:

> the development of agriculture, forestry, mining and hydroelectric power, the general economic development of the interior of British Columbia, protection of the environment or endangered species, the building of infrastructure and the settlement of foreign populations to support those aims, are the kinds of objectives that are consistent with the purpose and, in principle, can justify the infringement of aboriginal title.

He went on to say that indigenous rights need not always be given priority in such cases, but instead that the fiduciary duty owed by the Crown entailed

---

1   *Delgamuukw v British Columbia* [1997] 3 SCR 1010.
2   Dussault and Erasmus, *Report of the Royal Commission*, vol. 1, p. 169.

'an altered approach to priority' under which the government demonstrates that priority is reflected in the way in which resources are allocated to the original holders of the land. This could be achieved, for example, by conferring fees simple[3] or licences so that the aboriginal peoples could take part in the proposed schemes. He concluded that:

> This aspect of aboriginal title suggests that the fiduciary relationship between the Crown and aboriginal peoples may be satisfied by the involvement of aboriginal peoples in decisions taken with respect to their lands. There is always a duty of consultation ... The nature and scope of the duty of consultation will vary with the circumstances. In occasional cases, when the breach is less serious or relatively minor, it will be no more than a duty to discuss important decisions that will be taken with respect to lands held pursuant to aboriginal title. Of course, even in these rare cases when the minimum acceptable standard is consultation, this consultation must be in good faith and with the intention of substantially addressing the concerns of the aboriginal people whose lands are at issue. In most cases, it will be significantly deeper than mere consultation. Some cases may even require the full consent of an aboriginal nation, particularly when provinces enact hunting and fishing regulations in relation to aboriginal lands.

The question of the degree of consultation required came before the Supreme Court again in 2004 in two cases, *Haida Nation v British Columbia (Ministry of Forests)* and *Taku River Tlingit First Nation v British Columbia (Assessment Director)*,[4] which together provided a clearer set of rules on what was required of the Crown. In *Haida,* McLachlin CJ used the concept of the honour of the Crown to underpin Canada's obligations – 'a precept that finds its application in concrete practices'. The principle requires that the Crown must act honourably in all its dealings with aboriginal peoples and its purpose is to bring about and maintain reconciliation of the pre-existence of aboriginal societies with the claimed sovereignty of the Crown. This gives rise to the fiduciary duty which requires that the Crown act always in the best interests of the aboriginal peoples over whose lands it has discretionary control. The honour of the Crown, she said, 'infused the processes of treaty making and treaty interpretation', and means that: 'The Crown must act with honour and integrity, avoiding even the appearance of "sharp dealing".'

Chief Justice McLachlin explained that the purpose of this principle is to secure and maintain the peace and friendship of the indigenous people concerned. She said that section 35 of the Constitution Act 1982 represents this promise and 'it is always assumed that the Crown intends to fulfil its promises'.

---

3   Freehold title to the land under the common law.
4   *Haida Nation v British Columbia (Ministry of Forests)*, [2004] 3 SCR 511, *Taku River Tlingit First Nation v British Columbia (Assessment Director)*, [2004] 3 SCR 550.

She concludes that the promise is realised and the claims of sovereignty reconciled 'through the process of honourable negotiation'. This implies that the Crown must act honourably in defining the rights it guarantees and in reconciling them with other rights and interests. Thus, the Crown has a duty to consult and where possible accommodate:

> The Crown, acting honourably, cannot cavalierly run roughshod over Aboriginal interests where claims affecting these interests are being seriously pursued in the process of treaty negotiation and proof ... To unilaterally exploit a claimed resource during the process of proving and resolving the Aboriginal claim to that resource, may be to deprive the Aboriginal claimants of some or all of the benefit of the resource. That is not honourable.

McLachlin CJ says that true reconciliation can only flow from the Crown's honourable dealing with land and resources over which it has taken *de facto* control from the aboriginal people concerned. This means that the duty to consult arises as soon as aboriginal rights are asserted, not when they are finally proven. Once this duty arises, the nature of the consultation, at a minimum, must be consistent with the honour of the Crown, acting in good faith to provide meaningful consultation appropriate to the circumstances. However, she goes on to point out that there is no duty to agree and that aboriginal claimants must also act in good faith, especially when agreement is not reached.

The Chief Justice then introduces the concept of a spectrum of what is required in particular circumstances. This would start with minor incursions on a weak claim to title over limited rights. In such cases, which she considered to be rare, the Crown need only give notice, disclose information and discuss any issues raised by the Aboriginal people. At the far end of the spectrum, there will be a strong *prima facie* claim, the infringement will be highly significant to Aboriginal people and the risk of damage which cannot be compensated will be high. In such a case meaningful consultation may require the opportunity to make submissions, formal participation in the decision-making process, and provision of written reasons to show what impact their concerns had on the decision-making process. She suggested that mediation and arbitration procedures might be appropriate.

Next, the judge cited the New Zealand Ministry of Justice *Guide for Consultation with Maori*, 1997:

> Consultation is not just a process of exchanging information. It also entails testing and being prepared to amend policy proposals in the light of information received and providing feedback. Consultation therefore becomes a process which should ensure both parties are better informed ... Genuine consultation means a process that involves:
>
> • Gathering information to test policy proposals
>
> • Putting forward proposals that are not yet finalised

- Seeking Maori opinion on those proposals
- Informing Maori of all relevant information upon which those proposals are based
- Not promoting but listening with an open mind to what Maori have to say
- Being prepared to alter the original proposal
- Providing feedback both during the consultation process and after the decision-process.

She added that genuine consultation may suggest an amendment to Crown policy to bring about accommodation. What is required is a balancing of conflicting interests. This New Zealand model is more comprehensive than current Canadian practice as demonstrated in the consultation clauses in land settlement agreements and, if adhered to, constitutes a model of good practice.

Any challenge to Crown policy on the grounds of lack of, or inadequate, consultation should be dealt with under Canadian administrative law, when the question for the court would be 'whether the regulatory scheme or government action, viewed as a whole, accommodates the aboriginal right in question; and in information and consultation, reasonableness must be the test and efforts must be proportionate to the strength of the aboriginal case'.

Michael Asch asks: 'If Indigenous peoples had legitimate sovereignty when Europeans first arrived, how did the Crown legitimately acquire it?', pointing out that Lamer CJ in *R v Van der Peet*,[5] and then in *Delgamuukw*, asserted that a basic purpose of constitutionalising aboriginal rights was 'the reconciliation of the pre-existence of aboriginal societies with the sovereignty of the Crown' – rather than the other way round.[6] In *Taku*, in which McLachlin CJ also gave the judgment of the Supreme Court, she added that 'the purpose of s35(1) of the Constitution Act 1982 is to facilitate the ultimate reconciliation of prior Aboriginal occupation with *de facto* Crown sovereignty'. Asch points out that she replaced the words 'pre-existence of aboriginal societies' with 'prior aboriginal occupation' and prefixed 'the sovereignty of the Crown' with the words *'de facto'*. This appears to be the court's own attempt to reconcile the differing views of the Crown and the indigenous peoples over ownership of the land.

In the *Taku* case, the Taku River Tlingit First Nation claimed that they were not properly consulted when the province of British Columbia granted a certificate which permitted the reopening of an old mine on their land. The province had followed the guidelines of the Environmental Assessment Act 1992. The Taku River Tlingit were invited to participate in the project

5   *R v Van der Peet,* [1996] 2 SCR 507.
6   Asch, *On Being Here,* p. 32.

committee and were given the original submission for review and comment. They were active members of the project committee, apart from a short period of time when they opted out of its proceedings to pursue other solutions to their requirements. They met directly with the mining company on several occasions to raise concerns and receive information. The company paid for extensive archaeological and ethnographic studies to assess the impact of the mine and ancillary development on the Tlingit traditional way of life. Under these circumstances, the Chief Justice concluded that there had been adequate consultation and accommodation of the aboriginal concerns.

In the subsequent Supreme Court decision in *Mikisew Cree First Nation v Canada (Minister of Canadian Heritage)*,[7] Binnie J again emphasised the importance of the honour of the Crown: 'The honour of the Crown infuses every treaty and the performance of every treaty obligation.'

The significance of the duty to consult as laid down in modern treaties has been further underscored by the Supreme Court of Canada in *Beckman v Little Salmon/Carmacks First Nation*.[8] The definition of 'consult' found in the Little Salmon/Carmacks First Nation Final Agreement[9] considered in the case is exactly the same as that in the Innu New Dawn Agreement in Principle. This in itself calls into question the various governments' willingness to negotiate open-mindedly with the indigenous peoples whose land they are taking and to deal with each group according to its individual circumstances.

In *Little Salmon/Carmacks*, the Supreme Court was divided, Judges McLachlin and Binnie taking the majority view established by them in previous cases and emphasising the duty imposed on governments under the concept of the honour of the Crown. Speaking for the minority, Deschamps J took a harder, more pragmatic line. The minority proposed that, once the terms under which consultation was to take place were defined in the treaty, these terms, and all other terms agreed, must prevail. Because modern land claims treaties were contractual, the common law duty to consult only applied when no such terms were specified. Speaking for the majority, Binnie J held that the modern treaty was not intended to be a complete code and that the honour of the Crown applied independently of the expressed or implied intention of the parties as recorded in the treaty. Nevertheless, he held that:

> The content of meaningful consultation 'appropriate to the circumstances' will be shaped, and in some cases determined, by the terms of the modern land claims agreement. Indeed, the parties themselves may decide therein to exclude consultation altogether in defined situations and the decision to do so would be upheld by the

7   [2005] SCR 69.
8   [2010] SCC 53.
9   *Little Salmon/Carmacks First Nation Self Government Implementation Plan*, 29 Sept. 1997, www.gc.ca.

courts where this outcome would be consistent with the maintenance
of the honour of the Crown.

The Supreme Court acknowledged the differences between the historic treaties,
where Binnie J said that the court had to resort to principles such as the honour
of the Crown to ensure a fair outcome, and the modern treaties – starting with
the James Bay and Northern Quebec Agreement (JBNQA) in 1975.

> Modern treaties … while still to be interpreted and applied in a
> manner that upholds the honour of the Crown, were nevertheless
> intended to create some precision around property and governance
> rights and obligations. Instead of *ad hoc* remedies to smooth the way
> to reconciliation, the modern treaties are designed to place Aboriginal
> and non-Aboriginal relations in the mainstream legal system with its
> advantages of continuity, transparency and predictability.

This raises the question: advantages for whom? These treaties certainly produce
predictability and continuity for the Crown, but the negotiation process under
which the terms were 'agreed' produces no transparency. Yet the Supreme
Court found that: 'Where adequately resourced and professionally represented
parties have sought to order their own affairs, and have given shape to the duty
to consult by incorporating consultation procedures into a treaty, their efforts
should be encouraged and, subject to such constitutional limitations as the
honour of the Crown, the court should strive to respect their handiwork.'

If a challenge were mounted by the Innu, the precedent of *Little Salmon/
Carmacks* would make litigation to challenge the validity of the New Dawn
terms, rather than the validity of the agreement itself, a much riskier course
of action.

The minority judgment given by Deschamps J frames the modern treaty as
a grant to the governments of land owned by the aboriginal group. He defines
the duty of consultation as provided in the treaty as a contractual duty, rather
than a constitutional one designed to prevent the infringement of aboriginal
rights. He looks at the duty to consult as it applies at three stages of negotiation
of a land claims treaty: at the initial stage to protect the constitutional rights of
aboriginal people, in the medium term to favour negotiation of the framework
for exercising those rights, and in the long term to assist in reconciling
aboriginal interests with mainstream interests. To allow an interpretation of a
Final Agreement which negated its written provisions would be to compromise
rather than foster reconciliation.

Judge Deschamps proposes that the Crown's fiduciary duty has 'paternalistic
overtones', and suggests that in modern times the ability of aboriginal people to
conduct their own affairs should be recognised and the principle of the honour
of the Crown should not be invoked to enable them to disregard their treaty
obligations. This is an astounding volte-face. If such treaties were treated by the
Crown as a grant from the aboriginal people, they would be negotiating from
a document drawn up for and on behalf of the aboriginal people concerned,

the terms would be different for each negotiation, and the Crown could not remain inflexible on the terms.

In this particular case an individual was challenging the territorial government's right to infringe his established right to hunt and trap over land in order to grant an agricultural licence to a settler. The granting of the licence required prior consultation with the Little Salmon/Carmacks nation. The case concerned a procedural point on the appropriate level of consultation, for which the individual invoked the honour of the Crown. Judge Deschamps' assertion that the claimant was 'Reneging on the treaty' seems an inappropriate term for the nature of this case.

A fiduciary duty of this nature has no basis in paternalism. Such duties have been invoked in the case of business partners and companies of equal standing. Similarly, the Royal Proclamation established a fiduciary duty between sovereign nations under which the aboriginal peoples of the time were in a superior position to the newly-arrived settlers. The duty arose because the British Crown took responsibility for the disposal of aboriginal land. Deschamps goes so far as to claim that aboriginal parties had such superior bargaining power that Europeans had no choice but to accept the terms they dictated. This is clearly not borne out by the historical record.

Deschamps J distinguishes the *Little Salmon/Carmacks* case from *Haida* and *Taku* on the grounds that *Little Salmon/Carmacks* concerns a treaty which grants rights to the Crown under provisions to which it has freely agreed. Under such a treaty, all parties are bound by its contractual terms under 'the imperative of legal certainty'.

Earlier in the same year, the court was divided on the status of a provision in the James Bay Agreement. In *Quebec (Attorney General) v Moses*,[10] the court had to decide whether a provision in the James Bay Agreement prevailed over federal legislation. The case was brought by the Cree because if an environmental impact assessment of a proposed mining operation had to be made under federal fisheries law, rather than under the provisions of the James Bay Agreement, there was no requirement of consultation with the aboriginal people. The case was resolved by a compromise under which the majority of the court ordered that the federal requirements prevailed but with the additional requirement of the right of the Cree to be consulted.

The reasons for decision of the Supreme Court in *Little Salmon/Carmacks* also reflect a shift in attitude regarding the concept of the honour of the Crown in relation to modern treaties. In their dissenting judgment, Lebel and Deschamps JJ acknowledge that:

> First and foremost, the Agreement must be interpreted broadly and liberally, in a manner consistent with the government's fiduciary

10 [2010] 1 SCR 557: Ted Moses was one of the Cree negotiators of the James Bay and Northern Quebec Agreement.

obligations to the Cree. Nevertheless, the interpretation must reflect a reasonable analysis of the parties' intentions and interests, taking into account both the historical context and the legal context of the Agreement. Finally, where two or more interpretations are reasonably possible, the interpretation most consistent with the interests of the Aboriginal signatories must prevail.

The dissenting judges rehearse the interpretive criteria set out in *R v Marshall*,[11] including the provision that technical or contractual interpretations of treaty wording should be avoided. This, they claim, with some support from the majority of the court, applies only to the historic treaties. They claim that the rationale for this approach is that the negotiation of the historic treaties was 'marked by significant differences in the signatories' languages, concepts, cultures and world views'. This, they claimed, had no place in the negotiation of modern treaties. Yet the evidence set out in the succeeding chapters of this study demonstrates that not only are these differences current, but they are a tool in governments' negotiation process.

These dissenting opinions underpin the governments' case for any future challenge to the terms of a land claims agreement. Dissenting opinions by their very nature are not binding on future courts, but such an opinion from the Supreme Court is highly persuasive. If it is accepted by a future court and leads to a decision in favour of the governments, it will pass into binding Canadian case law.

Deschamps J in *Little Salmon/Carmacks* challenged the assertion that 'in treaty negotiations the Crown and Aboriginal parties have deeply divergent points of view on the objectives of legal certainty', attributing this to the adversarial nature of court proceedings. In effect, this challenges any entitlement of the aboriginal people to respect for their world view, beliefs and culture. Perhaps it points to a suspicion that those aboriginal people who claim to represent their peers at the negotiating table have become detached from the values that those people hold dear.

Tsilhqot'in Nation v British Columbia[12]

Having further developed the concept of the honour of the Crown in *Haida* and *Taku*, in *Tsilhqot'in*, McLachlin CJ, with the agreement of a court of eight senior judges, makes a clear statement that full beneficial ownership of aboriginal lands rests with the aboriginal title holders. This goes a long way towards clarifying the Supreme Court's approach to modern treaties and shows the long-awaited understanding of what a fiduciary duty entails in relation to land – something which the courts have been reluctant to spell out in earlier cases. The Crown can enjoy no rights over the land for its

11   [1999] 3 SCR 456.
12   *Tsilhqot'in Nation v British Columbia*, [2014] SCC 44, [2914] 3 SCR 256.

own benefit. This means that indigenous groups can decide how their land is to be used, provided that they use it in ways which will preserve use and enjoyment of the land for future generations. This is a new definition of the nature of indigenous title to land, in that this decision places more emphasis on the rights of future generations, which have not been fully taken into consideration in earlier cases. We must wait to see how this is developed by future litigation.

However, the Crown's right to encroach on indigenous land for purposes which are justified by a 'compelling and substantial public purpose and are not inconsistent with the Crown's fiduciary duty to the Aboriginal group' (at para 2) remains intact; but perhaps with more emphasis on the fiduciary duty. The decision raises the possibility of a redefinition of what constitutes 'compelling' and substantial objectives. The purpose of a justification principle, the Chief Justice asserts, is to promote reconciliation between Canadians and the indigenous peoples who live alongside them. Thus, despite a change of emphasis, her position falls well within the 'Citizens Plus' approach to the resolution of indigenous land rights which will be discussed in the final chapters. Nevertheless, the decision will encourage indigenous nations to pursue restitution of their land rights through the court.

McLachlin CJ first gives a summary of her conclusions, which include:

- aboriginal title confers the right to use and control the land and to reap the benefits flowing from it;

- where title is asserted, but has not yet been established, section 35 of the Constitution Act 1982 requires the Crown to consult with the group asserting title and, if appropriate, accommodate its interests;

- once title is established, section 35 of the Constitution Act 1982 permits incursions on aboriginal land only with the consent of the aboriginal group, unless they are justified by a compelling and substantial public purpose and are not inconsistent with the Crown's fiduciary duty to the aboriginal group;

- for purposes of determining the validity of provincial legislative incursions on lands held under aboriginal title, this framework displaces the doctrine of interjurisdictional immunity [defined at para 131 of the 1982 Act as follows: 'the doctrine of interjurisdictional immunity applies where laws enacted by one level of government impair the protected core of jurisdiction possessed by the other level of government']; and

- in this case, the province's land use planning and forestry authorisation were inconsistent with its duties owed to the Tsilhqot'in nation. [para 2]

Her starting point is the existing state of the law as laid down in *Delgamuukw*, which she restates at para 14:

> The principles developed in *Calder, Guerin* and *Sparrow* were consolidated and applied in *Delgamuukw v British Columbia* ... This Court confirmed the *sui generis* nature of the rights and obligations to which the Crown's relationship with Aboriginal peoples gives rise and stated that what makes Aboriginal title unique is that it arises from possession *before* the assertion of British sovereignty, as distinguished from other estates such as fee simple that arise *afterwards*. The dual perspectives of the common law and of the Aboriginal group bear equal weight in evaluating a claim for Aboriginal title.

She adds that, in the subsequent case of *Haida*, it was decided that the Crown had both a moral and a legal duty to negotiate in good faith to resolve land claims and that 'the governing ethos is not one of competing interests but of reconciliation'. [para 17]

At para 24, she points out that the court has never considered whether a semi-nomadic group has title to lands. She reminds the court that the *Delgamuukw* criteria for aboriginal title were based on occupation prior to assertion of European sovereignty. Three characteristics must apply: 'It must be sufficient, it must be continuous (where present occupation is relied on) and it must be exclusive.'

McLachlin CJ considered these to be useful lenses through which to assess occupation but warned that 'the court must be careful not to lose or distort the Aboriginal perspective by forcing ancestral practices into the square boxes of common law concepts, thus frustrating the goal of translating pre-sovereignty Aboriginal interests into equivalent modern legal rights'. [para 32]

In considering sufficiency of occupation, the Chief Justice says that the court must look to both aboriginal and common law principles. She accepts Brian Slattery's argument that in considering sufficiency from an aboriginal perspective, the court must take into account the 'group's size, manner of life, material resources, and technological abilities, and the character of the lands claimed'. [para 35]

Added to this, from the common law perspective, the court must consider possession and control of the lands. The Chief Justice points out that under common law this extends beyond sites that are physically occupied to lands that are effectively controlled. [para 36]

She proposes that the test for sufficiency is as follows:

> To sufficiently occupy the land for purposes of title, the Aboriginal group in question must show that it has historically acted in a way that would communicate to third parties that it held the land for its own purposes. This standard does not demand notorious or visible use akin to proving a claim for adverse possession, but neither can the

occupation be purely subjective or internal. There must be evidence of a strong presence on or over the land claimed, manifesting itself in acts of occupation that could reasonably be interpreted as demonstrating that the land in question belonged to, was controlled by, or was under the exclusive stewardship of the claimant group. As just discussed, the kinds of acts necessary to indicate a permanent presence and intention to hold and use the land for the group's purposes are dependent on the manner of life of the people and the nature of the land. Cultivated fields, constructed dwelling houses, invested labour, and a consistent presence on parts of the land may be sufficient, but they are not essential to establish occupation. The notion of occupation must also reflect the way of life of the Aboriginal people, including those who were nomadic or semi-nomadic. [para 38]

At para 41 she says that a culturally sensitive approach to this question is required, and that: '... A culturally sensitive approach suggests that regular use of territories for hunting, fishing, trapping and foraging is "sufficient" use to ground Aboriginal title, provided that such use, on the facts of a particular case, evinces an intention on the part of the Aboriginal group to hold or possess the land in a manner comparable to what would be required to establish title at common law.'

She defines continuity as follows: 'Continuity simply means that for evidence of present occupation to establish an inference of pre-sovereignty occupation, the present occupation must be rooted in pre-sovereignty times.' [para 46]

She then turns to the establishment of exclusivity of occupation and defines this as follows:

> Exclusivity should be understood in the sense of intention and capacity to control the land. The fact that other groups or individuals were on the land does not necessarily negate exclusivity of occupation. Whether a claimant group had the intention and capacity to control the land at the time of sovereignty is a question of fact for the trial judge and depends on various factors such as the characteristics of the land in question. Exclusivity can be established by proof that others were excluded from the land, or by proof that others were only allowed access to the land with the permission of the claimant group. The fact that permission was requested and granted or refused, or that treaties were made with other groups, may show intention and capacity to control the land. Even the lack of challenges to occupancy may support an inference of an established group's intention and capacity to control. [para 48]

At para 50 the Chief Justice points out that the burden of establishing aboriginal title lies with the aboriginal group concerned. This entails identifying how pre-sovereignty rights and interests can properly find expression in modern common law terms. Moving on from *Delgamuukw*, she asserts that: 'Occupation sufficient to ground Aboriginal title is not confined to specific sites of settlement but extends to tracts of land that were regularly used for hunting, fishing or otherwise exploiting resources and over which the group exercised effective control at the time of assertion of European sovereignty.' [para 50]

As Bruce McIvor observes, 'the government's myopic focus on dots-on-a-map is now indefensible'.[13]

Establishment of aboriginal title remains a question of fact for the Chief Justice. [para 52]

> This decision is the latest in a line of cases beginning with *Delgamuukw* which attempt to balance and to reconcile aboriginal title with common law title. McLachlin CJ is bound by the precedent set in these earlier cases but she is the first to acknowledge that, although the Crown has an underlying title to aboriginal lands, because of the fiduciary duty owed by the Crown the full beneficial interest in the lands lies with the aboriginal people. In her words, this means that: '... Aboriginal title is a beneficial interest in the land: *Guerin* at p 382. In simple terms, the title holders have the right to the benefits associated with the land – to use it, enjoy it and profit from its economic development. As such, the Crown does not retain a beneficial interest in Aboriginal land.' [para 70]

This means that the Crown has no right to benefit in any way from aboriginal land – all the benefits belong to the aboriginal group and the Crown's title is an empty title. She further contends that: '*Terra nullius* [that no one owned the land prior to European assertion of sovereignty] *never applied to Canada* as confirmed by the Royal Proclamation 1763 ... The Aboriginal interest in land that burdens the Crown's underlying title is an independent legal interest, which gives rise to a fiduciary duty on the part of the Crown.' [para 69] (emphasis added)

All that remains to the Crown according to precedent are two elements:

- a fiduciary duty owed by the Crown to aboriginal people when dealing with aboriginal lands; and

- the right to encroach on aboriginal title if the government can justify this in the broader public interest under section 35 of the Constitution Act 1982. [para 71]

I dispute this second point – the plain words of section 35 make no provision for justification on public policy grounds. The list of activities which can be justified by governments also remains unchanged – resource extraction, land for settlement and hydro-electricity. There is no indication whatsoever in section 35 that incursions into aboriginal title can be justified. But McLachlin CJ accepts the decision in *R v Sparrow* which wrote into this provision a government's right, in the interests of reconciliation, to justify incursions into aboriginal land and rights on a public benefit argument.

---

13   B. McIvor, 'The Age of Recognition: The Significance of the Tsilhqot'in Decision', 27 June 2014, First People's Law.

At para 72, she approves La Forest J's dictum in *Delgamuukw* that aboriginal title 'is not equated with fee simple [common law] title; nor can it be described with reference to traditional property law concepts'.

Thus, she concludes: 'Aboriginal title confers ownership rights similar to those associated with fee simple, including the right to decide how the land will be used; the right of enjoyment and occupancy of the land, the right to possess the land, the right to the economic benefits of the land, and the right to pro-actively use and manage the land.' [para 73]

Her next point is of the utmost importance: there is an important restriction on aboriginal title. It is a collective title 'held not only for the present generation but for all succeeding generations'. [para 74] She explains: 'This means that it cannot be alienated except to the Crown or encumbered in ways that would prevent future generations of the group from using and enjoying it.' [para 74]

This is a departure from earlier jurisprudence, in that previously collective title was only spoken of as applying to members of the present generation. McLachlin CJ speaks of the collective title as the 'pre-sovereignty incidents of use and enjoyment that were part of the collective title enjoyed by the ancestors of the claimant group' and points out that land use is not restricted to traditional uses: 'Aboriginal title holders of modern times can use their land in modern ways, if that is their choice.' [para 75].

The aboriginal right of control over aboriginal land means that governments and others seeking to use the land must *obtain the consent* of the original title holders. [para 76]

This is the most accurate analysis of the fiduciary duty owed by the Crown to the aboriginal peoples of Canada to be handed down by the Supreme Court of Canada. Nevertheless, the Crown's power to justify infringement of aboriginal rights remains virtually intact. McLachlin CJ reiterates the requirements for a justification argument as follows:

- that the government discharged its procedural duty to consult and accommodate;

- that its actions were backed by a compelling and substantial objective; and

- that the governmental action is consistent with the Crown's fiduciary obligation to the group. [para 77]

Thus, the requirement of free, prior and informed consent which applies to a fiduciary is still reduced to the duty to 'consult and accommodate'. We have seen in *Little Salmon/Carmacks* that, where there is a land settlement agreement in place, this duty is defined and further diluted by the provisions of that agreement. Further, the spectrum of the consultation laid down in *Haida* remains intact.

There appears to be a conflict between, for example, permitting hydro-electric development on aboriginal land and leaving it free for future generations of title holders, especially as in para 80 the Chief Justice spells out that what is required is: '… both a compelling and substantial government objective and that the government action is consistent with the fiduciary duty owed by the Crown to the Aboriginal people'. [para 80]

She confirms that the compelling and substantial objective of the government *must be considered from the Aboriginal point of view*. [para 81] (emphasis added)

In the next part of her reasons for decision, McLachlin CJ reasserts her purpose, as in previous cases, of promoting reconciliation between aboriginal rights and the rights of Canadian society as a whole. This, she says, is the purpose of the doctrine of justification. [para 82] However, she introduces a new criterion: 'incursions on Aboriginal title cannot be justified if they would substantially deprive future generations of the benefit of the land'. [para 86]

In para 87 she introduces the concept of proportionality.

The Crown's fiduciary duty demands that the government goes no further than necessary to achieve its goal (minimal impairment) and *that the benefits that may be expected to flow from it are not outweighed by the adverse effects on the Aboriginal interest* (proportionality of impact). (emphasis added)

> Next, McLachlin CJ reaffirms the Crown's duty to 'consult in good faith' before any incursion onto aboriginal land. [para 89] At the claims stage, prior to establishment of aboriginal title, the Crown owes a duty to consult in good faith and, if appropriate, to accommodate aboriginal interests. Where a claim is strong, e.g. immediately before a court is to declare the existence of title, the government must take 'appropriate' care to preserve aboriginal interests. [para 91]

Once title is established, '*it may be necessary for the Crown to reassess prior conduct in the light of the new reality in order to faithfully discharge its duty to the title-holding group*'. (emphasis added) The Chief Justice gives the example that, if the government has proceeded without the consent of the aboriginal group prior to establishment of title, it may be required to cancel a project and, if legislation has been passed to allow the project, this will be inapplicable to the extent that it infringes aboriginal title. [para 92] This does not meet the standard set by the United Nations Declaration on the Rights of Indigenous Peoples which, very late in the day, Canada endorsed. Whether this is because this point was not argued before the court is not known, but this seems likely.

In the case of the Tsilhqot'in, the group had a strong *prima facie* claim to the land at the time of government action and the intrusion was significant. Therefore, significant consultation and accommodation were required. [para 93] Now that title is established, the Tsilhqot'in had the right to determine the use to which the land is put and to enjoy its economic fruits. She spells out that this is not merely the right of first refusal to participate in the governments' plans – it is the right to *proactively use and manage the land* [para 94] (emphasis added).

Turning to the question of interjurisdictional immunity – in this case, whether provincial laws apply to aboriginal lands – McLachlin CJ says that there are restrictions on the applications of such laws, as laid down in *Sparrow*, namely:

- whether the limitations imposed by the legislation are unreasonable;

- whether the legislation imposes undue hardship; and

- whether the legislation deprives the aboriginal people of their preferred means of exercising their rights. [para 104]

These are not the only reasons for invalidating the legislation as far as aboriginal peoples are concerned, but unless the infringement of aboriginal title caused by the legislation is censured by the court, provincial laws of general application will apply to aboriginal lands. [para 106] However, she concludes at para 141 that, unless governments can justify their legislation under section 35 of the Constitution Act 1982, aboriginal rights are a limit on both federal and provincial jurisdictions. These remarks were made *obiter dicta* – i.e. they were not essential to the decision handed down in the case. They are therefore persuasive in future court decisions, but not binding. It has been suggested that these dicta were included in the reasons for decision in order to secure a unanimous verdict.[14]

The *Tsilhqot'in* decision has been criticised by Professor Robert A. Williams.[15] He points out that 'what the court is saying is that your government can come in and infringe on your title as long as it has a compelling justification'. I would go further and submit that if indigenous peoples – such as the Innu in Labrador – settle a land claim, under the present system principles of justification do not even apply. As has been seen in the dissenting judgments in *Little Salmon/ Carmacks*, the indigenous group will be held to what they have signed.

The only way for indigenous rights to be fully upheld is to go to court for a declaration in the wake of *Tsilhqot'in*. Whether any court would be prepared to rule that the justification argument approved in *Sparrow* was spurious is problematical, but McLachlin CJ, by linking justification so explicitly to section 35(1), has created an opening for such an argument. Harry Swain and James Baillie point out that the law enacted in section 35(1) is entirely

---

14 N. Bankes and J. Koshan, '*Tsilhqot'in*: What Happened to the Second Half of Section 91(24) of the Constitution Act 1867?', 7 July 2014, ablawg.ca/2014/07/07/tsilhqot'in-what happened-to-the-second-half.

15 'American law professor: Aboriginal title decision is no game changer', 23 July 2014, *Chronicle and Herald Nova Scotia*.

judge-made, and future decisions of the Supreme Court could provide a new interpretation.[16]

They go on to point out that corporations and investors are unlikely to proceed on projects on indigenous land unless there is resolution of the issues, whether through an agreement between the indigenous group and the Crown, a court case or negotiation.[17] The most likely course of action would be a negotiation where the governments come to the table with a set agenda and the indigenous group is no further forward because it has to commit to the consultation provisions in the agreement itself.

At the same time as the *Tsilhqot'in* decision was handed down, the Conservative Harper government was backing off from the Comprehensive Land Claims process. It is claimed that the government was instead focussing its efforts on assimilation of indigenous governance into federal and provincial structures. According to Russell Diabo, its principal purpose was to 'terminate the constitutionally protected and internationally recognized Inherent Aboriginal and Treaty Rights of First Nations'.[18] Whether this will change materially under the Trudeau administration remains to be seen.

The Harper policy is borne out by an article on the *Guardian* website by Martin Lukacs[19] which reports that, since 2008, the Department of Aboriginal Affairs and Northern Development Canada has been trying to evaluate the 'significant risks' posed to Canadian plans to attract C$650 billion of investment to the extractive industries on indigenous lands. The government is seeking to evade Supreme Court decisions such as *Tsilhqot'in*. In the article, Arthur Manuel, chair of the Indigenous Network on Economies and Trade, is quoted as follows: 'The Harper government is committed to a policy of extinguishing indigenous peoples' land rights, instead of a policy of recognition and co-existence. They are trying to contain the threat that our rights pose to business-as-usual and the expansion of dirty energy projects. But our legal challenges and direct actions are creating economic uncertainty and risk, raising the heat on government to change its current policies.'

It is further pointed out that 'native land claims scare the hell out of investors'.

In the same article, Martin Lukacs claims that the federal government 'has spent far more fighting aboriginal litigation than any other legal issue – including $106 million in 2013, a sum that has grown over the last several years'. At the

16 H. Swain and J. Baillie, '*Tsilhqot'in v British Columbia* and Section 35', *Canadian Business Law Journal* 56 (2015) pp. 264–79 at pp. 267–8.
17 Ibid., p. 274.
18 R. Diabo, 'Canada: Prime Minister Harper launches First Nations "Termination Plan"', www.globalresearch.ca?canada_prime_minister_harper, 10 Jan. 2013.
19 M. Lukacs, 'Aboriginal rights a threat to Canada's resource agenda, documents reveal', *True North*, reproduced in the *Guardian*, 4 Mar. 2014.

same time, Lukacs reports, the government is cutting funding to indigenous groups who seek to fight land claims.

It would appear that the fight for land to which indigenous groups are entitled has reached a new phase. Legislation will always trump litigation and the economic stakes may be high enough for the federal government to risk legislation which will extinguish indigenous rights to land which has not already been the subject of a settlement agreement.

Kenneth Coates and Dwight Newman suggest that '… what the Supreme Court has highlighted at a fundamental level is that Aboriginal communities have a right to an equitable place at the table in relation to natural resource development in Canada. Their empowerment through *Tsilhqot'in* and earlier decisions has the potential to be immensely exciting as a means of further economic development in Aboriginal communities and prosperity for all.'[20]

Their work is a call for academics and lawyers to be accurate in their analysis of the case.

Grassy Narrows First Nation v (Ontario) Natural Resources[21]

Two weeks after the decision in *Tsilhqot'in*, the doctrine of interjurisdictional immunity was further eroded when the Supreme Court of Canada was called upon to adjudicate on the role of the federal government in supervising the granting of logging licences over indigenous land in Ontario. The case concerned Treaty 3 land. The original treaty had been concluded between the Crown in Right of Canada and the ancestors of the Ojibwa people and included a right for Canada to 'take up' lands within the treaty area for the purposes of development. These lands had been ceded to the Crown subject to indigenous rights to hunt, fish and trap on these lands until they were taken up. In 1894, the right to take up the lands for development passed to the province of Ontario and from that time Ontario had issued licences over the land. In 2005, the Ojibwa challenged the granting of a forestry licence issued by the province, claiming that this should have been subject to the supervision of the federal government. The licence was for clearcutting of forest on lands over which Treaty 3 granted the Ojibwa rights to continue their traditional use of the land. Clearcutting would severely affect the exercise of these rights.

The trial judge held that there should have been a two-stage procedure under the scrutiny of the federal government which, by section 91(24) of the Constitution Act 1867 retained jurisdiction over 'Indians and lands reserved for Indians' in accordance with the Royal Proclamation of 1763. The Ontario Court of Appeal overturned the trial judge's decision and, on appeal to the

---

20 K. Coates and D. Newman, *The End is Not Nigh: Reason over alarmism in analysing the* Tsilhqot'in *decision* (Ottawa: MacDonald-Laurier Institute Papers Series, Sept. 2014).

21 [2014] SCC 48.

Supreme Court of Canada, that court also held that this two-stage procedure was not necessary. The province had the power to take up the land without reference to the federal government.

Controversially, McLachlin CJ concluded that, in the negotiations for Treaty 3, such a two-tier stage was not envisaged and that, following 1894, beneficial ownership in the treaty land lay with Ontario. She referred the court to her earlier decision on this point in *Tsilhqot'in*. Again, she emphasised that any action on the part of Ontario with regard to the treaty lands was subject to the justification criteria laid down in *Sparrow* and *R v Badger*, as developed in *Tsilhqot'in*. Following *St Catherine's Milling v R*, a case which also concerned Treaty 3, she pointed out that the treaty had been made between the Ojibwa and the Crown, not the Ojibwa and the Government of Canada. [para 33] She interpreted 'the Crown' to include the provincial government. Further, she said, section 91(24) does not give Canada authority over the take-up of land for purely provincial purposes such as forestry, mining and settlement. [para 37] Since the possibility of acquisition of the land by the province was 'patent', if those drafting the treaty had wanted Canada to have a supervisory role, the treaty would have said so. [para 40] She pointed out that the province had been exercising its right to take up the land for 100 years without any previous objection on the part of the Ojibwa.

McLachlin CJ emphasised that, in exercising jurisdiction over Treaty 3 lands, the provincial government must exercise its powers in conformity with the honour of the Crown and is subject to the Crown's fiduciary duties [para 50], and is also subject to the duty to consult and accommodate. This is spelled out in greater detail than in *Tsilhqot'in* at para 54:

> Where a province intends to take up lands for the purposes of a project within its jurisdiction, the Crown must inform itself of the impact the project will have on the exercise by the Ojibway of their rights to hunt, fish and trap, and communicate its findings to them. It must then deal with the Ojibway in good faith and with the intention of substantially addressing their concerns [*Mikisew*, at para 55; *Delgamuukw v British Columbia*, at para 168]. The adverse impact of the Crown's project (and the extent of the duty to consult and accommodate) is a matter of degree, but consultation cannot exclude accommodation at the outset. Not every taking up will constitute an infringement of the harvesting rights set out in Treaty 3. This said, if the taking up leaves the Ojibway with no meaningful right to hunt, fish and trap in relation to the territories over which they traditionally hunted, fished and trapped, a potential action for treaty infringement will arise [*Mikisew*, at para 48].

Although the province will be under the same obligation to justify and then to consult and accommodate as the federal government, this decision overrules the long line of cases cited above[22] in which the law was settled that the federal government had the final say on dealings in indigenous land under section 91(24). It removes a necessary line of defence of indigenous rights which goes to the very essence of the Royal Proclamation of 1763, in that the Crown stood between indigenous peoples and settlers where there was a conflict of interests. As is obvious in Labrador in disputes over the hunting rights of Innu resident in Quebec, the federal government can play a very valuable role in the protection of indigenous rights against the ambitions of a province.

Bruce McIvor, counsel for the Wabauskang First Nation, interveners in the proceedings, points out that freedom to deal directly with the Ojibwa may place a greater constitutional responsibility on the province to ensure that consultation is sufficient. He says that for a government objective to be compelling and substantial, it must be considered from both the public and indigenous perspective and it must be deemed that the infringement on indigenous rights is necessary. Further, the Crown, be it represented federally or provincially, is constrained by the requirement that the land must be preserved for the use and benefit of future generations and its objective must be consistent with the Crown's fiduciary obligations. This, he suggests, would preclude the interpretation of treaties as extinguishment documents.[23] Cathy Guirguis and Senwunk Luk, partners in Olthuis, Kleer Townsend (lawyers to the Innu in Labrador), point out that the restrictions placed on the Crown's ability to justify its use of indigenous land in *Tsilhqot'in* and *Grassy Narrows* fall short of the international standards of free, prior and informed consent required under the United Nations Declaration on the Rights of Indigenous Peoples. They also suggest that the Ojibwa were only prepared to co-operate over Treaty 3 if they could retain their way of life, and that they were promised that their harvesting rights could continue forever without significant interference. This was accepted by the trial judge.[24]

In the recent *Desautel* case,[25] both the British Columbia Court of Appeal and the Supreme Court of Canada applied a purposive interpretation of section 35(1) of the Constitution Act 1982 and, with some dissent in the SCC, established that ancestral rights applied even if the indigenous people concerned had moved outside Canada's national boundary. Further, if those people chose to live on a reserve as the least bad possible option, that did not constitute willingness to give up their land and rights.

22 See B. McIvor and K. Green, 'Stepping into Canada's Shoes: *Tsilhqot'in*, *Grassy Narrows* and the Division of Powers', 67 (2016) UNBLJ 146–67, at p. 148.

23 Bruce McIvor, 'What *Tsilhqot'in* and *Grassy Narrows* Mean for Treaty First Nations', 14 June 2015, First Peoples' Law.

24 C. Guirguis and S. Luk, 'Supreme Court Releases Decision in *Keewatin*', 11 July 2014, www.oktlaw/blog/supreme-court-releases-decision-in-keewatin.

25 [2019] BCCA 152 and [2021] SCC 17.

In October 2010, Desautel, a citizen and resident of the United States of America, was charged with hunting without a licence contrary to section 11(1) of British Columbia's Wildlife Act and hunting big game while not being a resident of the province contrary to section 47(a) of the Act. He defended the charges on the basis that he had an Aboriginal right to hunt, as he is a member of the Lakes Tribe of the Colville Confederated Tribes based in the State of Washington, a successor group of the Sinixt people, and he shot the elk within the ancestral territory of the Sinixt in British Columbia.

At trial, it was accepted that the date of first contact between the Sinixt and Europeans was in 1811. At that time, the Sinixt were engaged in hunting, fishing and gathering in their ancestral territory, which extended into what is now Washington State to the south, and into what is now British Columbia to the north, and until around 1870, the Sinixt continued to exercise their inherent rights in Canada. For various reasons, the Sinixt people moved to the United States. The trial judge did not find that the move was voluntary. Until 1930, they continued to hunt in British Columbia, despite living in Washington State, but continued to have a connection to the land where their ancestors hunted in British Columbia. Applying *R v Van der Peet*, the trial judge held that Dessautel was exercising an aboriginal right to hunt for food, social and ceremonial purposes. Desautel's aboriginal right was protected, despite his people's departure from the Canadian part of their traditional territory and notwithstanding a period of dormancy in the exercise of the right. The trial judge held that the right was infringed by the Wildlife Act and the infringement was not justified. Desautel was acquitted. The Supreme Court confirmed the trial judge's approach to section 35(1) with the outcome deciding that the phrase 'aboriginal peoples of Canada' can include aboriginal groups that are now outside Canada.

The potential impact of the United Nations Declaration on the Rights of Indigenous Peoples (UNDRIP) under the doctrine of the honour of the Crown

The court in *Tsilhqot'in* and *Grassy Narrows* did not hear testimony based on UNDRIP, because it has still not passed into Canadian law. However, Canada has endorsed the Declaration and therefore, if the Crown's fiduciary duty is to be fully observed, upholding the honour of the Crown demands that UNDRIP's principles are fully implemented, in accordance with the preamble of the Declaration, and in particular:

> *Concerned* that indigenous peoples have suffered from historic injustices as a result of, *inter alia*, their colonization and dispossession of their lands, territories and resources, thus preventing them from exercising, in particular, their right to development in accordance with their own needs and interests,

Recognizing the urgent need to respect and promote the inherent rights of indigenous peoples which derive from their political, economic and social structures and from their cultures, spiritual traditions, histories and philosophies, especially their rights to their lands, territories and resources,

...

Recognizing that respect for indigenous knowledge, cultures and traditional practices contributes to sustainable and equitable development and proper management of the environment.

(The full text of the Declaration can be found in Appendix B.)

The Coalition on the United Nations Declaration on the Rights of Indigenous Peoples explains:

> The purpose of the UN Declaration was to codify the minimum universal standards for the protection of Indigenous Peoples' human rights by all states – *not* by creating new rights, but by providing 'a contextualized elaboration of general human rights principles and rights as they relate to the specific, historical, cultural and social circumstances of indigenous peoples'. The UN Declaration incorporates norms and standards that already form part of customary and conventional international law and is grounded in fundamental human rights principles such as non-discrimination, self-determination and cultural integrity.[26]

UNDRIP provides an independent benchmark against which to assess government commitment to true reconciliation of indigenous land rights. It should be remembered that, according to Article 43, the United Nations Declaration on the Rights of Indigenous Peoples sets *minimum* standards for states in their dealings with indigenous peoples. Canadian delegates sat at the UN negotiating table attempting, with the other Anglo-Saxon nations whose colonising ancestors annihilated or assimilated indigenous peoples who stood in the way of the foreign settlement of their lands, to minimise the effects of UNDRIP.

Canada's immediate response to the Declaration was, according to Chuck Strahl, then Minister of Indian Affairs, that it was 'unworkable in a Western Democracy under a constitutional government'. He went on to explain: 'In Canada you are balancing individual rights versus collective rights. By signing, you default to this document by saying that the only rights in play here are the rights of First Nations. And of course, in Canada, that's inconsistent with

---

26 Coalition on the United Nations Declaration on the Rights of Indigenous Peoples (Joint Submission), *Renewing the Federal Comprehensive Land Claims Policy*, 27 Nov. 2014.

our constitution. In Canada, you negotiate on this because Native rights don't trump all other rights.'[27]

What Chuck Strahl appears to ignore is that the Declaration concerns the recognition of existing prior rights, which governments have hitherto ignored with impunity. His reference to negotiation demonstrates the determination of the federal and provincial governments to continue to hold all the cards, particularly in light of Article 19 which requires governments to secure the consent of their indigenous peoples to matters of public policy, and Articles 26 and 27 which appear to allow the reopening of apparently settled land claims. By contrast, the Nordic democracies, which have strong indigenous populations represented by indigenous parliaments, signed up immediately to the Declaration. Of the four nations who initially refused to endorse the United Nations Declaration, Australia and New Zealand did tardily accept their responsibilities. President Obama signified his willingness to consider endorsement by the United States.

The Canadian government endorsed the Declaration on 23 November 2010, within a week after the delivery of the final judgment in *Little Salmon/ Carmacks* discussed above. UNDRIP has the potential to put relations between aboriginal and non-aboriginal Canada on a basis which would enable the parties to proceed on a more equitable footing to resolve the difficulties besetting this troubled relationship. Endorsement is a significant concession, but it remains to be seen how fully, if at all, the Declaration will be implemented or supported in the Canadian courts. On 3 March 2010 in the Speech from the Throne, it was announced that Canada will 'take steps to endorse this aspirational document in a manner fully consistent with Canada's constitution and laws',[28] words which were used at the time of endorsement. To settler Canadians this may be an 'aspirational document', but to indigenous peoples across the world it represents what is due to them. During the drafting of the Declaration, Canada diluted UNDRIP's power by amending the wording of Article 21 with the addition of the words 'where appropriate', so that the obligation on the part of the state to ensure continuing improvement of the economic and social conditions of indigenous peoples remained under the control of national governments. In any event, interpretations of the Declaration's provisions are the remit of individual nation states. And in Canada, as yet there appears to be no real commitment to repeal the Indian Act or to adopt the recommendations of the Royal Commission on Aboriginal Peoples (RCAP).

Article 19 of the Declaration provides that: 'States shall consult and cooperate in good faith with the indigenous peoples concerned through their

27 *National Post*, 13 June 2007.
28 Speech from the throne, 3 March 2010, *Debates (Hansard) No 1 40(3)*, House of Commons.

own representative institutions in order to obtain their *free, prior and informed consent* before adopting and implementing legislative or administrative measures that may affect them,' hence the indigenous calls for negotiation to be based on FPIC.

Free, prior and informed consent is a standard taken from the law on fiduciaries and, as we shall see when we consider the duties of lawyers and consultants below, has been well defined through the common law case system. So far as it applies to indigenous peoples, Adem Kassie Abebe points out that: 'States should refrain from implanting new, all-embracing modes of decision-making. Consultations should be culturally appropriate, recognising indigenous peoples' own traditional decision-making processes.'[29]

Article 19, together with Articles 25–27, has the potential to reform the entire land claims negotiation process and to give the Innu greater equality of bargaining power. Article 25 recognises and upholds 'the[ir] distinctive spiritual relationship with their traditionally owned ... lands', a relationship effectively denied by Deschamps J. More significantly, it upholds their responsibilities to future generations. In endorsing UNDRIP, Canada reaffirms its existing responsibilities.

   Article 26 recognises that indigenous ownership of lands and territories includes ownership of resources now being targeted by the extractive industries, and provides that states must recognise and protect these rights.

   Article 27 of UNDRIP provides that: 'States shall establish and implement, in conjunction with indigenous people, a fair, independent, impartial, open and transparent process ...'

Article 8 (b) of the United Nations Declaration on the Rights of Indigenous Peoples says: 'States shall provide effective mechanisms for prevention of, and redress for ... any action which has the aim or effect of dispossessing them of their lands, territories or resources,' and Article 10 stipulates: 'Indigenous peoples shall not be forcibly removed from their lands or territories. No relocation shall take place without the free, prior and informed consent of the indigenous peoples concerned and after agreement on just and fair compensation and, where possible, with the option of return.'

In Canada, the whole negotiation process is undermined by the dominance of Canadian culture – in that the Band Councils which are the basis of the indigenous representation and decision-making process are actually a Canadian

---

29 A.K. Abebe, *The Power of Indigenous Peoples to Veto Development Activities: The Right to Free, Prior and Informed Consent (FPIC)* (Saarbrücken: VDM-Verlag, 2010), p. 10.

construct. Elders I spoke to pointed out that this was not the way in which the Innu chose their leaders according to their own tradition, which was much more consensual and involved the elders to a greater extent. Under Article 18 of UNDRIP, indigenous peoples have the right 'to participate in decision-making in matters which would affect their rights through representatives chosen by themselves in accordance with their own procedures, as well as to maintain and develop their own indigenous decision-making institutions'.

As the case for recognition of indigenous land rights, and other rights, in Canada is given yet greater public airing through the work of the Truth and Reconciliation Commission (TRC) and through UNDRIP, Canadian governments should also bear in mind Article 40 of the Declaration: 'Indigenous peoples have the right to access to and prompt decision through just and fair procedures for the resolution of conflicts and disputes with States or other parties, as well as to effective remedies for all infringements of their individual or collective rights. Such a decision shall give due consideration to the customs, traditions, rules and legal systems of the indigenous peoples concerned and international human rights.'

As we move on to consider the government's conduct of modern treaty negotiations and settlements, we shall see how far short Canada is falling in this respect.

In the minds of the Canadian judiciary, there appears to be some confusion over the true meaning of the term 'reconciliation'. The Final Report of the TRC, in its Call to Action 52 (ii) demands that: 'Once Aboriginal title has been established, the burden of proving any limitation on any rights arising from the existence of that title shifts to the party asserting such a limitation.'[30]

The Report approves dicta of RCAP spelling out that the restoration of civic trust is essential to reconciliation and goes on to say that, in order to forge peaceful relations, as the party who breached the trust, Canada has the 'primary obligation' to do the work needed to gain the trust of the aboriginal peoples. The TRC was set up in order to begin the process of forging a new relationship.

By contrast, the judiciary appears to have limited its task of reconciliation to the need to reconcile the purported title of the Crown in Right of Canada with the prior title of indigenous peoples to their ancestral lands in what is now Canada. Unless and until this confusion is resolved, decisions of the Supreme Court will continue to fall short of implementing the honour of the Crown. Speaking of the meaning of reconciliation to the TRC, Elder Fred Kelly told its members:

> Where government refuses to implement Aboriginal rights and the original spirit and intent of the treaties, the citizens of Canada must take direct action to forcefully persuade its leadership. Treaty making

30 Dussault and Erasmus, *Report of the Royal Commission*, vol. 6, p. 91ff.

and memoranda of agreement are simply the stage-setting mechanisms for reconciliation. There must be action … [A]ll Canadians have treaty rights … It is upon these rights and obligations that our relationship is founded.[31]

In almost every case since *Guerin v R*, the judiciary has paid lip service to the fiduciary duty and to the concept of the honour of the Crown but has never confronted the magnitude of the debt that the breach has created. It would seem that the 'honour of the Crown' rests on something less than observance of a duty of the utmost good faith. As Rotman points out: 'It is arguable that the Crown's obligations have become even more stringent as a result of the ascent of the Crown in the political and economic structure of Canada at the expense of the aboriginal peoples and in direct contravention of its fiduciary duty to them.'[32]

However, by contrast, as we shall see in the following chapters the Crown in Right of Canada has become increasingly able to disregard those duties with impunity.

When the present Liberal government was elected, Justin Trudeau was quick to prioritise his government's relationship with indigenous peoples. On 14 February 2018, Trudeau announced to parliament his government's intention to introduce a new legal framework to recognise and implement indigenous rights.[33] The announcement was short on detail but Trudeau cited a consultation process with Canada's original peoples which would lead to legislation before the next general election. Following town hall meetings across Canada, he announced an end to the colonial approach to indigenous relations and the implementation of the rights of indigenous peoples: 'Reforms are needed to ensure that among other things Indigenous peoples might once again have confidence in a system that has failed them all too often in the past.'

He noted that it was 35 years since his father's government had introduced section 35 of the Constitution Act, something which that government only agreed to after 'outspoken advocacy' by the indigenous peoples: 'Now imagine the mounting disappointment, the all too unsurprising and familiar heartache and the rising tide of anger when governments that had promised so much did so little to keep their word. You see, Mr Speaker, the challenge then as now is that while section 35 recognizes and affirms aboriginal and treaty rights, those rights have not been implemented by our governments.'

Perhaps this initiative was prompted by the decision in *Tsilhqot'in*, because one of the reasons Trudeau gave for this new initiative was that failure to recognise indigenous rights led to many lengthy court cases, trending towards

31 Dussault and Erasmus, *Report of the Royal Commission*, vol. 6, p. 34.
32 Rotman, *Parallel Paths*, p. 146.
33 'Trudeau promises legal framework for Indigenous rights: Transcript', *Macleans*, 14 February 2018.

full recognition and definition of these rights. Timely legislation on federal terms could enable the governments to retain some control over the process, including the retention of the justifications on public policy grounds upheld by *Delgamuukw v British Columbia*. Nevertheless, Trudeau acknowledged that, through Bill-C262, his government was committed to full implementation of UNDRIP without qualification:

> We signed agreements with First Nations, Inuit and the Metis Nation outlining how we will work together to identify each community's distinct priorities and how we will work together to develop solutions. We established a working group of Ministers to review our federal laws, policies and operational practices to ensure the Crown is meeting its constitutional obligations and adhering to international human rights standards including the UN Declaration on the Rights of Indigenous Peoples.[34]

This, he said, was just a start. What he was proposing was a programme for the next 150 years and beyond and the foundation for this must be recognition and implementation of indigenous rights. And so he announced that his government would develop a full partnership with First Nations, Inuit and Metis to develop a legislative framework for this purpose based on national consultation. He acknowledged that a solution coming from Ottawa alone would not achieve very much. In future all government legislation would be based on the results of this consultation and framework. The framework would introduce mechanisms to enable the recognition of indigenous self-government and 'ensure full and meaningful implementation of treaties and other agreements'. It would develop ways to rebuild native communities and introduce new dispute resolution mechanisms. Trudeau reassured parliament that this would not entail amendment of the Constitution Act, even though it was intended to replace policies like the Comprehensive Land Claims Policy. These sweeping changes, he announced, would be implemented with a few months' consultation and legislation in place by 2019.

Now that Bill C-15 is proceeding through parliament, it is hoped this will be possible in light of the existing recommendations contained in the RCAP Report and the Truth and Reconciliation Commission (TRC) Report. Justice Minister Jody Wilson-Raybould, a former Assembly of First Nations regional chief, was quick to voice her support: 'What our Prime Minister is doing is ensuring that Section 35 is a full box of rights to be filled up by First Nations, Metis and Inuit across the country.'[35]

This may well be Trudeau's intention, but what will happen when the proposed legislation comes up against the all-too-powerful resource extraction

34 'Trudeau promises legal framework', *Macleans*.
35 Quoted in J.P. Tasker, 'Trudeau promises new legal framework for Indigenous people', *CBC News*, 15 Feb. 2018, http://www.cbc.ca/news/trudeau-speech-Indigenous-right-1.4534679.

industry lobby in a world where corporations control budgets big enough to sink any such initiative?

Indigenous leaders and politicians remain sceptical that any legislation will come into effect. Romeo Saganash, a Cree New Democratic Party MP who introduced Bill C-262, a private member's bill to adopt UNDRIP, commented: 'While I appreciate the prime minister's words today, we need to make sure that this time it is for real. One of the most unacceptable things politicians can do is quash the hope of the most vulnerable in our society. We've faced 150 years of broken promises. Guess what? We will not let that happen again for the next 150 years.'[36]

Georges Erasmus, one of the RCAP commissioners, pointed out that Trudeau makes no reference to indigenous land: 'I didn't hear him say, you know, that Aboriginal people need a significant land base in this country in order to do what they need to do. It's much tougher for him to do because land obviously is controlled by the provinces ... [but] there's lots of places in Canada where we need to open up the whole concept of land equity for First Nations.'[37]

Erasmus also questioned Trudeau's commitment to free and prior and informed consent.

Grand Chief Arlen Dumas of the Assembly of Manitoba Chiefs wrote: 'We need a government that will not impose any more of their ideas, but will support First Nations to direct our own futures. We must ensure that our rights are protected from further erosion in any in any process going forward.'[38]

Noting that the Trudeau government had had two years in which to act upon its commitment to implement the findings of the TRC and UNDRIP, Grand Chief Sheila North added: 'Asking First Nations to commit to working with Canada is not an action plan. Decision-making is key, commitment is key, and the word "partnership" – it must be a real partnership.'[39]

Russell Diabo fears that the government wants to 'weaponize' recognition of indigenous rights and control the content of those rights.[40] Elsewhere he describes Justin Trudeau's initiatives as 'a top-down, non-transparent approach to federal Indigenous policy' designed to 'modify, convert and extinguish the inherent sovereignty of First Nations'.[41] He believes that the new policy will

36 Ibid.
37 D. McCue, 'Trudeau's vow on Indigenous rights is "long time coming", says Royal Commission co-chair', *CBC News*, 18 Feb. 2018.
38 D. Robertson, 'Trudeau promise to bolster Indigenous rights gets mixed reception', *Winnipeg Free Press*, 15 Feb. 2018.
39 Ibid.
40 Quoted in J. Barrera, 'First Nations leaders react with caution to Justin Trudeau's Indigenous rights plan', *CBC News*, 15 Feb'. 2018.
41 R. Diabo, 'When moving past the Indian Act means something worse', 22 Sept. 2017.

be implemented through individual agreements which will nullify the inherent right to self-government. He points out that '… the modern high-profile conflicts between First Nations and Crown governments were led by grassroots Indigenous peoples, and not Indian Act band councils: Oka, Ipperwash, Gustafsen Lake, Burnt Church, Grassy Narrows, Caledonia and Elsipogtog.'

The protest movement Idle No More took time to respond to Trudeau's announcement. On 7 September 2018, they issued a reply to the government's *Statement on Recognition & Implementation of the Inherent & Treaty Rights of Indigenous Peoples Framework Legislation*. In the background information issued with their statement, Idle No More say:

> In order to re-colonize First Nations into assimilated 'Indigenous Canadians', the Trudeau government has unilaterally imposed 10 Principles on Indigenous Relationships and started to dissolve the Department of Indian Affairs. Trudeau has imposed two new federal departments over First Nations to implement a new law and policy Framework … The Framework is a collection of federally imposed law and policy designed to terminate our pre-existing sovereignty and collective rights as Indigenous Nations and get us to surrender to Crown sovereignty as ethnic minorities, also known as Indigenous Canadians NOT as Indigenous Nations.

In the statement itself they call out the government for promising self-determination when it intends only self-government with limited powers. Pointing out that the indigenous nations have had no say on what has gone into the Framework, they say they must hold out for a relationship based on free, prior and informed consent and give the following call to action: 'This federal legislation must be stopped and a new process started that is based upon our original instructions from the Creator; our pre-existing sovereignty; our Aboriginal Title; our historic Treaties; our internationally recognized right to self-determination; and the restoration of our stolen lands, territories and resources, or restitution for lands, territories and resources not returned!'

On 3 December 2020, Bill C-15, *The United Nations Declaration on the Rights of Indigenous Peoples Act* (known as CANDRIP) was introduced in the Canadian House of Commons by the Minister of Justice and Attorney General of Canada. It is now undergoing its second reading, and will then be scrutinised at the committee stage before returning to the House of Commons for its third reading and then receiving Royal Assent. Under Bill C-15, in consultation and co-operation with indigenous peoples, the federal government must take the steps to ensure that Canadian law is consistent with UNDRIP, implement an action plan and prepare an annual report on its implementation.

One of the main stumbling blocks to full implementation is Article 19 of UNDRIP stipulating that free and prior informed consent is the standard by which governments should deal with decision-making with regard to indigenous land and interests. Yet in a backgrounder, the Government of Canada maintains that 'If passed, this legislation would not change Canada's existing duty to consult indigenous groups, or other consultation and participation requirements set out in other legislation like the new Impact Assessment Act [2019]. What it would do is inform how the Government approaches the implementation of its legal duties going forward. Additionally, it would do so in a way that provides greater certainty over time for Indigenous groups and all Canadians.'[42] If, as this statement suggests, governments intend to continue in their bad old ways, litigation is sure to follow. In British Columbia, where a similar Act has been in force since 2019, BC government communications are full of phrases such as 'in the interests of reconciliation' but it is apparent that the intention is that matters should be conducted in much the same way as before the law was changed. The way in which UNDRIP, or some diluted form of it, across Canada, remains firmly in the hands of the federal governments whose responsibility implementation is. As writer and activist Ken Coates puts it:

> We're now seeing across the country where communities, municipal governments are saying 'Let's take UNDRIP as an organizing principle.' But in both cases the challenge has, I think, been a simple one – how do you take these really good, broad principles with which almost everybody can agree and change them for immediate action?
>
> We start seeing pushback. People say, 'well you know we didn't really mean that, we never really wanted to go that far', and so what we actually have now is a country where the public conversation is very much informed by truth and reconciliation, at this point to a lesser degree by UNDRIP … where Canadians are wrestling with this question of how do we get rid of hundreds of years of discrimination and brutal treatment of indigenous peoples.
>
> Until we actually do something about it on a practical level, then we're just making ourselves feel good about what UNDRIP represents and truth and reconciliation. So our challenge is to actually make this stuff real and we're not doing as well with that as we should.'[43]

A First Nations speaker reminded us that 'consent is the best form of certainty that anybody could ask for. When you start looking at development costs that go into the millions and tens of millions, hundreds of millions, or billions of dollars, certainty is absolutely essential if you want to do that.'[44]

---

42 Government of Canada backgrounder on Bill C-15, 3 Dec. 2020.
43 Canada's Implementation of UNDRIP Commitments: What Will it Mean for Business and the Economy?, 13 Apr. 2021, Wilson Center, https://www.wilsoncenter.org/event/canadas-implementation-undrip-commitments-what-will-it-mean-business-and-economy.
44 Ibid.

I always thought that they were insulting our people in some way because it's not their land or they have joint rights on that land. If they don't have exclusive rights to that land, at least they should have considered our views and be respectful or asked the government if we wanted to surrender our lands because at least we should have had choices as a society about that. But they don't insert any provisions in those treaties that affect the rights of the Innu. But they were careless, I believe, but they would say, I heard somewhere, that the Crees or the Inuit were acting under duress, that we were forced to sign this. Well we were under the same situation and we didn't surrender our rights.

The Cree and the Inuit taking the money is like stealing the land. Selling the land is prostitution – it is selling your soul.

Flooding ruined our traditional way of life – animals, fish, poisoned by mercury – we cannot repair the damage done.

Canadians don't want to know about our rights – they just want to kill our case.

When the government wants talks to break down they can always do it. It was always like that.

Part Three
The modern treaties and Canada's
Comprehensive Land Claims Policy

Chapter 10

The James Bay project: 'The Plot to Drown the Northern Woods'[1]

Indigenous culture in North Eastern Quebec

Originally, before the Quebec provincial government and its commercial corporations required the land for resource extraction, the Innu shared the whole of the Ungava Peninsula with the Cree and the Inuit and other indigenous peoples. The Cree and the Innu spoke different dialects of the same language, intermarried, and respected each other's rights to hunt, trap and fish on the shared land.

When in 1668 the Hudson's Bay Company (HBC) established its first trading post on James Bay, the relationship between indigenous peoples and settlers was one in which the settlers were dependent on the indigenous people for food and local knowledge as well as for the supply of furs and, as a consequence, the indigenous people were left to lead a virtually autonomous life.

Boyce Richardson and Harvey Feit, a journalist and anthropologist respectively who worked with the Cree in the time immediately before their land was taken for the James Bay hydro-electricity project, both describe the Cree's use of the land they had shared for millennia with the Innu as the tending of a garden.

Boyce Richardson's film, *Job's Garden,* made in 1972 just before its Cree subject, Job Bearskin, gave evidence before Judge Albert Malouf, follows Job onto his land. There he traps beaver and demonstrates before the camera the traditional skills of the hunting way of life which enable him to provide for his family from the land.

---

1   This is the title of a book by Boyce Richardson, *James Bay – The Plot to Drown the Northern Woods,* published in 1972 simultaneously by The Sierra Club, San Francisco and New York, and Clarke Irwin & Company Limited, Toronto and Vancouver.

Harvey Feit[2] expands on the garden analogy, quoting an unidentified Cree speaker in the negotiations for the James Bay settlement: 'Land is like a garden to the Indians, everything grows, life [is] sustained from the garden. Dam the river, and the land is destroyed. No one has a right to destroy land except for the Creator.'[3]

Feit explains that the purpose of this metaphor is to show the similarities with and differences from the white man's relationship to and perceptions of ownership of the land, and that the metaphor refers not only to possession of the land 'but also to its productiveness, to Cree inheritance of the land and to the care that goes into protecting and using the land'. According to Feit, this signifies 'that for the Cree, hunting, like gardening, not only cares for but restores the land and renews its productivity'.[4] Feit goes on to say that this metaphor runs counter to the media coverage and the propaganda of Hydro-Québec to the effect that Northern Quebec was an uninhabited wilderness.

The 'garden' which is the subject of the film is the territory around Lake Caniapiscau, which was also the hunting land of the Aster family and other Innu now settled in Matimekush Lac John. Brother and sister François and Mani Aster, in extreme old age, described for me an attachment to the land as deep as Job Bearskin's.[5] They remember travelling the 750-mile round trip from the Gulf of St Lawrence to Lake Caniapiscau where François learned to hunt and Mani the women's skills of the traditional life. Both were life-long campaigners to recover their lost land.

Louis-Edmond Hamelin describes the Innu's use of the whole of the Ungava Peninsula as follows: 'Within the peninsula and over the centuries the North Shore Innu-Montagnais have shown a mega-territorial awareness by hunting caribou up to Ungava Bay and by using the "great portage" which leads to the Mistassini and on to James Bay.'[6]

The James Bay project

In 1970, Robert Bourassa, premier of Quebec, had decided to put Quebec on the map as a thriving progressive, potentially independent nation. He aimed to achieve this with the construction of a series of hydro-electric dams on the four major rivers which feed into the James Bay arm of Hudson's Bay. When he

2   H. Feit, 'The Power and the Responsibility: Implementation of the Wildlife and Hunting Provisions of the James Bay and Northern Quebec Agreement', in S. Vincent and G. Bowers (eds.), *James Bay and Northern Quebec: Ten Years After* (Montreal: Recherches amérindiennes au Québec, 1988), p. 424ff.
3   Ibid., p. 425.
4   Ibid., p. 426.
5   Interviews MA7 March 2009 and FAS10 Sept. 2009, Matimekush.
6   L.-E. Hamelin, 'The Agreement and Quebec: Totality, Polity and Behaviour', in A.-G. Gagnon and G. Rocher (eds.), *Reflections on the James Bay and Northern Quebec Agreement* (Montreal: Editions Québec Amérique, 2002), p. 179.

announced his proposed scheme, Bourassa claimed that the Quebecois lacked control of their economy, which resulted in poverty and underdevelopment.[7] His stated aim at the time was to escape from Quebec's state of economic inferiority.[8]

The scheme would entail the flooding of the traditional hunting grounds shared by the Cree, the Inuit, and the 11 communities,[9] two in Labrador and nine in Quebec, which then made up the Innu Nation. The Innu had used lands in the territories to be affected by the dams since time immemorial[10] up to the time of the flooding of their land. Initially, all the indigenous peoples affected by Bourassa's proposals met them with incredulity, strong in their core belief that land was given for all humankind to share and was not a commodity which could be bought or sold or owned. Working with the Indians of Quebec Association,[11] the Cree and Inuit went to court seeking an injunction to stop the initial works of construction together with a declaration establishing their rights to the land affected. In contrast to the Cree 'garden' analogy, Bourassa's approach to the development of the James Bay region lacked care for the land and its people.

In *James Bay: The Plot to Drown the Northern Woods*, Boyce Richardson notes that there was no press conference and no background material available to the press, as is normal after such an announcement. His assessment is that this was a 'nakedly political move'[12] on Bourassa's part. Bourassa had made an election pledge to create 100,000 jobs and he saw the James Bay project as one way of fulfilling this promise. Bourassa announced that the project would cost C\$2 billion. Immediately following the announcement, Hydro-Québec, the provincial electricity corporation, started to undertake feasibility studies. Next, two engineers were commissioned to ascertain the best way of achieving the project and to find ways of improving the employment figures with preliminary projects building roads and infrastructure. They had less than four months in which to complete their reports. Within six weeks of delivery, Bourassa announced to his cabinet that the project would proceed.[13] Richardson goes

7   Feit, 'The Power and the Responsibility', p. 427.
8   B. Richardson, *Strangers Devour the Land* (White River Junction, VT: Chelsea Green, 1991), p. 9.
9   There are in fact more than 11 communities – some share a negotiating team, as is the case of Matimekush and Lac John, which are now separate reserves.
10 Occupation and possession of land since 'time immemorial' establishes full ownership – for indigenous land in Canada, this means ownership pre contact with settlers.
11 R. MacGregor, *Chief: The Fearless Vision of Billy Diamond* (Markham, Ontario: Viking Press, 1989), pp. 38–9.
12 Ibid., p. 10.
13 Ibid., pp. 16–17.

on to note a distinct lack of preparation for the project,[14] with no adequate mapping of the region and no attempt to involve the indigenous peoples whose land it was. A sudden decision was made to start the project on the La Grande River rather than on the Nottaway, Rupert and Broadback Rivers as first intended. It emerged that Bourassa's intention had been to exclude Hydro-Québec from the project altogether and hand it over to private companies, but in the event it transpired that financial backing for the project would only be forthcoming if it was led by Hydro-Québec.

Most importantly, Richardson claims, the developers had no knowledge of the ecology of man-made lakes.[15] There were no preliminary environmental impact studies, merely the work of an inexperienced task force after the decision to proceed had already been taken. The task force admitted it knew very little about the area around the La Grande River. The potential effects on the weather arising from the creation of such huge expanses of water were not considered, nor was the possibility that the sheer weight of the impounded water might, as elsewhere, cause earthquakes. The environmental impact assessment finally produced referred only to the impact of the dams, not of the lakes.[16] By March 1972, the predicted cost of the project had escalated from C$2 billion to C$6–10 billion. Richardson concludes: 'It is bitterly ironical that so irrational a decision was made in so precipitate a way by the first Cabinet ever to have been highly educated in the ways of the modern, technological world.'[17]

On the question of job creation, Bourassa claimed that the initial stages of the project would provide 125,000 jobs. This proved to be an unattainable target, but a year later he nevertheless boasted that in all 55,000 jobs had been created of the initially promised 100,000. In fact, the figure was nearer 23,000.[18] Of the 56,000 jobs promised for the La Grande project, only 12,000 materialised. No comparative cost analysis was made to ascertain whether the electricity to be supplied from James Bay was competitive with that from the nuclear projects in Ontario and elsewhere.

Four young Cree, led by Robert Kanatewat, instructed lawyer James O'Reilly to seek an injunction on behalf of the Cree and Inuit to bring a halt to the devastation of their land. As we shall see in the next chapter, the injunction was granted by Judge Albert Malouf but quickly suppressed by the Quebec Court of Appeal.

14 Ibid., pp. 44–8.
15 MacGregor, *Chief: The Fearless Vision*, Chapter 5.
16 Ibid., p. 118.
17 Ibid., p. 112.
18 Ibid., p. 146.

I was happy because I was always looking forward to going back to our homeland, into the country, because I was a child and I was always excited to see animals, all kinds of animals. It was funny to see those animals, I was happy to see those animals, like beaver, bear, partridge, all these little animals were roaming on the land. I could see them and was pretty excited to see that. I enjoyed eating Indian food a lot – the food from our land. That's why it makes me happy to think about that – to remember – I was happy to live that life.

> Learning from the elders makes me proud of who I am and who we are as a people because there are a lot of bravehearts. We are a very strong people, going to different places on the land, covering long distances, vast areas of our homeland. I have heard people talking about going, for instance, to Nain, to George River, to Goose Bay, to go to other trading posts on the Caniapiscau Lake or up near the Cree land. That tells you the distance they covered and how strong and fit they were. And listening to the elders telling their stories, it's as if I was there, part of their journey, that's how I feel and I am very proud of it. We should be proud of our grandparents because they were strong, fit, courageous people, that's what they were. And the land was a very difficult terrain.

Chapter 11

The Malouf judgment

Initially, the Cree and Inuit applied to the Superior Court of Quebec for an interlocutory injunction to stop the James Bay project. In the case of *Chief Robert Kanatewat et al. v La Société de développement de la Baie James et al. et La Commission hydro-électrique de Québec* [1974] RP 38[1] the application was heard by Judge Albert Malouf. In his 200-page judgment he considered 10,000 pages of transcribed evidence from 167 witnesses, with 312 exhibits produced before the court. In addition, we have two detailed lay accounts from Boyce Richardson[2] and Roy MacGregor,[3] who were both in court for the proceedings.

At the outset, Judge Malouf stated clearly the scope of his powers to grant the injunction, explaining that the applicants were seeking an interlocutory injunction, an order to the respondent corporations to cease the preliminary works on the James Bay project until the rights of the Cree and Inuit could be considered in a full court hearing. Such an injunction is granted when a judge decides that it is necessary to preserve the status quo in a case where continuation on the part of the respondents would prejudice the position of the applicants. The judge explained that an interlocutory injunction was granted on different criteria from those applicable to an application for a final injunction. All Judge Malouf had to consider was whether the construction project would have a sufficiently serious effect on the rights of the Cree and Inuit to the extent that it must be stayed in order to preserve those rights until the court could make a final decision on their validity. The granting of an interlocutory injunction did not establish rights. It proceeded on the basis that the plaintiff presented a good arguable case that such rights existed. The injunction simply preserved those potential rights intact. On this basis, the court could only consider the effects of the construction works currently undertaken, not the effects of the James Bay project in its entirety.

---

1   The case was reported in French only and in the Quebec law reports, which had limited circulation.
2   Richardson, *Strangers Devour*.
3   MacGregor, *Chief: The Fearless Vision*.

Judge Malouf described the land affected, lying between the Ontario border in the west, the 49th parallel in the south, the Gulf of St Lawrence in the east and the 55th parallel in the north, comprising 133,000 square miles, a fifth of the entire area of Quebec – an area twice the size of England and 60 per cent of the size of France.

The judge accepted evidence that the major part of Quebec lies in the sub-Arctic, characterised by a hard climate, subject to large fluctuations in temperature during winter and summer. In that region there are fewer species of animals. The number and types of vegetation are limited and their regeneration is usually slow. The Rupert, Great Whale, La Grande and Eastmain Rivers all had rapids which were very important for fish stocks. Other rivers in the territory would also be affected, including the Caniapiscau which flowed 200–250 miles through narrow gorges. Around the La Grande River, there were a great number of lakes, including Lake Caniapiscau (where families from Matimekush Lac John had hunted for generations).

Judge Malouf said that, at full capacity, the James Bay project would produce three times the power of the Upper Churchill Falls in Labrador, then the largest hydro project on the American continent. This was another part of Nitassinan, the Innu homeland, taken for hydro development without the consent of the indigenous people.[4] In total, the project envisaged the construction of four plants, four dams, 18 diversions and control structures and 80 miles of dykes. By the end of 1975, the project would become irreversible.

The judge assessed the total population of Cree and Inuit affected by the project at 9,302. Since they were the only peoples who were parties to the case, populations of other indigenous groups who used the James Bay lands were not included. He accepted the evidence of anthropologists Ignatius Larusic and Harvey Feit that the Cree had occupied their territory at least since the 17th century (the time of initial contact with Europeans) and that they had lived on that land continuously since that date.

Judge Malouf dismissed the idea proposed by the respondent governments that the Cree were a warlike people, an assertion frequently made (and accepted by the judge at first instance in *Delgamuukw v British Columbia* 20 years later) in order to justify the right of settlers to take the land for themselves. On the contrary, he found that relations between white people and Indians had always been very good and very friendly.

The judge admitted the 14 treaties adduced by the applicants as aids to the court in its determination of the nature and extent of the land rights of the Cree and Inuit, especially in relation to their dealings with the Crown. The Court also considered the Loi de l'Extension des Frontières de Québec passed on 1 April

---

4   In Arthur Lamothe's *Mémoire Battante* series of films about the Innu, made in the 1970s, Mathieu André from Matimekush Lac John is seen looking over the new Churchill dam, lamenting the disappearance of Innu land under the waters.

1912 (the 'Law of 1912'). This extended the limits of the province of Quebec to incorporate Rupert's Land; land which before Confederation was ceded to the Hudson's Bay Company (HBC). The Law of 1912 contained the following clause, which informed his conclusion that the 14 treaties presupposed that the indigenous peoples of Canada had rights which they could negotiate away:

> 2c. The Province of Quebec shall recognise the rights of the native peoples in the territory … in the same way and shall ensure the delivery of these rights in the same manner that the government of Canada has heretofore recognised them and delivered them up.

Judge Malouf interpreted the words 'government of Canada' to include the James Bay Development Corporation and its associates because they were owned and controlled by the province of Quebec.

The second issue raised by section 2c was the nature and extent of the territorial rights of the Cree and Inuit who asserted a real (freehold) property right, a right which included the rights of usufruct and possession.[5] The section recognised that the Cree and Inuit could cede the land to no one but the Crown, and so the plaintiffs claimed that the province of Quebec could not develop the land without having obtained the cession of the native rights which affected it.

Noting Lord Haldane's dictum in the ruling *In Re Southern Rhodesia v Commissioner for Native Affairs*[6] that 'there are indigenous peoples whose legal conceptions, though differently developed, are hardly less precise than our own. When once they have been studied and understood, they are no less enforceable than rights arising under English law', Judge Malouf went on to consider the Law of 1912 and the obligations it conferred on the province of Quebec. He reviewed the position of the Canadian government vis-à-vis the lands to be ceded and observed that a 1910 Order-in-Council revealed the federal government's intention that the Quebec government would enter into a treaty with the native peoples for the cession of their lands. The Quebec government had argued that a treaty was not necessary. However, in a further Order-in-Council the Canadian government reiterated that terms should be offered to the native peoples 'for a relinquishment of their rights and title to the territory'. From this, the judge concluded that the legislation showed clearly and precisely that the province of Quebec had consented to recognise the rights of the native inhabitants of the land. Judge Malouf now had to determine what these rights were and in what manner the Canadian government had obtained their release.

The judge noted that, when Charles II of England made the grant of exploitation of the land to the Governor and Company of Adventurers of England, which became the HBC, the native peoples were already occupying

---

5   The rights to take the fruits of the land, e.g. to hunt, to gather berries.
6   [1919] AC 211.

most, if not all, of the territory. Both English and French authorities were concerned to recognise native rights at this time. They recognised the right to hunt and fish in all the unoccupied territories. As beneficiaries of indigenous trapping, they had no desire to disturb this right except in places where the land was needed for white settlers and, in these cases, they entered into treaties under which the Indians ceded all or part of their land rights.

Judge Malouf referred to the case of *Calder v Attorney General for British Columbia* in which, earlier that year, Judge Hall had reviewed the nature and extent of native title in detail, and he summarised the points which were relevant to the case now before him. He noted that, as early as the 17th century, the Crown had ordered its governors not to upset or disturb the Indians in the possession of their lands. In particular, he referred to the instructions given to Governor Murray of Quebec: 'And you are upon no account to molest or disturb them in the possession of such parts of the said province as they at present occupy or possess ...'

He further noted that immediately after Confederation the British imperial government took steps to terminate the jurisdiction of the HBC over the territory ceded to it by Charles II. This was acknowledged as part of the Confederation by the British North America Act, 1867. Set down in an Order-in-Council, the terms and conditions of this transfer included a provision to the effect that the Crown and the Canadian government would assume responsibility for any indemnity which might be paid to the Indians for the use of their land. Attached to the same Order-in-Council was a schedule containing the Address to the Queen of the Senate and Chamber of Commons of Canada which included the following request: 'And further that before the transfer of the lands in question [including Prince Rupert's Land] to the Government of Canada, the claims of the Indian tribes for lands required for the purpose of colonisation, shall be considered and regulated in conformity with the principles of equity which have uniformly guided the English Crown in its relations with the aboriginal peoples.'

Judge Malouf then began a review of the past Indian treaties. In all the 14 treaties adduced as evidence before him, the Indians had agreed to cede, release and surrender to the Crown all the land included in the territory described in the treaty. In most of the treaties the Crown recognised the right of the Indians to continue to hunt, trap and fish over the ceded territory. The judge held that, although it was not necessary to define exactly the nature of the Cree and Inuit title to the land for a decision on whether to grant the injunction, the judgments he had examined nevertheless demonstrated that they had enjoyed possession and occupation of the land together with personal and usufructuary rights.

Further, taking into consideration the obligations assumed by the province of Quebec under the terms of the Law of 1912, together with the fact that all other lands ceded to the Crown had been secured by a treaty, the only way in which Quebec could develop or otherwise open up the lands to colonisation was with the prior consent of the Cree and Inuit. It was irrelevant that, because the land had formerly been ceded to the HBC, it was not within the scope of the Royal Proclamation. This was, first, because the government of Canada had treated all Indians as having an interest in their lands and, second, because of the obligations imposed by the Law of 1912. The judge also decided that the land rights of the Cree and Inuit had never been extinguished, as evidenced by the Order-in-Council of 1907 which expressly reported this.

The Cree gave evidence that:

- they, their fathers and grandfathers trapped, hunted and fished in the greater part of Northern Quebec;

- the diet of Indian and Inuit populations consisted above all of food which they hunted, fished and trapped, known as 'country food'. The proportion of country food consumed as opposed to shop-bought food was 90 per cent;

- the Cree and Inuit ate all the land animals and fish that they caught, including caribou, moose, bear, marten, beaver, rabbit, fox, squirrel, snow partridge, lynx, diver and otter. From the sea they took whale and seal in small quantities and a great variety of fish including trout, salmon, whitefish, arctic char, vairon, pike and sturgeon. They also hunted a large variety of birds, most importantly geese;

- several heads of family were full-time hunters and trappers, some were part-time. Most, if not all, of the rest hunted and trapped near the reserve on a part-time basis. They had used 75 per cent of their territory within the last five years;

- they fished in many of the lakes and rivers. A particular mention was made of the fishing near the first rapids on the La Grande River and between the first and second rapids, places where great quantities of fish were caught;

- the rivers were used as water routes which permitted them to go to their traplines and elsewhere with ease during the summer and winter;

- several among them had salaried employment;

- several of their deceased relatives had been buried along the rivers near to lakes and to their traplines;

- their religion was centred on the hunting of animals, and the killing of each animal has a religious significance for them; and

- they were happy with their way of life and strongly opposed to the hydro-electric project.

The respondent corporations challenged this evidence, pointing out the indigenous reliance on salaried employment, social security benefits and food bought from the store. One witness, Thérèse Pageau, went so far as to claim that in 1972–1973 each family in Fort George received C$10,167 – but this included the cost of all services and infrastructure together with the provision of roads and old-age pensions. This method of calculation was rejected by the judge, who said that to include the costs of provision of such services in the income of the individual defied logic. It was wrong to apply such a calculation to the Cree and Inuit when it was never applied in the calculation of the incomes of any other individual. Several Cree and Inuit attested that they had never received an income of C$10,000 in all their lives. The judge then also pointed out that, just because the Cree and Inuit bought provisions from the store, this did not mean that they were not dependent on hunting. This led the judge to conclude that:

- the Cree and Inuit who occupied the territory and the adjacent lands had hunted, trapped and fished there since time immemorial;

- they had exercised these rights on a large part of the territory and on the adjacent lands, including setting their traplines, and fishing in the lakes, rivers and streams;

- these occupations were still of great importance for them and constituted a way of life for a great number of them;

- their diet was dependent, at least in part, on the animals which they hunt and trap and on the fish which they catch;

- the sale of the animals for fur represented a source of revenue for them; and the animals which they trap and hunt and the fish which they catch represent, if measured in dollars, a form of additional revenue;

- the skins of certain animals were used for clothing;

- they had a unique concept of the earth. They made use of all its fruits and products including all the animal life there and any interference would compromise their existence as a people; and

- they wished to continue in their way of life.

After reviewing in detail the evidence of biologists, ecologists, geographers and engineers from both sides, the judge concluded that the Cree and Inuit were justified in fearing that their rights were in danger of being prejudiced. Danger to flora and fauna was already occurring. Much greater damage would be caused by the works currently being undertaken.

The judge concluded that the evidence showed that these works would have an adverse effect on the birds, fish and animals, and on aquatic life in general. The number of animals would be significantly reduced. The native people would no longer be able to hunt, trap or fish in the affected territories. The ecological balance which existed in the territory would be seriously compromised. The entire ecosystem, which had taken 8,000 years to develop, would be destroyed. It would take at least 30 to 50 years for a new wetland habitat to re-establish.

One argument put forward by the development corporations was that they enjoyed Crown immunity as agents of the Crown, but the judge held that immunity does not protect an agent of the Crown which exceeds its authority. Reviewing the terms of Bill-50, which created the James Bay Development Corporation and defined its powers, he concluded that the James Bay Energy Corporation, as a subsidiary company, was not protected. He found that the corporations were only authorised to operate in the territory defined in Bill-50. Since some of the works were being carried out in basins outside the defined territory, the corporations were acting outside the scope of their powers and thus did not enjoy Crown immunity. Similarly, Hydro-Québec had exceeded its powers and could not take advantage of a privative clause[7] in the Hydro-Québec Act, which exempted it from proceedings by way of injunction.

Judge Malouf also found that the Cree and Inuit had brought proceedings within a reasonable time and that there was no delay which would preclude the granting of the injunction.

Having previously discussed the damage which would occur to the flora and fauna, the judge found that, if the works were to continue, a tort and an irreparable prejudice would be caused to the Cree and Inuit. It would not be possible to give back life to the fish and animals which would die, and it would no longer be possible to restore the vegetation which would be destroyed. The evidence had shown that it would take many, many years before the flora and fauna were re-established. Further, if the court were to allow the respondents to continue the works, a state of fact would soon be created which would render any final or permanent injunction ineffective. It would thus be physically impossible to return the parties to their current positions. Because of the nature and extent of the works which were being undertaken and which were projected for the months to come, the project would become irreversible at the end of that year. On the other hand, there was doubt as to whether the prejudices suffered by the respondent corporations, if the injunction were granted, were of the nature of irremediable losses.

The general rule was to allow the parties to remain in their respective positions until their respective rights were determined by the final judgment. The judge held that, in carrying out these works, the respondents had succeeded in changing the status quo which existed between the parties at the time of the institution of the proceedings. Further, they had the intention to continue the works according to their production schedule. The continuation of the works would cause a state of fact which could not be remedied adequately by a final judgment. The judge had no doubt that it would be preferable for the parties

---

7   A clause which exempts the party from liability.

to remain in their respective positions until their rights were determined by the full hearing.

Since the Cree and the Inuit had established a clear right to occupation of the land, it was not strictly necessary for Judge Malouf to consider the balance of convenience between the parties, but since this was an issue of importance to the respondent corporations, the judge took time to consider the case which they put forward. The balance of convenience is considered in order to establish whether a party would suffer unduly if an injunction were granted.

The judge held that the respondent corporations had of their own accord commenced work on the project without taking account of the opposition expressed by the applicants. Even after the institution of the present proceedings, the respondents continued the project and spent large sums of money. This was a very unfortunate decision. The respondents knew that the Cree and Inuit were in possession of the territory and the adjacent lands. They also knew that the Indians and the Inuit occupied and made use of the land. They took the risk to proceed with the works. No one had forced them to do this. It would have been much more prudent to await the decision of the court.

The corporations' case rested on the amount of money they would lose if the works were suspended. However, on an examination of the figures, supplemented by the production in evidence by the Cree and Inuit of the corporations' construction contracts with third parties, the court found that these sums were greatly inflated. The contracts showed that, in the event of a suspension of works, the corporations were not obliged to compensate the contractors. The figure for purchase contracts claimed by the corporations was reduced on examination of the evidence from C$9 million to C$1 million. Claims for preliminary research on the project were dismissed, as were claims for interest incurred on loans for the project. Only items of expenditure in the immediate future were taken into consideration. Amounts expended on the construction of roads which would be lost as a result of the suspension were considered to be very small. The judge considered claims by Hydro-Québec for interest on investment in the development corporation to be too remote. None of these sums could be taken into account when assessing the balance of convenience, nor could the projected needs of Quebec in 1980 for electricity.

In addition to the financial arguments, the corporations claimed that the project would only affect a small proportion of indigenous land and that the Cree and Inuit could exercise their rights elsewhere. However, the judge held that it was not the magnitude of the region which was important but more the use which the applicants made of those particular places where the works were proposed. Their argument on this subject could not be sustained because the evidence revealed that the lands, the lakes, the rivers and the streams affected by the project were of extreme importance to the applicants. Further, if the works were to continue, a state of affairs would arise which would render any final injunction ineffective because it would be impossible to restore the status quo. The pursuit of the works would lead to a fait accompli.

Turning to the losses which would be suffered by the Cree and Inuit were the injunction not granted, Judge Malouf concluded that in many cases such losses would be not only devastating but also irreparable. Although he found it difficult to compare the monetary losses of the corporations with the losses which the Cree and Inuit would suffer, he held that the right of the applicants to pursue their way of life in the lands subject to the litigation far surpassed any consideration given to monetary loss. For these reasons, even if he had had to consider the balance of convenience, the judge said that he would say that the balance of convenience swung in favour of the Cree and Inuit. In conclusion, Judge Malouf granted the interlocutory injunction and ordered the James Bay Development Corporation, James Bay Energy Corporation and Hydro-Québec to cease all operations on the hydro-electric project until after the matter could be brought to full trial.

Judge Malouf's order was overturned by the Quebec Court of Appeal just one week later. The decision to reverse Judge Malouf's carefully considered decision was taken only on the grounds of a public interest argument, that the interests of all Québécois should have priority over those of the few indigenous people affected. This was an issue dealt with in the original application citing case law to demonstrate that public interest should not be taken into account when balancing the needs of the parties.

Although largely unreported, the Malouf judgment is of the utmost importance for several reasons.

Firstly, it is revealing in its very detailed assessment of the magnitude of the project and the catastrophic effect that it would have on the ecology of the region, described by one witness as equivalent to a major natural catastrophe. Hélène Lajambe described it as the first ecological judgment in the world.[8]

Secondly, Judge Malouf makes the case for an Indian title which rests on primary and secondary legislation of the British and Canadian governments. This was read together with the implications of the treaties by which the federal government extinguished Indian title and which gave minimal compensation in return.[9] If the federal government had held title to the land, there would have been no need for the treaties which ceded it.

The case also reveals the approach to indigenous rights taken by the federal and provincial governments, the James Bay Corporations and Hydro-Québec. It is clear that the respondents did not consider these rights and had no real answer to the case put together by the lawyers for the Cree and Inuit. Indeed,

---

8   In Vincent and Bowers (eds.), *James Bay and Northern Quebec*, at p. 47.

9   For an account of the negotiations for Treaty 8, see R. Foumoleau, *As Long as This Land Shall Last: A History of Treaty 8 and Treaty 11 1870–1939* (Calgary: University of Calgary Press, 2004, 2007) (originally published in 1975).

witnesses for the respondents admitted that their prime consideration was the production of electricity, not the preservation of the area's ecology, let alone the livelihood of the indigenous peoples and their respect for the land and its creatures. Their calculation of potential pecuniary damage which would result from an order to cease work was grossly exaggerated. It required only examination of the construction contracts with third parties by the lawyers for the Cree and Inuit to demonstrate that the damage suffered would be minimal in comparison with the sum claimed. Albert Malouf had not been afraid to 'speak truth to power' but the Quebec provincial government experienced little difficulty in finding a forum to deliver the answer it needed. This is just one instance in a consistent pattern of action by Canadian federal and provincial governments in cases concerning the establishment of indigenous rights.

The Cree felt they had no alternative but to accept the government's ultimatum and settle, giving the Malouf decision perhaps its most important role as the basis on which the James Bay and Northern Quebec Agreement was negotiated and, through this, becoming the foundation of Canada's Comprehensive Land Claims Policy. The subsequent negotiations were seen by some as the negotiation of an out-of-court settlement in the light of the original Malouf judgment, since the appeal decision was not handed down until after the settlement had been negotiated.[10] Speaking ten years later, James O'Reilly, solicitor to the Cree, acknowledged that, without the Malouf judgment, the Cree and Inuit would have been at the mercy of Robert Bourassa and that 'the forces against the Indians and the Inuit in the quest for recognition and conservation of their way of life were overpowering'.[11]

He spoke of the significance of the judgment in forcing governments to the negotiation table:

> The judgment of 15th November 1973 marked a turning point in the attitude of the government of Quebec. If the government wished to respect the schedule, it could no longer afford to take the chance that it would be the courts that would decide whether the project proceeded or not. Moreover, if the judge who had heard over seven months of proof dealing with the question of Indian rights, as with other questions, had concluded against the government of Quebec, there was at least a risk that the Supreme Court of Canada might eventually affirm such a judgment.[12]

O'Reilly goes on to point out that the Malouf judgment was ground-breaking, preceding *Calder* – where the decision was delivered during the hearing for the

---

10   For example, R. Dupuis, 'Should the James Bay and Northern Quebec Agreement Serve as a Model for Other First Nations?' in T. Martin and S.M. Hoffman (eds.), *Power Struggles: Hydro Development and First Nations in Manitoba and Quebec* (Winnipeg: University of Manitoba Press, 2008), p. 215.

11   J. O'Reilly, 'The Role of the Courts in the Evolution of the James Bay Hydroelectric Project', in Vincent and Bowers (eds.), *James Bay and Northern Quebec*, p. 30.

12   Ibid., p. 35.

interlocutory injunction. It also preceded the moratorium imposed by Thomas Berger on the Mackenzie Valley pipeline.

In 1975, after the negotiations were completed and an Agreement in Principle was in place, the Court of Appeal delivered its judgment on the merits of Judge Malouf's findings.[13] The decision of the court was written by Judge Turgeon who had delivered the decision to overturn the interlocutory injunction in 1973. The reasons he gave were much the same, stating his task as 'to expand to forty pages' his previous four-page judgment.[14] The judgment accused Malouf of ignoring the evidence in chief[15] of the corporations' witnesses, choosing to accept only the evidence given by the respondents under cross-examination, and claiming that he made 'grave errors' in his assessment of the evidence before him on, *inter alia*, effects of erosion and effects on the beaver, and saying that he made 'many mistakes' and 'false interpretations'. Justice Turgeon noted that of the 27,000 people living in the James Bay area affected, 21,000 were white, and he accepted the spurious claims of witness Thérèse Pageau that between 75 and 80 per cent of the Cree relied on shop-bought food, even accepting her estimate of a C$10,167 income per annum. The higher court ignored the rule that it should not interfere with the findings of fact of the judge at first instance, holding that Malouf's finding that the flooded lands were of great importance to the Indians was irrational, claiming that the scientific witnesses for the Cree and Inuit were giving evidence on matters which were 'entirely outside their field'.[16] Finally, on what purports to be legal argument, a travesty of the close consideration of the issues by Albert Malouf, Judge Turgeon held that, since there was no mention of Indian rights in the charter of the HBC, he had serious doubts about the existence of any Indian rights to the land.[17] Turgeon J tells us that 'judges and authors had held that the Royal Proclamation of 1763 created rather than confirmed aboriginal land rights'. No sources were identified. He went through each of the statutes and orders leading to the Law of 1912 and gave an interpretation diametrically opposed to that given in the first instance, concluding that, even if there were aboriginal rights over the land, no one could say what they were. He dismissed the effect of *Calder* because the judges were divided 3:3. On the issue of balance of convenience, Turgeon J took only economic inconvenience into consideration. Further, he pointed out that the harm to caribou was only predicted to occur after 1979, that caribou could find their own territory and that they were not affected by fluctuations of water levels, as predicted by the Cree and Inuit at the interlocutory injunction hearing.

13 *Société de Développement de la Baie James et autres v Chief Robert Kanatewat et autres* [1975] CA 166.
14 Richardson, *Strangers Devour*, p. 311.
15 Evidence given in response to questions from the witness's own legal representative.
16 Ibid., p. 315.
17 Ibid., p. 316.

Nevertheless, it was too late by then to stifle the potential of the Malouf judgment to influence the way in which the governments dealt with the Cree and Inuit. This Court of Appeal decision was itself overturned by the Supreme Court of Canada in *Manitoba (AG) v Metropolitan Stores (MTS) Ltd and others*.[18] James O'Reilly, lawyer to the Cree, points out that they were given leave to appeal from this judgment but, since by that time the James Bay and Northern Quebec Agreement was in place, they took the matter no further.[19]

18   [1987] 1 SCR 110.
19   O'Reilly, 'The Role of the Courts', in Vincent and Bowers (eds.), *James Bay and Northern Quebec*, p. 31.

Canadians are consumers so they rely on our resources – I would try as much as possible to protect my land rights and not extinguish them.

The land is going to belong to our grandchildren.

I don't think the better lifestyle in other communities is a reason for us to sign.

Signing away your rights is like signing away your culture.

We never signed anything.

Everyone else has signed and we are in the middle of it and that is what is making us poor here.

How can we deal with companies and governments without abandoning our land?

It's good not to sign because we can't sell our rights. It's not something you can sell.

People told me that, as chief, I didn't bring much, but what I tried to do was address the social problems. I tried to bring respect to the community.

If we don't do something now, we will be really poor – they don't know we are here.

We live by technology and it is blocking us.

My priority would be to keep young minds occupied – to try to get them away from gambling. We must break the cycle.

My priority as chief was to look at how people were living and to let them live a little more safely. I wanted to do something about drink and drugs. I tried to get them work.

Chapter 12

Negotiating the James Bay and Northern Quebec Agreement

The governments and their commercial partners came to the negotiating table with a fixed agenda, including a clause in the agreement which would extinguish all indigenous rights in the land affected with the exception of those specifically 'granted' in the agreement itself. The land given up by the Cree, the Inuit and later the Naskapi stretched as far as the Labrador border. The Innu, their leaders adhering to the belief that indigenous rights also brought *responsibilities* for the land, left the negotiating table. If they gave up their land in this way, they were giving up their identity and culture.

Armand Mackenzie, former chief negotiator for the Strategic Alliance, spoke of his uncles' leadership of the initial James Bay negotiations on behalf of the Innu:

> In 1975 I heard it from my Uncles Alexandre and Gaston McKenzie, [that] they were asked to sign the treaty but they said no, they would prefer to act as a group with the other Innu and, moreover, they didn't agree with the extinguishment provisions. So therefore they said no and [the Cree and Inuit] have always the chance to say no and for me the argument that they were always acting under duress ... well, it's a legal argument I guess. But down the road when you look at it we were under the same critical situation and we had to make a choice and we said no.[1]

By leaving the negotiating table, the Innu were written out of this troubled history and there is little reference in the literature on the James Bay Agreement to either their involvement or to their lost rights.

In his biography of Grand Chief Billy Diamond, Roy MacGregor[2] describes how the task of negotiation on behalf of the Cree was taken up by three young Cree leaders in their twenties. Billy Diamond, Philip Awashish and Ted Moses, who had been educated together at residential school, worked with the older and more experienced Chief Robert Kanatewat. There is no similar record of the negotiations on behalf of the Inuit. MacGregor draws a contrast between the negotiators and their elders, who spent ten months of the

1   Interview MB3, March 2009.
2   MacGregor, *Chief: The Fearless Vision.*

year hunting out on the land and on whose wisdom and knowledge of the land
the young men relied. Boyce Richardson describes the elders, who were flown
back from their hunting camps by the governments when their consent was
needed in order for the negotiations to proceed:

> Weather-beaten and ragged from their months of hard work in the
> bush, the hunters gathered in the school auditorium, and when they
> got to their feet they spoke of only one thing, their land. They spoke
> with the passion, feeling and perception of poets. They talked about
> the purpose that the Creator had when he created the earth and put the
> animals on it and gave them to the Indians to survive on. They talked of
> how they had worked and suffered for the land, and of how the animals
> and the land had helped them to survive. They talked about the white
> man, and his thoughtless ways, his failure to ask their permission before
> he invaded their lands, the things they had silently observed him do
> over the last two decades. Over and over again they reported their
> affection for the land and the knowledge that its destruction meant
> their destruction.[3]

Nevertheless, the Cree soon discovered that only minimal recognition was
given to their desire to continue their traditional way of life. Richardson notes
that: 'the young Crees who had mobilized their people for the fight now had
to confront the complex task of giving flesh to the intricate and bewildering
agreement they had negotiated. To say that they found the federal and provincial
governments slippery as they tried to pin them down to the letter and spirit of
what had been agreed would be an understatement.'[4]

The government and the James Bay Development Corporation presented
the Cree, Inuit and Innu negotiators with a set agenda. Initially, the governments
offered compensation of C$100 million and 2,000 square miles of land (one
square mile per family of five).

The young Cree negotiators, bound by the indigenous tradition that the
elders made major decisions on behalf of the group, delayed their response to
the governments' terms until their elders could be consulted on their return
from the land where they still practised migratory hunting. They were ill-
prepared to present their own long-term claims because they had spent the
previous years building up sufficient political cohesion to argue their case before
the court. Although Toby Morantz points out that in the time immediately
before they signed agreements with the governments the Cree and Naskapi
were experiencing extreme poverty,[5] Richardson observes that the Cree had
no interest in monetary compensation. All that they were concerned with was

---

3   Richardson, *Strangers Devour*, pp. 307–8.
4   Ibid., p. 329.
5   T. Morantz, 'L'Histoire de l'est de la baie James au XXe siècle: A la recherche d'une
    interprétation', *Recherches amérindiennes au Québec* XXXII, no. 2 (2002), p. 69.

what was to happen to their land. Tired of waiting for the elders to return, the governments paid for them to be flown back.

As Harvey Feit explains,[6] the state and its commercial partners set the means of communication in such negotiations in a way which precluded the Cree and Inuit from asserting their cultural practices. Their needs could only be expressed in images of the dominant Canadian culture. Further, Feit endorses James C. Scott's observation that the governments' claimed duty to serve the common good erodes any minority's attempt to further its rights and protect diversity.

Work on the project was proceeding, and the Cree felt they had no alternative but to accept the governments' final offer of C$225 million[7] and exclusive rights to 14,000 sq km of land (Category I Lands). They retained limited rights to hunt and fish over a further 150,000 sq km (Category II & III Lands) but ceded all rights in 908,000 sq km of ancestral land. The Cree and Inuit also received a measure of self-determination which gave them control over education, health and social services. They ran a programme which paid hunters and trappers to hunt and trap for the whole community. As Chief Billy Diamond explained at the time: 'The Cree people all understand that the province must be allowed to build the hydro-electric project in the James Bay area … We realize that many of the friends we have made during our opposition to the project will label us as sellouts … I hope you can all understand our feelings, that it has been a tough fight, and our people are still very much opposed to the project, but they realize that they must share the resources.'[8]

This does not sound as though the James Bay and Northern Quebec Agreement (JBNQA) was signed under duress, but Boyce Richardson claims: 'One has to remember that the original Agreement was signed under heavy duress. With the dams already being built, the Crees had either to sign, and get some money and some breathing space to prepare for the full weight of what the industrial world was proposing to dump on them – its wealth, technology, and insatiable appetite for energy – or hold out, and be completely swallowed.'[9]

By the time of the signing, the Innu were long gone from the negotiating table, their rights extinguished by the indigenous signatories and the governments alike.

The JBNQA was the first of the so-called 'modern treaties'. Unlike the numbered treaties, its provisions were set out in detail in 480 pages and the

6   Feit, 'The Power and the Responsibility', p. 412.
7   Aboriginal & Northern Affairs Canada, *James Bay and North Eastern Quebec Agreement, Annual Report 1999–2000*, www.aadnc.gc.ca, accessed 7 Dec. 2011.
8   Richardson, *Strangers Devour*, p. 321.
9   Ibid., p. xvi.

Cree and Inuit had lawyers and consultants to advise them.[10] J.R. Miller suggests that an additional pressure on the Cree and Inuit to reach a relatively speedy settlement was the possibility that the federal government might refuse to make further loans to cover the legal costs of the negotiations if they held out for all that they hoped to achieve through the land claims settlement.[11]

The Naskapi sign

To the dismay of the Innu of Matimekush Lac John, in 1979 the Mushuau Innu, relocated from the area around Fort Chimo, signed a separate agreement and became the Naskapi Nation. They too received a share in the James Bay revenues. They were allocated land on which to build their own village, Kawawachikamach, 15 kilometres from Matimekush Lac John. On the signing of their agreement, the Naskapi received C$75 million. The land they were given under the agreement was traditional hunting territory of the Matimekush Lac John Innu, just as some of the land assigned to the Cree and the Inuit in the earlier agreement was Innu land. The Matimekush Innu were deeply offended by the way in which the agreement was signed – they believed by stealth, and without consulting them or taking into account their rights. At the time, the Matimekush Lac John Band Council was sharing premises on the old Matimekush reserve with the Naskapi Band Council. Yet the latter said nothing to the Innu about the deal they had struck.[12] A female Innu elder who worked at the joint Band Council offices at the time recalled:

> I can remember when I started working for the Band Council, the Naskapis and the Montagnais were together in the same building. That was about the time when they signed. I didn't really understand what was happening but suddenly they had more money. They would show us cheques. I asked them why. I didn't understand why [the Innu] called them the people who sold their land. That's when I began to see Naskapi with cheques and things written on the backs [of their jackets].

> After they signed, about two years later, the offices were still together, I was working with Ruby from the Naskapi. Boxes came in marked 'Conseil de Bande Naskapi' and they had offices in Montreal. The boxes came from there. The boxes were full of office equipment. Their office in Montreal had closed down because they had signed and when they opened the box it was all expensive office equipment and we were all laughing about it because we didn't really understand what was happening.

---

10   R. Dupuis, 'The James Bay and Northern Quebec Agreement: An Agreement Signed in the 20th Century in the Spirit of the 18th', in Gagnon and Rocher, *Reflections*, pp. 137–43.

11   Miller, *Compact, Contract, Covenant*, p. 261.

12   Interview FBS1, 30 Sept. 2009.

Later on, we started seeing that Innu land was affected too. We didn't know that our land was affected when they signed but later on we figured out that our land was sold too. Then there was a community meeting and that's what we were talking about and then I began to understand what was happening.[13]

Another elder said: 'With the stroke of a pen, within four hours, they killed thousands of years of Innu occupation on this land – and it took only four hours. The ceremony takes four hours to sign away the rights of the people who were historically here. They killed the culture, the way of life of that people.'[14]

Having been displaced from the northern parts of the Ungava Peninsula, the Naskapi living in what is now Kawawachikamach were easy targets for Canada's policy of divide and rule because they had already lost their traditional lands in the north. When the Naskapi signed the North Eastern Quebec Agreement in 1979, they were allotted lands with which they had little or no former connection.

The lands stretching from Schefferville west to Hudson's Bay, but especially around the now inundated lands of Lake Caniapiscau, were much loved hunting and travelling routes for Innu travelling north from Sept-Iles up the rivers draining into the St Lawrence. When the Cree, Naskapi and Inuit signed up to the JBNQA, in the eyes of the governments and of Hydro-Québec they also extinguished the rights of the Innu to those lands, making them subjects of *de jure* unilateral extinguishment. The people of Matimekush and Lac John now have only small reserves and no recognised claim to lands extinguished by this agreement. The Cree Naskapi Act of 1984 gave the Cree and Naskapi Band Councils greater local powers of administration over the Category 1A lands, the lands over which they had limited powers under the Indian Act. Renée Dupuis suggests that the Act 'almost completely displaced the Indian Act'.[15]

13 Ibid.
14 Interview MA11, March 2009.
15 Dupuis, *The James Bay and Northern Quebec Agreement*, p. 140.

It's everybody's land. If someone wants to drink water or eat the food, they are not going to say don't go there if it's their land. It's every culture's land. What I can't accept is that the government is not using it for that reason. It is destroying it all and it is only for money.

When the others signed, we didn't exist any more in the eyes of Quebec.

Signing didn't make the Naskapi any happier.

Whenever they extinguish our rights, the government extinguishes our culture.

I was glad the chief didn't sign. So was he.

It's good not to sign because we can't sell our rights. It's not something you can sell.

There is not enough money for us all to take our kids to the country.

The James Bay Agreement was signed when I was 14 and I knew I didn't want it – I saw the elders go off to Ottawa. I didn't understand why the Cree signed.

We are miserable when we see our land given away to others and the privileges they receive when they sign agreements.

The Cree and Naskapi signed for themselves but they signed away our land.

Chapter 13

The aftermath of signing the James Bay and Northern Quebec Agreement

Having signed the agreements, the Cree entered into what Toby Morantz[1] calls a state of 'bureaucratic colonialism'. Many of the Cree communities opposed the signing, as acknowledged by Chief Billy Diamond, but the Grand Council of the Crees decided, in what could not be considered a genuinely free choice, that it was better to have more security in their hunting and fishing rights and to have a share in the revenues of the hydro-electric projects. Later he was to become one of those who saw that the Cree had been misled as to the effects of signing: 'If I had known in 1975 what I know now about the way solemn commitments become twisted and interpreted, I would have refused to sign the Agreement. Protection of the environment has become a farce.'[2]

In the years following the signing of the James Bay Agreement,[3] Hydro-Québec and the governments ignored or broke terms of the agreement, a signal failure to uphold the honour of the Crown. The Cree and Inuit began to realise that the promises of environmental protection were being ignored by the corporations. There were numerous court cases and renegotiations in unsatisfactory conflict resolution on single issues. Boyce Richardson claims that the corporations manipulated the court process.[4]

In 1981, a committee was set up to establish whether the governments had complied with both the spirit and the letter of the agreement. This followed Cree and Inuit claims that the governments had failed to honour their social and economic provisions. The ensuing Tait Report identified the main impediment to effective implementation of the JBNQA as a lack of dispute resolution procedures.[5]

One unforeseen consequence of the James Bay project was the levels of methyl mercury in the impounded water. Methane from the plant life

---

1   Morantz, 'L'histoire de l'est de la baie James', p. 63.
2   Ibid., p. 31.
3   See Vincent and Bowers (eds.), *James Bay and Northern Quebec: Ten Years After*.
4   Ibid., p. xviii.
5   G. McKenzie, 'Implementation of the James Bay and Northern Quebec Agreement and Chronology of Important Events', in Gagnon and Rocher, *Reflections*, p. 203.

decomposing in the trapped waters combined with organic mercury already in the soil to produce methyl mercury. Levels in the waters in the James Bay area reached six times the safe level for human consumption.[6]

Another unfortunate consequence was that in 1984 10,000 caribou drowned due to a sudden release of water from the Caniapiscau Reservoir during the seasonal migration of the George River herd. Hydro-Québec claimed that this was an 'act of God'.[7] But in comments to a conference held to mark the tenth anniversary of the signing of the agreement (see below), Michael Barrett, an administrator working on the implementation of the environmental regime, said that there had been no built-in monitoring of the Caniapiscau Reservoir even though they should have been monitoring the increase in flow.[8]

The conference at which Michael Barrett made his comments was organised ten years after the signing of the JBNQA to assess the social and environmental impacts of the James Bay projects.[9] Paul Wilkinson, who chaired the proceedings, identified that the ensuing problems resulted not from questions of land rights but from issues of native identity. He suggested that relations between native and non-native peoples were the major stumbling blocks.[10]

John Ciaccia, who had been chief negotiator for the Quebec provincial government in the original negotiations admitted that, because of the way in which the negotiations had been framed, there had been too much emphasis on the financial benefits for the indigenous signatories and not enough on aboriginal rights, which were not even defined in the ensuing agreement.[11] He went on to remark on the way in which bureaucracy hampered proper environmental protection: 'On paper, everything is in place, but the regime has not really proven implementable, and should in any case be modified in the light of new environmental practice.'

However, he claimed that the main problem was that the agreement had not been implemented properly, and that the government had not fulfilled its obligations, especially in relation to funding. The agreement, he maintained, had not put an end to the era of paternalism.

Speaking later in the day, anthropologist Harvey Feit said that, although the Cree hunters had spent more time in the interior and more young people were encouraged to follow the hunting way of life since the signing of the agreement, they often felt that they had no effective role in decision-making about development activities that affected them. They had believed that the

6   Richardson, *Strangers Devour*, p. x.
7   Ibid., p. xi.
8   Reported in Vincent and Bowers (eds.), *James Bay and Northern Quebec: Ten Years After*, p. 124. See also Samson, *A World*, p. 119.
9   Reported in Vincent and Bowers.
10 Vincent and Bowers, p. 12.
11 Reported in Vincent and Bowers, pp. 12–14.

agreement would change this state of affairs.[12] Hunting was disrupted in many ways by the development and there was a perception among the Cree that hunting was getting harder. He stressed the importance of the traditional knowledge of the older hunters, which should play a part in the decision-making process.[13] He noted that increased incomes from employment on the project had brought greater consumerism in Cree villages.

As for wildlife management, Harvey Feit said that little had changed since the signing of the agreement. He said that lack of funding from Quebec for wildlife research was limiting its extent and that research requested by the indigenous peoples which was both reasonable and necessary was not undertaken.[14] He concluded that decisions relating to wildlife management were driven by political rather than ecological concerns and that 'conservation of wildlife had not been assured by the agreement, primarily because of incomplete implementation by governments.'[15] He also noted the administrative and legalistic rather than conservationist nature of the co-ordinating committee's decision-making.[16]

Speaking on behalf of the Cree, Albert Diamond spoke of the way in which the Cree were called on to implement programmes, but when they asked for reimbursement of their costs this was refused.[17] Alan Penn commented on the difficulty in integrating the indigenous groups into the decision-making processes, saying that this would take 15–25 years rather than ten.[18] He spoke of the communication gap between north and south. He too mentioned that the agreement was principally concerned with administration and noted that its administrative procedures failed to adapt in the light of experience during implementation. In this climate, research on ecological issues 'faded away' so that, for example, mercury levels were not measured. Advisory committees were put in place instead of proper research. There were also language difficulties, because committee proceedings were conducted in French whereas the Cree spoke English. Finally, very little had been done to monitor what was going on on the ground.[19]

Billy Diamond claimed that Cree aboriginal rights were never extinguished under the JBNQA. He claimed that the Cree had merely given permission for the James Bay project to take place on their land, enabling the Cree to take part in modern industrial development. Nevertheless, the description

12 Feit, 'The Power and the Responsibility', p. 76.
13 Ibid., p. 80.
14 Ibid., p. 82.
15 Ibid., p. 84.
16 Ibid., p. 87.
17 A. Diamond, 'The Costs of Implementing the Agreement', in Vincent and Bowers, *James Bay and Northern Quebec: Ten Years After*.
18 Vincent and Bowers, *James Bay and Northern Quebec: Ten Years After*, p. 127.
19 Vincent and Bowers, *James Bay and Northern Quebec: Ten Years After*, pp. 124–31.

of the Category III lands in the agreement specifically states that these lands are owned by the Crown in Right of Quebec and that, while hunting and fishing rights are reserved to the Cree and Inuit, rights to the exploitation of the land for forestry, mining and tourism are shared. Category III lands comprise 908,000 sq km.

One of the Cree who had sought the Malouf injunction, Billy Diamond, also said that, whereas the Cree had worked hard to make the project work, Canada and Quebec were conspiring *not* to make the agreement work.[20] Eric Gourdeau took up the point about non-extinguishment, saying that the only aboriginal rights which had been extinguished were those of Quebec's aboriginal people who were not signatories to the agreement.[21] James O'Reilly maintained that all that had been conceded were the Cree and Inuit rights to the exclusive use of the land.[22] Yet, on the ground, the Cree land was flooded and its ecology ruined.

Opening the first workshop of the conference, Pierre Lepage pointed out that the land signed away under the agreement had been shared by other indigenous groups: the Algonquin, Attikamekw, Montagnais (Innu) and the Inuit who lived in Labrador.[23] Robert Pratt spoke about Bill C-9, which would extinguish all the rights of third parties in the James Bay lands.[24]

Nobody attended the conference to represent the Innu. Both Gaston McKenzie, who had been chief negotiator for the Conseil Attikamekw-Montagnais (CAM), the group which pursued negotiations for the recovery of the lost lands of the Attikamekw and Innu, and Alexandre McKenzie, chief negotiator for the Innu domiciled in Matimekush Lac John, were invited but failed to attend.[25] It was left to William Anderson of the Labrador Inuit Association to describe the exclusion of the third parties as a 'massive betrayal', expressing his frustration that: 'If Quebec parties insist on treating the claimants as beggars, as people who are being granted new rights, and reminding us that we are in a position of weakness, the process of affirmation of our rights will be a degrading and resented experience.'[26]

Paul Charest,[27] the anthropologist working with CAM, said the Innu of Schefferville had tried to bring an action to stop Bill C-9 (something which Robert Pratt had earlier described as 'near impossible'). Later, Pratt said that

20   Ibid., p. 144.
21   Ibid., p. 146.
22   Ibid., p. 152.
23   Ibid., p. 28.
24   R.A. Pratt, 'Third-Party Native Rights and the James Bay and Northern Quebec Agreement', in Vincent and Bowers, *James Bay and Northern Quebec: Ten Years After.*
25   Vincent and Bowers, *James Bay and Northern Quebec: Ten Years After*, p. 69.
26   Ibid., p. 70.
27   Ibid., p. 72.

the claim had been dismissed on the grounds that the federal government had the legal right to extinguish claims with or without compensation. Charest estimated that 15–20 per cent of the James Bay land belonged to third parties. He spoke of the difficulty for the Innu from Schefferville in hunting, trapping and fishing on their traditional territories, which had been allocated to the Cree and Naskapi under the JBNQA. Taking up these themes the following day, he went on to add that the expenditure on housing, health and education in Cree and Inuit communities drew funding away from the non-signatory indigenous groups. The agreement also gave the signatories preferential access to the governments involved, since they had been better able to organise themselves and to form a political lobby.

Joseph Guanish, Chief of the Naskapi who had moved from Schefferville to Kawawachikamach, on lands allocated to the Naskapi under the North Eastern Quebec Agreement, made the following observation: 'A land claims settlement that does not create or guarantee a healthy economic basis for its beneficiaries is so seriously flawed as to risk becoming harmful to the long-term interests of those beneficiaries.' [28]

He claimed that the North Eastern Quebec Agreement, which brought the Naskapi into the James Bay Agreement, was negotiated by them on the basis that Schefferville remained a prosperous mining town. But the Iron Ore Company mine was closed in 1982, ruining their economy, and unemployment among the Naskapi rose to 85 per cent.[29] He concluded that the North Eastern Quebec Agreement had been of no benefit to the Naskapi economy, on the basis that the Innu – who did not sign – had received the same assistance in compensation for the closure of the mine. The Naskapi had subsequently wanted to return north to where they had lived from 1929–48, but the government had insisted that they remain in the Schefferville region. Now were bound to their village just outside Schefferville because they could not exercise their North Eastern Quebec Agreement rights anywhere else.

Another symposium was held in 2001 to take stock of the implementation of the JBNQA over the course of its first 25 years.[30] Albert Diamond,[31] having listed the many successful projects and improvements to living standards in the Cree communities, concluded by saying how much more there was to be done in the areas of community development, sanitation and housing.

Reporting on the symposium, Sylvie Vincent noted that no Naskapi were present and that there was no representation from any of the indigenous groups

28 J. Guanish, 'The Lessons of the Agreement', in Vincent and Bowers, *James Bay and Northern Quebec: Ten Years After*, pp. 187–8.
29 Ibid.
30 Proceedings reported in Gagnon and Rocher, *Reflections*.
31 A. Diamond, 'Territorial Development in the James Bay and Northern Quebec Agreement: A Cree Perspective', in Gagnon and Rocher, *Reflections*, p. 56ff.

who were not signatories, and no mention of them during the proceedings. She reported a boycott of the symposium by Ted Moses and other Cree, who were at that time involved in renegotiations with the Quebec government.[32]

Louis-Edmond Hamelin summed up the implementation of the agreement 25 years on as follows:

> Could the 1975 Agreement have generated greater benefits? The answer has to be Yes, given the restrictive circumstances of the process: insufficient deliberation in general, lack of northern geopolitical experience, too little time dedicated to drafting of the report (only two years starting in 1973), predominance of administrative concerns, obligatory linguistic conformity with a non-Aboriginal legal framework, vast areas to be covered by the planning, lack of preparation on the part of institutions and individuals for the implementation of contractual provisions, absence of arbitration mechanisms, and lack of equivalents for Cree, Inuit, French and English terms. All these factors hampered a more thorough conceptualisation and understanding of the things to be changed.[33]

The Paix des Braves

In 2002 a new accord was signed by the James Bay and North Eastern Quebec parties known as the Paix des Braves, following the recommendations of the Royal Commission on Aboriginal Peoples. In line with recent developments in the Comprehensive Land Claims process elsewhere, under this new treaty the Cree received a further C\$125 million and guarantees of apprenticeships, employment and support for Cree business enterprises.

With the signing of the Paix des Braves, the Cree and Inuit were said to become partners of the Quebec and federal governments with greater recognition of their rights in the land, but still under the regime of the James Bay Agreement. It was claimed that the accord was designed to ensure that corporations like Hydro-Québec took Cree and Inuit needs fully into account.[34]

The Paix des Braves was based on four principles:

- respect for Cree values and traditional way of life, including their requirement for sustainable development;

- greater Cree autonomy and self-determination in economic development;

---

32 S. Vincent, 'Vingt-cinq ans après sa signature: un symposium sur la convention de la Baie James et du Nord québécois', *Recherches amérindiennes au Québec*, XXXII no. 1 (2002), p. 93.

33 Hamelin, 'The Agreement and Quebec', p. 188.

34 T. Martin, 'Hydro Development in Quebec and Manitoba', in Martin and Hoffman, *Power Struggles*, p. 33.

- partnership between the Cree Nation and the province of Quebec; and

- the setting up of a dispute resolution and mediation system specific to the James Bay Agreement, in order to avoid the need for recourse to the courts.[35]

Perhaps the most significant change brought in by the Paix des Braves is that it is couched in terms of a 50-year lease, rather than insistence on extinguishment of all indigenous rights in the land.

As Romeo Saganash, at the time a member of the Grand Council of the Cree, pointed out:[36] 'Real "partnership" demands genuine equality of status and equity of outcomes between the partners. No true partnership can exist when one party exerts power over and possesses rights at the expense of the other. What characterizes a true partnership is the agreement on a common set of goals – shared objectives with equitable results, which require the respectful cooperation of the parties in order to be achieved.'

Earlier, he had also commented that partnership can be used to disguise what is really going on, including dispossession. He distinguished the Paix des Braves from indigenous land claims settlements in that it is not based on surrender and extinguishment, and made the questionable claim that the James Bay and Northern Quebec Agreement did not require the Cree to give up their land rights.

Renée Dupuis[37] is more critical of the Paix des Braves, however, suggesting it may be, in fact, merely a transfer of power between the federal and provincial governments without the creation of authoritative governance structures in Cree, Naskapi and Inuit communities. Further, it confers powers on regional authorities which are not directly accountable to local populations. She has also questioned whether the decentralised structures created for health and social services for the local communities actually improved living conditions in the subsequent years. Finally, 30 years after the JBNQA was signed, Dupuis called on the Quebec government to critically appraise its relations and policy regarding the Cree and Inuit before it embarks on future negotiations with the Attikamekw, Innu and Quebec-Algonquin peoples.

There was a further settlement in 2007 when the Cree received another C$1,050 million, plus a further C$300 million as compensation for proposed amendments to the Cree Naskapi Act.[38]

Reflecting on this situation, Kathleen Wootton told Boyce Richardson: 'It's very sad to see how we Cree have been corrupted by money – that is all our

35 Wera and Martin, *Power Struggles*, p. 70.
36 R. Saganash, 'The *Paix des Braves*: An Attempt to Renew Relations With the Cree', in Martin and Hoffman, *Power Struggles*, p. 205.
37 R. Dupuis, *The James Bay and Northern Quebec Agreement*, p. 222.
38 Richardson, *Strangers Devour*, p. xix.

politicians and tallymen talk about now. While I agree that the Cree should be entitled to some compensation for the impacts we have to tolerate, it is sad to see some tallymen refusing to share the money with other family members. It seems that we, as a people, have lost the value of sharing.'[39]

On 2 June 2012, at the tenth anniversary celebration of the Paix des Braves and bookended by self-congratulatory speeches on both sides, Dr Matthew Coon Come, former Grand Chief of the Cree Nation and former National Chief of the Assembly of First Nations, couched his support for the Paix des Braves in less hubristic terms, pointing out that:

> The Paix des Braves is also an ending. It marks the end of a certain paradigm, a certain framework which defined the relationship in the past. Sometimes we called that relationship 'colonial'; sometimes we called it 'paternalism'; and sometimes we called it 'cultural genocide'. In an era when we were excluded from development of the resources on our traditional territory and when development took place without our consent; when we were excluded from certain basic and fundamental rights – even the right to vote – and excluded from the management of our own affairs; and sent to residential schools forbidding us to speak our language; these were not inaccurate characterisations.[40]

In the 37 years between the signing of the James Bay Agreement and the tenth anniversary of the Paix des Braves, the Innu of the Strategic Alliance continued to suffer the indignities and exclusion described by Dr Coon Come. In his foreword to a collection of papers comparing the effects of hydro-electric developments in Quebec and Manitoba, John Bonner describes how, since the coming of the hydro-electric projects:

> … old values have disappeared. Elders are not as respected as they used to be, there is less closeness, respect, mutual aid in families, there is more quarrelling, more squabbling. Even worse, now violence, drug and alcohol abuse are common in our community, while thirty years ago we didn't know anything about these. White diseases. It is despairing to see our young people being ruined by all these imported behaviours. The worst is that we cannot do much to stop that social disaster.[41]

Bonner goes on to speak of the way in which villages wait for the governments to provide new housing to ease the overcrowding, wasting time arguing for the money – time which could be better spent building the housing for themselves.

While at pains to assign no blame to the Cree, the Naskapi or the Inuit and demonstrating respect for their right to reach a settlement, many of the Innu interviewed in 2009 claim that the signatories to the James Bay Agreements are no better off than those who refused to sign. They say that although the

39   Ibid., p. xx.
40   Grand Council of the Crees, *10th Anniversary Celebrations of the 'Paix des Braves'*, Speaking Noted for Grand Chief Dr Matthew Coon Come.
41   Martin and Hoffman, *Power Struggles*, p. 16.

upfront lump sums that they receive in return for their signatures give them more opportunities to improve their lives, they are simply equivalent to the annual sums paid to the non-signatory Band Councils by the Department of Aboriginal Affairs. This is borne out to an extent by the words of John Bonner. The main difference in the quality of life in Cree, Inuit and Naskapi villages is that they have a degree of self-determination, provincial schooling for their children and access to funding for private enterprise and employment opportunities rather than the tight annual budgets received by the Innu who continue to be wards of the Crown.

The last word should go to Cree Chief Allan Happyjack, who gave evidence to the Royal Commission on Aboriginal Peoples in 1992 that the Cree have borne a large part of the costs and reaped few of the benefits of the massive James Bay hydro-electricity project. Speaking for all indigenous peoples dispossessed under the James Bay agreements, he says:

> Our trees are gone. When the trees are gone, the animals are gone and all the land is destroyed. They all came from the outside, from non-native economic development. That is where we have our problems, with our hunting and fishing, our traditional way of life has been affected and these developments cause other problems, from alcohol and drug abuse, but you have also heard about the dams and flooding on the territory. You heard about forestry and those people that are leaders of Quebec and Canada – they are the ones that are letting the developers come into our territory to do what nobody has asked us, asked for our consent, or to talk about it. Nobody asked us for our consent, if we approve or are in favour of these projects.

Allan Happyjack gets to the heart of the matter. Without free, prior consultation, and, in a case as significant as the flooding of the northern woods, free and prior informed consent, it would appear that there can never be reconciliation in a situation where the majority of the people affected are excluded from negotiations.

Money is given to other communities but never to this one – we are helpless.

> Our young people have nothing. If we had money, we could do things for the young people. (Weeps) We need the government to do something about it. We should show kids today how to live in the country.

I would try to create a system to redistribute the traditional food – food from *nutshimit*. I would try to create a system whereby country food would be redistributed within the community. I would try to educate people or teach them how to cook, how to prepare Indian country food so that people like me or others would learn how to prepare Indian food, because surprisingly there are a lot of people who don't know how to prepare country food in the traditional way. I would have stores so that people who want country food could just go to the freezer and get some.

> I think that was the start of where we were cut off from our traditional way of life. That was the starting point and there were a lot of pressures put on … the parents to send their children to the residential schools. In the sense that they were not receiving any support from the government or the church. They were not receiving any help. Because that's where we started to lose our language, our culture. And that's where the government, in its actions, in its plan, tried to make sure that the Innu would become like white people, not any more Innu. Their children would become like white people.

They are drilling three hours north of here – that's where the big caribou herd passes. In Matimekush they are drilling right next to the cemetery, but our leaders do nothing about it.

> When Labrador signs the [New Dawn] Agreement they will have money, but we have no resources to fight our claims.

Chapter 14

The Comprehensive Land Claims Policy

With the decision in *Calder v Attorney General for British Columbia* which acknowledged that the indigenous peoples of British Columbia retained title to their land since it had never been sold, ceded or conquered, the federal government had to put in place a negotiation process which would give them as much control as possible over the land they intended to exploit. At the same time, as we have seen, negotiations were proceeding for the James Bay and Northern Quebec Agreement which was finalised in 1975.

On 8 August 1973, the federal government issued a statement of policy in which it attempted to 'signify the Government's recognition and acceptance of its continuing responsibility under the British North America Act for Indians and lands reserved for Indians'.[1] The statement signalled the federal government's willingness to negotiate land claims in those territories which were not already the subject of a treaty and which had never been sold, ceded or conquered. This had particular application in Quebec, Newfoundland Labrador, and British Columbia. The statement continued: 'The Government is now ready to negotiate with authorized representatives of these native peoples on the basis that where their traditional interest in the lands concerned can be established, an agreed form of compensation or benefit can be provided.'

Three government claims policies were developed: the Comprehensive Land Claims process, which deals with claims relating to unextinguished aboriginal title; the Special Claims process, which relates to claims for compensation for breach of lawful obligations on the part of the federal government, such as failure to fulfil treaty obligations or improper alienation of aboriginal assets; and a third category introduced in 1993 to deal with 'administrative solutions or remedies to grievances that are not suitable for resolution or cannot be resolved through the Specific Claims process'.[2]

The Report of the Royal Commission on Aboriginal Peoples (the 'RCAP Report'), finally published in 1996, lists the procedures common to all three policies:

1   Statement made by the Honourable Jean Chrétien, Minister of Indian Affairs and Northern Development on claims of Indian and Inuit people, 8 Aug. 1973.
2   Dussault and Erasmus, *Report of the Royal Commission*, vol. 2, part 2, p. 534.

- The burden of proving a claim is on the aboriginal claimants.

- Government determines the validity of the claim (without prejudice to any position that it might subsequently advance in court proceedings).

- Government can accept a claim as an alternative to litigation; litigation takes claims outside the scope of the policies.

- Government decides the parameters of what can be negotiated.

- Existing claims cannot be renegotiated.

- Government determines the basis for compensation.

- Negotiation funding can be provided to claimants in the form of loans.

- Third-party interests are not to be affected by a claims settlement.[3]

By stipulating these procedures, the federal government has ensured that it keeps tight control on the negotiation process, with very little option for any indigenous group except to agree to the terms or to have development of the group's land proceed over their heads.

Further, while the James Bay Agreement was reached relatively swiftly, albeit with flaws which remained unresolved for 25 years or more, agreements under the claims policies typically take much longer. For example, despite the landmark court case of *Calder* as far back as 1973, the Nisga'a Nation's Final Agreement was not reached until 1998. The Gitxsan and Wet'suweten nations are still negotiating their settlement 25 years after the decision in their favour in *Delgamuukw v British Columbia*. In May 2020 the Wet'suweten reached an interim agreement with the British Columbian and federal governments but, as yet, no Final Agreement is in place for either nation. The Oka crisis, a stand-off in the province of Quebec between the Mohawk people of Kahnawake and armed police when, in 1992, a Mohawk burial site was obtained by developers who intended the land for a golf course, was the trigger for the Royal Commission on Aboriginal Peoples. The RCAP Report also points out that the cause of the Oka crisis was total frustration at the lack of progress on a land claim which the Mohawk had been pursuing for two centuries.[4]

The federal government would only accept six claims into the process at a time, and then only after the group in question had established to the government's satisfaction that it had occupied the land exclusively and continuously since before contact. Only then would the few groups be admitted to what was, and is, a very one-sided process in the Crown's favour.[5]

---

3   Ibid.
4   Dussault and Erasmus, *Report of the Royal Commission*, vol. 2, part 2, p. 235.
5   Miller, *Compact, Contract, Covenant*, p. 265.

As we shall see, until such time as any finalised agreement is in place, development and exploitation continue apace and rights are granted to third parties with no informed consent or even consultation of the recognised owners of the land – despite the governments' acceptance that the indigenous peoples concerned have a valid claim to the land. The indigenous peoples fund their claims through loans taken from the federal government. As the years pass, these loans mount up, making it impossible for the indigenous parties to walk away from a negotiation table where the odds are heavily stacked against them, for fear of having no resources with which to repay the loans. By contrast, the federal government has retained powers to abandon the negotiations whenever it chooses, or to refuse to entertain a claim.

The Comprehensive Land Claims process

On receipt of advice from the Minister of Justice, it is for the Minister of Indigenous Affairs to decide whether or not to accept a land claim. The indigenous group submits the claim, which initially only has to comply with requirements which are comparatively broad – that they were not already treaty people, and that they were a distinct group who had occupied the land traditionally and continued to do so, and could produce a map identifying the boundaries of the land claimed.

Following the decision of *Baker Lake v Minister of Indian Affairs and Northern Development*[6] in 1979, the Royal Commission adopted the criteria which the claimant group must satisfy, as laid down by the federal court in that case:

- It is and was an organised society.

- It has occupied the specific territory over which it asserts aboriginal title from time immemorial. The traditional use and occupancy of the territory must be sufficient to be an established fact at the time of the assertion of sovereignty by European nations.

- The occupation is largely to the exclusion of other organised societies.

- There is continuing use and occupancy of the land for traditional purposes.

- Aboriginal title and rights to use of resources have not been dealt with by treaty.

- Aboriginal title has not been extinguished by other lawful means.

The court in *R v Sparrow* stipulated that the decision to extinguish title 'by other lawful means' must be 'clear and plain'. The RCAP Report points out

6   *Baker Lake v Minister of Indian Affairs and Northern Development* [1979] 107 DLR (3rd) at 513.

that the stringency with which these criteria are applied depends on other political factors.[7]

In practice, every negotiation for a modern treaty seeks to extinguish all pre-existing indigenous rights with the exception of those specifically provided in the new treaty. In return for extinguishment, the indigenous group gets access to very limited rights to land, resources, revenue-sharing and a financial settlement which in no way represents the value of the land and resources they are relinquishing. Any settlement is as close as possible to the sovereignty which the federal government purports to exercise in the first place.

The process was reviewed in 1985 with the findings of the Coolican Report. The report struck at the heart of the problem: 'The federal government has sought to extinguish rights and to achieve a once-and-for-all settlement of historical claims. The aboriginal peoples, on the other hand, have sought to affirm the aboriginal rights and to guarantee their unique place in Canadian society for generations to come.'[8]

Its recommendations included taking a starting point which acknowledged aboriginal land rights; and designing a process which was fair and less drawn out, subject to external review, which allowed for negotiations for self-government, and which provided for effective implementation of the negotiated settlements. As we shall see, despite criticism from international bodies and indigenous organisations, the federal government came up with an illusory alternative to extinguishment and placed the burden of negotiation with the indigenous group on the corporations who moved in to exploit the resources. Only in British Columbia has an outside review body been put in place (the British Columbia Treaty Commission), and its powers are so limited that it has little impact on the treaty process.

In a memorandum written on behalf of the Algonquin Nation secretariat and circulated widely to chiefs across Canada,[9] Russell Diabo lists the stipulations of governments when negotiating under the Comprehensive Land Claims Policy which indigenous nations must agree to:

- accept the extinguishment (modification) of aboriginal title;

- accept the legal release of Crown liability for past violations of aboriginal title and rights;

- accept the elimination of Indian reserves by accepting lands in fee simple;

- accept removing on-reserve tax exemptions;

7   Dussault and Erasmus, *Report of the Royal Commission*, vol. 2, part 2, p. 537.
8   Task Force to Review Comprehensive Land Claims Policy (the 'Coolican Report'), 1985, Ottawa, DIAND, p. 30.
9   R. Diabo, Briefing Note to ANS Council of Chiefs & Grand Chiefs on *Aboriginal Title/Rights vs Federal Comprehensive Land Claims Policy*, 11 Feb. 2013.

- respect existing third-party interests (and therefore agree to elimination of aboriginal title territory without compensation);

- accept (to be assimilated into) existing federal and provincial orders of government;

- accept application of Canadian Charter of Rights and Freedoms over governance and institutions in all matters; and

- accept funding on a formula basis being linked to own-source revenue.

These are matters which are rarely raised in public meetings designed to explain the terms of a modern treaty to those outside the charmed circle of negotiators and consultants. When in September 2012 the Harper government announced its intention to cut core funding to indigenous political organisations, Russell Diabo called on the 93 nations involved in negotiations under the Comprehensive Land Claims process to suspend their talks and to work towards a change in Canada's land claims policies to 'recognize and affirm' rather than to extinguish indigenous land rights.[10]

Writing in 2003, Paul Nadasdy tells us that the negotiators for the Kluane First Nation Final Agreement in the Yukon worked to find a solution to the need of the Kluane to continue to hunt over their traditional lands. They came up with a usufruct which allowed the Kluane to continue to hunt over land now assigned to the Crown. However, he questions whether this is sufficient to fulfil the need of the Kluane to preserve their special relationship with the land:

> We have seen ... how difficult it is to translate the beliefs, practices and values through which First Nations peoples relate to animals into the language of scientific resource management. This difficulty arises in large part from the need to compartmentalize and distil these beliefs and practices so as to include them in the management process. The attempt to translate the cultural realities of First Nations peoples' relationships with animals into the language of 'hunting rights' entails similar processes of compartmentalization and distillation ... This compartmentalization, useful though it may be from the perspective of legal theory, ignores the fact that some of these different types of rights may be incompatible.[11]

Following the outcome of the *Tsilhqot'in Nation v British Columbia* case in June 2014, Bruce McIvor spelled out to the Union of British Columbia Indian Chiefs[12]

---

10 R. Diabo, 'Harper Launches Major First Nations Termination Plan as Negotiating Tables Legitimize Canada's Colonialism', *The Bullet*, e-bulletin no. 756, 10 Jan. 2013.

11 P. Nadasdy, *Hunters and Bureaucrats: Power, Knowledge, and Aboriginal–State Relations in the Southwest Yukon* (Vancouver: UBC Press, 2003), pp. 243–4.

12 B. McIvor, 'Legal Review of Canada's Interim Land Comprehensive Claims Policy', firstpeopleslaw.com, 4 Nov. 2014.

the changes needed to the Comprehensive Land Claims Policy as a result of the decision. His starting point was the government's policy document, *Renewing the Comprehensive Land Claims Policy: Towards a Framework for Addressing Section 35 Aboriginal Rights*, which had been released on 29 August 2014. He concludes that the policy document is deficient in the wake of *Tsilhqot'in* because it fails to change the process under which aboriginal title is recognised and preserved, it ignores the move towards the requirement for consent to development on indigenous land, it 'imposes a unilateral approach which is inconsistent with Canada's fiduciary relationship ... and its obligations to act in good faith in negotiations', and it fails to work towards reconciliation. One of McIvor's recommendations is that: 'The policy should be clear that there will be no pre-determined limits on negotiations or any resulting agreements, including with respect to the exercise of Aboriginal rights, the scope of possible economic benefits from resource development, or the exercise of Indigenous self-government.'

Christopher McKee points to the existence of certain terms of any agreement which are excluded from the Final Agreement itself. This means that they have no constitutional protection. As will be seen with the Impacts and Benefits Agreements which accompany the New Dawn Agreement, these cover all the commercial aspects of development of indigenous land – economic and employment opportunities, and loans.[13] The development corporations offer the economic and employment opportunities and often the province provides the loans.

The Coalition on the United Nations Declaration on the Rights of Indigenous Peoples, comprising a wide range of indigenous organisations together with Amnesty International Canada and the Society of Friends, in its response to the policy document raises the fact that there is no mention of consent in the document, and no acknowledgement that the Crown has no beneficial interest in aboriginal-title lands. The policy documents ignore 'international standards' – i.e. the United Nations Declaration on the Rights of Indigenous Peoples (UNDRIP) – observing that, 'The federal government cannot evade the rule of law, as determined by Canada's highest court.'[14]

Another conclusion of the Coalition is that: 'It is unconscionable to perpetuate a process, where governments steadfastly refuse to alter unreasonable positions, while debts and interest continue to build and further impoverish disadvantaged and dispossessed Peoples ... Some have suggested that this relationship of indebtedness amounts to a form of *extortion*.'

---

13 C. McKee, *Treaty Talks in British Columbia: Negotiating a Mutually Beneficial Future* (2nd edn) (Vancouver: UBC Press, 2000), p. 102.

14 Coalition on the United Nations Declaration on the Rights of Indigenous Peoples (Joint Submission), *Renewing the Federal Comprehensive Land Claims Policy*, 27 Nov. 2014.

The Specific Claims process

The notion of 'Specific Claims' stems from a 1969 White Paper, which included a proposal that the 'lawful obligations' of the Crown in Right of Canada to the country's indigenous peoples with regard to claims which could be settled by 'specific relief'. Whereas under the general law land and land rights are held to be capable of settlement by way of monetary compensation only as a last resort, under the Specific Claims process the Crown seeks to settle all such indigenous title claims with a sum of money. In a paper prepared for the Department of Indian Affairs, G.V. La Forest suggests that '... we are not so much concerned with a legal obligation in the sense of enforceable in the courts as with a government obligation of fair treatment if a legal obligation is established to its satisfaction'.[15]

Lawful obligations can arise from non-fulfilment of treaties or agreements; a breach of obligations under the Indian Act and its accompanying regulations; a breach arising from government administration of indigenous lands, funds or other assets; or an illegal disposition of Indian land. The claim can only be based on one or more of these breaches. Further, following G.V. La Forest's guidelines, instead of extending the claims process beyond what can be awarded in court, the Specific Claims Policy restricts the scope of grounds to what can be achieved through the courts. In any event, the Crown determines the validity of claims and restricts the amount of compensation available. It can also choose to abandon 'negotiations' if the lump sum it proposes in settlement is rejected.

In 1994, Coopers & Lybrand put forward the following criticisms of the process:

- The government is seen as having a conflict of interest (acting as both judge and jury).

- The policies incorporate restrictive criteria that lead to confrontation and inhibit flexible and creative solutions.

- The process is too time-consuming and too confrontational.

- It is not directed at ameliorating the original grievance.

- The government negotiates on a 'take it or leave it' basis.

- Settlements do not have a long-lasting or positive effect on communities.[16]

---

15   G.V. La Forest, *Report on Administrative Processes for the Resolution of Specific Indian Claims* (DIAND: 1979) (unpublished), p. 14, quoted in Dussault and Erasmus, *Report of the Royal Commission*, vol. 2, part 2, p. 545.

16   Coopers & Lybrand Consulting Group, *Draft Report on the Evaluation of the Specific Claims Negotiation and Settlement Process* (unpublished, 1994), quoted in Dussault and Erasmus, *Report of the Royal Commission*, vol. 2, part 2, p. 548.

The RCAP Report accepts these criticisms and further points out that the Specific Claims process does not deal with the underlying causes of the grievances of the indigenous peoples concerned.

Claims of a third kind are a sub-group of special claims for which the federal process is intended to provide 'administrative solutions or remedies to grievances that are not suitable for resolution or cannot be resolved through the Specific Claims process'. The RCAP Report points out that the only example of such a claim is the Kanesatake claim, which was the root cause of the Oka crisis, arising in 1990 but still unresolved when they reported in 1996.[17]

After the Oka crisis, some amendments were made: the budget for special claims was increased, claims of a small value went into a fast-track process, the bar on claims arising before 1867 was lifted and the Indian Claims Commission was set up. The Commission had powers to review government decisions which arose under the Specific Claims process, to review specific claims which had been rejected by the minister and to mediate between the parties over which criteria were to apply to the award of compensation. However, these powers were merely advisory.

The Indian Claims Commission and the Assembly of First Nations advocated changes to the Comprehensive Land Claims process as follows:

- an independent claims body should be created;

- the government should not have power to validate claims; rather, in order to remove any conflict of interests, a separate body should validate them;

- the independent claims body should negotiate claims in order to promote fairness in the process; and

- the independent claims process or some other body should have authority to break impasses in negotiations for compensation.

The Assembly of First Nations further proposed that:

- the independent body should have power to oversee the whole claims process from research and submission through to conclusion and implementation of settlements;

- the process should be fair and equitable, with the power to bind governments;

- there should be an appeal mechanism; and

- there should be independent funding.[18]

The RCAP Report criticised the adversarial attitudes which hindered the creation of policy which can genuinely fulfil the Crown's fiduciary duty, and commented that the Department of Indian Affairs had not abandoned its assimilationist

17 Ibid.
18 Dussault and Erasmus, *Report of the Royal Commission*, vol. 2, part 2, pp. 550–1.

mindset.[19] Nevertheless, pointing to the improved living conditions and prospects of the James Bay Cree and Inuit, the Royal Commission concludes that negotiation is a better way forward than the court process.[20] The question may be asked: better for whom? The Commission's point is that courts cannot decide the detailed terms required to settle land claims – but the reality is that neither can the representatives of governments and indigenous groups who negotiate starting from a one-size-fits-all document and on a take-it-or-leave it basis. The Royal Commission looks forward to a future in which the Specific Claims Policy can be dispensed with because treaties will include an effective dispute resolution clause.

In their work with the Yupik people, Phyllis Morrow and Chase Hensel point to the ethno-centrism of the governments, corporations and advisers involved. They perceive indigenous beliefs about the flora and fauna which they have managed for millennia to be 'non-rational' without being aware of their own cultural bias: 'The regulators canonize the biological model of population dynamics even when, as is often true in the Arctic, population figures are sketchy, variables are numerous, and the dynamics are not well understood, all leaving sufficient room for the undue influence of Western beliefs in making actual management decisions.'[21]

Working with the Kluane people, Paul Nadasdy describes the indigenous perception, which privileges 'the primary role of personal experience, the non-sentential nature of that knowledge, the importance of animals as teachers … the importance of patience'.[22]

Morrow and Hensel noted that the more the Yupik took a stand for their traditions in negotiation, the more they presented an 'anosynchronic view of themselves' and the more dependent the negotiators became on the lawyers and consultants. Thus, the negotiations focussed on the more assimilated aspects of modern indigenous life to the exclusion of their tradition. Because they speak English, wear clothing from catalogues and use modern technology, they are expected to conform to the same norms as Euro-Canadians and to lose their aboriginal rights. This in turn leads them to question the authenticity of their own identity.[23]

The Canadian public's point of view

When the Nisga'a Treaty was negotiated in British Columbia, Canadian public opinion was deeply suspicious of the rights 'granted' to the Nisga'a and

19   Ibid., p. 555.
20   Ibid., p. 562.
21   P. Morrow and C. Hensel, 'Hidden Dissension: Minority–Majority Relationships and the Use of Contested Terminology', *Arctic Anthropology*, 29(1) (1992): 45.
22   Nadasdy, *Hunters and Bureaucrats*, p. 108.
23   Morrow and Hensel, 'Hidden Dissension', p. 41.

other indigenous groups. Before the decision in *Calder*, British Columbia had consistently refused to acknowledge indigenous land rights. The provincial government embarked on a vigorous public relations exercise.[24] When the vote was held to ratify the treaty, Canadian businesses, backed by the press, were vociferous in expressing the opinion that it was undemocratic to exclude them from the vote. The campaign in opposition to the treaty, which led the call for a province-wide vote on the issue, relied on many inaccuracies and appealed to the fears of Canadians. Ponting records that this campaign of fear eventually turned public opinion against the protesters. In any event the government's greater financial resources enabled it to run an effective polling campaign which turned public opinion in its favour. The government campaign cost C\$7.6 million.[25] Yet Christopher McKee tells us that polling in the run-up to the Nisga'a Treaty put the ruling New Democratic Party at an all-time low.[26]

There was a vigorous anti-treaty movement led by a former attorney general of the province and a local radio station. The logging and forestry industries in British Columbia were initially deeply opposed to the granting of any land rights to indigenous peoples, but came to realise that the settlements gave greater certainty as to the ownership of land. The commercial fishing lobby was never reconciled to indigenous ownership of land.[27] However, taken all in all, it would appear that in the 21st century settler Canadians are better disposed towards land settlements, as they open the way to resource exploitation on native land, which in turn provides more much-needed jobs.

Extinguishment

Historically, acquisition of indigenous lands by the Crown has always been seen as an extinguishment of indigenous rights in the land, and the first step in the process of transferring it into private ownership. The Royal Commission on Aboriginal Peoples urges the Crown to take heed of its positive obligation to protect indigenous lands and resources, concluding that it must allow indigenous peoples much greater control over their territories and resources. It advocates that the Crown abandon its insistence on extinguishment and that the burden of proof of ownership of land should pass from the indigenous people to the governments who seek to take their lands. Further, it says that the government should not place arbitrary limits on the compensation available to settle specific claims. It reminds the Crown that 'Aboriginal rights do not exist by virtue of Crown title; they exist notwithstanding Crown title ... A fiduciary

---

24 For an account of this, see J.R. Ponting, *The Nisga'a Treaty: Polling Dynamics and Political Communication in Comparative Context* (Toronto: Broadview Press, 2006).

25 Ponting, *The Nisga'a Treaty*, p. 35.

26 McKee, *Treaty Talks*, p. 106.

27 See Miller, *Compact, Contract, Covenant*, p. 274.

should not attempt to destroy what it is required to protect.'[28] Moreover, in order to make indigenous communities viable, it calls for significant expansion of the aboriginal land base, together with greater access or control over lands and resources outside the boundaries of that larger land base.[29] The Royal Commission further points out that indigenous peoples regard land and its resources as *living* things which require respect and protection.[30]

Finally, the RCAP Report says that: 'There must be a presumption in such negotiations that Aboriginal signatories did not intend to consent to the blanket extinguishment of the Aboriginal rights and title by agreeing to a treaty relationship.'

Back in 1994, the federal government had considered the option of not insisting on such an extinguishment. In 1995, it released a fact-finding report, *Canada and Aboriginal People: A New Partnership*, also known as the Hamilton Report. Hamilton concluded that extinguishment was not necessary in order to achieve future certainty in relation to the land. This could be achieved instead by mutual assurances of good faith and an effective dispute resolution provision in the Final Agreement, together with the inclusion of an amendment process. He also believed that less convoluted language in modern treaties and shorter, plainer documents would contribute to greater certainty.

Hamilton's report did not consider that: '... there are any circumstances that warrant even a partial extinguishment or surrender of Aboriginal rights whether one is dealing with Aboriginal rights in general or more specific Aboriginal rights with respect to land and resources'.[31]

Tom Berger had also 20 years previously raised the issue of extinguishment, and what it means to indigenous peoples, when he delivered his 1977 report following the Mackenzie Valley Pipeline Inquiry: 'Native people desire a settlement of native claims before a pipeline is built. They do not want a settlement – in the tradition of the treaties – that will extinguish their rights in the land. They want a settlement that will entrench their rights to the land and that will lay the foundations of native self-determination under the Constitution of Canada.'[32]

28   Dussault and Erasmus, *Report of the Royal Commission*, vol. 2, part 2, p. 569.
29   Ibid., p. 423.
30   Ibid., p. 436.
31   Dussault and Erasmus, *Report of the Royal Commission*, vol. 2, part 2, pp. 542–3.
32   Berger, *Northern Frontier, Northern Homeland*, p. xxii.

Asch and Zlotkin[33] point to the conflicting positions of the Crown and indigenous peoples, in that the Crown sees extinguishment as essential in resolving outstanding issues while the indigenous peoples see it as a block to resolution of fundamental issues at the negotiating table. They call for an approach which reconciles these differences, and in particular a starting point which recognises the validity of indigenous title. They remind us of the dictum in *R v Sparrow* to the effect that sovereignty and underlying title was vested in the Crown. Thus, the court had never made an attempt to define indigenous land rights until the matter came before it in *Tsilhqot'in*. It has thus historically been easy for the Crown to rely before the court on an argument that indigenous rights are uncertain and a barrier to economic development, and that therefore they should be extinguished either by agreement with the peoples concerned or by unilateral government act.

So far as the Innu of Matimekush Lac John are concerned, all their rights to their traditional lands have been extinguished by unilateral government Act, as we shall see in the following section. Perhaps the most insulting feature of this government policy is that the government insists that certainty is necessary for the future of the *indigenous* people who, the government says, are happy to exchange their broad rights over large areas of land which they know intimately and have a duty to protect for limited rights to a very small parcel of land, those rights having been prescribed in a very one-sided Final Agreement.[34] Paul Nadasdy says that the Canadian approach to land claims settlements is nothing more than 'an attempt to incorporate Aboriginal peoples' unique relationship to the land into the existing legal and political institutions of the Canadian state'.[35]

There have been countless indigenous criticisms of extinguishment, strong condemnation by Canada's own Royal Commission on Aboriginal Peoples, and a recommendation for the policy's abandonment by the United Nations Human Rights Committee in light of its incompatibility with Article I of the International Covenant on Civil and Political Rights. On 1 November 2002, the Committee on the Elimination of Racial Discrimination noted in its concluding observations that:

> The Committee views with concern the direct connection between Aboriginal economic marginalization and the ongoing dispossession of Aboriginal people from their land, as recognized by the Royal Commission. The Committee notes with appreciation the assurance

---

33   M. Asch and N. Zlotkin, 'Affirming Aboriginal Title: A New Basis for Comprehensive Claims Negotiations', in M. Asch, (ed.), *Aboriginal and Treaty Rights in Canada: Essays on Law, Equality and Respect for Difference* (Vancouver: UBC Press, 1997), p. 209.

34   For a discussion of the indigenous perspective on extinguishment, see Asch and Zlotkin, *Affirming Aboriginal Title*, p. 214ff.

35   Nadasdy, *Hunters and Bureaucrats*, p. 223.

given by the delegation that Canada would no longer require a reference to extinguishment of surrendered land and resource rights in any land claim agreements. The Committee requests that in the next periodic report, information be provided on the significance and consequences of limitations imposed on the use by Aboriginal people of their land.[36]

Currently, the legal framework of land claims agreements gives virtually no room for manoeuvre for any indigenous party that may feel aggrieved by any of the provisions in the agreement itself. However, if they look outside the Canadian state system, they will see that there is a considerable body of opinion that finds these land claims procedures unacceptable. Since 2005 the Assembly of First Nations has challenged the extinguishment requirement, which is now contrary to Articles 8(b) and 10 of UNDRIP, and which should also be considered in the light of Article 19, which requires fully informed prior consent.

These three Articles of UNDRIP would, should they ever pass into Canadian law, prevent Canada and its provinces from introducing extinguishment clauses such as the 'certainty' clause in the New Dawn Agreement in Principle (AIP), signed but as yet unratified by residents in the two Innu villages in Labrador.

Article 8 (b) of UNDRIP says: 'States shall provide effective mechanisms for prevention of, and redress for … any action which has the aim or effect of dispossessing them of their lands, territories or resources', and Article 10 states: 'Indigenous peoples shall not be forcibly removed from their lands or territories. No relocation shall take place without the free, prior and informed consent of the indigenous peoples concerned and after agreement on just and fair compensation and, where possible, with the option of return.'

The certainty and indemnity clauses in the New Dawn AIP amount to another, more insidious, form of extinguishment and impose even more restrictions than the old and much-discredited policy – most bizarrely in binding indigenous peoples' actions and court authority in the future. In 2005, the UN Human Rights Committee's country report on Canada commented specifically on this, especially as it relates to the Innu peoples:

> The Committee, while noting with interest Canada's undertakings towards the establishment of alternative policies to extinguishment of inherent aboriginal rights in modern treaties, remains concerned that these alternatives may in practice amount to extinguishment of aboriginal rights. (Articles 1 and 27)

---

36 UN Committee on the Elimination of Racial Discrimination (CERD), *Concluding Observations of the Committee on the Elimination of Racial Discrimination: Canada. 01/11/2002.*

> The State party should re-examine its policy and practices to ensure they do not result in extinguishment of inherent aboriginal rights. The Committee would like to receive more detailed information on the comprehensive land claims agreement that Canada is currently negotiating with the Innu people of Quebec and Labrador, in particular regarding its compliance with the Covenant.[37]

With particular reference to the Comprehensive Land Claims process, the Report condemns Canada's insistence on 'full and final certainty', which it says is unattainable. The Report observes: 'An overarching concern is that the Government appears to view the overall interests of Canadians as adverse to aboriginal interests, rather than encompassing them.'

It highlights the minimal attention which the Canadian government pays to aboriginal rights and its adversarial approach in negotiations. Stephanie Irlbacher-Fox tells us that the Dehcho First Nation, among the first to sign a land settlement agreement, found an alternative solution: 'The Dehcho First Nation and Canada intend their relationship to be based on mutual recognition and sharing and to achieve this mutual recognition and sharing by agreeing on rights rather than by extinguishing rights.'[38]

The UN Human Rights Committee report criticises the mounting costs for all parties, in particular the loans with which the government saddles indigenous parties. These stood at more than C$700 million at the time of the Special Rapporteur's investigation and, the Report observes, remain owing even if the government withdraws from the negotiations.

The UN report also highlights the fact that delays in the negotiations can mean that the indigenous people must stand by and watch their land destroyed by mines or dams with no agreement in place. This is exactly what has happened at Muskrat Falls.

Momentum for this criticism of Canada's policies, which many indigenous groups see as a perpetual lack of good faith, is steadily building. In February 2012, the Assembly of First Nations and other independent groups travelled to Geneva to submit an alternative report to the one submitted to the Committee on the Elimination of Racial Discrimination by the Canadian government. They alleged that the Canadian government has not, as required, consulted with indigenous groups or NGOs and had produced a sanitised version of events in Canada. Specifically, Chief Wallace Fox of the Onion Lake Cree Nation argues that Canada cannot claim title to much of the land it asserts to possess, that it continually confiscates indigenous lands which even under

37   United Nations Human Rights Committee, *Concluding observations of the Human Rights Committee: Canada. 02/11/2005*, Eighty-fifth session, New York: United Nations, Point 8.
38   Irlbacher-Fox, *Finding Dahshaa*, p. 65.

the treaties were not ceded, and that it is not meeting other requirements to ensure that indigenous peoples live free from discrimination.[39] In 2017, in its conclusions to its report on Canada, CERD called upon Canada to 'prohibit the environmentally destructive development of territories of Indigenous Peoples, and to allow Indigenous Peoples to conduct independent environmental impact studies'.

Liberal Prime Minister Justin Trudeau is only now fulfilling his promise to pass UNDRIP into domestic law but, despite the fact that this would drive another nail into the coffin of unilateral extinguishment, it will come too late for the Innu resident in Labrador. In the next section, we will look further at their struggle to recover their lost James Bay lands and the position of all Innu with regard to Tshash Petapen, the New Dawn Agreement.

---

39 See Léo-Paul Dana et al., 'Towards a better understanding of Aboriginal/Indigenous rights and their impact on development: An application of regulation theory', Academy of Management (AOM), August 2016, https://hal.archives-ouvertes.fr/hal-02089156/document.

My community gets nothing because they didn't sign. Why do we have to sign away our rights to be part of the wealth of the country?

> The Innu Nation has nine communities – before it was only one. Now it is divided into three groups – west, east and middle. The groups are not all at the same stage. The government plays with them – it doesn't act in good faith.

I always thought that they were insulting our people in some way because it's not their land, or they have joint rights on that land. If they don't have exclusive rights to that land, at least they should have considered our views and be respectful or asked the government if we wanted to surrender our lands – because at least we should have had choices as a society about that. But they don't insert any provisions in those treaties that affect the rights of the Innu. But they were careless, I believe, but they would say, I heard somewhere, that the Crees or the Inuit were acting under duress, that we were forced to sign this. Well, we were under the same situation and we didn't surrender our rights.

> We are miserable when we see our land given away to others and the privileges they receive when they sign agreements.

It is a big insult what the governments have done to our people. They have insulted our people by letting this happen. By letting other people have our rights, by signing away our rights, the Canadian government has acted. The government gives service with one hand but takes something back with the other – gives programmes and services but takes away our rights.

> The government fails to tell the real story about the Indian people.

Part Four
The Innu experience of the
Comprehensive Land Claims process

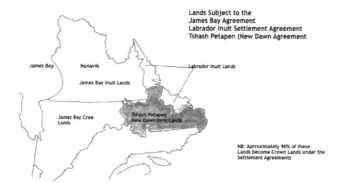

Map 2: Quebec-Labrador Peninsula showing the land acquired as Crown lands under the James Bay and Northern Quebec Agreement, the North Eastern Quebec Agreement, the Labrador Inuit Settlement Agreement and the Tshash Petapen (New Dawn) Agreement in Principle on which there is as yet no Final Agreement. Only 10 per cent of the land remains as indigenous land in fee simple after the signing of these agreements, which purport to 'grant' land to the peoples.

FIGURE 1

Map of Labrador Peninsula from author's survey showing approximate distribution since 1850 of local groups or bands of Montagnais-Naskapi and Eskimo. The blank areas on the northern and eastern coasts are, or were, occupied by Eskimo. As late as the eighteenth century the latter existed on the north shore of the Gulf of St. Lawrence west at least to the longitude of Anticosti Island (from *American Anthropologist*, Vol. XXXIII, 1931).

Map 3: Frank Speck's map of the Quebec-Labrador Peninsula showing the distribution of the land under Innu (both Montagnais and Naskapi) ownership and control. A version of this map was used in support of the Conseil Attikamekw-Montagnais land claim. Note that Speck allocates only the most northerly territory to the Inuit.

Chapter 15

'All that is left to us is the terms of our surrender': negotiations to recover lost Innu lands

In 2009, at the time of the interviews conducted by this study in Matimekush Lac John, when the Innu elders looked back on the building of the James Bay dams they spoke of the lost lands in much the same way as Cree elders had spoken to Boyce Richardson: 'The earth is respectful. My mother walked through the land. We didn't take more than we needed from it. It's our life they are taking away from us. We are destroying the land. It is alive but we don't respect it. I see the old people crying – but the earth still has a lot to give. It is tired now. The land is sad. I go to the country to pray and talk to the plants. When the wind blows, it is as if they are talking to you too.'[1]

They spoke of their frustration that their rights were ignored:

> So the Crown takes decisions or decides about the land as if we were non-existent, invisible on the land, and so government takes decisions and then governments decide about the use of the land, the occupancy of the land without the consent of the Innu, without the Innu being informed, as if the Innu were non-existent and where our family hunting grounds are. The Inuit are having jurisdiction on our land as if we were no longer there, non-existent, so ... it is very, very disturbing. I am not upset towards the Eskimos, I'm much more upset with the government because of the way they handle this situation, the way they use the restriction, because it is a form of manipulation.[2]

The Innu families in Matimekush Lac John spoke of their lost lands. Since they were no longer involved in the negotiation process, they had received no notice of the flooding of their lands around Lake Caniapiscau and arrived one year to find that not only was the land flooded but also the graves of their ancestors. For them this was indeed a catastrophe:

> My family, our uncles, our great-uncles were ... their burial sites were desecrated ... they were exhumed and we had to perform another ceremony back in Sept-Iles. They kept the human remains for a while in Montreal to study the bones. I don't believe that you do that to a

1   Interview MB2, Sept. 2009.
2   Interview MFC6, March 2009.

people, and we were affected as a family at the Caniapiscau reservoir
that was their hunting grounds that were flooded. There was no
compensation whatsoever – any form of consideration – no – and I
think this issue has still to be addressed …[3]

A former chief said:

I always thought at least, from our grandfather or my father, that they
were insulting our people in some way because it's not their land – or,
if they have joint rights on that land, if you don't have exclusive rights
to that land, at least they should have considered our views and be
respectful or asked the government if we wanted to surrender our lands,
because at least we should have had choices as a society about that. But
they don't insert any provisions in those treaties that affect the rights of
the Innu. But they were careless.[4]

And an elder told me:

I know there is a lot of food there and a lot of money but if they kill
everything what am I supposed to do? The land – that's how I used
to live, how I used to eat. There is wildlife, there's fish and now it's all
becoming one lake because of all the dams. All that was different lakes
[but] because of the dams it's all one now. My land didn't change but
other people's land got washed out in the flood. It used to be someone's
land but now it's under the water. There are trees you can see in the
water. They are all breaking the land and killing the trees. The trees
are really dirtying the water too. When the trees get wet, they stink
and now the fish won't eat from the water. You must know how the
trees smell. Where they cut the trees they stink and they are not getting
cut. They are just there under the water and they stink more. It's really
bad that the land is going that way. It's all breaking up. I guess the
government wants us to be like them, like Canadians.[5]

A hunter said:

It's theft. It's stealing the land and violating our identity to the land. My
family, the Grégoires, they were affected by those transactions on the
land in the sense that all the water was diverted to our hunting grounds
and they flooded everything. All the Innu hunting grounds. So we are
affected by the creation of those reservoirs on our homeland. All the
good places for caribou hunting, for fishing, were flooded. It's ruining
our traditional way of life. It's ruining the animals. The fish are ill, like
from the mercury poison. It is killing our way of life and so we can't
bring it back to the way it was before. We can't repair the damage done.
You just can't do it.[6]

3   Interview MB2, March 2009.
4   Interview MB4, March 2009.
5   Interview MA8, March 2009.
6   Interview MD6, Sept. 2009.

The background to the Innu comprehensive land claim to James Bay lands

When the Cree, Naskapi and Inuit signed away their indigenous rights, in the eyes of the governments and of Hydro-Québec they also extinguished the rights of the Innu to those lands, making them subjects of *de jure* unilateral extinguishment. When the Naskapi were invited to the negotiating table to make their own settlement, the Innu of Matimekush Lac John received the same invitation. The Innu insisted that they would not negotiate without the inclusion of Innu from all the other Quebec and Labrador villages and, when this was refused, they chose solidarity with their Innu relatives over a place at the negotiating table for their sole benefit.[7]

Thus, the people of Matimekush and Lac John now have only a small reserve, which is government-owned, and no recognised claim to lands taken from them by the James Bay and Northern Quebec Agreement (JBNQA) or to their other lands in Labrador. There have been repeated, but unsuccessful, attempts to gain recognition of Innu aboriginal title to some of the lands signed away by the Cree and Inuit, with the governments eventually telling the Innu that they must negotiate directly with the Cree and Inuit for the return of their lands.[8] Forty years of negotiations have achieved nothing, because the government insists that rights not expressly provided for in any agreement are extinguished; but, until comparatively recently, all Innu communities have categorically refused to agree to such an extinguishment, either over the JBNQA lands or their territories in Labrador.

In the records held at the Tshakapesh Institute in Uashat, there are files recording the meticulous correspondence between the Conseil Attikamekw-Montagnais (CAM) and the federal Department of Indian Affairs and Northern Development (DIAND), as well as with the governments of Quebec and Labrador on the progress (or lack of it) of negotiations on three issues: recovery of the James Bay lands, the closure of the town of Schefferville after the mine had ceased to function, and the rights of the Innu who live in Quebec to continue to hunt and trap on their traditional lands over the border in Labrador. The CAM files are incomplete because, following CAM's division into smaller negotiating units in 1992, the correspondence was divided and held by the individual villages to which individual documents referred.[9]

For most of the time between the loss of the James Bay lands and the break-up of the CAM, Gaston McKenzie from Matimekush was the chief negotiator

---

7   R. Dupuis, *Tribus, Peuples et Nations* (Montreal: Les Editions du Boréal, 1997), p. 91.

8   Interviews MD4 and MD2, Sept. 2009.

9   There is also a CAM archive in La Tuque, Quebec, to which I did not have access.

for CAM and Alexandre McKenzie, his brother, the Chief at Schefferville.[10] CAM represented the nine Innu bands who lived in the Lac St Jean region and along the St Lawrence North Shore as well as at Matemekush Lac John, and three Attikamekw bands in the St Maurice region of Quebec. For the first 25 years of the negotiations, Innu from either side of the Quebec–Labrador border were united with the Attikamekw at the negotiation table. Like most organisations representing indigenous peoples in Canada – such as the Assembly of First Nations and its predecessors, the Innu Nation in Labrador and Mamit Innuat in western Quebec – CAM was funded by the Canadian government.[11] Although ostensibly a benefit, this has adverse repercussions on the nature of representation and the freedom of representatives to negotiate truly independently.

CAM prepared a claim submission for DIAND which was presented in April 1979, but of which only a summary remains on file.[12] The document pointed out that the Innu and Attikamekw were forced to couch their claim in the terms of the dominant society, that the governments were well aware of the nature and validity of their claims, and that their situation might worsen now that the provincial governments were taking their land.

The summary document continues:

> It seems strange that while the rights of the Attikamekw and Montagnais have been continually eroded through the interests and activities of the dominant society, the native people are nevertheless obliged to bear the burden of proof of the existence of these rights, and the extent of the damages to their culture and their territories.
>
> The Attikamekw and Montagnais do not understand why jurisprudence takes into account only European written law, ignoring the principles of the unwritten law of the native people; nor why the European notion of private property must take precedence over the concept of collective or communal ownership on which native societies are based.[13]

The claim is based on occupation of the land since time immemorial,[14] as upheld in 1966 by the Dorion Commission on the integrity of the land claims of the Quebec government, in 1974 by the Malouf judgment, in 1975 by the JBNQA, and in testimony before the DIAND Standing Committee on Bill-C9. The Innu claim approximately 200,000 square miles of land, 25 per cent of

10 Although we arranged to meet several times, Alexandre McKenzie, who was still a member of the Matimekush Lac John Band Council in 2009, and one of its negotiators, never kept these appointments.
11 See Samson, *A Way of Life*, p. 30.
12 Fonds d'Archives CAM, Boîte 5800-6-8.
13 *Summary of Claim Submission of the Conseil Attikamekw-Montagnais*, Office of Native Claims, 1 May 1979.
14 This is a legal term supporting a claim to the equivalent of a fee simple interest. In Canada 'time immemorial' means before contact with Europeans.

which is over the provincial border in Labrador,[15] which has been used by themselves and their ancestors. They also seek the right to self-determination. They do not accept the option of assimilation. Twenty per cent of the James Bay lands were claimed to belong to the Attikamekw and Innu. CAM was prepared to accept that other lands were subject to overlapping claims, noting that Clause 2.14 of the JBNQA provides for '… negotiations with other Indians or Inuit who are not entitled to participate in the compensation and benefits of the present agreement, in respect to any claims which such Indians or Inuit may have with respect to the Territory'.

CAM refers to archaeological evidence that the land has been occupied by its ancestors for 8,000 years, and also points to the records of Jesuit missionaries which indicate the presence of Attikamekw and Innu in the territory on their arrival. For evidence of recent use and occupancy, CAM refers to the maps and lists of hunting territories provided by Frank G. Speck.

The Innu claim that native territorial rights should include subsurface rights, as found by Judge Thomas Berger in relation to the Mackenzie Valley Pipeline Inquiry, and on this basis claim the right to all the resources on their lands. They reject the governments' claim that these rights should be restricted to the usufructuary rights of hunting, gathering and trapping. Further, they say that their rights have been continuously eroded since first contact: firstly through the fur trade, forestry and agriculture, and since the 1920s through large-scale hydro-electric development which has taken more than 1,000 square miles of native land. The summary points out that, at the time of submission, these incursions were continuing with well-advanced plans for hydro-electric projects on the five rivers along the North Shore. It noted that the Attikamekw and Innu had never authorised the exploitation of the iron ore found near Schefferville, all of which fell within their territory and which has had a serious social impact on the environment and the native communities affected. Sports hunting, private fishing clubs and outfitting organisations have also had a detrimental effect on wildlife and on native hunting. They note that the Quebec provincial government refuses to recognise any native rights to the land and has permitted its exploitation without their consent.

CAM summarised its arguments by putting forward the following 11 demands:

- In view of the cultural autonomy before arrival of Europeans, desire for recognition as peoples having the right to self-determination

- As descendants of the first inhabitants of the lands in question, a request for recognition of sovereignty rights on these lands

15   There were no copies in the summary of the maps included in the full submission.

- Refusal to accept definitive extinguishment as a precondition of any agreement

- Request for compensation for all past and present violations of territorial rights

- Opposition to any proposed development of resources on Attikamekw-Montagnais lands until Attikamekw-Montagnais rights are recognised

- Desire for control of any future development of their lands and resources

- Wish to give priority to development of renewable resources, over that of non-renewable resources

- Desire to see the economic benefits resulting from control of development on their lands ensure the economic, social and cultural well-being of future generations

- Desire to assume control of all aspects of their own development, so that this control will no longer be exercised by the dominant society

- Wish to orient their development in accordance with the traditions and values inherited from their ancestors

- Wish to deal in the future as equals with the governments of the dominant society, and not to be considered any longer as inferior peoples.

The summary concludes with CAM's stated intention to commission two comprehensive surveys on 1) the nature of their traditional rights and the past and present use of their lands by both native and non-native peoples, and 2) a proposal for a programme of socio-economic development which would further Attikamekw-Montagnais autonomy in economic, social and educational matters.

Evidence in support of the CAM claim

The first of these surveys, on land occupation and use, of which there is a summary in the Tshakapesh Institute files, was carried out by Richard Dominique under the general supervision of Paul Charest, at the time a CAM adviser.[16] Eight anthropologists, eight technicians and 59 native researchers worked on the project. Drawing on the work of Frank G. Speck and on the records of the province of Quebec, the survey identified the land used by the Innu in recent times as lying between longitude 57–75 degrees W and latitude 47–57 degrees N, and covering an area of 571,000 square kilometres; although the report also pointed out that 'among the Montagnais, neither land nor society are

16   Fonds d'Archives CAM, Boîte 5800-6-8.

closed entities'. The survey further pointed to the Innu's 'linguistically distinct toponymy' for all the geographical features of the territory which they claimed.[17]

The summary included a description of the communication networks over Nitassinan:

> Waterways, portage routes, paths, winter routes, camps, meeting places, and locations for leaving messages for passers-by are described. There is also a list of twenty-six roads and paths that covered the area at the time. Some are still being used, although such use is infrequent because the harnessing of waterways and rapid expansion of logging roads have led the Montagnais to opt for other modes of travel. The modern world is being introduced. The presence of numerous cemeteries in the area is also mentioned.

Although no maps have been included in the summary, the writers comment that the maps in the full survey more or less reproduce those of Frank Speck. Although the survey notes the lack of archaeological research on the Quebec-Labrador Peninsula, by looking at the pattern of deglaciation and subsequent afforestation of the region, the writers conclude that it would have been populated starting from a time between 11,000 and 6,000 years ago. Caribou would be found in coastal regions from between 8,000 to 5,000 years ago, but not on the interior plateau before 5,000 to 4,500 years ago.[18] Tools, effigies, amulets and figurines found at grave sites in the region, together with hunting tools and stone axes, knives and needles pointed to occupation from 9,000 to 7,000 years ago onwards, with occupation of the valley of the River Moisie, where the Innu who now live in Matimekush Lac John originated, from 6,000 years ago. There were settlements along the Labrador coast and the Côte-Nord between 3,500 and 1,500 years ago, whose people lived on marine life and occasional hunting expeditions into the interior. These prehistoric populations are considered to be the ancestors of the present Innu population.[19] The report further stated that, according to Jesuit sources, the Montagnais lived along the St Lawrence River between Quebec City and Tadoussac (where Samuel Champlain made his first landing in 1603) and along the Gulf of St Lawrence between Pessamit and Moisie.

The full report, titled in French *Occupation et utilisation du territoire par les Montagnais de Schefferville*, was published in 1983.[20] In a comprehensive survey of land use by the Innu,[21] the report follows trade relations between Europeans and the Innu from the 17th century up until 1850, observing that

17 F. Boivin, Assistant Negotiator for CAM, *Summary of the Documents Dealing With the Occupation and Use of Attikamekw and Montagnais Territory*, Nov. 1989.
18 Ibid., p. 4.
19 Ibid., p. 10.
20 R. Laforest, *Occupation et utilisation du territoire par les Montagnais de Schefferville* (Rapport de recherche soumis au Conseil Attikamekw-Montagnais, 1983).
21 Ibid., pp. 29–49.

the native people were never dependent on this trade because of the presence in the area of the great herds of caribou in the Caniapiscau, Delorme and Opiscoteo regions, together with the George River herd, which provided subsistence for Innu families. However, from the 1830s caribou populations in the forests declined due to fires in the interior and warm winters when the ice was thin. By 1860 all game populations were in serious decline. By the end of the 19th century, nearly half the forest in the interior had been destroyed in less than 30 years. Some of the fires were caused by human intervention, both native and non-native. This decline continued until the 1930s, when numbers of fur-bearing animals were seriously affected. Some of this decline was due to better trapping technology available to the native people and commercial pressures to over-exploit the animal populations.

The report traces the modern history of the Sept-Iles Band after the closure of Fort Nascopie on Attikamagen Lake near modern-day Schefferville in 1868, when the band was first formally recognised. From that time the Sept-Iles Innu, formerly the Michikamau and Ashuanipi bands, made their summer camp at Sept-Iles near to the Hudson's Bay Company (HBC) trading post, together with those Innu who came down the Moisie from the interior. In 1909 the Sept-Iles reserve came into being. By 1926 there were approximately 26 families at Moisie (Maliotenam) and 200 Innu at Sept-Iles (Uashat). By 1950 there were approximately 800 Innu at Sept-Iles. During this period the annual journey to the north continued and the fur trade allowed the Innu credit to acquire clothing and food. This also meant that hunters could equip themselves for the journey north and repay sums borrowed when they returned with the fur. However, since the HBC had a monopoly on trade with the Innu, it could control the price offered for furs and this could have serious consequences for the Innu. Because they had to repay their debts to the store, they became dependent on trapping rather than hunting for their subsistence. In addition, the Innu had to compete with non-native hunters.[22]

In 1941 an airbase was constructed at Goose Bay, and many of the Innu settled nearby abandoned trapping in that area and took salaried employment. Along the Côte-Nord the situation was less acute, because even at the end of the 1940s there were only 15 white trappers operating in the region. The majority of Innu at Sept-Iles thus pursued their traditional life in the first half of the 20th century, albeit subject to diminishing resources. It is these resource constraints which led to their participation in the fur trade, which alone did not produce enough to live on due to the continually reducing prices for furs. Alongside the fur trade, from 1867 onwards there was also mining development. The first such mine was at Moisie, which produced high-quality steel; however, this enterprise was dependent on the American markets and was

22 Laforest, *Occupation et utilisation*, p. 58.

always subject to the demands of American steelworks. When the Americans raised import duties, the Moisie works closed.

Then, the report continues, during World War I Reuben d'Anglois, a surveyor working on behalf of Toronto financiers, discovered in the region not the precious metals they were seeking but substantial deposits of iron ore. However, it was not until there was a large enough market in the United States that these were exploited. For example, in 1929 deposits were discovered around what became the municipality of Schefferville, but nothing was done during the years of the Great Depression. It was not until 1939 that the Labrador Mining and Exploration Company joined with the McKay (Quebec) Exploration Company to exploit the deposits in this region. Hollinger North Shore Exploration was formed in 1942 and the M.A. Hanna Coal and Oil Exploration Company in 1943. Exploration camps were constructed on Lake Knob in 1945 and the Quebec North Shore and Labrador Railway was constructed, together with a hydro-electric plant on Lake Menehek, 25 miles from Schefferville.

By this time World War II had depleted American stocks of iron and steel. In 1949 the Iron Ore Company of Canada was formed, a company which, despite its name, was registered in the United States. In fact, this was a company formed and directed by all the exploration companies. There were 417 million tonnes of ore to be exploited. The workforce rose to nearly 7,000 and the municipality of Schefferville grew to accommodate them with houses, churches, a store, a school and a hospital. The town was incorporated in 1960. Despite this expansion, however, there were rumours of closure of the mine from 1960 onwards because the iron ore did not correspond to the requirements of the American markets. When more suitable iron ore was found in Latin America, the Iron Ore Company announced the closure of the mine in autumn 1982.

Against this backdrop, from 1947 onwards Innu from Sept-Iles began to move north, first to work on the construction of the exploration camp and the railway and ultimately to work in the mines. In 1956 the Naskapi were relocated, first to their own encampment and subsequently to the same Lac John reserve where the Innu had been relocated. The reason given in the report for the movement of the Naskapi from the north to Schefferville was so that they could fill jobs in the mine. Despite this, however, in July 1962 there were only 69 Innu and 38 Naskapi employed in the mine.

Turning to land use by the Innu of Schefferville, the writers of the report pointed out that Innu from Moisie were tempted to settle in Schefferville by the government in the first place by promises of access to their ancestral lands in the region, and became known as the Naplek Unnut ('Knob Lake Innu'). In 1966 the Dorion Commission allocated traplines to the Schefferville Innu families according to where their fathers had hunted.

There follow chapters on the ecology of the region, the daily and annual round of life out on the land and further toponymic evidence. Turning to the shared nature of the use of land, the writers explain that, while family groups were closely associated with certain areas by their superior knowledge of the terrain and were best able to exploit its resources, others could hunt on that land with the permission of the captain of that group. If the family were not on their land, there was no need to seek permission. The territory was not only managed by small groups in portions of the land, it was also managed in its entirety so that its resources could best be exploited.[23]

From 1956 until 1982, following their move to Schefferville, the Naplek Innu (newly named in the report, but not elsewhere) perceived themselves as restricted, or even prevented, from exploiting certain parts of their territory. During this period, hunting and fishing were no longer considered the basis of their economy. The ecological consequences of industrialisation and the damage caused to the territory, together with government interference and the influx of non-native people, meant that a new social model replaced the traditional way of life. The writers noted the political dimension to these changes. There was no consideration of the traditional way of life of the Innu, because Quebec had never recognised the right of the Innu to self-determination.

The report concluded that the signature of the James Bay and Northern Quebec Agreement and the North Eastern Quebec Agreement had consigned the Innu to the status of third parties, and all their rights in the land had been extinguished. This had been done in a disproportionate way – all that the state was concerned to do was to preserve its own full sovereignty over the land. The Naplek Innu had to submit themselves to certain rules contained in these agreements, which would exclude the Innu from portions of their territory unless they obtained permission from the signatories.

The Ashuanipi Corporation

After the break-up of negotiations and the demise of CAM, the Innu resident in Labrador pursued their own land claim while the Innu of Central Quebec – Uashat, Maliotenam and Matimekush Lac John – continued to pursue their land claims in the James Bay development area and in Labrador through the Ashuanipi Corporation. The Corporation was named for a lake which is at the centre of hunting territory shared by all Innu but which, under the New Dawn Agreement, will be signed over to the governments by the Innu who live in Labrador. Initially, I was invited to observe these negotiations but they closed very shortly after the invitation was issued. Nevertheless, I was able to interview some of the Matimekush Lac John Innu involved in the negotiations over the years and to learn of the seriousness of their approach and of the way in which they were frustrated by having to deal with set agendas and intransigent governments.

---

23   Laforest, *Occupation et utilisation*, p. 173.

One former chief, involved in the negotiations in the early 2000s, explained that there were differences between the Innu chiefs even though they were conducting a joint negotiation:

> I was involved in the Ashuanipi Corporation. The way I was involved was that we tried as much as possible to work together with other Innu communities. I wanted to address extinguishment – all the Innu area is subject to extinguishment provisions and I hoped somehow we could work together as Innu, as a group, one people, gather all these communities together. But there was a lot of mistrust between the Innu or even between the chiefs, who don't want to deal with the real issues at times, who don't want to address those issues because you don't want to hurt the other chiefs' feelings or don't want to be perceived as someone who is attacking a fellow chief, and it's very hard to be open about those issues. There is always this idea that we have to take our time, discuss calmly those issues, but it is as if it is impossible to confront those issues or confront other chiefs with those issues and I always had this belief that it's not only this community that is affected by the extinguishment provisions – it is all the Innu people. So that's what I was hoping – that, somehow, we would work round this with common sense. This didn't happen. They have created one, two, three, four tables of negotiations. That was one aspect. The other aspect with these negotiations is that you have to know what you want. You have to have a set objective. If you don't know what you want, if you don't know what principle you will rely on to negotiate those issues … well, you will end up negotiating forever with no result. We didn't have that. We didn't know where we were going.
>
> You have to deal with the community, the people, the grassroots. You have to know what they want and that's another challenge. So you don't know that. Then there's all the infighting between the employees, the lawyers – who knows best and so on. You have all these disputes. You have the hidden interests as well – that sometimes there are people who want to preserve their contracts or something. They have their own interests, all those lawyers, consultants, employees. They have their own self-interest. How do you deal with them?
>
> And when you try to address certain issues with the other chiefs and when you want to discuss face to face with another chief, you are accused of not trusting the advisers. And there is always this dispute between the consultants – one consultant to another, one lawyer to another, one employee to another. So you have all these different layers of difficulties. That's how I got involved. It's complex. Those are the issues, the situation you have to deal with when you are a chief.
>
> Out of someone's misery you will be able to manipulate [them] easily because that person somehow wants to get out of that misery. Governments play on that with the aboriginal communities. They

know that they are weak, fragile mentally, and they are therefore susceptible to manipulation.

The main problem with those negotiations is that you have to deal with the governments and they come up with a set of principles, a pre-set rule or objective, and it's up to you to accept it or not. All that is left to us is the terms of our surrender.

I didn't agree with that and I always told the negotiators to go with the mindset that we are the rightful owners and that we should not agree to terms of a surrender. The fundamental problem that underlies the negotiations is those pre-set rules. Because the federal negotiators come up with examples, they will tell you what they did in other places with other nations. But we have a right to have our own views on this and to say [that] for us it is different. You were always stuck with the thought that you either take the money or resign.

I tried to listen as much as possible to the elders, their advice or opinion on this issue. They were always telling me that extinguishment was never to be accepted – in the James Bay Agreement, for instance, to never accept it. Always lead with the assumption that your rights are alive. Always lead with the assumption that you are negotiating existing aboriginal rights. Don't accept the fact that people are giving you money in return for accepting extinguishment. So I always led with this assumption or this ideal whenever I was meeting other groups or in my work with government and negotiators. So we gathered and initiated those first discussions with the Inuit, the Naskapi and the Cree and then, when I was meeting them, I was always standing my ground in the sense I was telling them we were rightful owners of those lands and I was repeating this over and over again up to the point that people understood that what we were saying was true. Because at some point the Inuit said, 'You are absolutely right. We were just occupying the coastline. So we didn't go into the interior of the lands.' With the Cree it was the same. We spoke in our own languages and we somehow managed to understand each other. It was an evolving process whereby we were using our elders to try to come up with some form of agreement between the nations involved. Then somehow … and I don't want to put blame on anyone or give names [and the translator detected a lot of regret in the tone of his voice] I think we missed something there because some people didn't agree with the process. I would have liked back then to have the right resources to work with me, the right people to work with me, and somehow it wasn't possible. This work that we tried to do with the other chiefs in this native or indigenous environment was picked up by a bunch of lawyers and they screwed up the whole thing.

Probably we could have convened with the other Indigenous nations, the Cree, the Inuit, the Naskapi, probably we would have been able to agree on something. Maybe it wouldn't have [had] any legal value but to the international community it would have some form of value because it would have been an agreement between indigenous nations and the government probably would have put in their policies the legal framework. We were working on something and, despite the governments' position on the indigenous agreement, we could have told the world community that this is what happened in this part of the world and it might have offered a solution. Unfortunately, we didn't agree that [regretfully].

I regret the fact that in all the discussion with the Naskapi, Inuit, the Cree, I regret the fact that I was not able to see any gains. It was not possible for me to move forward the negotiations in discussions with other leaders.[24]

This chief was not the only one to observe the counter-productive involvement of lawyers and consultants. Sitting in on the land claims negotiations in Labrador in the 1990s, Colin Samson notes:

A rather different kind of knowledge, often both abstract and predictive, is required to be produced in order that the Innu document their land claims case and beat back the continual threats posed by a host of industrial projects on their lands. What is important to their case, especially in the eyes of advisers, is that representations of their knowledge, land and identity be presented to the state in terms that functionaries can easily grasp and that pose no serious ontological challenges to the scientific materialism upon which so much Western knowledge of the world is predicated.[25]

He continues:

For the Innu to be able to participate in the comprehensive land claims procedures, much of the funds paid to Innu Nation are distributed to non-Native lawyers, environmental scientists, and anthropologists, who help prepare the land claim. This procedure involves the federal government subsidizing Euro-Canadian professionals to prepare a 'case' for the Innu. This 'case' has to be intelligible to government bureaucrats and is therefore conveyed, presented, and packaged to conform to the various expectations of state protocol. The advisers are intermediaries not so much *for* the Innu, but *between* Canada and the Innu.

The Innu of the Ashuanipi Corporation and its successor the Strategic Alliance are experienced, skilled negotiators who would prefer to do the talking themselves rather than rely on the lawyers and consultants that the governments insist are there to advise them. They believe that this arrangement swallows up funding that could be used for more meetings and longer sessions. Those experienced in these negotiations[26] told me that the governments come with a fixed agenda and negotiate on the basis that other communities have signed up

24   Interview MAS5, Sept. 2009.
25   Samson, *A Way of Life*, p. 58.
26   Interviews MB2 in March 2009 and MD2, MD4, MAS5 in Sept. 2009.

to their set, pre-drafted terms of agreement and therefore the terms cannot be changed. The Innu, represented by the Strategic Alliance, have suggested a 50-year lease so that resources can be exploited while they retain title to the land, but this has fallen on deaf ears – although a similar arrangement was permitted on Cree land.[27] The Innu negotiators realise that they must keep the grassroots involved and informed, but this is difficult because of the complexity of the documentation. Over a cup of coffee in Rita's Café in Matimekush, one Innu land claims negotiator gave me a masterclass:

> When you are negotiating, you have to be able to gather different perspectives, different opinions, in the community and when confronted with the Canadian government and Quebec and Labrador. You have to seek common ground and try to come up with solutions. If you meet an obstacle, you don't want to leave it. You ask yourself, 'How can we overcome it? What can we discuss? What are our thoughts? How can we overcome this? What is the hope of our talks? What are we going to discuss about this?'

> We are talking about societies, we are talking about land. We are talking about a treaty which will survive for 200 years, and you have to have all these things in mind when you are negotiating and I am saying these things because I was a negotiator. I went to law school, I went to the bench, I read books, I learned from experience and you don't become a negotiator overnight, you don't just put people there. It takes years. I remember when we had the government who were changing negotiators, they would educate those negotiators, for a couple of months, six to 12 months. And that's fine – you have all those years for all those discussions.

> We need to change the policy that is approved by Cabinet. We need to change decisions, the Royal Commission [on Aboriginal Peoples] for instance, the new alternatives for the native people. It's an educational process. When we have new negotiators, we have new dynamics. We have to retrain the person, we have to teach, whether it's native or non-native. We have to tell them here's what we did over the last ten to fifteen years or the last five years and these are the elements we agreed and this is what we are about to agree. You talk about culture, economic development, you talk about the water rights, you talk about the resource rights, fiscal, taxation, self-government powers – and with the self-government powers you are talking about justice, health, social services, education, labour rights, anything. You can't just take this on and learn it in a few months, even if you have good will, it takes years of experience to have a depth and 360 degrees of good vision.

> When you are involved in the negotiations, each party has its own objectives: the Innu, the Quebec and the federal governments. The federal government wants the Indians to pay taxes and the Indians have

27 Interview MD2, Sept. 2009.

their [status] cards. They want us to integrate into Canadian society. The Quebec government want us to confirm that they have jurisdiction over the land and that we will integrate in some way their rules, legislation and so on, and from the Innu ... they just want to confirm their existing rights to the land – that they were there and because they were there they are entitled to certain rights – not to all kinds of rights because they interact with the Francophones and the Anglophones of Canada. When you are negotiating you have to bear in mind those principles.

When we had high-level negotiations in the late 1990s up to 2000 whereby three communities out of nine in Quebec signed an agreement based on the work that we did on certainty provisions or non-extinguishment provisions, we were looking for a certainty model. A certainty model is the Quebec government, the federal government saying to us, 'Do you want to know once and for all, forever, what are your Aboriginal rights?' Because Canada wants to confirm its sovereignty on the land, [and] the same with the Quebec government, they want to know. 'Tell us in 400 pages or 300 pages what are your land rights as an Aboriginal person in Canada, in Quebec or in Labrador.' And what we'd always say was that you can't do that – as a Canadian can you define your rights, all of your rights and then you're going to say that's it, once and for all this is it?

You can't change the constitution, you can't change the law, you can't change any rule or regulation. The same with Quebec – what are your rights as Quebecers? You made a referendum in the early 1980s and [then] you made another and another. Can you say once and for all that you are not going to pass anything in the future? No. See – well, it's the same for us. We have a right to evolve as a society or as a group so the extinguishment provisions or the certainty models are just not right – you can't ask aboriginal groups to surrender forever their land rights. So we have to come up with something that doesn't imply extinguishment in any way, form or ... indirectly or directly ... and so we work on certainty models and then unfortunately some of the lawyers who work on behalf of the Innu don't understand totally the concept and they came up with the [New Dawn] Agreement in Principle which is extinguishment by definition. Nothing in this agreement extinguishes the rights of the Innu but – there are a lot of buts – it's like the Nisga'a model or other models for certainty, but some intelligent people say there are extinguishment provisions indirectly in this form and then for that reason we won't sign this Agreement in Principle.[28]

The land use and other reports prepared for CAM referred to above set out clearly and comprehensively the basis of the Innu land claims in a way which refutes Canadian claims to ownership of the land, yet despite (or perhaps because of) this, the negotiations never reach a satisfactory conclusion for any indigenous parties, be they Cree, Inuit, Attikamekw or Innu. Whenever

28   Interview ME3; see also Irlbacher-Fox, *Finding Dahshaa*, pp. 57–9.

progress appears to be made that is not on terms pre-set by the governments, the negotiations collapse. For example, the last person to be appointed chief negotiator by the Matimekush Lac John Band Council told me:

> Our office [the Ashuanipi Corporation] was closed in May 2009 because the government of Quebec doesn't want to discuss aboriginal rights. That's why they cut the money and our office was closed. When I was a negotiator we once had a meeting in Kawawachikamach [Naskapi village] and we needed C$600,000 and the government gave us only half a million dollars. With that we could only have two meetings to get Inuit, Naskapi, Cree and Innu to discuss the Quebec agreement and the impact on us. What we wanted was the recommendations of the elders on what the issues are for them and how to fix the agreement, and [with] no money [there were] no meetings after that.

He also spoke of the difficulty of explaining the long and complicated negotiation documents to the people who would be called on to ratify any agreement:

> In the past there could be no information, no translation. The clauses were not well explained to the community. It is hard for a person to understand who has not reached grade 5 [in school]. Some of them didn't finish their schooling. Maybe more than 50 per cent, and the agreement is important for them, for their community, but they cannot know what it says. They can't read. They can't translate it into Innu. It is hard for them to understand. We try to translate word by word. We have five ways to reach people: by post, meetings, radio stations, newspapers and to see someone in their house. We try to explain very well the contents of the agreement, small agreement or big agreement. We take time to explain.
>
> It's hard for the young people because, you know, when you take the agreement it has 24 chapters and when you look at that in detail it is hard to summarise that for the people here. Only specialists can summarise that. It is hard for ordinary people because there are different views from young men or women or for a man who is related to the Naskapi. There are 30–40 people here who have Naskapi blood. That's why half the community has a different opinion from others who are not beneficiaries of the [North Eastern Quebec] Agreement.

This negotiator, I was told, had been in post for only three months before the finance was withdrawn. The same informant went on to say that the mindset of the Innu, especially those from Uashat, had changed so that they now favoured a settlement through the court, feeling that it was time to move on from the frustrations of the past 40 years of wasted effort at the negotiating table.[29] There are rivalries among those who hold power and those who seek power, dissent on the best approach to negotiation, and persistent anxieties arising from the close relationship with and proximity to the Naskapi.

29   Interview MD4, Sept. 2009.

Yet, prior to the *Tsilhqot'in Nation v British Columbia* decision in 2014, the prospect of mounting a successful court case was also fraught with uncertainty. As one interviewee told me:

> There are seven signatories to the agreement: Cree, Naskapi, Inuit, two governments, Hydro-Québec and Transénergie. If we decide to go to court it's going to take maybe 12–15 years to finish that and if we use the agreement maybe we could take five years to finish that case. I think there are a lot of items to fix. One is hunting and fishing and economic development – mining, forestry, everything that we used before as Montagnais [Innu] people. I know it is hard for the Naskapi and Montagnais to discuss that because it is politics. When you talk about politics it is hard to do this between nations and I know elders are respectful to each other but the young people are angry about the agreement in the Montagnais community and Naskapi community because for the Naskapi there was no information given to the young people at that time. In our time, we heard a lot about the Quebec agreement, the Cree and Inuit nations. Because when you talk about the James Bay Agreement, it would be easy to find issues to agree on but Quebec doesn't want to reopen that case because everybody knows that they made a mistake and Canada, which holds the land in trust, doesn't respect what the Crown has to do for the Indians. The two governments don't use the same way to listen to nations like the Montagnais people.

The accounts given above demonstrate a process which is tantamount to the systematic destruction of a community. There are many problems relating to the loss of Innu identity directly linked to the loss of their lands and hunting culture. Many of the people I interviewed told me they felt that they were invisible to the Quebec government and that their rights counted for nothing.

In 2008, at the fourth annual Séminaire Nordique Autochtone held at Mushuau Nipi (Indian House Lake) on the George River, Romeo Saganash, then a member of the Grand Council of the Crees and now a New Democratic Party politician, challenged Matimekush Chief Réal McKenzie over his people's decision to leave the James Bay negotiating table, claiming that, had the Innu stayed, they could have negotiated more compensation for the loss of their lands. However, Anne-Marie André, an Innu teacher, film-maker and elder, explained to me that the decision to withdraw was unanimously backed by the Innu in every community – they held to their belief that no amount of money could compensate for the loss of land which was not theirs to give away.

In this chapter, we have seen how the Innu resident in Central Quebec have grouped and regrouped in negotiations to recover their lost lands in Quebec. We have seen the strong case they put forward for their ownership of the land since time immemorial – in this case not just a phrase of legal shorthand but the reality of ownership and control for thousands of years over the land they claim. At the same time, the Newfoundland Labrador government has employed game wardens to harass from their hunting lands Innu who were once accorded resident status in Labrador, while refusing to come to the negotiating table or to recognise these rights in any way – another stain on the honour of the Crown.

The only small success at the negotiating table came when the Innu of the Ashuanipi Corporation met with chiefs and negotiators from the Cree and Inuit communities with no lawyers and consultants present. Without these outsiders to fuel dissent, the indigenous leaders made progress in acknowledging the rights of the Innu to their expropriated lands. Then the federal government withdrew funding. During the final negotiations for the New Dawn Agreement, the leaders of the Innu Nation in Labrador distanced themselves from the continuing struggle of their relatives in Quebec and disparaged their attempts to assert their hunting rights. In an article in *Le Devoir* in 2003, Armand Mackenzie noted how the Ottawa and Quebec governments had already split the nine Innu villages in Quebec into separate groups under their policy of divide and rule.[30]

We shall see further in the next chapter the degree to which the once-close relationship between the Innu has deteriorated.

---

30 A. Mackenzie, 'Commission parlementaire sur l'entente Québec–Ottawa–Innus – Manque de transparence et manque d'unité chez les Innus', *Le Devoir*, 20 Jan. 2003.

I am saddened to see how impoverished we are and when I see how the government is treating the other Indian communities, the neighbouring communities. They are always handing out money to the other communities whether in Goose Bay or Sept-Iles or to the Naskapis. They have recreational facilities for their children. They have pools, whereas in our case we have nothing, and we see all our kids hanging out in front of the bar or outside the community store begging for money, you see all your kids outside the Hotel Royale. It's an insult to us. It's an insult to who we are in this community. It is very insulting. It's a big offence to do what they did to this community, as the government did. Should we be envious of all the improvements to their lifestyle or the betterment of their communities with all these recreational facilities? The communities have all that, which is not the case with this community, and they have it because of these deals with the government or agreements or treaties with governments so they can improve their community's facilities. Should we be jealous? I don't know. Sometimes I look with envy and am jealous that they have all this and at the same time I applaud the fact that this community have continued to maintain that they wouldn't sign the treaty with the government. I applaud it because it makes me proud that they haven't signed away all rights in our culture. Signing away your rights is like signing away your culture. I am getting to a stage when I will be an old man soon and I have in mind the future of all my children, my grandchildren, my great-grandchildren, and I think about what's their future. It is a big insult what the governments have done to our people. They have insulted our people by letting this happen. By letting other people have our rights, by signing away our rights, the Canadian government has acted. The government gives service with one hand but takes something back with the other – gives programmes and services but takes away our rights.

I regret the fact that in all the discussion with the Naskapi, Inuit, the Cree, I regret the fact that I was not able to see any gains. It was not possible for me to move forward the negotiations in discussions with other leaders. It is hard for ordinary people to understand the James Bay Agreement. It has 24 chapters and is highly technical.

Couldn't the Cree, Inuit and Naskapi have waited?

Chapter 16

The New Dawn Agreement

Background

The Innu who live in the two Labrador villages of Sheshatshiu and Natuashish have been negotiating under the Comprehensive Land Claims process since 1977. During this time, with no agreement in place, the federal and provincial governments have permitted major resource extraction projects on the land with little or no consultation of or consent from the Innu peoples who live on either side of the Quebec–Labrador border.

Their land claim has been negotiated against the background of expropriation of Innu land for resource development which, with no land claims agreement in place, took scant account of the needs and wishes of the Innu in what was, effectively, a unilateral extinguishment of their rights. Even filing the petition for a land claim does not prevent land from simply being taken.[1]

Until the Supreme Court decision in *Delgamuukw v British Columbia* in 1997, there were no clear rules about how conflicts over such lands could be adjudicated. In practice, what occurred in many places was that provinces simply allowed prospecting and other industrial and settlement activity on unceded lands as if the land were under full Canadian sovereignty. This is what has happened on Innu lands with the Upper Churchill hydro-electric project of the late 1960s, military activities undertaken from the NATO base at Goose Bay since World War II, the Voisey's Bay nickel mine in Labrador which was first prospected in 1993, and also continuous cabin building, sports fishing and hunting outfitters, road building, and municipal encroachments.[2] Financial compensation is the only remedy available to the Innu for such incursions into the lands over which they hold aboriginal title.

---

1 See Samson, *A Way of Life*, pp. 49–56.
2 Samson, *A Way of Life*, pp. 53–4, 96–102. See also C. Samson and E. Cassell, 'The Long Reach of Frontier Justice: Canadian Land Claims "Negotiation" Strategies as Human Rights Violations', *International Journal of Human Rights*, vol. 17.1 (2013): 1–21.

Initially, all Innu stood together to challenge the governments' seizure of their land for these earlier projects. However, when it was proposed by the New Millennium Capital mining company in the first decade of the 21st century to reopen the mines in the hills above Schefferville, the two Innu villages in Labrador decided, unlike the other Innu groups, to sign the New Millennium mining agreements. This was because they were in the later stages of negotiation for their own land claims agreement, Tshash Petapen, also known as the New Dawn Agreement, under which lands shared with the Innu of the Strategic Alliance and other indigenous groups would be ceded to the governments and their commercial development corporations for the primary purpose of mining and hydro-electric development. However, the land to be expropriated by the governments included other lands for which there was no immediate commercial purpose, including the area around Lake Ashuanipi, which is an important site for Innu who live on both sides of the border and has been shared for millennia. The justification criteria laid down in *Delgamuukw* and subsequent cases require that indigenous land be acquired for stated purposes, but the negotiation process obviates the need to satisfy these criteria because ratification of the settlement agreement is taken to signify consent (if not free, prior and informed consent) to the provisions of the agreement. Innu deals with New Millennium (for extraction) and the governments (for land) are kept entirely separate. The governments can capitalise on these agreements to take more land than is strictly necessary.

If the New Millennium and New Dawn agreements went ahead, the Innu in Matimekush Lac John would be left with no land other than their reserve land, which is owned by Canada and administered by the Department of Aboriginal Affairs.

After the dissolution of the Conseil Attikamekw-Montagnais in 1994, the Innu resident in Central Quebec and those who live in the two villages of Sheshatshiu and Natuashish in Labrador conducted separate negotiations with the federal and provincial governments. Although negotiations with the Innu of the Ashuanipi Corporation and later the Strategic Alliance in Quebec foundered on the question of extinguishment of land rights, the elected leaders and negotiators for the Innu Nation in Labrador began to entertain the possibility that it was better to settle with the government and receive at least some recognition of their land rights together with a brighter economic future and a degree of self-determination. This was a negotiating table to which the Innu who live in Quebec, but who had maintained and asserted land rights in Labrador, were invited – but again they refused to attend as they did not wish to compromise their title to the land.

The land claims settlement

Under the terms of the New Dawn Agreement in Principle (AIP), the Innu resident in Labrador are called upon to give up 90 per cent of the land in Labrador shared by all Innu in return for which they alone will receive C$115 million, made up as follows:

- C$85 million in compensation

- C$10 million for economic development

- C$10 million for a training and capacity fund

- C$10 million for a heritage fund.

By the time of ratification of the AIP, this overall figure had risen to C$117 million.[3] By deliberate design, rather than identify the land which is being ceded to the governments, the AIP is couched in terms of the land which the Innu will keep – masking the fact that the compensation offered in no way represents the value of the land and resources which are being signed away. If the representatives of the governments and their commercial partners had explained that the compensation was in full and final settlement for the loss of 90 per cent of Innu lands and that the Innu would only have limited control over the remaining 10 per cent, the outcome of the referendum might have been very different.

The summary of the agreement makes clear that the Innu are still negotiating for a higher compensation payment to include an amount for Canada's failure to fund their communities adequately since 1949 when Newfoundland and Labrador joined the Confederation. They are also seeking priority of access to federal contracts in addition to the limited priority they have been granted over Newfoundland and Labrador and Nalcor[4] contracts.

While giving up approximately 90 per cent of the Innu ancestral lands, the Innu beneficiaries of the AIP will retain 5,000 square miles of Labrador Innu Lands (known as 'LIL') over which an Innu government, to be created on the signing of the Final Agreement, will have effective control but no ownership of subsurface rights or rights to nuclear materials. The Innu beneficiaries will have rights to be consulted over development of subsurface interests on the basis of the definition of 'consult' discussed below. Such future exploitation will be subject to Impacts and Benefits Agreements, for which responsibility lies with the corporations.

This land is included within the Labrador Innu Settlement Area (known as 'LISA') together with another 9,000 square miles over which the Innu beneficiaries have limited rights including priority in hunting and fishing.[5]

3   AIP, Clause 23.3.1.

4   'Nalcor' is the Newfoundland and Labrador Corporation, which is the corporate arm of the province responsible for development on the New Dawn lands.

5   Defined in the AIP as 'the exercise by Participants [Innu beneficiaries] of the rights to Harvest Wildlife up to the full level required to satisfy the domestic requirements of Participants and Innu communal needs'.

The level of hunting and fishing permitted will, in the event of a dispute, be decided by a committee made up of representatives of the province and the Innu.

Already there are disputes between the Newfoundland Labrador government and the Innu who live in the two Labrador villages concerning the weakness of conservation measures proposed by the provincial government which take no account of the destructive nature of sports hunting, particularly of caribou.[6] Should other aboriginal groups assert their rights to hunt in LISA, the Newfoundland Labrador government will consult with the future Innu government before such rights are acknowledged. This places the Innu resident in Quebec in the same position in which they find themselves with the Naskapi over hunting and fishing rights in Quebec. The future Innu government will have the right to be consulted when applications are made for sports hunters' and outfitters' applications for hunting licences in LISA. They will also have the right of first refusal when new commercial wildlife operations are proposed.

When the New Dawn Agreement was explained to the Innu resident in Labrador, the PowerPoint presentation used at the poorly attended information meetings explained that 'a significant portion of the AIP is dedicated to defining the remaining rights to "harvesting" [i.e. hunting], land use, consultation and process'. What it fails to make clear is that such clauses severely restrict or extinguish existing rights. The determinedly upbeat tone of the presentation is negated by the language of the AIP itself. It is open to question whether, in the minds of the Innu attending the meetings, the impression would have been left that they retained rights over all their former lands.

The proposed Innu government will have the right to be consulted over further development. Existing third-party rights over both LIL and LISA lands are preserved. Rights to create further easements necessary for transmission lines and for access to subsurface rights are reserved to the provincial government.

In addition, the Innu beneficiaries have access for non-commercial hunting in the new Mealy Mountains National Park.

The Lower Churchill Falls project

The commercial aspects of the land claims settlement are contained in separate agreements. According to the Impacts and Benefits Agreements summary circulated before ratification of the AIP, the project will comprise two dams, one at Muskrat Falls and one at Gull Island, together with the transmission lines between them. There will also be high-voltage alternating transmission lines from Gull Island to the Strait of Belle Isle and from Gull Island to the Labrador border with Quebec.

6   'Innu Strategic Alliance clarify points', *CNW Telbec*, 17 March 2010.

The Gull Island power station, which now may never be built for economic reasons, will be located about 100 kilometres west of Sheshatshiu and will include a rockfill dam 325 feet high and 4,275 feet long. There will be an approach channel, intake, penstocks, turbines, generators, a tailrace, a spillway and a discharge channel. Its production capacity will be 2,250 megawatts, producing 12,000,000 megawatt-hours per annum and providing electricity for a million people.

The Gull Island reservoir will entail the flooding of the Churchill River from Gull Island to the Upper Churchill Project, a distance of 140 miles, with a projected rise of six inches which could increase to 16 feet in flood conditions. The surface area of the reservoir will be approximately 80 square miles.

The Muskrat Falls power station, sited approximately 20 miles from Sheshatshiu, will be a roller-compacted concrete dam comprising two sections, one north of the river approximately 104 feet high and 1,400 feet long and one south of the river 95 feet high and 1,055 feet long. This will include the same ancillary structures as at Gull Island. The Muskrat Falls reservoir will flood the Churchill River from the Muskrat Falls Dam to the Gull Island Dam, a distance of 37 miles. The normal rise will be six inches but could increase to 18 feet under flood conditions. The surface area of the reservoir will be 38 square miles.

The New Dawn Agreement in Principle

The New Dawn AIP was ratified by the Innu resident in Natuashish and Sheshatshiu in a vote in November 2011. The full 480-page text of the agreement was not available to those who voted, nor was the 80-page summary which had had limited circulation beforehand, including with the proviso that it was not to be shown to anyone outside the two Innu communities because of its 'commercial sensitivity'. This, in itself, precluded the Innu who were called upon to ratify the AIP from taking independent advice beforehand. Therefore, 2,500 Innu in the two villages in Labrador voted, on very little information, to sign away all Innu land in Labrador with the exception of small parcels which are the traditional lands of the influential families whose members were signatories to the AIP.[7]

Although the project is only now ready to become operational, separate commercial agreements (Impacts and Benefits Agreements) have already been entered into with Nalcor, the Newfoundland Labrador government's commercial arm, which will oversee the hydro-electric development at Muskrat Falls and Gull Island. The terms of these agreements reflect those in the 1999 Paix des Braves discussed in Chapter 13, but it is important to note that these are discretionary terms such that the Innu enterprises which take up the commercial contracts must be competitive with mainstream Canadian businesses. Employees must meet standards of competence based on provincial standards of education, rather than the inferior federal education and

7   Discussion of Maps 4 and 5 with Professor Colin Samson.

qualifications that Innu receive. Further, the Impacts and Benefits Agreements should be read in light of the qualification that these terms only apply 'where reasonable' – and of the fact that after the initial construction few permanent jobs will be available.

The official versions of both the summary and the full AIP are in English and French, not in Innu-Aimun. The burden of explaining the full implications of the agreement rests with the Innu themselves. There are no equivalent translations of the very technical terminology in Innu-Aimun. It has been left to a member of the Natuashish Band Council to translate the full agreement into the one language understood by all those called on to ratify it.[8] And, as will be seen below, the language of the AIP is not even comprehensible to fluent English speakers. The limited explanations that were given took place in poorly-attended public meetings in the two Labrador villages, and were based on the short and inaccurate PowerPoint presentation cited above.[9]

Yet there was a very high turnout for the ratification poll and a near-unanimous vote in favour of ratification. Anecdotal evidence suggests that each vote in favour was bought with a 'bonus' of C$5,000. This is supported by the following evidence.

The minutes of the meeting of the trustees of the Teshipitakan Fund,[10] a fund set up for future generations from the compensation paid for the Voisey's Bay nickel mine sited on Innu land, record authorisation of payments of the same amount in the following resolution: 'The Trust hereby agrees to apply for a loan for approximately $12,500,000 from the Bank of Montreal to provide a per capita payout of $5,000 to each member of the Innu Nation.'

The meeting of the trustees was held by teleconference and took place on 6 July 2011, less than a week after the New Dawn ratification vote. No reason is given in these minutes for the $5,000 payouts, which would have been of the utmost significance to households where the average income, according to the latest census, was C$12,000 per annum. It would appear that money intended to be held for future beneficiaries was taken from this unrelated trust fund, for no stated purpose which could be said to advantage those future beneficiaries.

---

8   Meeting with George Rich, Chief of Natuashish, June 2011.

9   Copies of this presentation and the summary referred to above were sent to Professor Colin Samson and passed on to the writer in confidence. A number (five or six) of Innu present in Sheshatshiu and Natuashish at the time of the information meeting have said that little information was available on which to make the decision whether to ratify. See also the simplistic explanation of the AIP given on the website of the lawyers representing the Innu Nation at oktlaw.com/labrador-innu-sign.

10   See 'Some Sheshatshiu Innu fear millions will be misspent', *CBC News*, 3 Mar. 2012. This article says that the NL Auditor General concluded he had no evidence that the money had been misspent – there was not enough detail in the previous year's accounts.

There was insufficient liquidity in the trust fund, such that the payments had to come from a loan. The payments were to be made to each resident of the two Labrador villages whether adult or child, so a family of five, for example, would receive C$25,000. By contrast, an earlier application for $24,000,000 from the same fund, for housing, did not proceed when such a purpose was declared by the trustees' lawyers to be outside the scope of the fund unless such a request resulted from a natural disaster. Here, a loan secured on the trust's assets was taken out to benefit existing adult members of the Innu Nation who were clearly not its intended beneficiaries. The trustees were advised that this present loan of C$12,500,000 would preclude them from coming back for any future advance from the trust fund.

It was never stated that the purpose of the C$5,000 payments was to fund a bonus for voting for the AIP ratification.[11] However, the timing of the payments, coming so soon after the vote itself, together with enquiries made of Matnen Benuen, one of the election monitors for the vote, who was asked specifically by Innu arriving to vote when the payments would be made, makes it very probable. Further, Gerald M. Sider notes that payments of C$5,000 each were made to the Labrador Inuit Association members on their ratification vote.[12] Payments of C$3,000 were also made to the Innu of Unamen Shipu (La Romaine) to secure their agreement to Hydro-Québec transmission lines across their land.[13]

Questions thus arise as to whether the AIP was validly ratified by an electorate who were kept in ignorance of both the full implications of the overall agreement, and the nature of the advice offered by their consultants and lawyers. This situation also raises the larger question of whether there was proper consultation, and whether it can be said that ratification, in the circumstances, can truly be described as the free, prior and informed consent of the Innu people.

There was no attempt whatsoever to consult the Innu represented by the Strategic Alliance even though the Newfoundland Labrador government was well aware of their claims to land in Labrador. This duty was not discharged by the initial invitation to negotiate, turned down on the question of extinguishment of rights, because there was no attempt to accommodate this requirement.

The primary question which arises with regard to the New Dawn AIP is whether there was sufficient consultation to enable the ratification vote to stand as the free, prior and informed consent to the cession of Innu land for

11   B. Cabana, 'Lies, Bribes, Harper and Dunderdale – the Evidence', 21 May 2013, rocksolidpolitics.blogspot.com/search/label/Harper.

12   Sider, *Skin for Skin*, p. 209. For a similar scenario, see L. Gehl, 'Deeply flawed process around Algonquin land claim agreement', *Policy Options*, 15 Nov. 2016.

13   J.-L. Lavallée, 'Des Innus soulignent le "courage" de l'ADQ', 22 Nov. 2011.

the purposes of the Lower Churchill Falls hydro-electric project, and whether the governments acted honourably throughout the Comprehensive Land Claims process.

Depriving the Innu of the vast majority of their land, over which the governments have been in negotiation for 33 years, must fall at the furthest end of McLachlin CJ's spectrum in the *Tsilhqot'in* case (see Chapter 8). The implications of the settlement are fundamentally life-changing to the Innu, whose subsistence and identity continue to lie in the use and protection of the land. Once the hydro-electric project is completed, the land will be lost to them forever and, as the Innu who live in Quebec continue to maintain, no price could or should be put on the land for which they are responsible.

These circumstances require that, in order for the honour of the Crown to be maintained, all Innu, not just those who live in Labrador, should have been consulted from the outset on the project. When those who live in Quebec raised objections, these should have been taken seriously and addressed. Their votes should have counted in the ratification of the AIP. Instead the governments, despite knowing that the Innu resident in Quebec had asserted their rights to land in Labrador, completely ignored them after they refused to join in the negotiations as a defence of their land rights. In pursuing this course, neither the governments nor the Innu resident in Labrador acted with honour.

Second, under the possible justifications listed by Lamer CJ in the *Delgamuukw* case, aboriginal land can only be taken for specific projects. The land demanded by the governments under the terms of the New Dawn Agreement extends far beyond that actually required for the Lower Churchill Falls project and includes land for which there is no immediate use, and thus its inclusion cannot be justified. This requirement is obviated by a negotiated settlement.

Instead of the Crown's insistence on the extinguishment of all land rights, according to these precedents and legal principles, there should have been a genuine attempt to find a way of proceeding with the project without extinguishing the rights, either through shared ownership or through a lease which acknowledged that the underlying title to the lands affected remained with all Innu, not just those resident in Labrador. The governments should also have considered the possibility of leaving full title to the land with the Innu, or a joint title, and, if this were not done, should have provided reasons why this was not possible. Any of these courses of action might have brought the Innu resident in Quebec back to the negotiation table.

Equally problematic is the fact that not only was there little attempt to ensure that all Innu called upon to ratify the agreement were fully informed, but the full agreement was not even circulated within the Innu villages. There was no opportunity for individual Innu to take independent advice. The negotiation process was conducted behind closed doors and, as stated above, availability of the documentation necessary for fully informed independent advice was not made available.[14]

As will be seen below from the discussion of individual clauses in the agreement, clauses which were hardly touched on, either in the PowerPoint presentation or in the summary of the AIP, were explained in favourable terms before the vote but were then rewritten in the AIP, with severe implications for the Innu. There can be no prior consent when the text of the agreement is not available to the beneficiaries until after ratification – and this in itself is sufficient to nullify ratification.

Although the United Nations Declaration on the Rights of Indigenous Peoples (UNDRIP) was endorsed by Canada prior to the signing of the AIP, it does not appear either that the Innu were advised as to its significance or that it had any impact on the final content. Although the notes accompanying the agreement leave many of the clauses open to negotiation, no mention is made of UNDRIP. Because its provisions are parallel to the fiduciary duties assumed in the Royal Proclamation of 1763, even before endorsing UNDRIP the Crown already had an obligation to deal with indigenous peoples involved in land claims negotiations according to the standards that UNDRIP imposes. At the very least, UNDRIP provides an independent benchmark for the conduct of governments dealing with indigenous peoples.

Perhaps the most pressing point of concern is that the AIP is stated to have no binding legal effect, but work is nearly completed at Muskrat Falls. Flooding of the land has already begun. It would appear that this is yet another land grab with no agreement in place. Although the Innu were given powers in the AIP to monitor any works on the project, the area has been fenced off and access denied to Innu except as workers. Signature of the Final Agreement is still pending and thus Nalcor has no rights on the land, only personal rights under the Impacts and Benefits Agreement it signed with the Innu Nation of Labrador. The Innu are in a stronger position than the James Bay Cree and Inuit because their rights to the land have been recognised through the negotiation process. This is particularly important in the current financial climate, when Newfoundland and Labrador settler Canadians are beginning to question the huge cost of the project[15] and particularly at a time when there is a decline in the need for electricity in the United States. The majority of the million people whose electricity needs will be supplied by the project live in the United States, not Canada. This could mean that at this late stage the entire project could be abandoned and the landscape will have been destroyed for no purpose.

14 See Samson, *A World*, p. 90.
15 See, for example: 'Credibility put to test', *Huffington Post*, 5 March 2013, and 'Innu Nation angry as former chief paid $1m in two years', Joe O'Connor, *National Post*, 13 July 2012.

When invoking the honour of the Crown, the Supreme Court's stated aim is to promote reconciliation. In the conduct of negotiations for the AIP and subsequent incursions onto what is acknowledged to be Innu land, the federal and Newfoundland Labrador governments have fallen short of this standard. The result has been what the courts feared – mistrust of the governments and their commercial partners and dissension within the two villages concerned. The way in which the federal and Newfoundland Labrador governments have failed to address the claims of the Innu who live in Quebec exemplifies the sharp dealing in which the Crown should have no part. With no information or consultation over the legitimate claims of the Innu resident in Quebec to lands in Labrador, there is no question that the governments have, in the words of Chief Justice McLachlin, 'cavalierly run roughshod' over the rights of the Innu.

The terms of the Agreement in Principle

Turning to the AIP itself, the definition of what constitutes consultation given in the New Dawn AIP reads as follows:

'Consult' means to provide:

To the Person being consulted, notice of a matter to be decided in sufficient form and detail to allow that Person to prepare its views of the matter;

A reasonable period of time in which the Person being consulted may prepare its views on the matter, and an opportunity to present its view to the Person obliged to consult;

Full and fair consideration by the Person obliged to consult of any views presented.

There is a further provision that written reasons must be given for failure to act upon any requirements that are not substantially incorporated by the developer.

Clause 2.7 of the AIP provides that the agreement exhaustively sets out Innu rights to be consulted and further that they will have no right to challenge the definition through the courts. Not only do these provisions fall short of the obligations to consult imposed by the Supreme Court of Canada in *Delgamuukw*, let alone the more rigorous analysis in *Haida Nation v British Columbia (Ministry of Forests)* and *Taku River Tlingit First Nation v British Columbia (Assessment Director)*, they do not come close to Article 19 of UNDRIP, which says: 'States shall consult and co-operate in good faith with the indigenous people concerned through their own representative institutions in order to obtain the *free, prior and informed consent* before adopting and

implementing legislative or administrative measures that may affect them.'
(emphasis added)[16]

This article would allow all Innu to challenge the validity of the ratification
of the agreement. They were never given the opportunity to scrutinise the full
document, in their own language, and to seek informed independent advice.

Yet, as discussed in Chapter 8, the significance of the duty to consult as
laid down in modern treaties has been approved by the Supreme Court of
Canada in *Beckman v Little Salmon/Carmacks First Nation*.[17] The definition of
'consult' found in the Little Salmon/Carmacks First Nation Final Agreement[18]
considered in the case is exactly the same as that in the New Dawn AIP. This in
itself calls into question the governments' willingness to negotiate freely with
the indigenous peoples whose land they are taking and to deal with each group
according to their individual circumstances.

The interpretative presumption in favour of the weaker party is specifically
excluded in the New Dawn AIP. Squatters' rights in the land are also excluded,[19]
except for those of third parties.

Should the federal and Newfoundland Labrador governments ever negotiate
over the New Dawn lands with the Innu represented by the Strategic Alliance,
it is unlikely that the terms offered to them would be any different from those
offered to the Innu Nation in Labrador. There is a striking similarity between
the terms of all the land claims agreements which have been the subject of
litigation. All that the Strategic Alliance can hope for is a new treaty making
them parties to the New Dawn Agreement, or monetary compensation for
the loss of their lands. Thus the terms of the New Dawn Agreement are of
importance to the Strategic Alliance even though these terms were negotiated
over their heads – because they would be required to accept similar terms.

Indemnity and release

The [Labrador] Innu government to be set up under the Final Agreement must
give an indemnity and release for 'all past claims known or unknown relating
to any act or omission prior to the agreement ...'

This is accompanied by an indemnity from all costs and damages arising
from any Innu challenge to the agreement. In the summary 'Innu' is defined as
only those Innu who live in Labrador. The definition is still under negotiation
for the Final Agreement, since clearly such a narrow definition is absurd. The
terms of the AIP make it clear that only Innu beneficiaries in the two Labrador

---

16 The full text of the United Nations Declaration on the Rights of Indigenous
Peoples is reproduced in Appendix B.
17 [2010] SCC 53.
18 *Little Salmon/Carmacks First Nation Implementation Plan.*
19 The rights of anyone who has occupied the land for 12 years or more without
objection from the landowner to claim title to the land.

villages are included within the definition. Thus Innu from both sides of the border face an effective deterrent from asserting their rights to challenge the clauses of which they had no knowledge, the PowerPoint briefing having been so restricted. Should they take action, any compensation available to them through their court action must be paid by the Innu Nation of Labrador.

The mechanics of the indemnity were explained in the PowerPoint presentation to the public meetings in Natuashish and Sheshatshiu in technical, unfamiliar English. It appears that these presentations took place after the terms of the AIP had been decided.[20] Again, they call into question the honour of the Crown and the integrity of the lawyers who allowed them to stand, the more so since the release and indemnity apply to all claims for compensation for the damage caused by the presence of methyl mercury and PCBs, which are addressed within the initial payment. The stated purpose of the release and indemnity is that the payments to the Innu under the Impacts and Benefits Agreements discussed below are in full and final settlement of all amounts to be paid but, as in all projects of this magnitude, there may be instances of negligence on the part of the corporations for which, under the general law of tort, liability cannot be excluded but nevertheless has been specifically excluded in this AIP.

Since 'equity looks to the substance rather than the form', a court might accept a challenge from disaffected Innu on the grounds that these provisions oust the jurisdiction of the court. Nevertheless, it is more likely that the court would take Deschamps J's view discussed in Chapter 9 that the Innu were free to negotiate such terms and cannot renege on them. In any event, the Innu Nation would have to pay any compensation, not the governments or corporations.

Extinguishment

Only six of the 28 PowerPoint slides are devoted to explanation of the 480-page AIP. The rest are devoted to the Impacts and Benefits Agreements to be entered into with the hydro-electricity corporations. One line is devoted to the concept of 'certainty'. In the final ancillary clauses in the summary can be found the following paragraph: 'The Final Agreement will detail the scope and extent of the release that the Innu will give to Newfoundland and Labrador and Canada in return for the constitutionally protected rights and the benefits set out for the Innu.'

In the AIP this provision becomes:

2.12.1 This Agreement will:

a. constitute the full and final settlement of the aboriginal rights of Innu in Canada, except in Quebec; and

20 Conversation with Anthony Jenkinson, resident of Sheshatshiu, Oct. 2011.

b. … exhaustively set out the rights of Innu in Canada, except in Quebec, that are recognized and affirmed by s35 of the Constitution Act 1982.

What is described as a 'release' in the summary becomes an extinguishment of all Innu rights in Labrador other than those specifically provided for in the Final Agreement. It should be noted that, under this provision, the Innu in Sheshatshiu and Natuashish are still free to pursue their claims to land signed away under the James Bay Agreement. But at the public meetings, the implications of the release and indemnity and the extinguishment clause were linked to the Impacts and Benefits Agreements (IBAs) rather than the land claims settlement.

Further expropriation

The summary available to community leaders on which the ratification vote was based mentioned that the boundaries of the LIL could be 'adjusted' to accommodate the needs of the Lower Churchill Falls project. It omitted to mention that the governments and corporations could expropriate a further 12 per cent of the LIL and could carry out further development on it. If this were ever taken before the courts, there is a danger that, under *Little Salmon/Carmacks*, the Innu would be held to be reneging on the Final Agreement if they raised the inadequate standard of consultation undertaken by the governments.

Warranties given by the Innu Nation

Under the AIP, the Innu Nation gives a warranty that:

2.25.1: It represents Innu and

In respect of the matters dealt with in the Agreement, the Innu Nation has the authority to enter, and it enters, into the Agreement on behalf of all Innu who have or may exercise any aboriginal rights, including aboriginal title, in Canada, or who may make any claim in respect of these rights.

It is difficult to see how the signatories could give this warranty in light of the secrecy maintained over the terms of the agreement, the lack of opportunity for individuals to seek independent advice and the attempts to influence the outcome of the ratification vote by incentives. The purpose of this clause is to place liability for any failure to seek the consent of a wider set of Innu voters on the shoulders of the Innu Nation and free the governments from any further liability after payment of the sums due under the land claims settlement.

Ratification of the Final Agreement will be conclusive proof of the consent of the Innu (as defined in the AIP) to the terms of the agreement. A vote in favour by 51 per cent of those entitled who actually vote will be sufficient ratification.

The above provision means that, if only 25 per cent of those entitled actually vote, the agreement would be ratified – hardly a resounding consent from the communities involved. In the vote on the AIP, however, this point proved to be nugatory, since the provision of a C$5,000 bonus payable for each vote ensured that turnout was very high.

Royalties

The Innu will receive a royalty of 25 per cent of the profits from the exercise of subsurface rights on LIL, and a smaller proportion of the annual revenues from subsurface resources from the LISA on the basis of 50 per cent of the first C$2 million dollars of revenue and 5 per cent of any revenues above that figure; and this despite the fact, as we shall see below, that the Innu are entitled under UNDRIP to the ownership of subsurface rights.

The military

There is a provision for access to the Innu lands by military personnel:

> 17A.5.3 Canadian forces personnel may enter, cross or remain on Labrador Innu Lands to carry out activities related to national defence and security in accordance with Federal Law; [Members of foreign armed forces serving with, or under the operational control of the Canadian forces may enter and cross Labrador Innu Lands to carry out training activities.]

The words in square brackets indicate text still under negotiation. This provision has been hotly disputed by the Innu beneficiaries. Overflying of Innu aboriginal land has been the subject of protests and demonstrations. The notes to the AIP reveal that Canada is insisting on that part of the clause which is shown in brackets. If this provision were removed, LIL would instead be subject to the national law to which all private landowners are subject with regard to access by the military.

Archaeology and burial sites

Before any archaeological activity takes place in the LISA, a permit must be obtained from a permitting authority, whose membership and constitution have yet to be negotiated but which represents the province, with a duty to consult the Innu government. The Innu government will control access to archaeology within LIL, with a duty to consult the provincial archaeological permitting authority.

For Innu burial sites, the Innu government must provide the permitting authority with a list of known sites in LIL and LISA and they can add to this list if more sites are discovered. However, if a site does not appear on that list, there will be no duty to consult the Innu before the site is disturbed. I would suggest that the honour of the Crown requires that the Innu must give their free, prior and informed consent whenever such a site is discovered, whether it appears on the list on not. However, the AIP does specify that when such remains are discovered by a permit holder, work must cease until permitted by the permitting authority – not the Innu government, which will only have rights of consultation. While title to archaeological material in LIL is vested in the Innu government, title to such material in the (much larger) LISA vests in the provincial government, even when that material is Innu. One effect of this provision is that since the land was shared by all Innu and other indigenous peoples, the Innu represented by the Strategic Alliance have no say in the fate of the archaeological remains and burial sites of their own ancestors. The AIP does at least bind the province to undertake to use reasonable efforts to ensure that artefacts held in collections in other provinces are repatriated and to facilitate access to such archaeological and ethnographic material.

Nalcor promised to clear the site of archaeological artefacts before work began at Muskrat Falls but, as I walked the old portage route towards the falls in November 2011 with Anthony Jenkinson, a local activist and archaeologist, he pointed to the many flags where he had found items which the Nalcor archaeologists had missed, and he found yet more as we continued along the edge of the lake at the head of the falls. More than 40,000 artefacts have been recovered from the ancient campsites which date back 2,000–3,500 years, making this a site of major importance.[21]

The Impacts and Benefits Agreements

While the province agrees to ensure that no development will be permitted without an IBA in place, the agreements themselves are between the development corporations and the Innu government. However, before granting development licences, the province must consult with the Innu government in accordance with the definition of 'consult' discussed above. Where the province awards development or ancillary contracts, they are subject to the same provisions as those imposed on the development corporations.

The stated aims of the Impacts and Benefits Agreements, according to the PowerPoint presentation, are:

- to be the means by which the Innu receive revenue from the Lower Churchill Falls project;

- to provide them with employment and training benefits and business opportunities; and

- to enable them to participate in environmental protection and management.

For Nalcor, the benefits are said to be:

---

21   'Artifacts recovered at Muskrat Falls', *Canadian Press* news agency, 21 Nov. 2013.

- aboriginal certainty and stability for the project; and
- the Innu release and indemnity for the effects of the project, which are stipulated to be irrevocable.

This release and indemnity is the first of the significant terms of the IBAs to be mentioned.

The presentation then lists the employment, training and business opportunities to be made available to the Innu, but fails to mention the provisos which effectively exclude many individuals and businesses from participating because of their lack of education, training and competitiveness. Targets are set and education and training opportunities and funding are promised, but the fact that the Innu will be competing with non-Innu is underplayed or ignored. These provisions are expanded in the summaries of the IBA and the Upper Churchill Redress Agreement (UCRA) which were circulated before ratification and where the qualified nature of these terms is clearer – for example, it is stated that Nalcor will provide jobs only to 'qualified Innu', 'if there are jobs available'. If there are no qualified Innu, Nalcor can hire whom it chooses. Moreover, union requirements will have priority over the employment provisions in the IBA. Innu employees will be entitled to only two weeks' paid leave per annum, to which they can add a further two weeks' 'cultural leave', but which would be unpaid. This would mean that, added to the time off in the normal work round, Innu employees could take six weeks in order to go hunting or pursue other cultural activities. In addition, the company agrees to provide workplace practices which are sufficiently flexible for traditional Innu activities.

So far as Innu businesses are concerned, Nalcor must use them for contracts worth a minimum of C$266 million for the planning and construction works at Gull Island and for at least C$134 million at Muskrat Falls; otherwise Nalcor must pay penalties – but these are small enough to make it commercially viable to fail in this obligation. In any event, the criteria on which it is possible to find an Innu business unqualified for the work are wide enough to make this obligation meaningless.

So far as environmental management is concerned, Nalcor has the final decision-making power, after having consulted the Innu. This means that the polluter is judge and jury over its own activities. There is provision for the company to exclude the Innu from areas where works are being carried out, and this includes imposing hunting restrictions. This appears to be the clause on which Nalcor is presently relying, ignoring the fact that the AIP is not the Final Agreement and therefore has no binding force – so the land on which they are encroaching is currently still Innu land.

In managing the environment, Innu traditional environmental knowledge will only be taken into account 'where it is relevant'.

Payments due to the Innu under the IBA will be paid into a trust whose beneficiaries will be the Natuashish and Sheshatshiu First Nations and the Innu Nation. The trustees will be members of the Innu Nation. Should the beneficiaries sue Nalcor, the trustees will indemnify the corporation to the amount of any sums awarded.

As with the AIP, ratification of the IBA took place without the voters having access to the full agreements. A key provision is that the Innu Nation must collaborate with Nalcor in preventing any demonstration against the works carried out and must assist the corporation in fighting any claim against it from an Innu individual. As will be seen in Chapter 18, the Innu took a relatively minor part in the protests against the Muskrat Falls project in 2017 precisely because of this clause.

Provisions for Innu participation in environmental management just meet the standards approved in the case of *Mikisew Cree First Nation v Canada (Minister of Canadian Heritage)*, because they provide for a joint Nalcor–Innu environmental committee, Innu environmental monitors and a dispute resolution process.

Under the separate Upper Churchill Redress Agreement, the Innu resident in Labrador receive financial compensation for the impacts of the Upper Churchill Falls development on their aboriginal rights and for adverse environmental effects. In return Nalcor and the province receive a similar release and indemnity as in the New Dawn Agreement. Up until 2041, the Innu receive an indexed annual settlement payment. After 2041 they receive 3 per cent of the dividends received by Nalcor. The summary of the UCRA also provides for the settlement payments and dividend share to be paid into a trust with the same indemnity provisions applying to the Churchill Falls (Labrador) Company – in which the Newfoundland Labrador government has a 68 per cent shareholding.[22] Under UCRA, residents of Natuashish and Sheshatshiu will also be entitled to free power up to a limit of 10,200 kWh per annum.

In this document, the reasons for the indemnity clause are explained more fully. First, the annual payments are intended to compensate for losses incurred by the Innu who live in Labrador and any further compensation awarded by a court would mean the Churchill Falls (Labrador) Company would be subject to double jeopardy. UCRA also states expressly that, with the exception of harms caused by methyl mercury, the Churchill Falls (Labrador) Company will be liable for damage and personal injury which is caused by the company or its employees. However, payments due under this agreement are not subject to independent scrutiny; they are certified by the company's own senior financial officer.

Included in the presentation are terms for the resolution of outstanding electricity bills in the two Labrador villages. Outstanding bills for individual

22 Upper Churchill Redress Agreement, Summary, p. 1.

Innu are to be settled by a deduction of 50 per cent of the outstanding amount from the payments under the IBAs, and 50 per cent from UCRA. However, despite the use of their land, it is clearly stated that they will be treated as any other Newfoundland and Labrador Hydro residential customers and no discount afforded them.

What does the *Tsilhqot'in* judgment mean for the Innu?

The title of the Innu Nation to land all over Labrador has already been acknowledged by the federal and provincial governments, so they do not have to establish title to land. However, they have already agreed to sign over the majority of their land to the federal government in an agreement which the government will claim was negotiated at arm's length by authorised representatives of the Innu. They will also say that they have the free, prior and informed consent of the beneficiaries of the agreement. Therefore, the following appear to be the grounds upon which the validity of the New Dawn Agreement can be challenged:

- If the text of the full agreement was withheld from the majority of the voters, their vote cannot be on the basis of fully informed consent.

- It is unclear whether there was genuine endorsement of the signatories by the Innu they represented.

- Bearing in mind that negotiations are still at the AIP stage, the land already flooded for hydro-electricity dams cannot be said to be available to succeeding generations of Innu, despite this commitment to future Innu being a key plank of the agreement.

The judge in *Tsilhqot'in Nation v British Columbia* spells out very clearly that free, prior and informed consent is required for all incursions onto aboriginal land *unless* such activities can be justified 'by a compelling and substantial public purpose and are not inconsistent with the Crown's fiduciary duty', in which case the duty is to consult and accommodate where possible the requirements of the aboriginal group concerned. Hydro-electric development is specifically mentioned as a justifiable use of the land by the governments.

Under the existing law, the lack of information available to voters and some irregularities in the voting process could invalidate the ratification – but the *Tsilhqot'in* case does not add much where a valid treaty is already in place. Upon signing of the Final Agreement, land will cease to be aboriginal land unless a successful challenge can be made to the question of valid ratification.

With regard to the James Bay lands, however, Innu title to the affected lands was ignored and then unilaterally extinguished by the governments. There was a strong *prima facie* case for aboriginal title to those lands, and thus at the very least a duty to consult in good faith and where possible accommodate; and, under UNDRIP, a requirement of free, prior and informed consent. In the circumstances, the governments realise that they have a much freer hand if they persuade indigenous parties to negotiate a treaty instead.

So far as the Innu of the Strategic Alliance are concerned (newly named also as the Innu Nation as a separate organisation representing the Innu who live in Central Quebec), however, the *Tsilhqot'in* judgment has more to offer. Incursions have been made onto both the James Bay lands and the Labrador lands to which they have laid claim. The federal and provincial governments have negotiated with them on the premise that they have aboriginal title to the disputed lands and, should they go to the court for a declaration of aboriginal title, then following the criteria laid down in *Tsilhqot'in*, their claim will be validated – and not only to lands where they are settled, but also to lands over which they migrate. Without their free, prior and informed consent to the surrender of lands to which they are entitled, in principle they could overturn the New Dawn Agreement and also have their rights to the James Bay lands recognised and compensated. Since the governments must take reasonable steps to accommodate the requirements of the aboriginal groups, they must cease to insist on extinguishment of all rights other than those contained in the agreements. For example, lands could be leased by the aboriginal group or held in joint ownership.

The Uashat mak Mani-utenam and Matimekush Lac John Innu First Nations have already challenged the Iron Ore Company, following conclusion of an agreement with the Innu Nation of Labrador for exploitation of lands which are the traditional territory of the challengers. They filed legal proceedings against the Iron Ore Company on 18 March 2013 on the same grounds as those applied in *Tsilhqot'in*.[23]

The *Tsilhqot'in* decision has been criticised by Professor Robert A. Williams.[24] He points out that 'what the court is saying is that your government can come in and infringe on your title as long as it has a compelling justification'. This suggests that, if indigenous peoples such as the Innu in Labrador settle a land claim under the present system, principles of justification do not even apply. As has been seen in the dissenting judgments in *Little Salmon/Carmacks* the indigenous group will be held to what they have signed.

The only way for indigenous rights to be fully upheld is to go to court for a declaration in the wake of *Tsilhqot'in*. Whether any court would be prepared to rule that the justification argument approved in *R v Sparrow* was spurious is problematic but McLachlin CJ, by linking justification so explicitly to section 35 (1) of the Constitution Act 1982 has created an opening for such an argument.

---

23   Canadian Newswire, 1 Aug. 2014.
24   'American law professor: Aboriginal title decision is no game changer', 23 July 2014, thechronicaalherald/novascotia/1224914-american-law.

After *Tsilhqot'in*, the Harper government backed off from the Comprehensive Land Claims process. It is claimed that the government is now focussing its efforts on assimilation of indigenous governance into the federal and provincial structures. Its principal purpose is to 'terminate the constitutionally protected and internationally recognized Inherent Aboriginal and Treaty Rights of First Nations'.[25]

This is borne out by an article on the *Guardian* website by Martin Lukacs[26] which reports that, since 2008, the Department of Aboriginal Affairs and Northern Development Canada has been trying to evaluate the 'significant risks' posed to Canadian plans to attract C$650 billion of investment to the extractive industries on indigenous lands. The government was seeking to evade Supreme Court decisions such as *Tsilhqot'in*. In the article, Arthur Manuel, chair of the Indigenous Network on Economies and Trade, is quoted as follows: 'The Harper government is committed to a policy of extinguishing indigenous peoples' land rights, instead of a policy of recognition and co-existence. They are trying to contain the threat that our rights pose to business-as-usual and the expansion of dirty energy projects. But our legal challenges and direct actions are creating economic uncertainty and risk, raising the heat on government to change its current policies.'

It is further pointed out by Manuel that 'native land claims scare the hell out of investors'. In the same article, Martin Lukacs claims that the federal government 'has spent far more fighting aboriginal litigation than any other legal issue – including $106 million in 2013, a sum that has grown over the last several years'. At the same time, Lukacs reports, the government is cutting funding to indigenous groups who seek to fight land claims. Although Liberal Prime Minister Justin Trudeau has throughout his years in office made reconciliatory approaches to the First Nations, little action has emerged to date. It would appear that the fight for land to which indigenous groups are entitled has reached a new phase. Legislation will always trump litigation and the governments' hands may soon be tied by the impending Canadian UNDRIP legislation.

One further word of warning on the effectiveness of UNDRIP, particularly relevant to the land claims process, was given when sociologist and former UN Special Rapporteur on Indigenous Peoples Rudolfo Stavenhagen criticised the negotiation process:

> Even more serious is the widespread practice of corruption in poor societies with great inequalities. Indigenous peoples are often the victims of corruption, and sometimes they become partners in corruption as well. Unless we work out the nuts and bolts of improving human rights mechanisms [UNDRIP] will remain an empty word, and it has to do with existing institutional structures, legal systems and

25 Diabo, 'Canada: Prime Minister Harper launches'.
26 Lukacs, 'Aboriginal rights a threat'.

power relationships which in turn relate to the wider social system in which Indigenous peoples are the historical victims of human rights violations to begin with.[27]

Having ratified the AIP by vote, the Innu who live in the two Labrador villages are beginning to question the terms of the New Dawn Agreement agreed over their heads, on the advice that this was the best deal they could get.[28] In particular, they note that valuable contracts are taken up by the signatories to the agreement instead of being processed by a co-operative for the benefit of all.[29] They are concerned that work is almost completed at Muskrat Falls in advance of a Final Agreement and are seeking an independent review of the full terms of an agreement which they ratified without full information as to its contents and implications.

Napess Ashini, a Sheshatshiu hunter and indigenous rights campaigner, observed:

> The New Dawn Agreement is just another Voisey's Bay Agreement, just another rip-off. A big financial benefit for just a few. Ninety per cent of us will not be getting anything, only short-term benefit for us all. Let's all THINK!!! Let's make sure that 90 per cent of us will not get the short end of the stick this time. Let's not be fooled by non-Innu consultants and legal advisers who tell us what to do. They dismantle and control our Innu history, culture, language, intellectual properties, etc. They make us weak and they want us to surrender our land to the Canadian government without resistance. The don't tell us what are [the] repercussions or ramifications in the long term. They are not our friends. I consider them as enemies. These are my comments. I will ask more questions when consultations take place in future.

It would appear that, as with the Dene,[30] who concluded a land settlement agreement in the North West Territories, those who sit at the negotiation table in Natuashish and Sheshatshiu ignored the concerns of the elders when recommending acceptance of the terms of the AIP.[31]

---

27 R. Stavenhagen, 'Making the Declaration Work', in C. Charters and R. Stavenhagen (eds.), *Making the Declaration Work: The United Nations Declaration on the Rights of Indigenous Peoples* (Copenhagen: International Working Group for Indigenous Affairs, 2009), p. 361.

28 Confidential enquiries from a number of Innu in Labrador and freely available on the 'Leadership Scandals' Facebook page.

29 See Samson, *A World*, pp. 95–7; also, Samson, 'Canada's Strategy of Dispossession: Aboriginal Land and Rights Cessions in Comprehensive Land Claims', *Canadian Journal of Law and Society*, vol. 31 (2016): 1–24, at pp. 4–6.

30 See Irlbacher-Fox, *Finding Dahshaa*, p.17.

31 See also J. Brake, 'Elder speaks out against Muskrat Falls' Innu leadership', *Newfoundland and Labrador Independent*, c. 14 Oct. 2016. The elder in question was Elizabeth, Peter Penashue's mother.

In November 2011, an individual band member challenged the validity of the recently held Band Council elections in Sheshatshiu. The matter went to court, where a federal judge ruled that elections to the Innu Nation, a public body, were subject to the court's scrutiny.[32] New elections had to be held, which produced a younger chief and Band Council members. Such an initiative marks another turning point away from the consensual governance of the elders of the Innu people, but simultaneously demonstrates a lack of faith in the Canadian Band Council system.

This brings us back to the concept of a fiduciary duty, which was applied first to those who took responsibility for the property of others, discussed in Chapters 7 and 8. Such a duty equally applies to those who represent the Innu resident in Labrador, and their lawyers and consultants. The fiduciary duty concept is scrupulous in excluding any element of unjust enrichment – however committed to their clients, no person who assumes a position of trust can benefit in any way from information or opportunities received as a result of that position except with the free, prior and informed consent of the beneficiaries. If even a single beneficiary fails to give that consent, whether through unwillingness or through incapacity, such consent is invalid.[33] This legal constraint would invalidate, for example, the use of the Voisey's Bay future beneficiaries' trust fund for the provision of the C$5,000 bonuses.

An examination of the Canadian Business Registries by Sheshatshiu resident Anthony Jenkinson shows that some of those who represented the Innu Nation have interests in the companies engaged to carry out the preliminary works on the hydro-electric project at Muskrat Falls.[34] They placed themselves ahead of those in Sheshatshiu and Natuashish who wished to tender for this work and ahead of the formation of co-operatives to take on this work for the benefit of the two communities as a whole.

Brad Cabana[35] published a list of donors to the election fund of Peter Penashue, who was instrumental in the Innu negotiations for the New Dawn Agreement and one of its signatories. Penashue was elected as Progressive Conservative MP for the region and became the first indigenous minister in the Harper administration. He was prosecuted for irregularities in the donations to his campaign and in 2013 had to resign both as minister and as MP.

Cabana's list notes the donations which were disallowed by the court. Many of these were from officers and employees of institutions with a close financial interest in the success of the Muskrat Falls project.

Public anger was also directed at Peter Penashue's brother-in-law, Paul Rich, a former chief at Sheshatshiu who, as CEO of Innu Development

32   *The Telegram*, 13 April 2014.
33   *Boardman v Phipps* [1967] AC 46.
34   Information received from Anthony Jenkinson, resident in Sheshatshiu.
35   B. Cabana, 'Political Donations', *Rock Solid Politics*, 16 April 2013.

Limited Partnership, a private firm set up to broker deals with non-indigenous companies who wish to do business on Innu land, was paid a salary of C$1 million over the course of two years.[36] Prosecution for fraud failed for lack of evidence.

Writing on the 'Uncle Gnarley' blog, Newfoundland and Labrador commentator Des Sullivan has also pointed up conflicts of interest and nepotism in the awarding of executive posts and contracts by Nalcor.[37]

As we have seen in Chapter 7, the test for breach of fiduciary duty was laid down in the English case of *Bray v Ford* by Lord Herschell, as follows:

1. The defendant is actually in a fiduciary relationship with the claimant – a relationship in which it is possible to exert undue influence;

2. the defendant obtained a benefit; and

3. there is a causal connection between the relationship and the benefit.

This test was subsequently adopted by Wilson J in the Canadian case of *Frame v Smith*.[38]

Those sitting around the New Dawn negotiating table were in an actual fiduciary relationship with the people they represented (the beneficiaries) and had scope for exercising discretion and power on their behalf. As elected members and their agents, lawyers and consultants, they had recognised professional relationships which required the standard of the utmost good faith. They were the only people who had access to the full text of the Agreement in Principle and IBAs, and they were the first to know of the business opportunities which would be available from the works. If they then used knowledge and opportunities (the benefit) received as a result of these positions to secure the business opportunities from which they are now profiting, there is a clear causal connection between these two sets of circumstances. However, there is no clear evidence for this. One federal negotiator interviewed by Stephanie Irlbacher-Fox told her: 'I have seen colleagues power-trip at negotiations; there are situations where they have pulled things off the table or refused to give on something that is well within their mandates. Sometimes it's strategic; sometimes it's just to bring the First Nations negotiator under control, or it's about their own ego, where they want to get back at a negotiator who made them angry.'[39] She reports that First Nations negotiators in the North West Territories regarded their consultants with suspicion and anger. It would seem that Chief Justice McLachlin's admonitions to act in treaty negotiations in a way consistent with the honour of the Crown passed them by.

36 *The National Post*, 13 July 2012.
37 'Is Nalcor Rife with Conflicts of Interest?', unclegnarley.blogspot,com, 23 Jan. 2017. See also B. Cabana, 'Riadh Ben Aissa, Danny Williams and SNC Lavalin', *Rock Solid Politics*, 10 April 2013.
38 [1987] 2 SCR 99.
39 Irlbacher-Fox, *Finding Dahshaa*, pp. 20–2.

Neither the legal partnership Olthuis, Kleer Townshend nor any of the other consultants to the Innu Nation have been approached in the research and writing of this text, and there is nothing to suggest that they have taken advantage of their position or acted in bad faith. However, *Boardman v Phipps*[40] makes clear that, even when the fiduciary acts to promote the best interests of the beneficiaries in acquiring these interests, it is still the case that without the free, prior and informed consent of all the beneficiaries, they cannot take any profit or advantage from the opportunities or knowledge received as a result of their insider knowledge. Where business arrangements acquired by the fiduciaries were acquired without such consent and the lawyers, consultants, negotiators and representatives are therefore liable to account for the profits made and advantages taken which came to them as a result of their relationship to the beneficiaries of the AIP. This conservative, proscriptive approach to the nature of fiduciary relationships was confirmed by the Supreme Court of Canada in *Galambos v Perez* in 2009.[41]

On the ratification of the AIP, C$115 million was payable to the Innu Nation – but accumulated fees and expenses of the lawyers and other consultants were deducted from this sum to the tune of C$60 million. By contrast, the figure for such fees accepted by the Supreme Court in *Beckman v Little Salmon/Carmacks First Nation* was C$7 million.[42] If the Innu Nation did not receive fully itemised bills to account for every item of this sum, they should call for these immediately. If they are not forthcoming, the Innu Nation can call for the fees to be 'taxed' by the professional bodies, who will scrutinise the accounts and reduce them if appropriate. Further, as fiduciaries, fees and expenses are subject to a test of reasonableness and can be challenged through the courts of equity.[43]

40 [1967] 2 AC 46.
41 312 DLR (4th) 220. For a discussion of the nature of fiduciary relationships in Canadian case law, see M. McInnes, 'A New Direction for the Canadian law of fiduciary relations?', *Law Quarterly Review* 121 (2010): 185.
42 At para 9.
43 See G. Watt, *Trusts & Equity* (Oxford: Oxford University Press, 2012), p. 361.

The government was so good it could even break up CAM. All the Band Councils worked together but the government broke it up, going after one Band Council at a time and offering them money. When they all worked together, no government was able to do that.

We can't find unity with other Innu any more and now suddenly the negotiations have closed.

You have to work on many fronts – even civil disobedience.

I look at the experience of the people from Labrador and most governments, Quebec or Labrador, they don't have the same type of history or relationship which Quebec has with its native people. The same with Newfoundland and Labrador. They don't necessarily have the same approach. We are both the same people, we are both Montagnais, we eat the same food, speak the same language. Governments have different priorities. Now with all these protests in Labrador, somehow the government decided to give something back to the Innu. They are literally throwing things to the Innu in some sort of redress or giving back something and they almost get whatever they want. It's like a baby – we give something to the baby because it yells and at some time the baby shuts up. So it's the same thing nowadays – the Labrador Innu are like their mouths are covered. They can't say anything because the Labrador government puts something into the mouth of the Labrador Innu. Quebec doesn't have the same approach to its native people, because we are still speaking up about the injustices which are happening in our homeland. But we don't hear as much from Labrador as we used to because the government has decided to shut them up – with mining programmes or whatever.

Chapter 17

The position of the Innu who live in Quebec

Innu in Matimekush expressed a sense of déjà vu when it came to consideration of the signing of the New Dawn Agreement in Labrador:

> The New Dawn Agreement? It's the second James Bay Agreement. It's the same thing. We are going to have a new map again because Indians from Sept-Iles and here have their own territories. It's the same as the [North Eastern] Quebec Agreement. The [Innu in Labrador] have a mining agreement for the Voisey's Bay project and with Hydro Labrador for the Churchill River and now with the government. I know for governments to negotiate with two communities it's easy. It's easy to persuade them. When you have nine communities, it is harder. People in Sheshatshiu, these are our own sisters and brothers. Are they going to be like the Naskapi are now – not wanting to be a nation with us? It's the same with the nation of Labrador, they don't want to know. Sheshatshiu has no territory near here. There are no cemeteries round here belonging to Sheshatshiu – only from here and from Sept-Iles.[1]

However, the New Dawn Agreement in Principle (AIP) does have an added dimension which closely affects the Innu in Quebec. At Clause 2.112 it provides that: 'Nothing in the Agreement shall be construed to affect, recognize or provide any rights under section 35 of the Constitution Act, 1982, for any Aboriginal People of Canada other than Innu.' [as defined under the AIP and restricted to Innu beneficiaries from Labrador]

In order to establish these rights, the Innu resident in Quebec whose lands are alienated by the New Dawn Agreement must take their case to a court of 'last resort' – which could mean to the Supreme Court of Canada, an extremely costly and lengthy undertaking. If they re-entered negotiations for their own land claim, their rights in Labrador could be acknowledged under that process but, under the terms of the AIP, would still have to be confirmed by the court.

While the Innu who live in Quebec say that the Innu in Labrador have abandoned their core beliefs in agreeing to sell the Labrador lands to the governments, the Innu who live in Labrador claim somewhat defensively that their relatives in Quebec were asked to join the negotiating table and share

1   Interview MFD7, Sept. 2009.

in any benefits from the New Dawn Agreement but refused. Nevertheless, under the New Dawn Agreement the Innu Nation are preparing to sign away lands which are shared and lands such as the land for mining on the outskirts of Matemekush in which the people of Sheshatshiu and Natuashish have little interest.

On 19 March 2010, Jean-François Bertrand, lawyer for the Strategic Alliance, wrote to Prime Minister Harper, Premier Danny Williams, Minister of Indian Affairs Chuck Strahl and the Innu negotiators as follows:

> We formally demand that the Government of Canada immediately cease any discussions and meetings regarding the possible execution of this treaty, since that would entail a flagrant breach of your fiduciary obligations to the Innu of Quebec.

> As in the case of the government of Newfoundland and Labrador, you are well aware that our clients have aboriginal title, aboriginal rights and treaty rights over that part of Nitassinan which is located in Labrador. However, negotiating with Innu Nation and the Government of Newfoundland and Labrador without prior consultation of the concerned Innu communities of Quebec, the Government of Canada has already breached its fiduciary obligations. The execution of a treaty would only compound this breach.

> Consequently, considering the foregoing, we demand that you cease immediately any discussions, meetings and communications regarding the execution of such a treaty and that you start the process anew and so as to enable consultation of the Innu communities in Quebec, their participation in such treaty negotiations and the recognition of their rights in Nitassinan.

However, the present author would suggest respectfully that what the lawyers should have been demanding in 2010 was that free, prior, informed consent should be given by their Innu clients in Quebec.

In 2011 informal discussions were held between the Newfoundland Labrador government and the Strategic Alliance regarding the rights claimed by the Strategic Alliance to lands in Labrador.[2] In November 2011 a meeting was held at the Band Council offices in Matimekush of representatives of all interested communities in Quebec to decide on a joint approach to the federal and Newfoundland Labrador governments.[3] As we have seen, there is a provision in the New Dawn AIP that the agreement will be amended to accommodate any successful court challenge from other native people, which includes a challenge from the Strategic Alliance.

---

2   Conversation with Armand MacKenzie, then negotiator for Uashat Maliotenam, Nov. 2011.

3   Preparations for this meeting were in progress when the author was working there in Oct. 2011.

The Innu village of Ekuanitshit, to the east of Sept-Iles, not part of the Strategic Alliance but a close associate, began a court challenge to the works at Muskrat Falls on 26 April 2012.[4] The community asked the court to set aside a decision of the federal government to grant permits to Nalcor for the Muskrat Falls project because the government had rejected the joint review panel's recommendations with regard to the rights of the Innu who live in Quebec. The panel had recommended a financial review and assessments of alternative sources of energy. The lawyer for the plaintiffs said that they were particularly concerned about the effect on the George River herd of caribou, which was reported by Survival International to have been reduced in size from 800,000–900,000 to fewer than 74,000.[5] Peter Penashue, then a minister in the Harper government, retorted that all outstanding legal issues had been addressed.[6] So far as is known, no involvement was offered to or sought by the Strategic Alliance, such is the governments' successful division of Innu in Quebec into eastern, central and western negotiating tables. On 24 April 2013, the case was dismissed. On 24 May, the Ekuanitshit Innu filed an appeal. Leave to appeal was refused in 2015.[7]

When the Voisey's Bay nickel mines were proposed in the early 2000s, all Innu stood together to try to stop the project because it would ruin the land. Innu from Matimekush Lac John united with the Innu of Sheshatshiu to circle the runway of the Goose Bay airfield, and they had previously been together to Rotterdam to protest against proposed NATO overflying.[8] Yet in 2008 when Chief Réal McKenzie of Matimekush Lac John asked Peter Penashue, then Chief in Sheshatshiu, for help to fight the opening of the new mines, no help was forthcoming.[9] When interviewed in 2009, at a time when the ratification of the New Dawn Final Agreement seemed imminent, one elder in Matimekush described relations between the Innu in Quebec and those in Labrador as follows:

> It seems to me that the governments have divided the Innu people into their separate communities. How can the Innu reunite? It's a very tough question. Off the top of my mind I can't give you a straightforward answer. It's really complex and difficult. I am pretty much concerned about the New Dawn Agreement about to be ratified by the Innu of Labrador because what it will do is cause an upset to our hunting rights and our hunting activities. Priority will be given to the Innu resident

4   *CBC News*, 26 April 2012.
5   www.survivalinternational.org/news/7967, accessed 2 May 2012.
6   'MP Dismisses Quebec Innu Complaint', *VOCM Local News*, 29 April 2012.
7   *APTN National News*, 5 March 2015.
8   Interview MFA7, March 2009. For accounts of the Goose Bay protests, see Samson, *A Way of Life*, Wadden, *Nitassinan: The Innu Struggle*, and also H. Brody's film *Hunters and Bombers* (1990).
9   Conversation with Chief Réal McKenzie, Aug. 2008.

in Labrador and [as for] those in Quebec – there will be no concern for
our position. I cannot see how people cannot see that we are the same
people – Innu from Quebec and Labrador are one nation.[10]

The 'negotiation' process shown in these chapters demonstrates the lack of good
faith and the failure of the federal and provincial governments to uphold the
honour of the Crown in their dealings with small indigenous nations who trust
their future to a negotiated land claims settlement. Settlement agreements are
shown to be one-sided, with all the cards held by the Crown – a position which
the governments continue to abuse in disregard of the honour of the Crown.

In the run-up to the signing of the New Dawn AIP, game wardens in
Labrador took steps to remove Innu hunters from Quebec from their long-
established hunting territory in Labrador. They threatened to burn down their
cabins, although the threat was later withdrawn. The response of the Innu was
to engage in a mass hunt in February 2010 in order to establish their rights.[11]

At about this time, the new iron mines were opening at Schefferville. The
Innu resident in Labrador signed the necessary agreements, but again the
Matimekush Lac John Innu did not and mounted roadblocks to the excavation
sites.[12] They were threatened by Chuck Strahl, then federal Minister of
Indian Affairs, with funding cuts unless they removed the barricades – saying
that unless they capitulated the government would withdraw its subsidy of
C$6 million from the Quebec North Shore and Labrador Railway (the
community's only affordable connection to the outside world) and also the
C$73 million promised to upgrade the railway (which was presumably mainly
for the benefit of the mining company). He also said the government would
renege on its promise of a round table to settle overlapping claims. Chief Réal
McKenzie's response was, 'We will not give in to this inexcusable and shameless
intimidation,' and he indicated that the chiefs were prepared to take the matter
of this federal intimidation to the G-20 and G-8 summits due to take place in
Toronto in June 2010.[13]

This approach was successful. The Strategic Alliance was able to reach
Impacts and Benefits Agreements with Labrador Iron Mines, Tata Steel and

10   Interview MA11, March 2009.
11   See Canada Newswire press release, http.//www.newswire.ca/en/releases/archive/
     March2010/17/c2596.html; also, 'Quebec Innu caribou hunt protests NL deal',
     CBC News, 21 Feb. 2010, http://www.cbc.ca/news/canada/newfoundland-
     labrador/story/2010/02/21; 'Des Innus en colère', *L'Actualité*, l'actualite.com, 21
     Nov. 2013.
12   'Quebec Innu protesters blockade iron works sites', *CBC News*, 4 July 2012,
     http://cbc.ca?newfoundland-Labrador/story/2012/07/04/nl-innu-blockade-iron-
     ore-704.html.
13   Press release, Innu Strategic Alliance, 'Mining conflict in Schefferville: The Innu
     denounce their intimidation by the federal government', www.newswire.ca/news-
     releases/policy-public-interest-latest-news/legal-issues-list/, 18 June 2012.

ArcelorMittal.[14] These negotiations have also provided an opportunity for the Innu of Matimekush Lac John to pursue their claims in Labrador. The first payments from Labrador Iron Mines and Tata Mines were used to pay off the Matimekush Lac John Band Council deficit. Further payments could finance court cases to recover both James Bay and Labrador lands, allowing the Quebec Innu to engage their own lawyers independent of the influence of the governments who, up until now, were the source of loans for legal and other advice. As part of the IBA compensation, the mining companies agreed to replace the infrastructure destroyed with the departure of the Iron Ore Company in the 1980s, including the provision of a new sports arena.[15]

Galvanised by the verdict in *Tsilhqot'in Nation v British Columbia*, the newly formed Innu Nation representing the Innu of Quebec have joined with the Attikamekw and Anishnabeg in a coalition which is calling for the renegotiation of the James Bay Agreement so that their rights in the land are recognised.[16] It remains to be seen whether they will take similar action to gain recognition of their rights to lands in Labrador.

Also in the wake of *Tsilhqot'in*, the Innu of the Strategic Alliance brought a court case against the Iron Ore Company, claiming $900 million for past exploitation of their traditional lands both in Quebec and in Labrador. The Iron Ore Company had recently concluded a similar deal with the Innu in Labrador, despite the fact that the compensation awarded them related to land which had always been recognised by the Innu as Strategic Alliance territory. Four years of negotiation to get compensation had proved fruitless. As the chief at the time in Matimekush Lac John put it: 'Governments and the mining industry allow other Aboriginal groups with no legitimate claim to our territory to encroach on our lands at our expense. We can no longer tolerate such an attitude which aims to capture our resources and the benefits which derive from them.'[17]

The chiefs of Matimekush Lac John, Uashat mak Mani-Utenam and Ekuanitshit also travelled to Europe to the headquarters of Rio Tinto, which now owns the Iron Ore Company mines, to attend their AGM in an initiative they called 'Pay the Rent'.[18] Rio Tinto's attempt to block the class action was

14   Press release, Innu Takuaikan Uashat Mak Mani-Utenam, 27 Feb. 2012.
15   Hugo Grandpré, 'Schefferville: l'aréna rouvre 30 ans plus tard', *La Presse*, Ottawa, 8 Feb. 2014.
16   Marie-Michèle Sioui, 'Des autochtones veulent renégocier la Convention de la Baie-James', *La Presse*, 13 Nov. 2014.
17   'Aboriginal Rights of the Innu in Labrador: the real Aboriginal title rights-holders call on IOC to sign an agreement', *Digital Journal*, 1 Aug. 2014.
18   'Des Innus en mission européenne contre la minière IOC', *Radio Canada*, 9 April 2015.

rejected by the Supreme Court of Canada. The case was then sent back to the Quebec Superior Court for trial.[19]

One new possibility advocated by Russell Diabo, in his capacity as adviser to the Algonquin Nation, is an alliance between all those who have refused to enter into comprehensive land claims negotiations. He believes their position following *Tsilhqot'in* is stronger than that of nations who are already negotiating land claims with the governments but, he says, they must start negotiating between and among themselves. They should 'establish a co-ordinating body with political and technical representation on it to ensure proper representation by Indigenous Nations Not Negotiating in the AFN-PN "high level" process on Comprehensive Land Claims Policy reform'.[20]

Already the indigenous peoples of the Ungava Peninsula are coming together to address the depletion in caribou numbers. Most Canadians involved in caribou conservation blame the indigenous hunters for the drop in the size of the George River and Wood herds but Nicolas Mainville, at the time a senior officer with Greenpeace, came out in support of the indigenous peoples, who have held meetings and press conferences to produce evidence that the depletion is not as serious as the government bodies claim. He adds that, in any case, the real cause is the forestry industry. He also points out that it is not just falling caribou numbers Canada should be concerned by – the entire fauna of the boreal forest is under threat.[21]

Although the federal and provincial governments deal with the Innu resident in Quebec through three separate negotiating tables with regard to land claims, chiefs from all the Innu villages in Quebec have been working together since 2013 to lobby the Quebec government to change its economic policy for the region so that caribou are no longer threatened by the forestry industry in the province. In September 2013, a round table was held in Nain, Labrador, with Inuit and Cree representatives, which produced a conservation plan based on both indigenous knowledge and scientific research. All Innu villages from both sides of the Quebec–Labrador border participated in the discussions. Sara Leo, president of the Nunatsiavut government, observed that: 'The profound respect and unity demonstrated by all those round the table is impressive. This is where our power lies and we have hope for the future of the caribou of the Ungava Peninsula.'[22] (author's translation)

19 R. Marowits, 'Supreme Court rejects Rio Tinto's efforts to dismiss Innu class action lawsuit', *The Canadian Press*, 15 Oct. 2015.

20 R. Diabo, *Briefing Note to ANS Council of Chiefs & Grand Chiefs on Aboriginal Title/Rights vs Federal Comprehensive Land Claims Policy*, 11 Feb. 2013.

21 Nicolas Mainville, 'Protection de nos forêts publiques: les scientifiques répliquent aux "faits" de l'industrie', blog, 15 April 2014.

22 Canada Newswire press release: 'La Table ronde sur le caribou de la péninsule Ungava, Nain, Nunatsiavut – 24–25 septembre 2013', 27 Sept. 2013.

This – environmental conservation – is one issue which strikes at the heart of indigenous existence and has engendered a high degree of co-operation despite the dissent over land claims. The PEW Trust records that 'the Peoples of the Ungava in 2013 created the Ungava Peninsula Caribou Aboriginal Round Table to improve caribou management across 580,000 square miles of Quebec, Labrador and Nunavik'.[23] However, where Nunavik hunters have refrained from hunting for several years, Innu hunters from Quebec continue to assert their rights to hunt in southern Labrador, albeit on a very small scale – nothing on the scale of sports hunting by American tourists.[24]

Christopher Alcantara, once a student of Tom Flanagan, poses the question, 'Why were the … Labrador Inuit able to complete comprehensive land claims agreements and why were the … Labrador Innu not able to complete them?' He points to the success of the James Bay Agreement which, he says, rested on the opportunities for resource development; but he also notes that many comprehensive land claims negotiations fail because: '… government actors have tended to have inflexible mandates, have lacked political will, or have failed to provide sufficient incentives for professional negotiators to complete agreements quickly'.

He also points to the inability of indigenous governments to harness the necessary resources to complete negotiations because of government interference with compulsory relocation and underfunding of indigenous communities. Other factors are the cultural difference which often results in provincial and federal governments perceiving themselves as 'representatives of the Crown meeting with minorities within Canada' rather than as negotiators seeking to acquire title to land from the rightful owners.[25] Certainly, all these factors are present in the background to the New Dawn Agreement negotiations.

Alcantara's own conclusion is that successful land claims negotiation requires a similarity of preferences of the parties involved, which results in a lack of confrontation – something of a statement of the obvious. Relations of all 11 Innu groups on both sides of the Quebec–Labrador border have their foundations in protest against resource exploitation over which they were not consulted. Alcantara points out that the revenues received by the province for development in Labrador dwarf the amounts paid to the indigenous groups on whose land development took place.[26] He suggests that the Labrador Inuit took a pragmatic, conciliatory approach to land claims whereas, for the Innu, recognition of their sovereignty was paramount.

23 *PEW Trust* magazine, 20 May 2019.
24 See 'It is not right: Possible hunt of protected Labrador caribou a recurring concern', *CBC News*, 3 Mar. 2021, and 'Illegal caribou hunt under investigation: Innu take responsibility, *CBC News*, 10 Apr. 2015.
25 C. Alcantara, *Negotiating the Deal: Comprehensive Land Claims in Canada* (Toronto: University of Toronto Press, 2013), pp. 4–5.
26 Ibid., p. 23.

Alcantara claims that the Innu resident in Quebec and those in Labrador became two separate groups, the division created by the provincial border.[27] This is patently not true – the Innu continued to work together until 1990, and in their relations in the 20th century they were united in protest. Alcantara identifies the turning point as the election of Peter Penashue as president of the Innu Nation in 1990.[28] Even under Penashue's leadership, negotiations moved slowly, mired in internal problems and disputes with the governments over their illegal use of Innu lands. In 1999, Alcantara tells us, the federal government suspended negotiations due to what were perceived as unreasonable Innu demands which did not adhere to the governments' imposed national standards – which is a clear indication that negotiations were not free and fair. They were reinstated when the provincial government wished to proceed with the Lower Churchill Falls project.

Alcantara identifies four factors necessary for a successful outcome for land claims negotiations:

- compatibility of government and aboriginal group goals

- minimal use of confrontational tactics by the aboriginal group

- strong aboriginal group cohesion as it relates to the treaty process

- positive government perceptions of aboriginal group capacity.

In other words, it seems that the indigenous group is judged to have 'capacity' when it has been sufficiently demoralised at the hands of the governments to capitulate. Yet, despite everything they have suffered at the hands of the governments, the Innu resident in Quebec have maintained their cohesion and resilience long enough to benefit from the *Tsilhqot'in* decision. In order to acquire the necessary 'cohesion', the governments had to divide off the only two Innu communities which would concede to demands which did nothing to uphold the honour of the Crown. Even then, 'cohesion' was a result of the death of a powerful leader, Ben Michel, who led those faithful to Innu core beliefs. Alcantara observes that Peter Penashue 'reduced the number of community consultations'.[29] He warns that: 'It may be that limited consultations lead to higher levels of distrust and conflict during the treaty implementation phase …'[30]

Can Alcantara really believe that the nine Innu villages in Quebec are less committed to the negotiation process, having stayed with it for 40 years? Even though he claims that 'government actors generally react negatively to confrontational tactics because such tactics tend to embarrass them and their

27 Ibid., p. 39.
28 Ibid., p. 53.
29 Alcantara, *Negotiating the Deal*, p. 67.
30 Ibid., p. 125.

governments',[31] can he honestly condone a requirement to abstain from peaceful protest when issues such as methyl mercury and quick clay arise, the consequences of which are described below?

31 Alcantara, *Negotiating the Deal*, p. 123.

It is unfortunate that this country has to rely on someone else's misery to force them to sign away their rights. When you look at it, with the level of their poverty, their socio-economic conditions, they come to a point when they want to sign a deal. Sometimes before stretching out their hands to give something to us – we look at it, what do we do, do we take it just to satisfy our immediate needs, say for housing or development, and in return sign away our rights? It's not an easy situation.

> Out of someone's misery you will be able to manipulate [them] easily because that person somehow wants to get out of that misery. Governments play on that with the aboriginal communities. They know that they are weak, fragile mentally, and they are therefore susceptible to manipulation.

It's hard for the young people because, you know, when you take the agreement it has 24 chapters and when you look at that in detail it is hard to summarise that for the people here. Only specialists can summarise that. It is hard for ordinary people because there are different views from young men or women or for a man who is related to the Naskapi. There are 30–40 people here who have Naskapi blood. That's why half the community has a different opinion from others who are not beneficiaries of the agreement. It is hard because when you see people going into the country, the Montagnais people going into the country and the Naskapi band and we have no money, you know, we each go into the country.

> I know in the West of Canada a lot of treaties have been signed … [but] even the Quebec agreement since it was signed, 50 per cent of the agreement was not respected, just like the others – Treaty 8, etc. If we sign an agreement with Quebec or Canada – the general [land claims] treaty – I know a few years later maybe half of the content of the agreement will not be respected. If we sign with the Quebec agreement, to fix the mistake that they did, I know 50 per cent will not be respected.

Chapter 18

Construction and protest at Muskrat Falls

In November 2016, the initial flooding of the reservoir at Muskrat Falls took place. It was delayed by protests, a hunger strike and sit-ins within the site perimeter. Despite the Newfoundland Labrador government's assertion that 'extensive pre-feasibility work, such as progression of the environmental assessment process'[1] had been undertaken, serious problems have emerged in the capture of such a vast area of water.

The North Spur

The North Spur is the site of the Muskrat Falls reservoir. The North Spur had potential as a natural dam and has been strengthened by substantial engineering works. Nevertheless, experts have declared it unsafe because the spur contains quick clay, a substance which is likely to collapse when the reservoir is flooded to a depth of five metres. Jim Gordon, a hydropower consultant who worked on dams in Newfoundland Labrador up until 2005, wrote as follows for the newspaper *The Telegram:*

> The North Spur is a natural hill 1,000 metres long connecting Spirit Mountain [a significant spiritual site for the Innu] to the north shore at Muskrat Falls, which includes three layers of sand and two of marine clay, all resting on a foundation of marine clay. When the Muskrat reservoir is filled, this hill will form part of the dam containing the reservoir.

> Marine clay is a type of clay found in coastal regions around the world. In the northern, deglaciated regions, it can sometimes be quick clay, which is notorious in being involved in landslides. Construction in marine clays thus presents a geotechnical engineering challenge.

> Marine clay is present around the southern half of James Bay. This persuaded Hydro-Québec to by-pass development on the Nottaway River, moving instead 300 kilometres north to the La Grande, at considerable added expense for access and transmission.

---

1   Newfoundland Labrador Government, 'Backgrounder – Muskrat Falls', 18 Nov. 2010.

In his article, Gordon refers to research carried out by Dr Stig Bernander, an expert in quick clay landslides. Bernander examined the North Spur and concluded that, if the dam were flooded to a depth of five metres, the safety of the dam would be severely reduced. On the basis of Bernander's examination, Gordon observes that:

> If the North Shore dam fails, there is the likelihood of loss of life in Goose Bay and Happy Valley and the river will divert to flow through the breach in the Spur.
>
> If the North Spur fails, Muskrat Falls will disappear and be left high and dry. The Muskrat Hydro facility would become a stranded asset, with (if feasible) a repair cost well over several billion dollars. Power would be interrupted for at least several years.[2]

Nevertheless, the Muskrat Falls flooding is scheduled to proceed to a depth of six metres on the grounds that, if it does not, the dam will be damaged by the winter ice.

Methyl mercury

Indigenous peoples and the settler community of Newfoundland and Labrador and beyond staged their most significant protest over concerns about increased levels of methyl mercury in the captured waters at Muskrat Falls. This came in the wake of a report from Professor Elsie Sunderland of Harvard University to the effect that mercury levels would double in the bodies of people living downstream from the plant. As with the James Bay project, she explained that when the soil underwater is cut off from oxygen, bacteria that convert mercury into methyl mercury flourish and this compound is concentrated in the bodies of fish and anything eating fish, including human beings, rather than being excreted.[3] Her report concluded that the dam waters would contain methyl mercury levels 'to the point that they exceed regulatory thresholds for exposure' and, although the majority of build-up would occur three years after the flooding of the reservoir, the effects would last for decades. This echoes the findings of the Lake Melville scientific report, which predicted that there would be a sharp increase in methyl mercury levels immediately after flooding and that levels could spike by 380 per cent. Methyl mercury is toxic to the human central nervous system.[4] Lake Melville is the large body of water from which the Innu and Inuit take the fish which provide a significant part of their diet.

2   J. Gordon, 'Muskrat Falls and the North Spur Controversy', *The Telegram*, 2 Jan. 2016.
3   I. Austen, 'Canada's Big Dams Produce Clean Energy, and High Levels of Mercury', *New York Times*, 10 Nov. 2016.
4   T. Roberts, *CBC News*, 18 April 2016; see also M. Troian, 'Neurological and birth defects haunt Wabaseemoong First Nation decades after mercury dumping', *CBC News*, 20 Sept. 2016.

The protesters (who could also be described as land protectors), a group made up of Innu, Inuit, Metis and settler Canadians, demanded that no flooding should take place until the dam was cleared, not only of vegetation but also of topsoil. This was a step which Nalcor was not prepared to take, even though the Newfoundland and Labrador Environment Minister acknowledged that this was the root of the problem.[5]

While Nalcor downplayed Professor Sunderland's findings and ended the study,[6] the provincial government responded by announcing that she would carry out another survey for them, a claim which was speedily refuted by Harvard University on her behalf.[7] However the province did order Nalcor to 'clear as much forest cover as possible' but this did not extend to clearing topsoil. In the meantime, Nalcor was bringing in workers by helicopter in order to circumvent the blockade.[8]

The protest was led, not by Innu who lived close by, but by the Nunatsiavut government. The Innu Nation's hands were tied because there was a clause in the Impacts and Benefits Agreement they signed with Nalcor providing that they would support Nalcor in the event of any protest against its activities.[9] Nevertheless, many Innu as individuals took part in the protest. Nine people were arrested from a blockade on the Trans-Labrador Highway outside the gates to Muskrat Falls and court injunctions were granted against the protesters, who nevertheless refused to give up until the charges were dropped and the vegetation was cut.[10] On 22 October, tactical units of the Royal Canadian Mounted Police were called in to evict the protesters, who were involved in only a peaceful protest and were instructed not to fight back. Later that evening the Newfoundland Labrador Premier, Dwight Ball, agreed to meet the leaders

5   C. Cosh, 'The Muskrat Falls fiasco – maybe you'd be protesting too', *Full Comment*, 24 Oct. 2016.
6   T. Roberts, *CBC News*, 18 April 2016. See also Sarah Cox, 'Mercury Rising: How the Muskrat Falls dam threatens Inuit way of life', 22 May 2019, *The Narwhal*, https://www.thenarwhal.ca/mercury-rising-muskrat-falls-dam-threatens-inuit-way-of-life/ and see Ryan Calder, 'Muskrat Falls hydroelectric project poses risks for Canada that are being ignored', 3 Oct. 2019, *The Conversation*, https://theconversation.com/muskrat-falls-hydroelectric-project-posos-risks-for-canada-that-are-being-ignored-122360 (Ryan Calder is one of the researchers from the Harvard project).
7   M. Boone, *CBC News*, 19 Oct. 2016.
8   A. Delaney and G. Barry, 'Muskrat Falls workers enter site by helicopter, bypass protester roadblock', *CBC News*, 20 Oct. 2016.
9   See above, p. 258.
10 Garrett Barry, 'NL Government, Labrador leaders make "significant" Muskrat Falls progress', *CBC News*, 25 Oct. 2016.

of the protest, and to postpone the flooding until he had spoken to the land protectors.[11]

At the meeting, Premier Ball announced the formation of an advisory committee made up of provincial, municipal, federal and indigenous leaders to monitor the project. The Nunatsiavut representatives claimed this as a victory and urged the land protectors to go home. Ball assured them that, 'Going forward, decisions will be made using science-based research,' and promised to order further clearing of the dam site.[12] The protesters were released without charge provided they agreed to stay clear of the Muskrat Falls site, and Nalcor began to raise the water levels.[13] Work at the site returned to normal.

One protester summed up the frustration of the land protectors at Muskrat Falls:

> I wonder what we will eat? A way of life gone.

> It just really hurts the heart that it has got to this point. I so hoped it would have been stopped by now, but if feels like we are not getting anywhere. But I still think that, with the cost of this project, and all the destruction, hopefully someone higher up than me will see the destruction and what's happening and they will just shut down the project.

Another said:

> We've had relocation and compensation. We've had residential schools and compensation. And now we're looking at methyl mercury and then compensation. Money doesn't pay for any of it. In the midst of all of it, we have lives that are devastated. We have social issues, and we're just contributing more to them. I think it's time that we just need to put our foot down and say enough is enough and stand up to some of the colonisation.[14]

Under the Impacts and Benefits Agreements (IBAs) accompanying the New Dawn Agreement in Principle (AIP), further compensation for methyl mercury poisoning is specifically excluded. Such compensation is covered in the sums paid on signing of the IBAs. Some commentators have linked the failure to address the concerns of the land protectors to the sincerity of Canada's promise of reconciliation and its lack of commitment to the adoption of the United Nations Declaration on the Rights of Indigenous Peoples (UNDRIP). Hans Rollmann observed:

11 'We Hold Muskrat Falls', *Newfoundland and Labrador Independent*, c. 22 Oct. 2016.
12 'Aboriginal leaders tell Muskrat Falls protesters to "go home" after meeting with Premier', *The Canadian Press*, 26 Oct. 2016.
13 *Globe and Mail*, 6 Nov. 2016.
14 S. Flowers and M. Kinney, quoted by J. Banks in 'Fear, anger, desperation plans dominate Muskrat Falls rally', *Newfoundland and Labrador Independent*, c. 30 Sept. 2016.

The manner in which Nalcor and the provincial government have responded to the Muskrat Falls crisis is simply not how things are done in 2016. They reflect the archaic and outdated approaches of previous decades and the backward-looking inability of those in office to adapt to the present.

The old heavy-handed approach simply doesn't work in an age of social media and international acknowledgement of Canada's need to change its relationship with indigenous peoples. But it's not surprising that the people in charge are stuck in the ways of the past.

Times have changed. But has the RCMP? Has the Government of Newfoundland and Labrador? The current events in Labrador are a true test of whether the country and its institutions have indeed changed.

...

In 2016, the year that Truth and Reconciliation is supposed to be an active principle in Canada's relations with Indigenous peoples, the Newfoundland and Labrador government is playing the centuries-old role of racist cowboy villain. It's an embarrassment to the province, and an embarrassment to the country.[15]

Playing into this stereotype, Nalcor's response to the impending ecological disaster is to promise to put up notices advising people not to eat the fish and to propose a scheme of compensation. By contrast, Pamela Palmater, a Micmac lawyer and indigenous rights activist, describes the comparable Lower Churchill Falls project in far stronger language: as 'a modern-day form of genocide'. She continues:

Look at every single court case that's dealt with Aboriginal treaty rights. [They take] anywhere between 20 and 25 years to get to Supreme Court of Canada. What do you think is going to happen during those intervening 25 years? The dam will be built, the poison will be done, people will be sick, and then we're talking about compensation. It's in part political strategy. Governments are able to delay dealing with any of these issues simply by making it go to court. Even getting a criminal charge could find its way all the way to the Supreme Court of Canada. But 25 years later? The trees are gone, the minerals are gone, the water is poisoned and the people are sick.[16]

Palmater also describes industrial projects such as Muskrat Falls as 'environmental racism'.

Financial concerns

In order to pay for the project, it is estimated that Newfoundland and

15 'Muskrat Falls and Canada's Promise of Reconciliation', 21 Oct. 2016.
16 H. Rollmann, 'Muskrat Falls a "modern-day form of genocide": lawyer', *Newfoundland and Labrador Independent*, c. 21 Oct. 2016.

Labrador and Nova Scotia will not see the benefits of cheap electricity until 2067 because, in the meantime, the electricity produced will have to be sold in the United States to pay off the seriously mounting debts which are being incurred.[17] Further, decisions on the need for power are politicised by the need to provide jobs in the maritime provinces. In the short term, there are ample jobs in the construction of the Muskrat Falls dam and the transmission lines of the 1,500-kilometre Maritime Link taking the electricity to the United States.

The initial budget for the Muskrat Falls project was C$6.2 billion. The viability of the project rested on high oil prices when oil was commanding US$100 per barrel. Elsewhere it is claimed that the projected oil price on which the project was recommended was US$150 per barrel.[18] By April 2016, the oil price had fallen dramatically while the cost of the project had risen to C$11.4 billion (including interest)[19] – and now requires a loan guarantee from the federal government of C$5 billion. By 2020, when the Muskrat Falls Report was published, this had risen to C$13.1 billion.[20] It is hardly surprising that, in a province of just half a million people, questions are beginning to be raised. At the same time, an audit by Ernst & Young exposed 'a tangled web of inadequate governance and out-of-control management ineffectiveness'.[21] Yet the provincial government and Nalcor appear to be safe in the knowledge that the project is too big to cancel although, at the same time, public trust in the provincial government is failing. Settler Canadians are joining the protests and, on two private visits to St. John's and Corner Brook in 2015 and 2016, the author noticed a marked change in the attitude of the settler communities there. In 2015, the locals were keen to impress on all who would listen the importance of the jobs the scheme would provide. In 2016, there was complete silence on the matter.

The incoming CEO of Nalcor, Stan Marshall, told CBC News on 24 June 2016: 'The original capital cost analysis, estimates and schedule was very aggressive and overly optimistic and just didn't account for many of the risks that were known, or should've been known, at the time. And the analysis, finally, relied on high energy prices which were projected to continue with the rise.'

17 R. Surette, 'Proposed Muskrat Falls project renews much-needed energy debate', rabble.ca, 22 Oct. 2012
18 D. Vardy, 'Judicial Inquiry Best Disinfectant for Muskrat Falls', unclegnarley. blogspot.com, 9 Feb. 2017
19 T. Roberts, *CBC News*, 24 June 2016.
20 David Maher, 'Muskrat Falls costs top $13.1 billion; Nalcor CEO says further increase possible', 28 Sept 2020, *Saltwire*, https://www.saltwire.com/ newfoundland-labrador/business/local-busin…top131-billion-nalcor-ceo-says-further-increases-possible-503057.
21 T. Corcoran, 'How Muskrat Falls went from a green dream to a bog of red ink', FP Comment, *National Post*, 22 April 2016.

He pointed to the lack of experience of Nalcor and its contractors of working in the cold, northern climate, but he too said that stopping the project was not a practical option.

Writing on the Uncle Gnarley blog – one of the outlets for Newfoundlanders' frustrations with the project – commentator David Vardy discussed the Ernst & Young report which claimed that Nalcor's costs had been significantly underestimated and that the schedule for completion could not be met. At this point, Vardy suggests, the government could have suspended the project and called for a full cost/benefit analysis. He said that the public had never been given the evidence base for continuing with the project. Vardy also claimed that Nalcor was awarding contracts outside the provisions of the Public Tender Act and without independent regulatory oversight to protect the interests of ratepayers.[22] Furthermore, he claimed that the entire Muskrat Falls project had been removed from the scrutiny of the Public Utilities Board.[23] On 9 February 2017, a guest contributor to the blog again proposed that, following warnings from the Joint Provincial/Federal Review Panel and the Public Utilities Board, there should be a full Royal Commission of Inquiry into why the project was sanctioned in the first place, the causes of its escalating costs and, perhaps most importantly, whether the initial cost estimates were falsified.

Local Labradorian activist Cabot Martin[24] points to another failure in the assessment of the viability of the overall Lower Churchill Falls project. Why, he asks, did Newfoundland and Labrador not consider the availability of wind power (a question also raised by the Innu negotiator in Matimekush), or a combination of wind power and the natural gas available under the Newfoundland Grand Banks? He also mentions shale gas technology – which in the years since the project was first mooted has made the Lower Churchill project redundant. While the gas alternatives add to Canada's greenhouse gases total, wind power is cleaner than hydro and does not present the problems posed by methyl mercury or the quick clay in the North Spur. Martin's claim is that these alternatives were never properly studied. He reports on a meeting at which Nalcor Vice President Gil Bennett claimed: 'The capital cost on Muskrat Falls first is driven by favourable construction characteristics at the site. So, we look at the physical characteristics of Muskrat Falls, the geotechnical conditions are favourable. We are on competent bedrock.'[25]

Martin claims that Nalcor failed to carry out 'even the most basic geotechnical investigations prior to Project Sanction'.[26] He has asked the minister to make

22   D. Vardy, 'Muskrat Falls: The Public Right to Decide (Part 1)', unclegnarley. blogspot.com, 17 Nov. 2016.
23   D. Vardy, unclegnarley.blogspot.com, 28 Jan. 2017.
24   C. Martin, *Muskrat Madness* (privately published, 2014).
25   Martin, *Muskrat Madness*, p. 31.
26   Ibid., p. 69.

available the Dam Safety Review and Emergency Preparedness Plan on which Project Sanction was based, but to no avail.[27]

Research by the UK's University of Oxford in 2014, which investigated 245 large dam projects, concluded that they are a risky investment, leading to soaring budgets which drown emerging economies in debt, fail to deliver the promised benefits and are not economically viable. Further, the leader of the study, Professor Bent Flyvbjerg, said that dams 'are not carbon-neutral, and they're not greenhouse-neutral' – because the vast quantities of concrete required in their construction leave an enormous carbon footprint, and flooded vegetation under the reservoirs produces methane, a greenhouse gas 20 times more potent than carbon dioxide.[28]

While the people of Newfoundland and Labrador are by now all too aware of the threats posed by the continuation of the Muskrat Falls project, Nalcor and the provincial government press on regardless. It is to be hoped that they never have to quantify the costs of proceeding until the project results in financial ruin and human catastrophe against the stated will of the people to end the project immediately.

Very late in the day, after irreparable damage has been done to the environment, a Public Inquiry began in Goose Bay with Judge Richard LeBlanc sitting as its Commissioner.[29] The inquiry considered how the project came to be sanctioned, its increasing costs and whether the provincial government was justified in excluding the project from scrutiny by the Public Utilities Board. The questions of methyl mercury poisoning and the stability of the North Spur were beyond the scope of the inquiry, as were questions of democratic deficit and process. The Innu Nation, Nunatsiavut government and the Conseil des Innus d'Ekuanshit were all given limited standing to attest to levels of consultation and the physical construction of the project.[30] Professor Flyvbjerg was one of those called to give evidence. The Inquiry examined 2.5 million documents and the Final Report was published on 5 March 2020[31] in six volumes and 1,000 pages.

The Commissioner found that the project was backed by a Conservative government who were determined to proceed through a lens of political bias and unrealistic optimism. He concluded that top bureaucrats failed to provide oversight of Nalcor's activities, exposing the citizens of Newfoundland Labrador

27 Ibid., p. 106.
28 L. Everitt, 'Do massive dams ever make sense?', *BBC News Magazine*, 11 March 2014.
29 *CBC News Newfoundland Labrador*, https://www.cbc.ca/news/canada/newfoundland-labrador/muskrat-falls-inquiry-begins-1.4845831 and 1.4819253.
30 Ashley Fitzpatrick, 'Muskrat Falls inquiry commissioner makes determination on standing', *Saltwire*, 17 Apr. 2018.
31 Richard D. LeBlanc, *Muskrat Falls: A Misguided Project*, 5 Mar. 2020, Commission on Inquiry Respecting the Muskat Falls Project, www.muskratfallsinquiry.ca.

to billions of dollars' worth of debt, and that Nalcor's CEO and his deputy took 'unprecedented steps to secure sanction of the project'. Commissioner LeBlanc held the removal of the NL Public Utilities Board 'unjustified and unreasonable'. The Report was handed to the police because of the possibility of criminal charges. NL Premier Dwight Ball said that the project 'became a runaway train that could not be stopped'.[32]

32 Terry Roberts, 'Scathing Muskrat Falls inquiry report lays blame on executives', 10 Mar. 2020, *CBC News*, https://www.cbc.ca/news/canada/newfoundland-labrador/muskrat-falls-inquiry-misguided -project-1.549169.

In the past they wanted to abolish Indian rights, but since 30 to 40 years ago, the universities and schools are taking the cases seriously – *Delgamuukw*, etc. – we have maybe ten or 12 cases. Our title cannot be extinguished now. All governments must respect that. We maintain that these decisions are right. That is why it took time in the past for the band to negotiate with the governments. And when we look at the government of Quebec or Canada I think they want to stick together – they want us to give them their land and respect their laws. That's what they are waiting for. That was happening in the beginning when Frenchmen or English explorers, with the church – they wanted to extinguish our religion and persuade us to be like white men. You know the Innu Nation has nine communities. Before it was only one. After the governments were able to separate the group to create three groups. The government tried to get agreement by this. The east are undecided like Ashuanipi and the west are going ahead. They have a lot of steps to go. The two others are just starting negotiations. I know what they did with the tribal councils. They want to accelerate the processes to have the treaty. But the groups are not at the same stage – they have to wait until the others finish. They have to wait a long time. They say we don't respect what we signed with them. It is not in the treaty. They play with you. They have cards on the table. They don't tell you the truth. They are not in good faith. They just want our signatures and to give us the money and they own the land. Because what's in the land is going to make them money – with our land. It's not the money from the land. It's government money. They are not going to share. Like I said, I once met a Cree leader in Quebec City. I took a walk with that man and I told him 'Look what the government did to your land. We didn't sign. They made a map. They gave you money. What they did was take the land, the river – they gave you small change.' It's like a wheel of fortune. You receive small change. Just a few dollars.

Part Five
'Citizens Plus' or parallel paths?

Chapter 19

Academic solutions

In recent years, academics have turned their attention to finding a solution which will reconcile the need to acknowledge indigenous rights in land with Canadian needs for economic expansion.

The Royal Commission on Aboriginal Peoples (RCAP) maintained that the foundation of Canadian/indigenous relations was that symbolised by the two-row wampum – two peoples living side by side in a spirit of equality, respect and dignity. Having led distinguished academic careers as defenders of indigenous rights, political scientist Alan Cairns and historian J.R. Miller now seek alternatives. They believe it is unrealistic to ignore the common history of the past 250 years, following which indigenous peoples no longer live entirely separate lives. As examples of this, the academics claim that indigenous people today are dependent on the wage economy or the social security payments made by the governments, that generations of children have now received Canadian schooling and that indigenous people enjoy the mechanical and technological advances which have been made over the centuries.

It was Cairns who developed the idea of 'Citizens Plus':[1] that First Nations should be treated as Canadian citizens with special extra rights because of the injustices of the past. Cairns found the governments' failure to stimulate public discussion on the findings of the RCAP Report of 1996 'disturbing and astonishing'.[2] He maintained that the indigenous population of Canada had been silenced and marginalised, and that the settler population did not hear their arguments.[3] He argued that RCAP's continuation of the concept of nation-to-nation dialogue (albeit with a consolidation of the indigenous population into just 80 nations) militated against the idea of a common citizenship and ignored the ties that had developed over time.[4] He adopted

1   A.C. Cairns, *Citizens Plus: Aboriginal Peoples and the Canadian State* (Vancouver: UBC Press, 2000).
2   Ibid., p. 5.
3   Ibid., p. 5.
4   Cairns, *Citizens Plus*, pp. 7–8.

the idea first mooted in the Hawthorn Report,[5] the precursor to the 1969
White Paper entitled *Statement of the Government of Canada on Indian Policy*,
which proposed that indigenous peoples should enjoy full Canadian citizenship
with additional special rights and that existing policies were discriminatory.[6]
Cairns proposed that there should be a continuing debate about the past and
that a real settlement of differences required that the settler population should
make amends.[7] This should include respect for and validation of traditional
practices.[8] As an example of the way in which the first peoples had no voice
in mainstream politics, Cairns observed that the chiefs' submissions to the
1969 White Paper had been totally ignored.[9] He noted the paternalism
which persisted in the Comprehensive Land Claims process.[10] Rejecting both
assimilation and the parallelism of the two-row wampum, he said:

> Neither the assimilationist paradigm nor the parallelism paradigm is
> capable of handling difference and similarity simultaneously. Neither,
> therefore is an adequate recipe for a future constitutional order that
> needs to recognize difference or reinforce similarity. The assimilationist
> paradigm says to Aboriginal peoples, 'You can only become full
> members of Canadian society by ceasing to be yourself.' The parallelism
> paradigm says to non-Aboriginal Canadians, 'You cannot expect to
> share a strong sense of citizenship with Aboriginal peoples for you and
> they are not travelling together.' Clearly, we can no longer deny our
> differences, but if this is all we have, and if we are unable or unwilling to
> try to transcend them in part, we have no basis for trying to reconstruct
> a common country.[11]

The problem with this idea is that there was never a common country in the
first place. Cairns advocates that multiple identities are retained in a citizenship
model, but with greater emphasis on the similarities.[12] Perhaps it would be
simpler, as Calvin Helin does, first to identify common goals such as prosperity,
independence and good health for indigenous communities.

There is also the consideration that the two-row wampum provides effective
links between its two strands in terms of equality, dignity and respect, which
should enable the celebration of similarities and closer ties where appropriate.

Endorsing the views of Canadian liberals such as Will Kymlicka and Charles
Taylor, the main thrust of Cairns's writing is towards greater involvement of
indigenous individuals in Canadian democracy. His concern is that nation-

5   *A Survey of the Contemporary Indians of Canada: Economic, Political, Educational
    Needs and Policies*, 1966.
6   Cairns, *Citizens Plus*, p.12.
7   Ibid., pp. 33–40.
8   Ibid., p. 44.
9   Ibid., p. 52.
10 Ibid., p. 64.
11 Ibid., p. 96.
12 Ibid., p. 109.

based treaty relationships in which indigenous/settler relationships are worked out by negotiations outside the parliamentary system 'nation to nation' isolates indigenous peoples and their differing needs both from mainstream policy-making and from the attention of the settler society.[13] He asks what will enable the two peoples represented by the two-row wampum to take a sustained responsibility for each other.[14] Part of this process, he says, would be for settler Canadians to take responsibility for past misdeeds.[15] But these are not past misdeeds. As long as there is no genuine attempt to address the consequences of indigenous land rights, this remains a present and future problem. Cairns notes with approval Peter Russell's remark: 'Native autonomy and integration must be treated not as choices but as parallel and interacting paths. The path of integration cannot be followed without positive regard for the benefits of participating in the life of the larger and newer society.'[16]

Dismissing the solution in Scandinavia of indigenous representation through the establishment of Sámi parliaments, Cairns concludes that the circumstances which supported nation-to-nation relations have vanished and that it is time to create a new model based on citizenship in order to move beyond the indifference which exists between the indigenous and non-indigenous nations.[17]

J.R. Miller agrees with Cairns that assimilation will not work and, in any event, has lost the support of the settler Canadian population. His solution is that indigenous peoples have to join the mainstream Canadian way of life,[18] in something resembling the multiculturalism offered to modern settlers from abroad rather than assimilation. Writing in 2004, he describes relations between government and First Nations organisations as 'poisonous and apparently intractable'.[19] He rejects the two-row wampum model, saying it is unsustainable in a situation where there are now 633 separate aboriginal nations,[20] but fails to point out that these are the federal government's concepts of 'nations'.

Miller proposes that the Citizens Plus approach would refashion native–non-native relationships recognising these social realities; an approach which,

---

13 Cairns, *Citizens Plus*, p. 135.
14 Ibid., p. 155.
15 Ibid., p. 118.
16 Ibid., p. 203, from P. Russell, 'Aboriginal Nationalism and Quebec Nationalism: Recognition Through Fourth World Colonization', (1997) *Constitutional Forum*, 8 (4) at p. 116.
17 Cairns, *Citizens Plus*, p. 210.
18 J.R. Miller, *Lethal Legacy: Current Native Controversies in Canada* (Toronto: McClelland & Stewart, 2004), p. 261.
19 Ibid., p. 275.
20 Ibid., p. 278.

he says,[21] 'seeks to establish a shared basis in Canadian citizenship, and to supplement it with arrangements that reflect both Aboriginal peoples' special needs and their claim to prior occupancy to consideration by newcomers'.[22]

This arrangement appears to fall far short of the equality, respect and dignity promised in the two-row wampum, certainly so far as equality is concerned. After long and distinguished careers supporting indigenous rights, these writers lend credibility to the governments' land claims practices despite the size of the land transferred into government hands by the new treaties – usually approximately 90 per cent of the land guaranteed to the indigenous peoples under the Royal Proclamation. They do not seem able to divest themselves of the colonialist propensity, pointed out by Will Kymlicka, to '[a]ssert their "principles" in the Empire without realising that what they were really seeking was to impose their own national forms, regardless of the historic life and culture of, and needs of, some quite different community. In short, they thought it sufficient to transplant, where the need was to translate.'[23]

Kymlicka goes on to point out that, in considering minorities within a state, it is wrong to equate the situation of immigrants to a country with that of peoples who were already there. Quoting Walzer, he points out that:

> ... [T]he process of voluntary immigrants differs from the assimilation of conquered or colonised national minorities ... In the latter case, it is wrong to deprive 'intact and rooted communities' that 'were established on lands they had occupied for many centuries' of mother-tongue education or local autonomy. Under these conditions, integration is an 'imposed choice' which national minorities typically (and justifiably) have resisted. The integration of immigrants, by contrast, 'was aimed at peoples far more susceptible to cultural change' for they were not only uprooted: they had uprooted themselves ... they had chosen to come.[24]

This is a distinction which seems to have escaped Cairns and Miller. However, Kymlicka does recognise the difficulty of accommodating indigenous groups within the state.[25] He also points to the propensity of liberal theorists to begin by talking about the moral equality of 'persons' but to end up talking about the equality of 'citizens' without even noticing the shift.[26] Kymlicka concludes that there can only be a true integration into one citizenry when all inhabitants of the state have a shared identity and a sense of common purpose, and that this model will not be possible in the case of the indigenous peoples of Canada

---

21 Ibid., p. 281.
22 Ibid., p. 283.
23 W. Kymlicka, *Multicultural Citizenship: A Liberal Theory of Minority Rights* (Oxford: Clarendon Press, 1995), p. 54.
24 Ibid., p. 63.
25 Ibid., p. 79.
26 Ibid., p.125.

until the 'deep diversity' of their cultures is recognised and honoured.[27] Surely, however, this integration is another form of assimilation and, in any event, in Canada would take centuries.

Tom Flanagan, one of the advisers to the most recent Conservative government, takes the assimilationist view that civilisation is an objective standard and that societies who live by it have greater power over their environment than those who are uncivilised. Clearly misinformed on legal precedent, Flanagan claims that only the Canadian state had sovereignty in Canada and Indian lands were held under the regime put in place by the state. For Flanagan there was no inherent Indian title.[28] He claims that 'European civilization was several thousand years more advanced than the aboriginal cultures of North America both in technology and in social organization. Owing to the tremendous gap in civilization, the European colonization of North America was inevitable and, if we accept the philosophical analysis of John Locke and Emer de Vattel, justifiable.'[29]

Flanagan also asserts that the doctrine of *terra nullius* has never been totally rejected in arbitrations across the colonised world and in particular was not in fact rejected in the Australian case of *Mabo v Queensland [No2]*.[30] However, the Canadian case of *Tsilhqot'in Nation v British Columbia* has now made it clear that there is no place for this doctrine in Canadian law.

In a text intended to influence government policy, he rejects what he calls 'Aboriginal Orthodoxy',[31] the idea that aboriginal peoples came to the American continent as early as 40,000 years ago, and notes their migrations within North America because of war and conquest, buffalo depopulations and the arrival of new people. Ignoring the significance of the phrase as legal shorthand for living on the continent before European contact, Flanagan concludes that aboriginal peoples cannot have lived there 'since time immemorial'.[32] He rejects the finding of the Supreme Court of Canada in *R v Van der Peet*[33] that aboriginal peoples can establish title to land because they were there before first contact, living in organised societies. The Royal Proclamation, he maintains, did not have the sanction of an elected parliament, and was issued over the heads of the settlers and of the Indian people. He describes the Proclamation as 'monarchist, imperialist and mercantile',[34] possibly unaware that foreign policy was the prerogative of the Crown and exercised by the monarchy up until the

27   Kymlicka, *Multicultural Citizenship*, pp. 189–91.
28   T. Flanagan, *First Nations, Second Thoughts* (Montreal: McGill–Queen's University Press, 2000), p. 46.
29   Ibid., p. 6.
30   Ibid., p. 57ff.
31   Flanagan, *First Nations*, Chapter 1.
32   Ibid., pp. 12–20.
33   [1996] 2 SCR 507.
34   Flanagan, *First Nations*, p. 121.

death of Edward VII in 1911. He makes the claim, in the face of 19th-century expansionism and of 20 years of Supreme Court of Canada decisions to the contrary, that Indians could not have ceded title to land and resources to the federal government by treaty because they had never owned the land.

He goes on to reject aboriginal rights to self-government, claiming that indigenous peoples had *de facto* become subjects of the Crown.[35] Flanagan regards European settlement as a fourth wave of migration, of a more powerful people who have the right to assume sovereignty.[36]

Flanagan supports the position set out in the 1969 White Paper that Indian status should no longer be recognised, hailing this as the beginning of a stage of 'negotiation and renewal'.[37] He goes on to reject the far more contemporary findings of RCAP that aboriginal peoples find themselves in their present state of deprivation due to the bad faith of settler Canadians and their governments; instead attributing it to their low level of development, taking as his authority the early Canadian anthropologist Diamond Jenness who, Flanagan asserts, considered the disparity between Europeans and native peoples to be 'huge'. This is his reason for rejecting RCAP's framework of equality in native/non-native relations.[38]

In his review of indigenous self-government,[39] Flanagan notes the unviably small size of many First Nations, leading to a shortage of skilled personnel and scarcity of financial resources. His answer to this is for bands to join together in some kind of tribal government. He describes abuses of leadership positions: meetings held off-reserve at considerable expense, the drawing of unreasonably high salaries, and nepotism. He points to fiscal mismanagement of band funds and harsh treatment of those members of the band who dare to question Band Council activities. Flanagan cites a number of isolated incidents in support of mismanagement which he appears to claim is present in all nations and Band Councils. However, he is right in his conclusion that they are all overloaded with bureaucracy and administration in comparison with Canadian local councils of similar size.

Another problem which Flanagan identifies is the level of government funding for aboriginal communities – whether in the form of fiscal transfers, land claims settlements or natural resource rents – all of which he claims are unearned income. The money comes, he says, without the need to work for it.[40] Flanagan claims that resource-related income is dependent on mere chance – these are windfall gains which improve cash flow but do not necessarily take

35 Ibid., p. 24.
36 Ibid., p. 25.
37 Flanagan, *First Nations*, p. 36.
38 Ibid., pp. 37–8.
39 Ibid., Chapter 6.
40 Flanagan, *First Nations*, p. 102ff.

the poorer members of the community off welfare.[41] He also notes that few of the well-paid jobs generated by resource extraction go to the members of communities who sign agreements.

He recommends that, as a start, aboriginal governments should be taxing their own communities, thus making themselves more accountable to their electorate.[42] In indigenous governance, leaders are accountable to the elders. His next step would be to privatise on-reserve housing, removing it as a source of undue influence exercised by Band Councils on their electorates. He notes that the most successful aboriginal governments are those where there is a separation of powers.[43] As more and more indigenous people move into wider Canadian society, Flanagan advocates that the reserve system be wound down, or at least that Band Councils should no longer be flooded with money – hardly a state which is felt to be the norm in Matimekush Lac John.

Flanagan identifies welfare dependency as the major barrier to improving of quality of life in indigenous villages. He tells us that 41 per cent of on-reserve Indians were on welfare in 1991.[44] He asks: 'If the band offers a place to live, if the government pays for every bit of health care, if some government jobs are available and there is a tradition of sharing the benefits with family members, and if all of this is tax-free, is it surprising that so many people stay on the reserves even if no real jobs are available there?'[45]

Flanagan approves the RCAP's solution of 'building aboriginal economies' because it would enable indigenous peoples to provide for their needs from their own resources and because it is pro-capitalist. Ultimately, however, he rejects the RCAP model because, he says, this kind of regional development tends to increase rather than reduce unemployment – corporations go bankrupt, debts go unpaid.[46]

Flanagan's ultimate conclusion is that what is necessary is better auditing, the creation of a 'politically neutral' body of aboriginal public servants, and self-funding through local taxation. He also floats the idea of dividing up the C$6.3 billion spent annually on indigenous funding and delivering it to individuals and families. Further, he advocates the breaking-up of Band Councils and the separation of the management of public services. His final suggestion is the introduction of individual property rights. The doctrine of the 1969 White Paper lives on.

41   Ibid., p. 184.
42   Ibid., p. 107.
43   Ibid., p. 109.
44   Ibid., p. 176.
45   Flanagan, *First Nations*, p. 177.
46   Ibid., p. 186.

Writing in 2011 with Christopher Alcantara and André le Dressay,[47] Flanagan turned his attention once more to individual property rights for indigenous peoples. With the support of a small number of West Coast Nations, he and his co-authors advocate the repeal of the Indian Act and its replacement with a First Nations Property Ownership Act which would give Band Councils the ability to mortgage, sell, lease or cede land to individuals without the lengthy bureaucracy attaching to the procedure under the Indian Act, some of which persists under the regime of the First Nations Land Management Act (FNLMA) 1999.

The 1999 Act went a long way to addressing the indignities and difficulties promulgated by the Indian Act, by repealing its clauses dealing with indigenous land. It allows indigenous groups to opt in to a regime under which they sign a framework agreement enabling them regulate the land and its environmental protection and natural resources without the Crown's approval. By 2016, 58 of the 633 First Nations had signed up to the system and another 60 had applications in the pipeline. No application is accepted by the government until a code of land management and funding has been agreed both by the members of the applicant First Nation and the government of Canada.[48]

Le Dressay, in his concluding chapters,[49] acknowledges that the FNLMA is an improvement on the Indian Act regime, clarifying land-use laws and creating a land registry system. He says the Act creates long-term tenure but does not create an indefeasible title. Most important, under the FNLMA, the process of releasing the land for exploitation takes only two years or so, in comparison with the 20 or more years it takes to settle a land claim.

Under the legislation proposed by Flanagan et al., indigenous land could be mortgaged, and its advocates believe this would make the use of indigenous land, in particular reserve land, more commercially viable – to the advantage of the band which holds the land. No mention is made by Flanagan either of the government's obligations under the Royal Proclamation or the United Nations Declaration on the Rights of Indigenous Peoples which, under a Liberal government, has finally begun the process of passage into Canadian law. This seems to be another attempt to circumvent the awkward fact that the Crown in Right of Canada holds only a paper title to indigenous land. It is difficult not to believe that the underlying purpose of this legislation would be the enrichment of those corporations and individuals intent on resource extraction. The authors note on the very first page the wealth which is tied up in indigenous land, and frequent references are made throughout the book to

47 T. Flanagan, C. Alcantara and A. Le Dressay, *Beyond the Indian Act: Restoring Aboriginal Property Rights* (2nd edn) (Montreal: Mc Gill–Queen's University Press, 2011).

48 See S. Boutillet, *An Unsung Success: The First Nations Land Management Act Policy Options*.

49 Flanagan, Alcantara and Le Dressay, *Beyond the Indian Act*, p. 151.

the economic advantages of indigenous access to 'the market', and to the need for certainty.

As with FNLMA, under the proposed legislation participation by interested First Nations would be optional. For those opting in, they would either own the reversionary title to the land or an 'allodial' title would be created which would mean that there was, in effect, no reversionary title. This, Flanagan says, would enable First Nations to grant fee simple titles to *individuals* (emphasis added).[50] The consequence of this would be that the individual could alienate land just as any settler Canadian could and, ultimately, the land could pass out of indigenous hands altogether. Referencing Hayek and his individualistic philosophy, Flanagan approves this system, comparing it to Margaret Thatcher's 'right to buy' social housing scheme in the United Kingdom, which has led to chronic public housing shortages in the country today.[51]

Despite recent Canadian Supreme Court judgments, in his section of the book Alcantara dismisses the force and effect of the Royal Proclamation, claiming that: 'There was no attempt at negotiation or even consultation with the natives of North America regarding the property rights which the Proclamation attributed to them.'[52]

What, then, it might be asked, was the purpose of the great gathering at Niagara at which wampum belts were distributed recording indigenous agreement to the terms of the Proclamation? Despite the ambiguity of the text, which Alcantara correctly points out, by taking control of the land to the detriment of the indigenous peoples the Crown assumed a fiduciary duty, and the parallel paths of the wampum belts indicated that in all other respects than control of alienation of the land, the indigenous peoples could continue on the land as they had before.

Le Dressay, in the third section of the book, has some interesting ideas as to the future. The proposed legislation would be based on a Torrens registration system which, unlike the FNLMA scheme, would guarantee title once registered. Having worked with First Nations wishing to take up the FNLMA opportunities, he notes that they see it as an escape from the inevitable poverty imposed under the Indian Act. Le Dressay sees the solution in private investment,[53] which he says would be more forthcoming with a more certain property regime. However, he points out that:

> Even economic development is a controversial goal because many First Nations fear it masks an agenda for the federal government to abandon its fiduciary obligations. These apprehensions are exacerbated because the business constituency within First Nations is small and many First Nations opinion leaders were educated in law or history rather than business or

50 Flanagan, Alcantara and Le Dressay, *Beyond the Indian Act*, p. 5.
51 Ibid., p. 16.
52 Ibid., p. 58.
53 Flanagan, Alcantara and Le Dressay, *Beyond the Indian Act*, p. 139.

economics. This is why all escapes [from poverty and the Indian Act]
generally require strong First Nations leadership and a voluntary approach
so that interested First Nations can make the break when they are ready.

Le Dressay's thesis is that the proposed First Nations Property Ownership Act
would reduce property transaction costs, afford First Nations 'clear underlying
and individual property ownership' and increase indigenous land values to a
level competitive with Canadian land values.[54] He compares this with the
benefits the Nisga'a Nation received under its land settlement. In that case,
the reversionary title to indigenous lands lies with the province, should the
Nisga'a Nation cease to exist. In their land management legislation, the Nisga'a
adopted the Torrens registration system but they are still working towards
registration which would protect individual title.

Looking at the detail of how a First Nations Property Ownership Act
(FNPOA) would work, Le Dressay identifies five prerequisites to escape from
the Indian Act:

a) It must be First-Nations-led.

b) It must provide First Nations with powers to replace parts of the
Indian Act.

c) It must support markets on First Nations land so that they become
independent.

d) It must be optional.

e) It must create First Nations institutions to facilitate takeover of
responsibilities from the federal Department of Indigenous and
Northern Affairs Canada.[55]

The FNPOA, he says, is not a reflection of the 1969 White Paper because it
promotes inalienable reversionary rights to indigenous title.

Where Flanagan gives a considered, albeit fairly shallow, argument from
his standpoint that Locke and Vattel provide a firm foundation for European
land rights and sovereignty in the New World, Frances Widdowson and Albert
Howard by contrast provide a disrespectful, ill-considered rant about what they
call 'the Aboriginal Industry' in *Disrobing the Aboriginal Industry: The Deception
Behind Indigenous Cultural Preservation*.[56] A number of academic writers
refused to offer their texts for publication by McGill following its acceptance
of this diatribe against all who seek a constructive solution to the situation in
which Canada's aboriginal peoples find themselves.[57] However, their views are

---

54   Flanagan, Alcantara and Le Dressay, *Beyond the Indian Act*, p. 162.
55   Ibid., p. 169.
56   F. Widdowson and A. Howard, *Disrobing the Aboriginal Industry: The Deception
Behind Indigenous Cultural Preservation* (Montreal: McGill–Queens University
Press, 2008).
57   Email correspondence with Camille Giret, University of Quebec at Chicoutimi.

representative of a significant proportion of the non-indigenous population of Canada and, again, seek to validate the governments' approach to the land claims and resource extraction process.

In the most pejorative language they can find, the authors dismiss traditional knowledge and oral history as irrelevant. In an introduction entitled 'Discovering the Emperor's Nudity', they give a description of the way in which traditional knowledge is presented before inquiries, usually in the form of recordings and notes of interviews with elders. They describe the way in which indigenous leaders are slow to get their points across, not understanding that they think before they speak. They dismiss these processes as unsystematic and their proponents as giving undue weight to cultural difference.[58] Even today, in the 21st century, they place indigenous peoples as still in the Stone Age, approving Lewis Henry Morgan's use of the terms 'barbarism', 'savagery' and 'civilization' to classify the various stages of human development.[59]

Widdowson and Howard describe the progress in establishing land rights which indigenous peoples have made through the courts, limited as it is, as 'stealthful'. Judges, they say with disapproval, are becoming more active.[60] They prefer the doubtful evidence of Sheila Robinson that the Gitksan and Wet'suweten had learned to live in ordered societies from contact with Europeans for centuries prior to official first contact – approved at first instance by Judge McEachern in *Delgamuukw*[61] – to that of anthropologists who have spent years in the field working with the indigenous peoples concerned. Robinson relied on her doctoral thesis on work with other peoples. She had never worked with the Gitksan or Wet'suweten.[62]

They claim that the cultural gap between indigenous communities and Europeans at the point of contact was that between the Neolithic and the later stages of capitalism. Since then, they continue, aboriginal peoples have been helped into the modern world with the advantages of 'the ministrations of the church for hundreds of years; they also use modern technology such as computers, pickup trucks, and cell phones'.[63]

At a time when the apparatus of the Truth and Reconciliation Commission was crossing Canada to take testimony on, and to commemorate the victims of, the Indian Residential Schools system, Widdowson and Howard assert:

58 Widdowson and Howard, *Disrobing the Aboriginal Industry*, pp. 5–12.
59 Ibid., p. 12.
60 Ibid., p. 85.
61 [1991] DLR (4th) 79.
62 Ibid., p. 101. For an analysis of the anthropologists' evidence in *Delgamuukw* see E. Cassell, 'Anthropologists in the Canadian Courts' in M. Freeman and D. Napier (eds.), *Law And Anthropology* (Oxford: Oxford University Press, 2008).
63 Ibid., p. 13.

> The most significant initiative with respect to this [assimilationist]
> agenda came to be the residential school system; removing aboriginal
> children from their communities was intended to reduce the
> impediment of a tribal and subsistence lifestyle on their development.
> Thus, the pace of the civilizing process could be increased and aboriginal
> peoples more effectively assimilated into the social fabric … Aside
> from the horrors of physical and sexual abuse, the church is accused
> of destroying aboriginal culture by forcing aboriginal children to speak
> English and adopt Christianity, by disrupting community child-rearing
> practices, and by subjecting aboriginal children to disciplines that were
> alien to their traditions.[64]

Unsurprisingly, the writers dismiss the widely held view that this project
amounted to cultural genocide. Anticipating a response supportive of their
'thesis', they ask the question: what would aboriginal communities be like if
they had not been subjected to residential schooling? The people of Matimekush
Lac John would provide them with an answer which might surprise them.

The other thrust of Widdowson and Howard's argument is that non-native
lawyers, anthropologists and archaeologists who work to enable indigenous
communities to improve their lot are not altogether altruistic and work in
what they call the 'Aboriginal Industry' for their own benefit. They point to
the 'altruistic posture' assumed by such people and maintain that this cloaks
the need to keep the people they purport to help in dependency. They claim
that some of these workers can be naively uncritical of Rousseau's concept
of the 'noble savage' while others see themselves strictly as professionals who
take up consultative roles. This second group, they say, can be cynical and
disinterested.[65]

They come closest to making their point that there is an aboriginal industry
when discussing the activities of consultants and the aboriginal leaders they
advise. They describe meetings where the consultants interpret and translate the
proceedings, and both consultants and clients receive sinecures and attendance
fees. They make sweeping claims of corruption in all native administration
and claim this is played down by the federal government.[66] They note the
disconnect between the aboriginal leadership and the grassroots people it
represents. They say this disconnect flows from the fact that funding for all
activities seeking to establish native rights comes from governments.[67] They
describe self-government as the basis for 'tribal dictatorships'.[68]

The writers portray dealings between settler Canadians and native peoples as
an Orwellian nightmare of double-speak. They end by describing the difficulty

64   Ibid., pp. 14–15.
65   Ibid., p. 20ff.
66   Ibid., p. 117.
67   Ibid., pp. 29–30.
68   Ibid., p. 106.

they had in finding a publisher for their vituperative, simplistic text, quoting an article in Canada's *Globe and Mail* newspaper in which the book was described as 'so full of mean-spiritedness and factual distortion as to make it not worth refuting in detail'.[69] Yet the online responses to newspaper coverage of stories of successful court cases and negotiated settlements with native nations display similar levels of vitriol. There are many settler Canadians, some of my own relatives among them, who are adamant that all native rights are 'granted' by the federal government and paid for out of settler Canadians' taxes. This is fuelled by a genuine sense of grievance that so much money is poured into proposed solutions with no real return.

With the airing of 'research' like this, the Canadian governments are relatively free to pursue their resource extraction policies safe in the knowledge that they have the backing of voters who feel native peoples have no entitlement to the land or its resources. As long as the federal government is able to perpetuate the myth that Canadian settlers are equally entitled to indigenous lands and that indigenous peoples do not work for their subsistence, they will have a mandate to take land and resources at will with no regard for the solemn undertakings given in 1763.

69 Ibid., p. 215.

Among all those groups that are around here I think that the government is creating a lot of prejudice against us. They undermine a lot of our rights. We are the poorest of the poorest in the sense that we are the last in line. If you look all around here – all the ore that has been exploited and the wealth generated and created and even today all the work that has been done on the exploration – we still haven't seen any benefit for our community and all of this is done without our knowledge or consent – without our prior consent. And this is our homeland.

> Unfortunately what happened is that without evidence or any proof, the Pierre Trudeau government signed deals with aboriginal groups, for example the Naskapi, without any evidence that they owned the land, and now it is the same with the Labrador Innu. They have no proof or claim that they are the rightful owners of the land that they are occupying right at this moment. I can say that this is my land.

I would have liked back then to have the right resources to work with me, the right people to work with me, and somehow it wasn't possible. This work that we tried to do with the other chiefs in this native or indigenous environment was picked up by a bunch of lawyers and they screwed up the whole thing.

> The fundamental problem that underlies the negotiations is those pre-set rules, because the federal negotiators come up with examples. They will tell you what they did in other places with other nations. But we have a right to have our own views on this and to say for us it is different. You were always stuck with the thought that you either take the money or resign.

The land would belong to the government if we signed. It is sad to see people signing over their rights to the government in return for money – they do not realise they are giving money to the government. Money given on signing doesn't last.

Chapter 20

Indigenous solutions: they talk, we listen

When I asked the Innu in Matimekush Lac John what they would say to settler Canadians about indigenous rights, the answer was unanimous – nothing, since settler Canadians never listen. In the 50 years since the notorious 1969 White Paper on Indian policy, the growing body of indigenous leaders and academics have come up with solutions which would go a long way towards reconciling the differing needs and values of both settlers and indigenous peoples – but these have largely been ignored.

In his seminal work in answer to the White Paper, Harold Cardinal[1] accused the Pierre Trudeau government of washing its hands of its responsibilities towards Indians. His criticisms still resonate today. He questions the sincerity of a government which protests at the persecution of minorities in other countries while 'ignoring the plight of Eskimo, Metis and Indians in their own country. There is little knowledge of native circumstances in Canada and even less interest. To the native, one fact is apparent – the average Canadian does not give a damn.'[2]

Cardinal goes on to point out the ethnocentric nature of Canadian society and its lack of vision, which leads it to promote its own culture and values to the exclusion of those of the indigenous peoples. He observes: 'Throughout the hundreds of years of Indian–government relationship, political leaders responsible for matters relating to Indians have been outstanding in their ignorance of the native people and remarkable in their insensitivity to the needs and aspirations of the Indians in Canada.'[3]

Writing before the 1973 decision in *Calder v Attorney General for British Columbia*,[4] before the implementation of the modern treaty process, and with national indigenous organisations in their infancy, he points to the usurpation

---

1   H. Cardinal, *The Unjust Society: The Tragedy of Canada's Indians* (Edmonton: M G Hurtig Limited, 1969).
2   Ibid., p. 3.
3   Ibid., p. 6.
4   Cardinal, *The Unjust Society*, p. 11.

of the aboriginal right to self-government and the endless promises of change
which are – even now – never fulfilled. Cardinal calls for both sides to abandon
negative attitudes towards each other and to end the long period of separation
from each other, and for settlers to accept Indians as individuals in their
own right who wish to work with the dominant society without the need to
assimilate. He declares that it is time for the white man to do the listening in
order to begin a purposeful dialogue.

While deploring the divisive and demeaning nature of the Indian Act,
Cardinal recognised that, with the implementation of the White Paper and
the abolition of the Act, Indians stood to lose a large part of their identity
and their rights under the old treaties. His thesis was that Indians must be
allowed to rebuild their social institutions themselves, with both social and
political leadership.[5] Canadians, he says, must fully accept Indian identity. In
response to Pierre Trudeau's assertion that, 'It is inconceivable that one section
of a society should have a treaty with another section of society. The Indians
should become Canadians as have all other Canadians,'[6] Cardinal answers:

> To the Indians of Canada, the treaties represent an Indian Magna
> Carta. The treaties are important to us because we entered into these
> negotiations with faith, with hope for a better life with honour. We
> have survived for over a century on little but that hope. Did the white
> man enter into them with something less in mind? Or have the heirs
> of the men who signed in honour somehow disavowed the obligation
> passed down to them?
>
> …
>
> While we find much to quarrel with in the treaties as they were signed,
> they are, we contend, important, not so much for their content as for
> the principles they imply in their very existence.[7]

Emphasising the importance and relevance of the treaties in the modern
day, Cardinal nevertheless calls for them to be renegotiated. He describes the
demotivating effects of the Indian Act, when all meaningful power over the
reserve lies with the Department of Indian Affairs, especially financial affairs,
provision of medical facilities, housing and education:

> … the Indian Act, that piece of colonial legislation, enslaved and
> bound the Indian to a life under a tyranny often as cruel and harsh
> as that of any totalitarian state. The only recourse allowed victims of
> the act is enfranchisement, whereby the Indian is expected to deny his
> birthright, declare himself no longer an Indian and leave the reserve,

5   Ibid., p. 25.
6   Ibid., p. 28.
7   Cardinal, *The Unjust Society*, p. 36.

divesting himself of all his interest in his land and people. This course of action is one that any human being would hesitate to take.[8]

Later Cardinal observes: 'Time and again, in the very department which was set up to protect our rights, decisions have been made that openly flaunt the treaties.'[9]

Cardinal's riposte also draws attention to the fact that indigenous peoples were promised full consultation on the contents of the 1969 White Paper, but this was never forthcoming (even though the government claimed it was, on the basis that it called meetings with indigenous leaders at which officials promised that consultation would come later).[10]

Like most writers, indigenous and non-indigenous, Cardinal also deplores the welfare trap; a view which, he says, is shared by the majority of Indian people.[11] He demands that indigenous people be put in charge of their own destiny, be allowed to set their own goals and create their own opportunities.[12] This, surely, is the true objective of the Royal Proclamation and the wampum belts; the Crown reserving to itself only the power to deal in indigenous land. Further, these are still the demands of the Innu of Matimekush Lac John 50 years on.

Most white people wishing to help, Cardinal says, know not what they do. If they wish to help, they should 'nourish the initiative of the Indian people' and not inhibit the growth of their potential.[13] Yet this is a message ignored with impunity by lawyers and consultants who tell indigenous people that surrender of their lands is the only game in town.

Cardinal insisted that there should be no repeal of the Indian Act until all indigenous rights were recognised in Canada. With the promise of Trudeau *fils* to pass UNDRIP fully into Canadian law, the first true steps of recognition have been taken, but it remains to be seen how this UN legislation will be implemented in Canadian domestic law. Like other indigenous writers, Cardinal called for positive recognition of Indian contributions to wider society.[14] Further, he said: 'Keep in mind, also, that no amount of preaching by the federal government about goodwill and acceptance of Indian values can change the attitude of Canadians generally unless the Indian achieves the position of economic self-sufficiency.'

8   Ibid., p. 45.
9   Ibid., p. 47.
10 Ibid., p. 123ff.
11 Ibid., p. 63.
12 Cardinal, *The Unjust Society*, p. 64.
13 Ibid., p. 91.
14 Ibid., p. 143.

This is a point expanded by Calvin Helin (see below). Cardinal also noted the way in which the White Paper attempted to deny the force and effect of the treaties, calling their provisions 'limited and minimal', and showing, he asserts, utter contempt. By contrast the Indians say that a plain reading of the treaties is 'inadequate and, more than that, unjust'.[15] He concludes that all trust of the Indians for the government has been lost.

Turning to land title, in the White Paper provision proposing that each indigenous community should have the right to decide the manner in which they intend to manage their land,[16] Cardinal foresaw the danger that proposals decided by one community would be imposed on others – exactly the effect of the modern policy with regard to comprehensive land claims.

Writing at much the same time as Cardinal, Vine Deloria turns the tables on the dominant North American society. In *We Talk, You Listen*,[17] he examines America (and Canada) in its relations with indigenous peoples with the same scrutiny usually applied to the first peoples. He points to the fissures forming in the American Dream with 1960s opposition to consumerism, the devastation of the environment and the Vietnam War. He observes that 'American society is unconsciously going Indian':[18]

> There is no doubt in my mind that a major crisis exists. I believe, however, that it is deeper and more profound than racism, violence, and economic deprivation, American society is undergoing a total replacement of its philosophical concepts. Words are being emptied of old meanings and new values are coming in to fill the vacuum. Racial antagonisms, inflation, ecological destruction, and power groups are all symptoms of the emergence of a new world view of man and his society. Today thought patterns are shifting from the traditional emphasis on the solitary individual to as yet unrelated definitions of man as a member of a specific group.[19]

Deloria is writing for the 'electric' age but what he says applies equally, if not more so, to the electronic age. He urges us to reflect on the meaning of the changes, attributing them in large part to the speed of modern communication and the supremacy of scientific knowledge. He says that, following the Depression, Americans lost faith in the American Dream.[20] America, like Canada, tried to end its federal responsibilities for the Indians.

---

15 Cardinal, *The Unjust Society*, p. 153.
16 Ibid., p. 159.
17 V. Deloria, *We Talk, You Listen: New Tribes, New Turf* (Nebraska: Bison Books, 1970) (republished 2007).
18 Ibid., p. 11.
19 Ibid., p. 15.
20 Deloria, *We Talk, You Listen*, p. 22.

Deloria believes that: 'The key to the communication gap is thus really quite simple. We must return to and understand the land we occupy. Communications have made the continent a part of the global village. The process must be reversed. The land must now define the role communications can play to make the country fruitful again.'[21]

Sadly, Deloria did not live to hear the voices from the protest groups Idle No More and Occupy joined in promotion of the values of their predecessors, who challenged the American myth and demanded a more human-scale approach to change.

Deloria calls for society to reject the 'conquest-orientated' interpretation of the American Constitution, saying that it should provide adequate protection of existing treaty rights and provide a balance between groups – as it has for conflicts between individuals.[22] He believes not in revolution, which he says tends to be self-destructive, but in change within the existing system.[23]

Deloria is also critical of both white liberals and militant leaders within the indigenous community. He says that ordinary folk within the different white and minority groups understand each other better than the leaders,[24] saying:

> The liberals who create havoc within the minority groups are people in the official structure, be it church or state, private or public organization, who wield tremendous amounts of power and who do not for a moment listen to anyone … These are [people] who beat people of goodwill into the ground by calling them do-gooders. By blasting the motives of the average man, the liberals within the power structure are able to raise themselves as knowledgeable, authority figures to whom the common citizen then cedes all power and funding sources, asking only that the problem be resolved.[25]

He asks for the inclusion of the 'others' – those like Indians who are never consulted on the big decisions that affect them relating to housing, roadbuilding and industrial development. He calls for greater understanding of the needs of the 'others' when such decisions are made. He calls for the recognition of the sovereignty of all minority groups so that group rights are recognised rather than the rights of individuals within the group.[26] Deloria concludes that the American Constitution did not meet the needs of government of the increasing settler population:

> The new government was immediately plagued with two problems – land acquisition and slavery. Without land it could not push west to

21 Ibid., p. 32.
22 Ibid., p. 43.
23 Ibid., pp. 62–4.
24 Ibid., p. 83.
25 Deloria, *We Talk, You Listen*, p. 84.
26 Ibid., p. 118.

develop itself, and without cheap labor in the South it could not settle the country. The Constitution, although based upon the freedom and equality of all mankind, did not extend those rights to every group. The social compact was created among Western Europeans and it spoke only tangentially of non-Europeans. Congress was given authority to deal with the original inhabitants on the basis of regulating commerce.[27]

It was only in 1871, at the end of the treaty process, that Indians were brought within the remit of the US Constitution, and even then not as individuals. As in Canada under the Indian Act, Indians in the US had to relinquish their indigenous rights in order to obtain emancipation. Deloria suggests that there is no need for a new Constitution, but for the recognition of rights in common as well as individual rights. However, while minority groups call for a pledge of faith from white society, white society continues to deal with minority groups on a contractual basis, as in the treaties. Nevertheless, he acknowledged that there had been more progress on this score among Indian groups since the formation of the Indian Claims Commission to deal with land claims.

Deloria also raises the issue of the rising power of corporations: 'The accumulation of capital, development of income, and distribution of profits characterizes the profit-making corporations. To achieve this goal, land and natural resources have been destroyed, communities dispersed or dominated, and social problems unwittingly created. The profit-making corporations have generally disclaimed any responsibility for the conditions created by their activities.'[28]

Does it not seem strange that Flanagan et al. do not turn their attention to what Deloria terms these 'organizations that produce income but have no social responsibility' before focussing their attention on the 'Aboriginal Industry'? Deloria also deplores the conflict between profit-making organisations and those not-for-profit organisations which try to assume social responsibility for the victims of capitalism – from which he predicts 'severe oppression' from the right or 'destruction of the economic system' from the left.[29] He sees the solution in a return to tribal government and community development corporations to manage the vast resources on indigenous lands. These moves would bring about a return to community-based governance. As to progress, he concludes:

> In recent years we have come to understand what progress is. It is the total replacement of nature by an artificial technology. Progress is the absolute destruction of the real world in favor of a technology that creates a comfortable way of life for a few fortunately situated people. Within our lifetime the difference between the Indian use of land

27 Ibid., p. 144ff.
28 Deloria, *We Talk, You Listen*, p. 153.
29 Ibid., p. 156.

and the white use of land will become crystal clear. The Indian lived with his land. *The white destroyed his land. He destroyed planet earth.* (Deloria's emphasis)[30]

This, he says, is the reason that settler society is re-forming into tribes of its own. Deloria's prediction was that mankind would not survive for 50 years from the time he was writing, 1970.

Taiaiake Alfred wrote his *Indigenous Manifesto*[31] following the Oka crisis. Through the trope of the Rotinohshonni ceremony of condolence, in his great polemic Alfred declares:

> Indigenous people today are seeking to transcend the history of pain and loss that began with the coming of Europeans into our world. In the past 500 years, our people have suffered murderous onslaughts of greed and disease. Even as history's shadow lengthens to mark the passing of that brutal age, the Western compulsion to control remains strong. To preserve what is left of our culture and lands is a constant fight. Some indigenous people believe the statements of regret and promises of reconciliation spoken by our oppressors. Some have come to trust and accept the world that has been created through the colonization of America. But those who find sincerity and comfort in the oppressor, who bind themselves to recent promises, must yield to the assimilationist demands of the mainstream and abandon any meaningful attachment to an indigenous cultural and political reality. And in so doing they are lost to the rest of us. Thankfully, those who accept the colonization of their nations are a small minority. Most people continue to participate in, or at least support, the struggle to gain recognition and respect for their right to exist as peoples, unencumbered by demands, controls, and false identities imposed on them by others.[32]

He says that affording indigenous peoples a 'reasonable' standard of life does nothing to end the 'European genocide' of 500 years while their nationhood is denied.[33] He calls for the induction of more 'special individuals' into the culture of leadership: people who understand and will abide by indigenous traditions, and will work to counter the vulgar, westernised leadership which has caused the current crisis in most indigenous communities. He does not see this as a return to the past but as invigoration of indigenous politics. He acknowledges that this will not be a uniform process across all nations.[34]

Alfred describes the fluid nature of indigenous political power and its respect for individual autonomy, which precludes the concept of sovereignty because on a matter of conscience no individual surrenders their power to

30   Ibid., p. 186.
31   T. Alfred, *Peace, Power and Righteousness: An Indigenous Manifesto* (Don Mills, Ontario: Oxford University Press, 1999).
32   Ibid., p. xi.
33   Ibid., p. xv.
34   Alfred, *Peace, Power and Righteousness*, p. 2ff.

decide for themselves to a superior authority. Unlike westernised governance, indigenous decision-making is consensual. There is no element of coercion.[35] In native politics, Alfred says: 'There is a division between those who serve the system and those who serve the people. In a colonial system designed to undermine, divide, and assimilate indigenous people, those who achieve power run the risk of becoming instruments of those objectives.'[36]

Nevertheless, he says the failure to confront these failures in leadership rests with the indigenous peoples themselves and that they have a responsibility to the ancestors to rebuild the foundations of nationhood – as he says, 'Native people can't cry their way to nationhood'.[37]

Alfred tells us that power exercised in the non-indigenous way involves the imposition of the leader's will on others and the satisfaction of personal motives using the ability to control resources such as service provision and connections to the outside world. He recognises that, in order for indigenous nations to withdraw from colonial power, they still have to deal with the state.[38] He counsels against adopting the western concept of sovereignty because of the sharp contrast between the concept of the 'state' and the indigenous concept of nationhood, where there is no absolute authority or hierarchy.[39] For example, in land claims, assertion of Canadian sovereignty over indigenous land and peoples underpins the power structure, and consequently perpetuates the colonial structure on which settler/indigenous relationships are based, such that 'any progress made towards justice will be marginal'. Alfred sees sovereignty as a legal fiction.

Where Flanagan and Alcantara are quick to promote the immediate gains which follow land claims settlements and the First Nations Land Management Act, Alfred presses for the long-term gains from returning to an indigenous form of government.[40] Alfred maintains that indigenous leaders '… know what's right; they have long known what's wrong as well, and what needs to be done. But they choose to suppress their knowledge and accept the dispossession and disempowerment that are part of being colonized. Wilfully ignoring what is ultimately the only resolution – to forsake good relations with the state – they join the conspiracy of silence that has perpetuated the historical injustice done to their people.'[41]

35 Ibid., pp. 25–7.
36 Ibid., p. 30.
37 Ibid., p. 35ff.
38 Alfred, *Peace, Power and Righteousness*, p. 47.
39 Ibid., p. 56ff.
40 Ibid., p. 97.
41 Ibid., p. 98.

Yet the leaders in Matimekush Lac John are paying the crippling price of holding out for their rights: by taking a stand, they remain wards of the Crown and subject to its whims in the matter of withholding finance.

Alfred recognises that economic development does not flow from money pumped into native communities but rather from learning, skills and business acumen and from taking control of indigenous lands and using them for the benefit of their true owners.[42] He deplores the 'aggressive manipulation of the state' in the modern treaty process,[43] which relies on settler ignorance, native apathy and the grooming of native leaders, all based on the false premise that Canada owns the land:

> In effect, the Canadian government arrogantly asserts ownership rights over the identity of indigenous nations. On the eve of the twenty-first century, Canada's final solution to the Indian Problem is to force indigenous peoples who have inhabited the land for millennia to do what no other people in the world is obliged to do: to formalize a definition of themselves and agree a set of criteria for determining membership that will not be subject to evolution or change as the group responds to the shifting realities of the political and economic environment.[44]

This is what the treaty principle of 'certainty' truly means. In brief, Taiaiake Alfred's manifesto is:

> In our relations with others, we need to engage society as a whole in an argument about justice that will bring about real changes in political practice. We need to convince others to join us in challenging the state's oppression of indigenous peoples. This will require a broad-based intellectual and political movement away from prevailing beliefs and structures. All actions in this effort – not just our own but those of everyone who supports us – must be inspired and guided by four principles. First, undermine the intellectual premises of colonialism. Second, act on the moral imperative for change. Third, do not cooperate with colonialism. Fourth and last, resist further injustice. Decolonization will be achieved by hard work and sacrifice based on these principles, in concert with the restoration of an indigenous political culture within our communities.

> These words are a manifesto, a challenge, a call for action. Don't preserve tradition, live it! Let us develop a good mind and do what is necessary to heal the damage done to us and bring back to life the culture of peace, power and righteousness that is the indigenous way.[45]

Calvin Helin echoes Alfred's call to action in his mantra 'Wai Wah!' – 'Just do it'. He too is deeply concerned at the levels of dependency and social

42 Alfred, *Peace, Power and Righteousness*, p. 116.
43 Ibid., p. 119.
44 Ibid., p. 123.
45 Ibid., p. 145.

dysfunction in indigenous communities although his proposed solution is not assimilation but, like Alfred's, a return to the old values of self-reliance. His starting point is the question: 'What can be done to make the lives of indigenous peoples better?'[46] Taking a much more pragmatic approach, he calls for an open and frank discussion of the problems besetting indigenous communities. He too says that the non-aboriginal 'hucksters' only add to the despair of the communities they claim to serve.[47] As the indigenous elders in Matimekush have testified, Helin claims that the Department of Aboriginal Affairs has promoted dependency with its firm hold on all expenditure in indigenous villages which remain wards of the Crown. His thesis is that these problems will never be overcome until the indigenous people take control of the situation,[48] as the best economic decisions are made by people who are spending their own money, creating their own wealth.[49] The indigenous peoples themselves must take responsibility for getting themselves out of the welfare trap.[50] This is a much more positive, constructive approach to the future of Canadian–indigenous relations than those of Flanagan and Widdowson.

He looks to pre-contact practices to find solutions for today, citing the trade between the peoples of the coastal and interior regions of what is now British Columbia in order to supply the needs of others.[51] In the absence of government welfare payments, Helin says that 'stark reality ensured that a fundamental level of organization and understanding pervaded the very grassroots of the tribal structure.'[52]

He too advocates the leadership style of the elders who paid close attention to the conditions of their people and gave good advice. Describing the current state of indigenous leadership, Helin concludes: 'The further problem with the manner in which governance is exercised in First Nations is that the system that has arisen is effectively a closed loop that concentrates all political power in the hands of chiefs at the same time as politically disempowering the great masses of community members ... This powerlessness directly contributes to the existing status quo of Aboriginal poverty.'[53]

This problem, he says, extends to the Assembly of First Nations, citing the failed attempt by Matthew Coon Come to have his successor chosen by direct election. The failure arose because the federal government threatened

46   Helin, *Dances with Dependency*, p. 30.
47   Ibid., p. 36.
48   Ibid., p. 128.
49   Ibid., p. 139.
50   Ibid., p. 167.
51   Ibid., p. 80.
52   Helin, *Dances with Dependency*, p. 82.
53   Ibid., p. 145.

to withdraw funding from the Assembly. This resulted in a situation in which chiefs are not accountable to their electorate but to the Department of Aboriginal Affairs. Helin says that a 'banana-republic-like mindset prevails in many communities'.[54] He sees new opportunities in the new definitions of meaningful consultation emerging from the Supreme Court.[55] He supports the initiative of the First Nations Land Management Act and the introduction of the First Nations Finance Authority, the First Nations Tax Commission, the First Nations Financial Management Board and First Nations Statistics because they promote 'a whole new fiscal framework for doing business on reserves'.[56] Yet, I would suggest, these are Canadian constructs, designed to bring indigenous economies into line with the mainstream.

All these writers, indigenous and non-indigenous, whatever their point of view, identify the same obstacles in the path to full indigenous emancipation in Canada:

- failure to honour the treaties;

- failure to repeal the Indian Act;

- the continued existence of the Department of Indian Affairs in its many forms;

- the Comprehensive Land Claims process;

- life on welfare payments;

- lack of education; and

- lawyers, consultants and leaders who do not negotiate in the true interests of the people they represent.

John Borrows goes much further. He returns to the principles laid down by Harold Cardinal in his 1969 book *The Unjust Society* and finds them as relevant at the beginning of the 21st century as they were in 1969. Yet where Cardinal and the Royal Commission on Aboriginal Peoples call for aboriginal control of aboriginal affairs, Borrows has even more radical solutions. Noting that, since Cardinal's text:

> All the while, Aboriginal citizenship with the land is being slowly diminished. The disfranchisement of our people (and our spirits) from the land, water, animals and trees continues at an alarming rate. Do we need a new story, new solutions? We do. We no longer need a revolutionary message for a transformative time: we need a transformative message in a reactionary time ... To preserve and extend

54   Ibid., p. 156.
55   Ibid., p. 189.
56   Ibid., pp. 201–2.

our participation with the land, it is time to talk also of Aboriginal
control of Canadian affairs.[57]

He calls on indigenous peoples, especially those in positions of authority, both
individually and in groups to incorporate indigenous ideals and perspectives
into mainstream thinking and thus expand indigenous influence throughout
Canada. It is no longer enough to leave this to the elders and teachers
within communities. What Borrows is calling for is not assimilation, but for
'Canadian citizenship under Aboriginal influence': 'Aboriginal peoples can
resist assimilation by applying their traditions to answer the questions they
encounter in the multifaceted pluralistic world they now inhabit.'[58]

Borrows returns to the theme of the wampum belts distributed at the great
gathering at Niagara in 1764, the Gus Wen Tah.[59] Rather than looking at the
two rows of purple beads representing the two separate nations, he looks at the
three rows of white beads in which they are embedded. He says that the three
white rows signify the importance of sharing and interdependence and stand
for peace, friendship and respect and the linking of the two cultures. Borrows
also speaks of the second belt which was present at Niagara, which depicted a
ship at one end of the belt and 24 Indians holding hands to reach the Quebec
shore. This belt was touched by the participants at Niagara and from it, he
concludes that it supports 'a notion of citizenship that encourages autonomy
and at the same time unifies us to one another and the lands we rely on'.[60]

In his book *Recovering Canada*,[61] Borrows deplores the uncritical acceptance
of the Canadian courts that indigenous lands are vested in the Crown and that
the Crown holds sovereignty and underlying title to these lands:

> Some Canadians do not realize that the nation is built upon a deeply
> troubling relationship with its original owners and governors. Many
> people assume that since their experience of life in Canada is one of
> fairness and justice, most people must experience life in Canada in the
> same way. However, Canada is a country that does not have an 'even'
> experience of justice. Aboriginal peoples have often been denied the
> essential legal rights in property (title) and contract law (treaties) that
> lie at the heart of our private law ordering. This should be of concern
> to all Canadians because such a basic failure of the rule of law presents

57 J. Borrows, 'Landed Citizenship: Narratives of Aboriginal Political Participation',
    in W. Kymlicka and W. Norman (eds.), *Citizenship in Diverse Societies* (Oxford:
    Oxford University Press, 2000), pp. 326–42 at p. 328ff.
58 Borrows, 'Landed Citizenship', p. 333.
59 See Borrows, 'Wampum at Niagara'.
60 Borrows, 'Landed Citizenship', p. 337.
61 J. Borrows, *Recovering Canada: The Resurgence of Indigenous Law* (Toronto:
    University of Toronto Press, 2002), p. 112.

a threat to the very fabric of our fundamental principles of order. If the rule of law cannot be relied upon to overcome the political and economic exploitation of Aboriginal peoples, what assurances do we have that it will not be equally vulnerable in situations involving non-aboriginal Canadians? … Aboriginal peoples might function like the miner's canary. When the most vulnerable among us suffer from the toxins present in our legal environment, their suffering serves as an important warning about the health of the larger legal climate.[62]

Borrows goes on to acknowledge that recognition of underlying aboriginal title would cause 'significant disruption' but points out that many Canadians are unjustly enriched through failure to uphold the rule of law in favour of the original owners and that there must be radical change: 'Nevertheless, seriously disrupting our socio-political relations is not the same thing as completely undermining those relations, especially when the correction of injustice may ultimately set the entire society on the path to a more peaceful and productive future.'[63]

Rather than simply offering a form of citizenship under the auspices of settler Canada, the state should recognise aboriginal sovereignty and incorporate indigenous law into the mainstream, giving it equal and, in some cases, superior force to Canadian law. This would get rid of the bias in Canadian law. Judges should examine aboriginal laws, oral tradition and perspectives in order to 'sustain Canada's constitutional text'.[64] True to his word, in September 2018 Borrows and Val Napoleon, another indigenous lawyer and academic, launched the first law degree teaching both Canadian law and indigenous law at the University of Victoria.

Borrows, like Helin, calls for indigenous groups to take on greater responsibility than that afforded indigenous peoples under the rights-based, 'clientelisation' process prevalent today. Instead, he says, citizenship should be interactive and reciprocal. For example, indigenous concepts of citizenship might deter Canadians from destroying the land – or indeed encourage them to adopt the indigenous core belief that the land is a living entity which should itself be treated with the respect and status due to any other citizen. What Borrows is calling for is 'Aboriginal control of Canadian affairs' so that their citizenship is pro-active rather than reactive,[65] saying that Canadian authorities must learn to share so that indigenous peoples have, not dominance, but the same privileges as settlers in an interdependent model of citizenship.

Borrows has some limited support for Flanagan's attitude to indigenous title: 'Clearly Professor Flanagan sees problems with concepts of Aboriginal citizenship that accentuate group rights, reinforce Aboriginal organizations,

62 Ibid., p. 114.
63 Ibid., p. 115ff.
64 Ibid., p. 123.
65 Ibid., p. 148.

and emphasize Aboriginal identity. While certain elements of his argument may seem to overstep the mark if one is concerned about fostering civic peace, his emphasis on concerns of stability and peace is worthy of attention.[66] Borrows acknowledges that there are legitimate concerns expressed by both Flanagan and Cairns over social cohesion if indigenous interests are protected to the exclusion of their relationships with settler society. Borrows sees the problem as one of promoting 'Aboriginal affairs for Aboriginal peoples'. What Borrows is trying to do is to promote this ideal together with aboriginal control of Canadian affairs: 'Refusal to recognize the interdependent nature of Aboriginal/non-Aboriginal peoples is also likely to provoke hostility and resentment from each group, alienating them further from their activity as citizens with the land. The simultaneous call for Aboriginal control of Canadian affairs could actually enhance citizenship.'[67]

Borrows concludes that the special indigenous relationship to the land should be reflected in any model of indigenous citizenship. Only then can there be any meaningful participation of indigenous people with settler Canadians and with each other.

66   Ibid., p. 155ff.
67   Ibid., p. 157.

In terms of my life, the message would probably be that we have the knowledge, the history, we have the connection to this land. We know that. We have all the good human resources that could help us to generate or struggle or fight to bring about the possibility to have our voices heard. We have the knowledge, we have the history, we have the connection to the land, we have all of these elements. What is lacking in my view is that we have no financial resources to struggle or mount a comeback or fight with the government. We don't have that because you can see we are poor. So all those rights are extinguished, resources are taken away without our consent.

> I am hurt and sad, very sad, of what happened to my people, my community, especially when I think of how my parents lived freely on this land. They had self-rule, they controlled very much their lives and there was a lot of respect, but nowadays you have all these aboriginal communities around here in our neighbouring nations, they signed their own deals, their own settlements, their own agreements and at the end they want to force this community to follow this path, make the same choice as a group, to sign away our rights and by doing so the government succeeds in extinguishing our rights, our culture, our way of life, our Indianity, and then they succeed in covering up all of who we are as a people, as a culture, as a distinct group so that they can forget forever about the culture, the Indian people that lived here.

The government is so evil that they plan to force us to sign away our rights by having other communities sign on our behalf. That's what they do. They just wave the money in front of our nose. They let us smell the money, they let us see the colour of money and then they say, 'You guys, you don't want to sign away your rights? OK, fine. We don't need you anyway. We'll ask the neighbouring communities to sign away your rights,' and that's really bad that they can do that.

> Our parents were there and recent history tells us that we were there first when the mines came, when the missionaries came over here, when they started to build runways, the train. It was the Innu who led them, working for prospectors, explorers, mining surveyors.

Chapter 21

'Citizens Plus' or parallel paths?

Innu attitudes to money, discussed in previous chapters, mean that large sums of money do not necessarily benefit indigenous communities. For many generations they lived off the land and its bounty, working hard for their livelihood. Centuries of subsistence living have taught them to live on what is currently available and to share resources, knowing that in times of trouble they too will be supported. When this philosophy is applied to large amounts of cash, the result is seen by settler Canadians as profligacy. The question remains how to extricate both settlers and native peoples from this situation.

The Hawthorn Commission as far back as 1963, and much more recently Alan Cairns and J.R. Miller, backed the 'Citizens Plus' model in which native peoples are treated as ordinary citizens with additional benefits given in recognition of their prior ownership of the land. The Royal Commission on Aboriginal Peoples, whose report took into consideration extensive research among and by aboriginal peoples, preferred the model of the two-row wampum: settlers and aboriginal peoples living separately side by side, according to their respective beliefs. This is reflected in Calvin Helin's proposed solution. Which would better enable aboriginal rights disputes to be resolved?

The Citizens Plus format is said to encourage a solution that is forward-looking. It proposes to give indigenous peoples a stronger voice in mainstream Canadian politics by recognising their rights as individual citizens of Canada so that their requirements are treated as equal to those of settler citizens. Cairns' solution is for settler Canadians to take greater responsibility for past treatment of indigenous peoples and their issues. However, this solution is still Canadian-centred and it is not specific as to how the realities of current settler–indigenous relations are to be addressed. Even taking on board Judge Murray Sinclair's remark that, 'It will take a long time to turn the ship round',[1] due to the overwhelming settler majority in Canada, it is doubtful whether with this approach the indigenous voice would truly be heard. There is no true reciprocity in this solution, no incentive to change the status quo. Kymlicka

---

1   Judge Murray Sinclair, Commissioner of the Indian Residential Schools Truth and Reconciliation Commission, in an address to the Origins Festival, London, 27 Oct. 2013.

and Norman point out that: 'The discourse on citizenship has rarely provided a neutral framework for resolving disputes between the majority and minority groups; more often it has served as a cover by which the majority nation extends its language, institutions, mobility rights and political power at the expense of the minority, all in the name of turning supposedly "disloyal" or "troublesome" minorities into "good citizens".'[2]

At heart, Citizens Plus is assimilationist. It is more than likely that the governments would retain their present control of indigenous policy. If the fiduciary duty assumed by the Crown had been honoured from the outset, governments could not have encroached in any way onto indigenous land without the free, prior and informed consent of its peoples. While it ill becomes Judge Lamer to declare in his reasons for decision in *Delgamuukw v British Columbia*, 'Let's face it, we're all here to stay', in any case (as the chief land claims negotiator in Matimekush told me) it was never the intention of the indigenous peoples to ask settlers to leave.

If settlement and resource extraction together with the numbered treaties and the modern settlement agreements had been approached in the spirit of the Royal Proclamation, this would not have precluded European use of indigenous land, but it might have given pause for thought before land was ruined for a few years of mineral extraction. The assimilationist experiment would not have devastated so many indigenous lives if the three tenets of equality, respect and dignity had been afforded the original owners of the land. These are the forgotten strands of the two-row wampum. Had there been respect for indigenous beliefs about stewardship of the land and if they had been given equal weight to European considerations in the development of pristine land, the excesses of those whose only motive is glory for the separatist state of Quebec or monetary profit for (often American) corporations might have been curtailed. John Borrows would not have to call for aboriginal involvement in Canadian government decisions which affect the wider population. It should be remembered that it is not only the indigenous peoples of Canada who object to the destruction of their environment for the profit of corporations and governments. As foreseen by Vine Deloria, two protest movements came to prominence in Canada in late 2011: Idle No More and the worldwide Occupy movement. They had very similar aims drawn from each of the parallel paths.

One interviewee in Matimekush asked me to consider what would have been the situation had the James Bay agreements not been signed. At the time of the Malouf Judgment, before the decision in *Calder v Attorney General for British Columbia* [1973] was published, there was as yet little discussion of the nature of aboriginal title to land. The Quebec Court of Appeal summarily dismissed the Cree and Inuit claim, overturning the Malouf judgment. The

2   Kymlicka and Norman, Introduction to *Citizenship in Diverse Societies*, p.10.

corporations would most likely have pursued a much more ambitious scheme, destroying more of the ecology and in total disregard of the needs of the people who had lived on the affected land for millennia. Most likely, like the Innu, the Cree and the Inuit would have been driven off the land with no resources with which to sustain their communities. Like the Innu who live in Central Quebec, they would have made their hunting journey only to discover their land flooded and their livelihood gone.

On the other hand, had the Royal Proclamation been honoured, all aboriginal peoples with an interest in the James Bay lands would have been properly informed and the project would have depended on their free, prior and informed consent. It would have been recognised automatically that the underlying title to the land was theirs.

The parallel paths model of co-existence was what the indigenous peoples were promised by the Crown. Even if this were not the case, the model offers greater advantages to both communities in that it frees each of them to flourish with all the advantages from their own cultures and to develop together. The parallel paths model should afford the indigenous population the same benefits as Citizens Plus, but without the extinguishment of their rights which the latter model would inevitably entail. The requirements to treat each other with equality, mutual respect and dignity provide the basis for the promotion of similarities between the two peoples – an approach which Cairns believes to be lacking currently. It is absolutely essential that the settler population of Canada learn the full truth about past dealings with indigenous land and how, on settlement in Canada, their governments made the new European inhabitants promises which were not theirs to give. Most important of all, Canadians must accept that the promises made in 1763 are binding today. Only then will they allow indigenous peoples the right to make decisions on behalf of all Canadians.

Final thoughts

Within the relationship set down in the Royal Proclamation, the Treaty of Niagara and the two-row wampum, which establish the fiduciary duty owed by the Crown in all its manifestations, Canada cannot establish title to any land which it has taken without the free, prior and informed consent of the indigenous peoples within its borders. This requirement is also a cornerstone of the United Nations Declaration on the Rights of Indigenous Peoples (UNDRIP). Since 1763, all decisions the Crown has made with regard to indigenous land should have been made in the best interests of the indigenous peoples alone. Where such interests conflict with those of settler Canadians, the rights of the indigenous peoples must prevail. The governments must disgorge any profits they have made as a result of their exploitation of indigenous land, however remote in time these are. That is the commitment which was given in the Royal Proclamation. However inconvenient this conclusion, this is the state of affairs which must be conveyed to Canada's settlers. Unless and until they understand what is owed to the native peoples, no satisfactory solution to the divide between the followers of the parallel paths can be found.

No native grouping has ever called for this, however. The contagion of neo-liberal capitalism has not entered into the beliefs of grassroots native peoples in the way it has affected some of their leaders. Treaties could and should be re-negotiated in the light of the fiduciary duties which were taken on by the Crown. Unilateral extinguishment of rights is not permitted under international human rights law, and this is confirmed by UNDRIP in the case of land rights. The claim of the people of Matimekush Lac John to their traditional lands must be honoured and the necessary adjustments made through a renewed treaty process, preferably backed with a decision of the court.

Resistance to the idea of a trans-Canada indigenous government must be overcome. This was a key recommendation of the Royal Commission on Aboriginal Peoples (RCAP) in its 1996 Report. The Sámi in Scandinavia have separate parliaments which work together with the national parliaments in Norway, Sweden and Finland. They pursue their parallel paths with the national bodies with respect and dignity, if not with full equality. They unite on issues which affect the whole of Sápmi, their traditional homeland.[3] This is a forum in which their traditional knowledge can be heard and acted upon. With an indigenous parliament in place in Canada, much of the policy-making would be taken out of the hands of individual chiefs and Band Councils and away from the Assembly of First Nations. There could be economies of scale and accountability which would ensure that funding was allocated more effectively, and the indigenous peoples of Canada would have the voice they need in mainstream politics. The Innu of Central Quebec, who believe they are the last to refuse to sign away their rights, would have those rights respected and could break free from being the wards of the Crown.

The people of Matimekush Lac John have stood up for their rights under the fiduciary duty owed to them by the Crown. They have remained true to their belief that they have responsibility for their land and its ecology. This they have done at great cost to themselves in terms of living standards, health and freedom to take charge of their own destiny. Yet not one of the 48 people I interviewed believed that it was wrong to refuse to sign deals which entailed the extinguishment of their rights. Psychologically they are the stronger for it.

In this work I have traced the development of indigenous law in Canada from its beginnings with the Royal Proclamation in 1763, when indigenous nations were strong. The meaning of the Royal Proclamation was confirmed by the wampum belts distributed at the meeting which led to the Treaty of Niagara

---

3   See H. Hannum, *Autonomy, Sovereignty and Self-Determination: The Accommodation of Conflicting Rights* (Philadelphia: University of Pennsylvania Press, 1990).

of 1764. The Crown gave a solemn undertaking that indigenous peoples would be free to live on their land in accordance with their tradition and world view. However this unwritten record, like much oral history of native peoples, has been ignored in the rush to take land for settlement and subsequently for resource extraction.

Under the Royal Proclamation, the Crown took to itself the responsibility for disposing of indigenous land. This was done for the benefit of the Crown in order that all settlers took their title to land from the Crown. Such an arrangement also precluded other interested European nations from buying up indigenous land. In agreeing to this, the indigenous peoples acted to their detriment, placing the Crown under a separate duty to treat indigenous lands as trust property. This means that the Crown received only an empty title to the lands, the full benefit resting with the indigenous people concerned. Yet it was not until the decision in *Tsilhqot'in Nation v British Columbia* – 250 years later – that this was acknowledged by the Supreme Court of Canada.

Looked at from the point of view of property law and equity and trusts law, the Crown in Right of Canada can, like any other body which finds itself under a fiduciary duty, be called on to account for all it has taken by way of lands, resources and profits from the indigenous beneficiaries of the relationship. The only exception to this is when the indigenous group concerned has given its free, prior and informed consent to the settlement and has received a fair market value for the land and resources expropriated. Neither of these preconditions appears to apply to any modern land claims settlement. In the case of the Innu who live in Quebec, they were not even informed when their land was taken.

Despite 250 years of assimilation, indigenous beliefs and values survive. Even among those who have chosen to settle land rights with the governments and corporations, the underlying values of sharing the land remain intact. In the James Bay Agreement, the Innu lost their lands in Quebec. Now they expect to lose their lands in Labrador, although they have joined together to fight through the courts to retain them.

The Conseil Attikamekw-Montagnais, Ashuanipi Corporation and Strategic Alliance negotiators have compiled an excellent, thorough and cohesive case for their right to the lands both in Quebec and in Labrador. Similar rights were recognised over the James Bay lands by Judge Malouf in 1974. He has been proved right by subsequent cases in higher courts whose decisions have extended the application of the Royal Proclamation to all indigenous land rights in Canada. He was also correct in his assessment of the environmental damage which follows in the wake of hydro-electric and other resource extraction projects. It was thus vital to federal and provincial governments planning to profit from such initiatives that this judgment be suppressed at the earliest opportunity.

Now, however, it is time for it to be revived and reconsidered. The decision in *Tsilhqot'in* has been handed down in time to give the Innu who object to the

New Dawn Agreement hope of recognition of their lost rights. However, any such settlement is likely to be worked out at the negotiation table. It would appear that the principle of justification on grounds of overriding public interest put forward in *R v Sparrow* is ill-founded, although further research is needed into the intention of parliament when it drafted section 35(1) of the Constitution Act, 1982.

Turning to the negotiations with the provincial governments which took place from the signing of the James Bay Agreement by the Cree, Inuit and subsequently the Naskapi, the records at the Tshakapesh Institute show that the Innu have withdrawn from negotiations for the recovery of their land whenever the federal and provincial governments have insisted that all rights not specifically granted in a forthcoming settlement be extinguished. Under the new rules in *Tsilhqot'in*, this is not a legitimate demand for the governments to make, since extinguishment is not necessary for the public purpose on which they rely as justification for taking the land. Insistence on an extinguishment clause (now renamed a 'certainty' clause) is a prime example of the governments' disregard of their fiduciary duty. At the same time, government insistence on negotiation from a fixed agreement with no attempt to address and accommodate the requirements of a particular indigenous group is a failure to uphold the honour of the Crown. Furthermore, failure to identify those who are selected to represent the indigenous group in a free and fair way, according to the procedures traditionally used by the group concerned, is not only a stain on the honour of the Crown – it is also a contravention of the standards laid down in UNDRIP. Where the federal government may regard UNDRIP as 'aspirational', the indigenous peoples intended to benefit from the rights it endorses have repeatedly called on the federal government to abolish the discriminatory Indian Act and replace it with legislation enabling UNDRIP to pass fully into Canadian law. Again, failure to do so is a breach of the Crown's fiduciary duty and a stain on the honour of the Crown.

Perhaps the most important evidence of the Crown's breach of fiduciary duty is given in the testimony of the Innu of Matimekush Lac John. They testify to the harm that government policies of assimilation and failed promises of improved conditions under the cash economy has inflicted on them. By allowing the Innu to fall behind in education, health, status and self-determination, the governments have ceased to acknowledge that they have any duty to improve their quality of life and ability to provide for their families. Despite having demonstrated their good stewardship of the land for which they feel responsible, the Innu also have to stand by and see that land destroyed for a few years of mineral extraction or for an eternity of artificial inundation. At the same time, they are blamed, either directly or indirectly, by both their indigenous neighbours and the governments for staying true to their beliefs rather than 'moving on'. The inhumanity and indignity they suffer through these processes is never taken into account at the negotiating tables.

Now the Innu of the Strategic Alliance expect to lose their lands in Labrador under the New Dawn Agreement. As discussed, the Newfoundland Labrador government has been aware for more than 30 years of the Quebec Innu claim to this territory. The ratification vote on the New Dawn Agreement is also invalid because there was no free, prior and informed consent to the acquisition of the lands or for the Lower Churchill Falls project from the Labrador Innu beneficiaries of the agreement. There is strong evidence that C$5,000 was paid for each ratification vote. The withholding of the full text of the Agreement in Principle from those called upon to vote on it also invalidates the ratification. Further, the Innu owners of the land, whether they are beneficiaries of the Final Agreement or not, are entitled to compensation for the destruction of the environment resulting from the Muskrat Falls project due to the commencement of construction without the Final Agreement in place.

The very purpose of the fiduciary duty created by the Royal Proclamation was to protect indigenous groups from the seizure of their land by settlers. The Proclamation is intended to shield the beneficiaries from unscrupulous dealing. For well over a century, governments and corporations were permitted to act as though indigenous peoples had no proprietary right to the land by the decision in *St Catherine's Milling v R*, but this decision has been overturned. *Tsilhqot'in* established that the principle of *terra nullius* never applied in Canada because, the court said, it was overridden by the Royal Proclamation. The court might also have said that it never applied because it was an invalid concept from the outset. The principles of equity which govern the law relating to fiduciaries demand that the highest standards of conduct are observed by the fiduciary towards the beneficiary at all times and in all ways relating to the beneficiaries. This is what the honour of the Crown comprises. Since the 2004 decision in *Haida Nation v British Columbia*, the Supreme Court has given prominence to this principle as a means to achieve reconciliation between the differing indigenous and settler relationships to the land. What the court has failed to do, however, is to lay down concrete principles under which land claims negotiations should be conducted.

There are many 'dead letters' in Canadian aboriginal law – the Report of the Royal Commission on Aboriginal Peoples, the Charlottetown Accord, the Kelowna Agreement and now UNDRIP. It would seem that they will soon be joined by the Report of the Indian Residential Schools Truth and Reconciliation Commission. These various documents all have one thing in common. They are directed towards honouring the Crown's promise in the Royal Proclamation of 1763 rather than towards a 'reconciliation' process through negotiation which enables Canada to exploit indigenous land. There can be no reconciliation unless the honour of the Crown is upheld and aboriginal peoples are given back the lands and rights they enjoyed before contact.

The Muskrat Falls dam stands as a symbol of the dire situation in which indigenous peoples find themselves. Now that the dam is completed and partially filled, the land can never be recovered and nothing can save it for those who hold true to the core belief that land is held on a sacred trust to be preserved for future generations. The last generation to lead a life according to indigenous tenets of belief and practice is fast dying out, and with them the wisdom which could help all Canadians to turn back the Doomsday clock and prevent the catastrophic genocidal and ecological disaster about to befall the indigenous peoples on 'Turtle Island'.

Rafael Lemkin wrote:

> Genocide has two phases: one, destruction of the national pattern of the oppressed group: the other, the imposition of the national pattern of the oppressor.[4]

In 1948, the United Nations rejected Lemkin's wider definition of genocide but, in the provisions of UNDRIP, many of the actions of state governments which are proscribed are genocidal under Lemkin's definition. It remains to be seen whether the current Trudeau government and the Canadian settler nation have the courage and commitment to turn away from its catastrophic path.

---

4   R. Lemkin, *Axis Rule in Occupied Europe* (New York: Columbia University Press, 1944), at p. 79; quoted in D. Short, *Redefining Genocide: Settler Colonialism, Social Death and Ecocide* (London, Zed Books, 2016), at p. 18.

When I read the treaties I think the last nation not to have a treaty is the Innu. Now the governments – Quebec and Labrador – want to make treaties to extinguish the rights but they don't sign treaties, the Innu are really strong. You can go on your land. It is very far. I think the land is sleeping. It hasn't disappeared – just sleeping. It will wait for us.

Appendix A: text of the Royal Proclamation

THE ROYAL PROCLAMATION OF 7 OCTOBER 1763

RSC 1985, App II, No 1

Whereas We have taken into Our Royal Consideration the extensive and valuable Acquisitions in America, secured to our Crown by the late Definitive Treaty of Peace, concluded at Paris, the 10th Day of February last; and being desirous that all Our loving Subjects, as well of our Kingdom as of our Colonies in America, may avail themselves with all convenient Speed, of the great Benefits and Advantages which must accrue therefrom to their Commerce, Manufactures, and Navigation, We have thought fit, with the Advice of our Privy Council, to issue this our Royal Proclamation, hereby to publish and declare to all our loving Subjects, that we have, with the Advice of our Said Privy Council, granted our Letters Patent, under our Great Seal of Great Britain, to erect, within the Countries and Islands ceded and confirmed to Us by the said Treaty, Four distinct and separate Governments, styled and called by the names of Quebec, East Florida, West Florida and Granada …

And whereas it is just and reasonable, and essential to our Interest, and the Security of our Colonies, that the several Nations or Tribes of Indians with whom We are connected, and who live under our Protection, should not be molested or disturbed in the Possession of such Parts of Our Dominions and Territories as, not having been ceded to or purchased by Us, are reserved to them, or any of them, as their Hunting Grounds. – We do therefore, with the Advice of our Privy Council, declare it to be our Royal Will and Pleasure, that no Governor or Commander in Chief in any of our Colonies of Quebec, East Florida, or West Florida, do presume, upon any Pretence whatever, to grant Warrants of Survey, or pass any Patents for Lands beyond the Bounds of their respective Governments, as described in their Commissions; as also that no Governor or Commander in Chief in any of our other Colonies or Plantations in America do presume for the present, and until our further Pleasure be known, to grant Warrants of Survey, or pass Patents for any Lands beyond the Heads of Sources of any of the Rivers which fall into the Atlantic Ocean from the West and North West, or upon any Lands whatever, which, not having been ceded to or purchased by Us as aforesaid, are reserved to the said Indians, or any of them.

And We do further declare it to be Our Royal Will and Pleasure, for the present as aforesaid, to reserve under our Sovereignty, Protection and Dominion, for the use of the said Indians, all the Lands and Territories not included within the lands of our said Three new Governments, or within the Limits of the Territory granted to the Hudson's Bay Company, as also all the Lands and Territories lying to the Westward of the Sources of the Rivers which fall into the Sea from the West and Northwest as aforesaid.

And we do strictly forbid, on Pain of Our Displeasure, all our loving Subjects from making any Purchases or Settlements whatever, or taking Possession of any of the Lands above reserved, without our especial leave and Licence for that Purpose first obtained.

And, We do further strictly enjoin and require all Persons whatever who have either wilfully or inadvertently seated themselves upon any Lands within the Countries above described, or upon any other Lands which, not having been ceded to or purchased by Us, are still reserved to the said Indians as aforesaid, forthwith to remove themselves from such Settlements.

And whereas great Frauds and Abuses have been committed in purchasing Lands of the Indians, to great Prejudice of our Interests, and to the great Dissatisfaction of the said Indians, In order, therefore, to prevent such Irregularities for the future, and to the end that the Indians may be convinced of our Justice and determined Resolution to remove all reasonable Cause of Discontent, We do, with the Advice of our Privy Council strictly enjoin and require that no private Person do presume to make any purchase from the said Indians of any Lands reserved to the said Indians, within those parts of our Colonies where, We have thought proper to allow Settlement; but that, if at any Time any of the Said Indians should be inclined to dispose of the said Lands, the same shall be Purchased only by Us, in our Name, at some public Meeting or Assembly of the said Indians, to be held for that Purpose by the Governor or Commander in Chief of our Colony respectively within which they shall lie, and in any case they shall lie within the limits of any Proprietary Government, they shall be purchased only for the Use and in the name of such Proprietaries, conformable to such Directions and Instructions as We or they shall think proper to giver for that Purpose

...

Given at our Court at St James's the 7th Day of October 1763, in the Third Year of our Reign

Appendix B: the United Nations Declaration on the Rights of Indigenous Peoples

The General Assembly

Guided by the purposes and principles of the Charter of the United Nations, and good faith in the fulfilment of the obligations assumed by States in accordance with the Charter,

Affirming that indigenous peoples are equal to all other peoples, while recognizing the right of all peoples to be different, to consider themselves different, and to be respected as such,

Affirming also that all peoples contribute to the diversity and richness of civilizations and cultures, which constitute the common heritage of humankind,

Affirming further that all doctrines, policies and practices based on or advocating superiority of peoples or individuals on the basis of national origin or racial, religious, ethnic or cultural differences are racist, scientifically false, legally invalid, morally condemnable and socially unjust,

Reaffirming that indigenous peoples, in the exercise of their rights, should be free from discrimination of any kind,

Concerned that indigenous peoples have suffered from historic injustices as a result of, *inter alia*, their colonization and dispossession of their lands, territories and resources, thus preventing them from exercising, in particular, their right to development in accordance with their own needs and interests,

Recognizing the urgent need to respect and promote the inherent rights of indigenous peoples which derive from their political, economic and social structures and from their cultures, spiritual traditions, histories and philosophies, especially their rights to their lands, territories and resources,

Recognizing the urgent need to respect and promote the rights of indigenous peoples affirmed in treaties, agreements and other constructive arrangements with States,

Welcoming the fact that indigenous peoples are organizing themselves for political, economic, social and cultural enhancement and in order to bring to an end all forms of discrimination and oppression wherever they occur,

Convinced that control by indigenous peoples over developments affecting them and their lands, territories and resources will enable them to maintain and strengthen their institutions, cultures and traditions, and to promote their development in accordance with their aspirations and needs,

Recognizing that respect for indigenous knowledge, cultures and traditional practices contributes to sustainable and equitable development and proper management of the environment,

Emphasizing the contribution of the demilitarization of the lands and territories of indigenous peoples to peace, economic and social progress and development, understanding and friendly relations among nations and peoples of the world,

Recognizing in particular the right of indigenous families and communities to retain shared responsibility for the upbringing, training, education and well-being of their children, consistent with the rights of the child,

Considering that the rights affirmed in treaties, agreements and other constructive arrangements between States and indigenous peoples are, in some situations, matters of international concern, interest, responsibility and character,

Considering also that treaties, agreements and other constructive arrangements, and the relationship they represent, are the basis for a strengthened partnership between indigenous peoples and States,

Acknowledging that the Charter of the United Nations, the International Covenant on Economic, Social and Cultural Rights and the International Covenant on Civil and Political Rights, as well as the Vienna Declaration and Programme of Action, affirm the fundamental importance of the right to self-determination of all peoples, by virtue of which they freely determine their political status and freely pursue their economic, social and cultural development,

Bearing in mind that nothing in this Declaration may be used to deny any peoples their right to self-determination, exercised in conformity with international law,

Convinced that the recognition of the rights of indigenous peoples in this Declaration will enhance harmonious and cooperative relations between States and indigenous peoples, based on principles of justice, democracy, respect for human rights, non-discrimination and good faith,

Encouraging States to comply with and effectively implement all their obligations as they apply to indigenous peoples under international instruments, in particular those related to human rights, in consultation and cooperation with the peoples concerned,

Emphasizing that the United Nations has an important and continuing role to play in promoting and protecting the rights of indigenous peoples,

Believing that the Declaration is a further important step forward for the recognition, promotion and protection of the rights and freedoms of indigenous peoples and in the development of relevant activities of the United Nations system in this field,

Recognizing and reaffirming that indigenous individuals are entitled without discrimination to all human rights recognized in international law, and that indigenous peoples possess collective rights which are indispensable for their existence, well-being and integral development as peoples,

Recognizing that the situation of indigenous peoples varies from region to region and from country to country and that the significance of national and regional particularities and various historical and cultural backgrounds should be taken into consideration,

Solemnly proclaims the following United Nations Declaration on the Rights of Indigenous Peoples as a standard of achievement to be pursued in a spirit of partnership and mutual respect:

Article 1

Indigenous peoples have the right to the full enjoyment, as a collective or as individuals, of all human rights and fundamental freedoms as recognized in the Charter of the United Nations, the Universal Declaration of Human Rights and international human rights law.

Article 2

Indigenous peoples and individuals are free and equal to all other peoples and individuals and have the right to be free from any kind of discrimination, in the exercise of their rights, in particular that based on their indigenous origin and identity.

Article 3

Indigenous peoples have the right to self-determination. By virtue of that right they freely determine their political status and freely pursue their economic, social and cultural development.

Article 4

Indigenous peoples, in exercising their right to self-determination, have the right to autonomy or self-government in matters relating to their internal and local affairs, as well as ways and means for financing their autonomous functions.

Article 5

Indigenous peoples have the right to maintain and strengthen their distinct political, legal, economic, social and cultural institutions, while retaining their right to participate fully, if they so choose, in the political, economic, social and cultural life of the State.

Article 6

Every indigenous individual has the right to a nationality.

Article 7

Indigenous individuals have the rights to life, physical and mental integrity, liberty and security of person.

Indigenous peoples have the collective right to live in freedom, peace and security as distinct peoples and shall not be subjected to any act of genocide or any other act of violence, including forcibly removing children of the group to another group.

Article 8

Indigenous peoples and individuals have the right not to be subjected to forced assimilation or destruction of their culture.

States shall provide effective mechanisms for prevention of, and redress for:

Any action which has the aim or effect of depriving them of their integrity as distinct peoples, or of their cultural values or ethnic identities;

Any action which has the aim or effect of dispossessing them of their lands, territories or resources;

Any form of forced population transfer which has the aim or effect of violating or undermining any of their rights;

Any form of forced assimilation or integration;

Any form of propaganda designed to promote or incite racial or ethnic discrimination directed against them.

Article 9

Indigenous peoples and individuals have the right to belong to an indigenous community or nation, in accordance with the traditions and customs of the community or nation concerned. No discrimination of any kind may arise from the exercise of such a right.

Article 10

Indigenous peoples shall not be forcibly removed from their lands or territories. No relocation shall take place without the free, prior and informed consent of the indigenous peoples concerned and after agreement of just and fair compensation and, where possible, with the option of return.

Article 11

Indigenous peoples have the right to practise and revitalize their cultural traditions and customs. This includes the right to maintain, protect and develop the past, present and future manifestations of their cultures, such as archaeological and historical sites, artefacts, designs, ceremonies, technologies and visual and performing arts and literature.

States shall provide redress through effective mechanisms, which may include restitution, developed in conjunction with indigenous peoples, with respect to their cultural, intellectual, religious and spiritual property taken without their free, prior and informed consent or in violation of their laws, traditions and customs.

Article 12

Indigenous peoples have the right to manifest, practise, develop and teach their spiritual and religious traditions, customs and ceremonies; the right to maintain, protect and have access in privacy to their religious and cultural sites; the right to the use and control of their ceremonial objects; and the right to the repatriation of their human remains.

States shall seek to enable the access and/or repatriation of ceremonial objects and human remains in their possession through fair, transparent and effective mechanisms developed in conjunction with the indigenous peoples concerned.

Article 13

Indigenous peoples have the right to revitalize, use, develop and transmit to future generations their histories, languages, oral traditions, philosophies, writing systems and literatures, and to designate and retain their own names for communities, places and persons.

States shall take effective measures to ensure that this right is protected and also to ensure that indigenous peoples can understand and be understood in political, legal and administrative proceedings, where necessary through the provision of interpretation or by other appropriate means.

Article 14

Indigenous peoples have the right to establish and control their educational systems and institutions providing education in their own languages, in a manner appropriate to their culture's methods of teaching and learning.

Indigenous individuals, particularly children, have the right to all levels and forms of education of the State without discrimination.

States shall, in conjunction with indigenous peoples, take effective measures in order for indigenous individuals, particularly children, including those living outside their communities, to have access, when possible, to an education in their own culture and provided in their own language.

Article 15

Indigenous peoples have the right to the dignity and diversity of their cultures, traditions, histories and aspirations, which shall be appropriately reflected in education and public information.

States shall take effective measures, in consultation and cooperation with the indigenous peoples concerned, to combat prejudice and eliminate discrimination and to promote tolerance, understanding and good relations among indigenous peoples and all other segments of society.

Article 16

Indigenous people have the right to establish their own media in their own languages and to have access to all forms of non-indigenous media without discrimination.

States shall take effective measures to ensure that State-owned media duly reflect indigenous cultural diversity. States, without prejudice to ensuring full freedom of expression, should encourage privately owned media to adequately reflect indigenous cultural diversity.

Article 17

Indigenous individuals and peoples have the right to enjoy fully all rights established under applicable international and domestic labour law.

States shall in consultation and cooperation with indigenous peoples take specific measures to protect indigenous children from economic exploitation and from performing any work that is likely to be hazardous or to interfere with the child's education, or to be harmful to the child's health or physical, mental, spiritual, moral or social development, taking into account their special vulnerability and the importance of education for their empowerment.

Indigenous individuals have the right not to be subjected to any discriminatory conditions of labour and, *inter alia*, employment or salary.

Article 18

Indigenous peoples have the right to participate in decision-making in matters which would affect their rights, through representatives chosen by themselves in accordance with their own procedures, as well as to maintain and develop their own indigenous decision-making institutions.

Article 19

States shall consult and cooperate in good faith with the indigenous peoples concerned through their own representative institutions in order to obtain their free, prior and informed consent before adopting and implementing legislative or administrative measures that may affect them.

Article 20

Indigenous peoples have the right to maintain and develop their political, economic and social systems or institutions, to be secure in the enjoyment of their own means of subsistence and development, and to engage freely in all their traditional and other economic activities.

Indigenous peoples deprived of their means of subsistence and development are entitled to just and fair means of redress.

Article 21

Indigenous peoples have the right, without discrimination, to the improvement of their economic and social conditions, including, *inter alia*, in the areas of education, employment, vocational training and retraining, housing, sanitation, health and social security.

States shall take effective measures and, where appropriate, special measures to ensure continuing improvement of their economic and social conditions. Particular attention shall be paid to the rights and special needs of indigenous elders, women, youth, children and persons with disabilities.

Article 22

Particular attention shall be paid to the rights and special needs of indigenous elders, women, youth, children and persons with disabilities in the implementation of this Declaration.

States shall take measures, in conjunction with indigenous peoples, to ensure that indigenous women and children enjoy the full protection and guarantees against all forms of violence and discrimination.

Article 23

Indigenous peoples have the right to determine and develop priorities and strategies for exercising their right to development. In particular, indigenous peoples have the right to be actively involved in developing and determining health, housing and other economic and social programmes affecting them and, as far as possible, to administer such programmes through their own institutions.

Article 24

Indigenous peoples have the right to their traditional medicines and to maintain their health practices, including the conservation of their vital medicinal plants, animals and minerals. Indigenous individuals also have the right to access, without any discrimination, all social and health services.

Indigenous individuals have an equal right in the enjoyment of the highest attainable standard of physical and mental health. States shall take the necessary steps with a view to achieving progressively the full realization of this right.

Article 25

Indigenous peoples have the right to maintain and strengthen their distinctive spiritual relationship with their traditionally owned or otherwise occupied and used lands, territories, waters and coastal seas and other resources and to uphold their responsibilities to future generations in this regard.

Article 26

Indigenous peoples have the right to the lands, territories and resources which they have traditionally owned, occupied or otherwise used or acquired.

Indigenous peoples have the right to own, use, develop and control the lands, territories and resources that they possess by reason of traditional ownership or other traditional occupation or use, as well as those which they have otherwise acquired.

States shall give legal recognition and protection to these lands, territories and resources. Such recognition shall be conducted with due respect to the customs, traditions and land tenure system of the indigenous people concerned.

Article 27

States shall establish and implement, in conjunction with indigenous peoples concerned, a fair, independent, impartial, open and transparent process, giving due recognition to indigenous peoples' laws, traditions, customs and land tenure systems, to recognise and adjudicate the rights of indigenous peoples pertaining to their lands, territories and resources, including those which were traditionally owned or otherwise occupied or used. Indigenous peoples shall have the right to participate in this process.

Article 28

Indigenous peoples have the right to redress, by means that can include restitution, or, when this is not possible, just, fair and equitable compensation, for the lands, territories and resources which they have traditionally owned or otherwise occupied or used, and which have been confiscated, taken, occupied, used or damaged without their free, prior and informed consent.

Unless otherwise freely agreed upon by the peoples concerned, compensation shall take the form of lands, territories and resources equal in quality, size and legal status or of monetary compensation or other appropriate redress.

Article 29

Indigenous peoples have the right to the conservation and protection of the environment and the productive capacity of their lands or territories and resources. States shall establish and implement assistance programmes for indigenous peoples for such conservation and protection, without discrimination.

States shall take effective measures to ensure that no storage or disposal of hazardous materials shall take place in the lands or territories of indigenous peoples without their free, prior and informed consent.

States shall also take effective measures to ensure, as needed, that programmes for monitoring, maintaining and restoring the health of indigenous peoples, as developed and implemented by the peoples affected by such materials, are duly implemented.

Article 30

Military activities shall not take place in the lands or territories of indigenous peoples, unless justified by a relevant public interest or otherwise freely agreed with or requested by the indigenous peoples concerned.

States shall undertake effective consultations with the indigenous peoples concerned, through appropriate procedures and in particular through their representative institutions, prior to using their lands or territories for military activities.

Article 31

Indigenous peoples have the right to maintain, control, protect and develop their cultural heritage, traditional knowledge and traditional cultural expressions, as well as the manifestations of their sciences, technologies and cultures, including human and genetic resources, seeds, medicines, knowledge of the properties of fauna and flora, oral traditions, literatures, designs, sports and traditional games and visual and performing arts. They also have the right to maintain, control, protect and develop their intellectual property over such cultural heritage, traditional knowledge, and traditional cultural expressions.

In conjunction with indigenous peoples, States shall take effective measures to recognize and protect the exercise of these rights.

Article 32

Indigenous peoples have the right to determine and develop priorities and strategies for the development or use of their lands or territories and other resources.

States shall consult and cooperate in good faith with the indigenous peoples concerned through their own representative institutions in order to obtain their free and informed consent prior to the approval of any project affecting their lands or territories and other resources, particularly in connection with the development, utilization or exploitation of mineral, water or other resources.

States shall provide effective mechanisms for just and fair redress for any such activities, and appropriate measures shall be taken to mitigate adverse environmental, economic, social, cultural or spiritual impacts.

Article 33

Indigenous peoples have the right to determine their own identity or membership in accordance with their customs and traditions. This does not impair the right of indigenous individuals to obtain citizenship of the States in which they live.

Indigenous peoples have the right to determine the structures and to select the membership of their institutions in accordance with their own procedures.

Article 34

Indigenous peoples have the right to promote, develop and maintain their institutional structures and their distinctive customs, spirituality, traditions, procedures, practices and, in the cases where they exist, juridical systems or customs in accordance with international human rights standards.

Article 35

Indigenous peoples have the right to determine the responsibilities of individuals to their communities.

Article 36

Indigenous peoples, in particular those divided by international borders, have the right to maintain and develop contacts, relations and cooperation, including activities for spiritual, cultural, political, economic and social purposes, with their own members as well as other peoples across borders.

States, in consultation and cooperation with indigenous peoples, shall take effective measures to facilitate the exercise and ensure the implementation of this right.

Article 37

Indigenous peoples have the right to the recognition, observance and enforcement of treaties, agreements and other constructive arrangements concluded with the States or their successors and to have States honour and respect such treaties, agreements and other constructive arrangements.

Nothing in this Declaration may be interpreted as diminishing or eliminating the rights of indigenous peoples contained in treaties, agreements and other constructive arrangements.

Article 38

States in consultation and cooperation with indigenous peoples shall take the appropriate measures, including legislative measures, to achieve the ends of this Declaration.

Article 39

Indigenous peoples have the right to have access to financial and technical assistance from States and through international cooperation, for the enjoyment of the rights contained in this Declaration.

Article 40

Indigenous peoples have the right to access to and prompt decision through just and fair procedures for the resolution of conflicts and disputes with States and other parties, as well as to effective remedies for all infringements of their individual and collective rights. Such a decision shall give due consideration to the customs, traditions, rules and legal systems of the indigenous peoples concerned and international human rights.

Article 41

The organs and specialized agencies of the United Nations system and other intergovernmental organizations shall contribute to the full realization of the provisions of this Declaration through the mobilization, *inter alia*, of financial cooperation and technical assistance. Ways and means of ensuring participation of indigenous peoples on issues affecting them shall be established.

Article 42

The United Nations, its bodies including the Permanent Forum on indigenous issues, and specialized agencies, including at the country level, and States shall promote respect for and full application of the provisions of this Declaration and follow up the effectiveness of this Declaration.

Article 43

The rights recognized herein constitute the minimum standards for the survival, dignity and well-being of the indigenous peoples of the world.

Article 44

All the rights and freedoms recognized herein are equally guaranteed to male and female indigenous individuals.

Article 45

Nothing in this Declaration may be construed as diminishing or extinguishing the rights indigenous peoples have now or may acquire in the future.

Article 46

Nothing in this Declaration may be interpreted as implying for any State, people, group or person any right to engage in any activity or to perform any act contrary to the Charter of the United Nations or construed as authorizing or encouraging any action which would dismember or impair, totally or in part, the territorial integrity or political unity of sovereign and independent States.

In the exercise of the rights enunciated in the present Declaration, human rights and fundamental freedoms of all shall be respected. The exercise of the rights set forth in this Declaration shall be subject only to such limitations as are determined by law and in accordance with international human rights obligations. Any such limitations shall be non-discriminatory and strictly necessary solely for the purpose of securing due recognition and respect for the rights and freedoms of others and for meeting the just and most compelling requirements of a democratic society.

The provisions set forth in this Declaration shall be interpreted in accordance with the principles of justice, democracy, respect for human rights, equality, non-discrimination, good governance and good faith.

Bibliography

Abebe, A.K., *The Power of Indigenous Peoples to Veto Development Activities: The Right to Free, Prior and Informed Consent (FPIC)* (Saarbrücken: VDM-Verlag, 2010)

Agamben, G., *Homo Sacer: Sovereignty, Power and Bare Life*, trans. D. Heller-Roazen (Stanford, CA: Stanford University Press, 1998)

Alcantara, C., *Negotiating the Deal: Comprehensive Land Claims in Canada* (Toronto: University of Toronto Press, 2013)

Alfred, T., *Peace, Power and Righteousness: An Indigenous Manifesto* (Don Mills, Ontario: Oxford University Press, 1999)

Asch, M. and P. Macklem, 'Aboriginal Rights and Canadian Sovereignty', (1991) 29 Alta Law Rev 498

Asch, M. and N. Zlotkin, 'Affirming Aboriginal Title: A New Basis for Comprehensive Claims Negotiations', in M. Asch (ed.), *Aboriginal and Treaty Rights in Canada: Essays on Law, Equality and Respect for Difference* (Vancouver: UBC Press, 1997)

Asch, M., *On Being Here to Stay: Treaties and Aboriginal Rights in Canada* (Toronto: University of Toronto Press, 2014)

Bankes, N. and J. Koshan, '*Tsilhqot'in*: What Happened to the Second Half of Section 91(24) of the Constitution Act 1867?', 7 July 2014, ablawg.ca/2014/07/07/tsilhqot'in-what happened-to-the-second-half…

Berger, T., *Northern Frontier, Northern Homeland: The Report of the Mackenzie Valley Pipeline Inquiry* (Ottawa: Ministry of Supply and Service, 1977)

Berger, T., *One Man's Justice: A Life in the Law* (Vancouver: Douglas & MacIntyre, 2002)

Blackstone, Sir W., *Commentaries on the Laws of England*, Book I (Oxford: Clarendon Press, 1765)

Blaser, M., 'Is Another Cosmopolitics Possible?', *Cultural Anthropology*, 31(4) (2016): 545–70

Boldt, M., *Surviving as Indians: The Challenge of Self-Government* (Toronto: Toronto University Press, 1993)

Borrows, J., 'Wampum at Niagara: The Royal Proclamation, Canadian Legal

History and Self-Government', in M. Asch (ed.), *Aboriginal and Treaty Rights in Canada*, pp. 155–72 (Vancouver: UBC Press, 1997)

Borrows, J., 'Landed Citizenship: Narratives of Aboriginal Political Participation', in W. Kymlicka and W. Norman, *Citizenship in Diverse Societies* (Oxford: Oxford University Press, 2000), pp. 326–42

Borrows, J., *Drawing Out Law: A Spirit's Guide* (Toronto: University of Toronto Press, 2010)

Borrows, J., *Recovering Canada: The Resurgence of Indigenous Law* (Toronto: University of Toronto Press, 2002)

Borrows, J. and L. Rotman, *Aboriginal Legal Issues: Cases, Materials & Commentary* (2nd edn) (London: LexisNexis Butterworths, 2003)

Brody, H., *Maps and Dreams* (London: Faber & Faber, 2002) (originally published 1981)

Brody, H., *The Other Side of Eden: Hunter-Gatherers, Farmers, and the Shaping of the World* (London: Faber & Faber, 2001)

Brownlie, R., *A Fatherly Eye: Indian Agents, Government Power, and Aboriginal Resistance in Ontario, 1918–1939* (Toronto: Oxford University Press, 2003)

Bryant, M.J., 'Crown–Aboriginal Relationships in Canada: The Phantom of Fiduciary Law' (1993) 27.1 *UBC Law Review* 19–49

Cabana, B., 'Lies, Bribes, Harper and Dunderdale – The Evidence', 21 May 2013, rocksolidpolitics.blogspot.com/search/label/Harper

Cairns, A.C., *Citizens Plus: Aboriginal Peoples and the Canadian State* (Vancouver: UBC Press, 2000)

Calloway, C.G., *The Scratch of a Pen: 1763 and the Transformation of North America* (New York: Oxford University Press, 2006)

Cardinal, H., *The Unjust Society: The Tragedy of Canada's Indians* (Edmonton: M G Hurtig Limited, 1969)

Cassell, E., 'Anthropologists in the Canadian Courts', in M. Freeman and D. Napier (eds.), *Law And Anthropology* (Oxford: Oxford University Press, 2008)

Chrisjohn, R., A. Nicholas, J. Craven, K. Stote, P. Loiselle, T. Wasacase and A. Smith, 'A Historic Non-Apology, Completely and Utterly Not Accepted', *Upping the Anti: A Journal of Theory and Action*, 2008

Coates, K. and D. Newman, *The End is Not Nigh: Reason over alarmism in analysing the* Tsilhqot'in *decision* (Ottawa: MacDonald-Laurier Institute Papers Series, Sept. 2014)

Cruikshank, J., *The Social Life of Stories* (Vancouver: UBC Press, 1998)

Deloria, V., *We Talk, You Listen: New Tribes, New Turf* (Nebraska: Bison Books, 1970) (republished 2007)

Diamond, A., 'The Costs of Implementing the Agreement', in S. Vincent and G. Bowers (eds.), *James Bay and Northern Quebec: Ten Years After* (Montreal: Recherches amérindiennes au Québec, 1988)

Diamond, A., 'Territorial Development in the James Bay and Northern Quebec Agreement: A Cree Perspective', in A.-G. Gagnon and G. Rocher (eds.), *Reflections on the James Bay and Northern Quebec Agreement* (Montreal: Editions Québec Amérique, 2002)

Dupuis, R., *Tribus, Peuples et Nations* (Montreal: Les Editions du Boréal, 1997)

Dupuis, R., *Justice for Canada's Aboriginal Peoples,* trans. R. Chodos and S. Joanis (Toronto: James Lorimer & Company, 2002)

Dupuis, R., 'The James Bay and Northern Quebec Agreement: An Agreement Signed in the 20th Century in the Spirit of the 18th', in A.-G. Gagnon and G. Rocher (eds.), *Reflections on the James Bay and Northern Quebec Agreement* (Montreal: Editions Québec Amérique, 2002)

Dupuis, R., 'Should the James Bay and Northern Quebec Agreement Serve as a Model for Other First Nations?', in T. Martin and S.M. Hoffman (eds.), *Power Struggles: Hydro Development and First Nations in Manitoba and Quebec* (Winnipeg: University of Manitoba Press, 2008)

Feit, H., 'The Power and the Responsibility: Implementation of the Wildlife and Hunting Provisions of the James Bay and Northern Quebec Agreement', in S. Vincent and G. Bowers (eds.), *James Bay and Northern Quebec: Ten Years After* (Montreal: Recherches amérindiennes au Québec, 1988)

Finn, P.D., *Fiduciary Obligations* (Sydney: The Law Book Company, 1977)

Finn, P.D., 'The Fiduciary Principle', in T.G. Youdan (ed.), *Equity, Fiduciaries and Trusts* (Toronto: Carswell, 1989)

Flanagan, T., *First Nations, Second Thoughts* (Montreal: McGill-Queen's University Press, 2000)

Flanagan, T., C. Alcantara and A. Le Dressay, *Beyond the Indian Act: Restoring Aboriginal Property Rights* (2nd edn) (Montreal: McGill-Queen's University Press, 2011)

Foucault, M., *Madness and Civilization: A History of Insanity in the Age of Reason,* trans. R. Howard (New York: Random House, 1965)

Foumoleau, R., *As Long as This Land Shall Last: A History of Treaty 8 and Treaty 11 1870–1939* (Calgary: University of Calgary Press, 2004, 2007) (originally published Toronto: McClelland & Stewart, 1975)

Francis, D., *The Imaginary Indian* (7th edn) (Vancouver: Arsenal Pulp Press, 2004)

Gagnon, A., *La Baie James indienne: Texte intégral du jugement du juge Albert Malouf* (Montreal: Editions du Jour, 1973)

Grant, A., *No End of Grief: Indian Residential Schools in Canada* (Winnipeg: Pemmican Publications, 1996)

Grégoire, P., *Relations entre le gouvernement de Terre-Neuve, le Ministère des Affaires Indiennes et les Montagnais, enregistrées à Sept-Iles au sujet de la trappe et de la chasse au Labrador 1960–1970 (Document préparé pour les comparutions en cour, novembre 1979)* (Conseil Attikamekw-Montagnais, Nov. 1979), Tshakapesh Institute Archive

Guanish, J., 'The Lessons of the Agreement', in S. Vincent and G. Bowers (eds.), *James Bay and Northern Quebec: Ten Years After* (Montreal: Recherches amérindiennes au Québec, 1988)

Hamelin, L.-E., 'The Agreement and Quebec: Totality, Polity and Behaviour', in A.-G. Gagnon and G. Rocher (eds.), *Reflections on the James Bay and Northern Quebec Agreement* (Montreal: Editions Québec Amérique, 2002)

Hannum, H., *Autonomy, Sovereignty and Self-Determination: The Accommodation of Conflicting Rights* (Philadelphia: University of Pennsylvania Press, 1990)

Helin, C., *Dances with Dependency: Out of Poverty Through Self-Reliance* (Woodland Hills, CA: Ravencrest Publishing, 2006, 2008)

Henriksen, G., *Hunters in the Barrens: Naskapi on the Edge of the White Man's World* (New York and Oxford: Berghahn Books, 1973)

Hind, H.Y., *Explorations in the Interior of the Labrador Peninsula* (Labrador: Boulder Publications, 2007) (first published London, 1863)

Irlbacher-Fox, S., *Finding Dahshaa: Self-government, Social Suffering, and Aboriginal Policy in Canada* (Vancouver: UBC Press, 2009)

Jones, G. 'Unjust Enrichment and the Fiduciary's Duty of Loyalty', (1968) 84 LQR 472

Kapesh, A.A., *Je suis une maudite sauvagesse*, trans. into French by José Mailhot, assisted by Anne-Marie André and André Mailhot (Ottawa: Editions Lemeac, 1976)

Kymlicka, W., *Multicultural Citizenship: A Liberal Theory of Minority Rights* (Oxford: Clarendon Press, 1995)

Kymlicka, W. and W. Norman (eds.), *Citizenship in Diverse Societies* (Oxford: Oxford University Press, 2000)

Lacasse, J.-P., *Les Innus et le territoire* (Quebec City: Les Editions du Septentrion, 2004)

LaForest, R., *Occupation et utilisation du territoire par les Montagnais de*

Schefferville (Rapport de recherche soumis au Conseil Attikamekw-Montagnais, 1983), Tshakapesh Institute Archive

Lepage, P., *Aboriginal Peoples: Fact and Fiction* (Quebec City: Commission des droits de la personne et des droits de la jeunesse, 2005)

Leacock, E., 'The Montagnais "Hunting Territory" and the Fur Trade', *American Anthropologist*, 56 (1954): Part 2, Memoir No. 78

Lemkin, R., *Axis Rule in Occupied Europe* (New York: Columbia University Press, 1944)

Locke, J., *Two Treatises on Government*, in P. Laslett (ed.), *Cambridge Texts in Political Thought* (Cambridge: Cambridge University Press, 1988)

Lukacs, M., 'Aboriginal rights a threat to Canada's resource agenda, documents reveal', *True North*, 4 March 2014, https://www.theguardian.com/environment/true-north/2014/mar/04/aboriginal-rights-canada-resource-agenda

MacGregor, R., *Chief: The Fearless Vision of Billy Diamond* (Markham, Ontario: Viking Press, 1989)

McFadyen, K., 'An Aboriginal Perspective on Canada's Human Rights "Culture"', *Cultural and Pedagogical Inquiry*, 4(1) (2012): 27–42

McInnes, M., 'A New Direction for the Canadian Law of Fiduciary Relations?', *Law Quarterly Review*, 121 (2010): 185

McIvor, B., 'The Age of Recognition: The Significance of the *Tsilhqot'in* Decision', 27 June 2014, firstpeopleslaw.com/indes.articles.158.php

McIvor, B., 'Legal Review of Canada's Interim Land Comprehensive Claims Policy', 4 Nov. 2014, firstpeopleslaw.com

McIvor, B., 'What *Tsilhqot'in* and *Grassy Narrows* Mean for Treaty First Nations', 14 June 2015, firstpeopleslaw.com/index/main/articles/php

McIvor, B. and K. Green, 'Stepping into Canada's Shoes: *Tsilhqot'in*, *Grassy Narrows* and the Division of Powers', 67 (2016) UNBLJ 146

McKee, C., *Treaty Talks in British Columbia: Negotiating a Mutually Beneficial Future* (2nd edn) (Vancouver: UBC Press, 2000)

Mackenzie, A., 'Commission parlementaire sur l'entente Québec–Ottawa–Innus – manque de transparence et manque d'unité chez les Innus', *Le Devoir*, 20 Jan. 2003

McKenzie, G., 'Implementation of the James Bay and Northern Quebec Agreement and Chronology of Important Events', in A.-G. Gagnon and G. Rocher (eds.), *Reflections on the James Bay and Northern Quebec Agreement* (Montreal: Editions Québec Amérique, 2002)

Macklem, P., 'First Nations Self-Government and the Borders of the Canadian Legal Imagination', (1991) vol. 36, *McGill Law Journal*, 382

Macklem, P. *Indigenous Difference and the Constitution of Canada* (Toronto: University of Toronto Press, 2001)

Mailhot, J., *The People of Sheshatshit: In the Land of the Innu*, trans. A. Harvey (St. John's: Institute of Social and Economic Research Press, 1998)

Mann, C.C., *1491: New Revelations of the Americas Before Columbus* (New York: First Vintage Books, 2006)

Martin, C., *Muskrat Madness* (privately published, 2014) www.muskratmadness.ca

Martin, T. and Hoffman, S.M. (eds.), *Power Struggles: Hydro Development and First Nations in Manitoba and Quebec* (Winnipeg: University of Manitoba Press, 2008)

Martin, T., 'Hydro Development in Quebec and Manitoba', in T. Martin and S.M. Hoffman, *Power Struggles: Hydro Development and First Nations in Quebec and Manitoba* (Winnipeg: University of Manitoba Press, 2008)

Miller, J.R., *Compact, Contract, Covenant: Aboriginal Treaty-Making in Canada* (Toronto: University of Toronto Press, 2009)

Miller, J.R., *Skyscrapers Hide the Heavens: History of Indian–White Relations in Canada* (Toronto: University of Toronto Press, 1991)

Miller, J.R., *Shingwauk's Vision: A History of Native Residential Schools* (Toronto: University of Toronto Press, 1996)

Miller, J.R., *Lethal Legacy: Current Native Controversies in Canada* (Toronto: McClelland & Stewart, 2004)

Monture-Angus, P., 'Considering Colonialism and Oppression: Aboriginal Women, Justice and the "Theory" of Decolonization', *Native Studies Review*, 63 (1999) 12(1)

Morantz, T., 'L'Histoire de l'est de la baie James au XXe siècle: A la recherche d'une interprétation', *Recherches amérindiennes au Québec* XXXII, no. 2 (2002)

Morrow, P. and C. Hensel, 'Hidden Dissension: Minority–Majority Relationships and the Use of Contested Terminology', *Arctic Anthropology*, 29(1) (1992): 45

Nadasdy, P., *Hunters and Bureaucrats: Power, Knowledge and Aboriginal–State Relations in the South-West Yukon* (Vancouver: UBC Press, 2003)

O'Reilly, J., 'The Role of the Courts in the Evolution of the James Bay Hydroelectric Project', in S. Vincent and G. Bowers (eds.), *James Bay and Northern Quebec: Ten Years After* (Montreal: Recherches amérindiennes au Québec, 1988)

Pagden, A., *Lords of All the World: Ideologies in Spain, Britain and France, c1500-c1800* (New Haven: Yale University Press, 1995)

Palmater, P., *Indigenous Nationhood: Empowering Grassroots Citizens* (Halifax and Winnipeg: Fernwood Publishing, 2015)

Partington, G., 'Thoughts on *Terra Nullius*', *Proceedings of the Samuel Griffith Society*, 19 (2007) 96, https://static1.squarespace.com/static/596ef6aec534a5c54429ed9e/t/5c9d76219140b781bed9 6b74/1553823268546/v19chap11.pdf

Ponting, J.R., *The Nisga'a Treaty: Polling Dynamics and Political Communication in Comparative Context* (Toronto: Broadview Press, 2006)

Pratt, R.A., 'Third-Party Native Rights and the James Bay and Northern Quebec Agreement', in S. Vincent and G. Bowers (eds.), *James Bay and Northern Quebec: Ten Years After* (Montreal: Recherches amérindiennes au Québec, 1988)

Richardson, B., *James Bay: The Plot to Drown the Northern Woods* (San Francisco/New York: The Sierra Club, and Toronto/Vancouver: Clarke Irwin & Company Limited, 1972) (published simultaneously)

Richardson, B., *Strangers Devour the Land* (White River Junction, Vermont: Chelsea Green Publishing Company, 1991)

Robertson, L.G., *Conquest by Law* (Oxford: Oxford University Press, 2005)

Rotman, L., *Parallel Paths: Fiduciary Doctrine and the Crow–Native Relationship in Canada* (Toronto: University of Toronto Press, 1996)

Rotman, L., 'Taking Aim at the Canons of Treaty Interpretation in Canadian Aboriginal Rights Jurisprudence', 46 (1997) UNBLJ 1

Rotman, L., 'Wewaykum: A New Spin on the Crown's Fiduciary Obligations to Aboriginal Peoples?', 31.1 (2004) *UBC Law Review* 219

Dussault, R., and G. Erasmus, *Report of the Royal Commission on Aboriginal Peoples* (Ottawa: Government of Canada, 1996), https://qspace.library.queensu.ca/spul/handle/1974/6874

Saganash, R., 'The *Paix des Braves*: An Attempt to Renew Relations With the Cree', in T. Martin and S.M. Hoffman (eds.), *Power Struggles: Hydro Development and First Nations in Manitoba and Quebec* (Winnipeg: University of Manitoba Press, 2008)

Saku, J., R. Bone and G. Duhaime, 'Towards an Institutional Understanding of Comprehensive Land Claim Agreements in Canada', *Etudes Inuit/Studies*, 22(1) (1998) 109

Samson, C., J. Wilson and J. Mazower, *Canada's Tibet – The Killing of the Innu* (London: Survival International, 1999)

Samson, C., *A Way of Life That Does Not Exist: Canada and the Extinguishment of the Innu* (London: Verso Books, 2003)

Samson, C. and D. Short, 'The Sociology of Indigenous Peoples' Rights', in L. Morris (ed.), *Rights: Social Perspectives* (London: Routledge, 2006)

Samson, C. and E. Cassell, 'The Long Reach of Frontier Justice: Canadian Land Claims "Negotiation" Strategies as Human Rights Violations', *International Journal of Human Rights,* (2012) IJHR 1–21

Samson, C., *A World You Do Not Know: Settler Societies, Indigenous Peoples and the Attack on Cultural Diversity* (London: Institute of Commonwealth Studies, 2013)

Samson, C., 'Canada's Strategy of Dispossession: Aboriginal Land and Rights Cessions in Comprehensive Land Claims', *Canadian Journal of Law and Society,* (2016): 1

Savard, R., *La Voix des autres* (Montreal: Editions de l'Hexagone, 1985)

Schouls,T., J. Olthuis and D. Engelstad, 'The Basic Dilemma: Sovereignty or Assimilation?', in D. Engelstad and J. Bird (eds.), *Nation to Nation: Aboriginal Sovereignty and the Future of Canada* (Concord, Ontario: House of Anansi Press Limited, 1992)

Seed, P., *American Pentimento* (Minneapolis: University of Minnesota Press, 2001)

Short, D., *Redefining Genocide: Settler Colonialism, Social Death and Ecocide* (London: Zed Books, 2016)

Sider, G.M., *Skin for Skin: Death and Life for Inuit and Innu* (Durham, North Carolina: Duke University Press, 2014)

Silberstein, J., *Innu: A la rencontre des Montagnais du Québec-Labrador* (Paris: Editions Albin Michel, 1998)

Slattery, B., 'Understanding Aboriginal Rights', *Canadian Bar Review,* (1987): 727

Smith, L.T., *Decolonizing Indigenous Methodologies: Research and Indigenous Peoples* (Dunedin: University of Otago Press, 1999)

Speck, F., *Naskapi: The Savage Hunters of the Labrador Peninsula* (Norman: University of Oklahoma Press, 1935 and 1977)

Sprague, D.N., 'Canada's Treaties with Aboriginal Peoples', (1996) Man LJ 341

Stavenhagen, R., 'Making the Declaration Work', in C. Charters and R. Stavenhagen (eds.), *Making the Declaration Work: The United Nations Declaration on the Rights of Indigenous Peoples* (Copenhagen: International Working Group for Indigenous Affairs, 2009)

Stevenson, L., *Life Beside Itself: Imagining Care in the Canadian Arctic* (Oakland: University of California Press, 2014)

Stevenson, M.C., *Ethics and Research with Aboriginal Communities* (Alberta: Sustainable Forest Management Network, 2009)

Swain, H. and J. Baillie, '*Tsilhqot'in v British Columbia* and Section 35', *Canadian Business Law Journal,* 56 (2015): 264–79

Thompson, P., *Sea-change: Wivenhoe Remembered* (Stroud: Tempus Publishing Limited, 2006)

Truth and Reconciliation Commission of Canada, *Final Report of the Truth and Reconciliation Commission of Canada, Volume One: Summary* (Winnipeg, Manitoba, 2015)

Tully, J., *A Discourse on Property: John Locke and his Adversaries* (Cambridge: Cambridge University Press, 1980)

Tully, J., *Strange Multiplicity: Constitutionalism in an Age of Diversity* (Cambridge: Cambridge University Press, 1995)

Tully, J., 'The Struggles of Indigenous Peoples for and of freedom', in A. Walken and H. Bruce (eds.), *Box of Treasures or Empty Box? Twenty Years of Section 35* (Penticton: Theytus Books, 2003)

Venne, S., 'Understanding Treaty 6: An Indigenous Perspective', in M. Asch (ed.), *Aboriginal and Treaty Rights in Canada* (Vancouver: UBC Press, 1997)

Vincent. S., and G. Bowers (eds.), *James Bay and Northern Quebec: Ten Years After* (Montreal: Recherches amérindiennes au Québec, 1988)

Vincent, S., 'Vingt-cinq ans après sa signature: un symposium sur la convention de la Baie James et du Nord québécois', *Recherches amérindiennes au Québec*, XXXII no.1 (2002): 93

Wadden, M., *Nitassinan: The Innu Struggle to Reclaim Their Homeland* (Vancouver/Toronto: Douglas & MacIntyre, 1991)

Waters, D.W.M., 'New Directions in The Employment of Equitable Doctrines: The Canadian Experience', in T.G. Youdan (ed.), *Equity, Fiduciaries and Trusts* (Toronto: Carswell, 1989)

Watt, G., *Trusts & Equity* (Oxford: Oxford University Press, 2012)

Weber, M., *The Protestant Ethic and the Spirit of Capitalism*, trans. T. Parsons (London and New York: Routledge, 1992) (first published 1930)

Wesley-Esquimaux, C. and M. Smolewski, *Historic Trauma and Aboriginal Healing* (Ottawa Aboriginal Healing Foundation, 2004)

Widdowson, F. and A. Howard, *Disrobing the Aboriginal Industry: The Deception Behind Indigenous Cultural Preservation* (Montreal: McGill-Queens University Press, 2008)

Youngblood Henderson, J. (S.), 'Empowering Treaty Federalism', (1994) 58 Sask L Rev 241

Youngblood Henderson, J. (S.),'Interpreting *sui generis* Treaties', (1997) 36 Alta Law Rev 46

Index

CPSIA information can be obtained
at www.ICGtesting.com
Printed in the USA
LVHW050155221021
701073LV00009B/38